MW01013208

The publication of this volume has been
made possible by a gift to the University
of California Press Foundation by

WILLIAM & MICHELLE LERACH

in honor of

DILLON LERACH

and his adopted hometown

Sky-high gratitude to these generous supporters, who made this atlas, and all the maps, writing, art, research, and more contained therein, possible:

Marty & Pamela Krasney
Samuel H. Kress Foundation
Lambent Foundation
Josh Mailman
Jonathan Rose
David Rumsey

NONSTOP
METROPOLIS

A NEW YORK CITY ATLAS

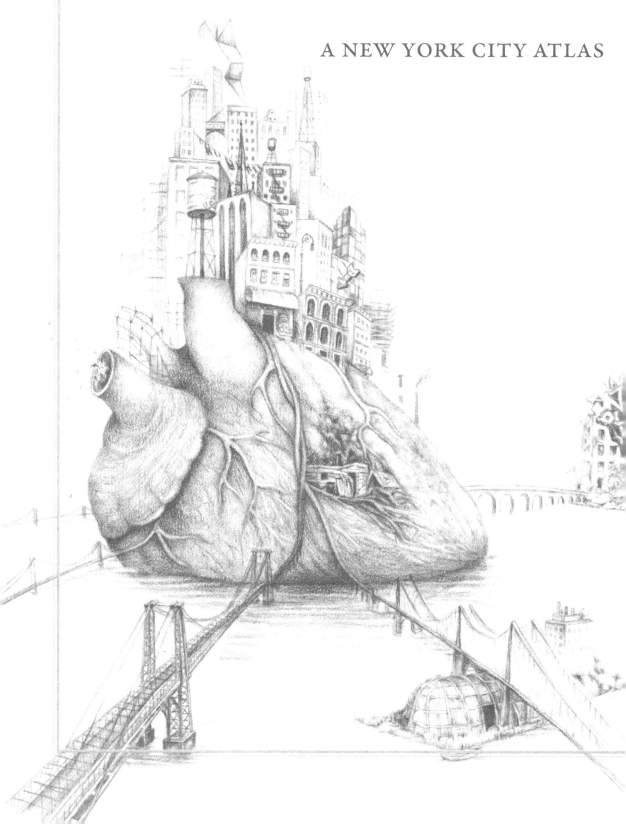

CHARTING THE GREAT CITY AND ITS BRIGHT CENTERS, ITS SHADY EDGES, ITS OUTSKIRTS, ITS MANY ISLANDS AND ARCHIPELAGO IDENTITIES, ITS FIVE BOROUGHS, ITS EIGHT HUNDRED OR SO LANGUAGES, ITS RIOTOUS PAST, GLACIAL ERAS, BROWN DECADES, GOLDEN AGES, CRASHES AND COLLAPSES, ITS PRESENT OF CEASELESS CHANGE AND DISPLACEMENTS AND REPLACEMENTS, AND ITS UNCERTAIN FUTURE; ITS INVISIBLE WOMEN AND UNSILENT MAJORITIES, THIRSTS AND GHOSTS, LIBRARIES AND NIGHTCLUBS, WALKERS AND SUBWAY RIDERS, BRIDGES AND TUNNELS, RECORD-SCRATCHERS AND MCS; ITS RADIO WAVES, ITS RICH AND ITS POOR, ITS RIOTERS AND WRITERS, ITS BANKERS AND DANCERS, ITS TRASH AND ITS TREASURES, ITS CARBON FOOTPRINTS AND CATAS-TROPHES, AND MANY RISES AND FALLS OVER THE YEARS; THE RESTLESS INHABITANTS OF A RESTIVE CITY AS MUCH DESTINATION AS POINT OF DEPARTURE, WHOSE LOCATION ON A CONTINENT'S COAST HAS NEVER PREVENTED ITS PEOPLE THINKING THEMSELVES OR THEIR METROPOLIS THE CENTER OF THE WORLD, IN TWENTY-SIX MAPS AND ESSAYS, ALONG WITH SOME ORAL HISTORIES AND ILLUSTRATIONS

EDITORS

REBECCA SOLNIT AND JOSHUA JELLY-SCHAPIRO

DESIGNER
Lia Tjandra

CARTOGRAPHER
Molly Roy

EDITOR-AT-LARGE
Garnette Cadogan

CHIEF RESEARCHER
Jonathan Tarleton

ADDITIONAL
CARTOGRAPHERS
Richard Campanella
Chris Henrick

PRINCIPAL
ARTIST
Alison Pebworth

ARTISTS
Bette Burgoyne
Hannah Chalew
Molly Crabapple
Alex Fradkin
Kelsey Garrity-Riley
Lady Pink
Duke Riley
Tino Rodriguez
Linnea Russell
Gent Sturgeon
Peach Tao

WRITERS
Sheerly Avni
Gaiutra Bahadur
Marshall Berman
Joe Boyd
Will Butler
Thomas J. Campanella
Daniel Aldana Cohen
Teju Cole
Joel Dinerstein
Francisco Goldman
Margo Jefferson
Paul La Farge
Lucy R. Lippard
Barry Lopez
Valeria Luiselli
Suketu Mehta

Mirissa Neff
Emily Raboteau
Sharifa Rhodes-Pitts
Luc Sante
Heather Smith
Astra Taylor
Alexandra T. Vazquez
Christina Zanfagna

ALSO FEATURING
Valerie Capers
Peter Coyote
Grandmaster Caz
Grandwizzard Theodore
Melle Mel
RZA

 UNIVERSITY OF CALIFORNIA PRESS

The publisher gratefully acknowledges the
generous contribution to this book provided by
Furthermore: a program of the J. M. Kaplan Fund.

Furthermore:
a program of the J.M. Kaplan Fund

University of California Press, one of the most distinguished university presses in
the United States, enriches lives around the world by advancing scholarship in
the humanities, social sciences, and natural sciences. Its activities are supported by
the UC Press Foundation and by philanthropic contributions from individuals
and institutions. For more information, visit www.ucpress.edu.

University of California Press
Oakland, California

Illustrations on half title and title pages by Alison Pebworth

Library of Congress Cataloging-in-Publication Data

Names: Solnit, Rebecca, editor. | Jelly-Schapiro, Joshua, editor. | Roy, Molly,
    cartographer. | University of California Press, publisher.
Title: Nonstop metropolis : a New York City atlas / editors, Rebecca Solnit and Joshua
    Jelly-Schapiro ; designer and compositor, Lia Tjandra ; cartographer, Molly Roy.
Description: 1st edition. | Oakland, California : University of California Press, [2016]
Identifiers: LCCN 2016015756 | ISBN 9780520285941 (cloth : alk. paper) |
    ISBN 9780520285958 (pbk. : alk. paper)
Subjects: LCSH: New York (N.Y.)—Maps. | New York (N.Y.)—Social life and
    customs—Maps. | Human geography—New York (State)—New York—Maps. |
    LCGFT: Atlases.
Classification: LCC G1254.N4 N7 2016 | DDC 912.747/1—dc23

LC record available at https://lccn.loc.gov/2016015756

Designer and compositor: Lia Tjandra
Cartographer: Molly Roy
Text: Garamond Premier Pro
Display: Garamond Premier Pro, Berthold Akzidenz Grotesk
Prepress vendor: Embassy Graphics
Printer and binder: QuaLibre

Manufactured in China

25 24 23 22 21 20 19 18 17 16
10 9 8 7 6 5 4 3 2 1

CONTENTS

CENTERS AND EDGES

REBECCA SOLNIT

THE TRINITY

A city is a machine with innumerable parts made by the accumulation of human gestures, a colossal organism forever dying and being born, an ongoing conflict between memory and erasure, a center for capital and for attacks on capital, a rapture, a misery, a mystery, a conspiracy, a destination and point of origin, a labyrinth in which some are lost and some find what they're looking for, an argument about how to live, and evidence that differences don't always have to be resolved, though they may grate and grind against each other for centuries.

Nonstop Metropolis is the last volume in a trilogy of atlases exploring what maps can do to describe the ingredients and systems that make up a city and what stories remain to be told after we think we know where we are. The project began in my hometown, San Francisco, and went onward to New Orleans, where I'd been drawn to report on Hurricane Katrina and stayed to fall in love with the various kinds of warmth and presence there, the way people show up. It was inevitable that the third city would be my mother's hometown, New York.

"America has only three cities: New York, San Francisco, and New Orleans. Everywhere else is Cleveland," Tennessee Williams famously remarked, though the United States has many cities and towns with their own centripetal force and spectacular communities, from Calexico to Montpelier. This trilogy of books—*Infinite City, Unfathomable City, Nonstop Metropolis*—was created in the belief that any significant place is in some sense infinite, because its stories are inexhaustible and the few that are well known overshadow the many worth knowing; because its meanings are innumerable; because a place is only an intersection between forces converging from various distances, from a little ways upriver to the other side of the world; because any place can be mapped in countless ways.

Each of us is an atlas of sorts, already knowing how to navigate some portion of the world, containing innumerable versions of place as experience and desire and fear, as route and landmark and memory. So a city and its citizens constitute a living library. None of the atlases in this trilogy pretends to be comprehensive; each instead is meant to illustrate a few of the myriad ways a city can be described and understood, and thereby to encourage you to recognize that beyond our maps—seventy in total in the three books—are endless other ways to map, describe, explore, and imagine cities, these three and every other one. The books are finite, but they try to indicate the infinite possibilities.

The fragments make the mosaic we mean by city, and each of us grasps and inhabits only part of the pattern. The complexity beyond comprehension is one of the marvels of great cities, their inexhaustible, ever-renewing mystery. This is why some city-dwellers become explorers, finding new and unknown phenomena in a process of discovery that need never end, since a thriving city forever renews and changes. New York in particular is rich in explorers and encyclopedists of this kind, spelunkers in the subways, charters of obscure phenomena, be they wildlife or languages, experts on the invisible cities of communications networks or ethnographic phenomena, wanderers and celebrants. It is as though New York were a sacred book and some of its citizens Torah scholars immersed in study and interpretation of a text they're convinced is the most fascinating on earth. We benefited from many of these passionate scholars in the course of making our own book about the place.

Every city is many places; the old woman and the young child do not live in the same city, and the rich and the poor, the pedestrian and the wheelchair-bound, black and white inhabit different but not completely separate realms. Ghettos and shtetls and barrios abound in cities where scale can segregate, but we mingle nevertheless, to some extent. In a city we are individually fish and together the water that each fish swims through.

As our editor-at-large, Garnette Cadogan, put it, "As I've circulated through New York's streets, nothing reveals the city's opposites in stark juxtaposition like the walk from the Upper East Side to the South Bronx, two neighborhoods separated by a brisk ninety-minute walk, or a quick twelve-minute subway ride. . . . To walk the streets from one to the other, as I often do, is to bear witness to a landscape of asymmetry." Pieces of cities are isolated from each other, though that isolation can mean opera-goers sweeping past the homeless; isolation can be a state of mind in a space of coexistence. Even in segregated cities, servants and caregivers cross over one way, police and profiteers another; even those who stay put in the slums or the palatial realms know they are defined by the place's others and the other places.

The three cities in our atlases share an isolation from the country around them. New York, New Orleans, San Francisco come close, each of them, to being island republics, not quite the Venetian Republic at the height of its powers, but not quite obedient, integrated parts of the United States either. They aren't even very firmly attached to the continent. New York City is in essence an Atlantic archipelago—a place comprising tiny islands, from the Isle of Meadows through the Brother Islands to Hart Island, and bigger ones like Staten Island and Manhattan, along with Brooklyn and Queens at the western end of Long Island. Only the Bronx is part of the continental United States.

San Francisco is the tip of a long peninsula, with weather, soil, species, and culture so distinct it comes close to having an island ecology and mentality, and until the two bridges across the bay were built in the 1930s, it was usually approached by water. New Orleans not only has the Mississippi on its south and Lake Ponchartrain on its north sides, but is surrounded by areas that are often mapped as though they were solid land but are really (as we made clear in the map "Waterland" in that atlas) marsh, wetland, bayou, swamp. There the most fundamental cartographic distinction between land and water falls apart in an encounter with stuff that's not quite either (and is itself falling apart on the fastest-eroding coastline on earth, as another map in that volume shows).

I once called San Francisco the anti-America in which America invents itself, and all three of the cities can be seen as immensely generative of new ways of living, thinking, dancing, singing that the rest of the country may mock or revile and think it rejects and then ten years later absorb without apology. All three have been hated by their surrounding regions as sin cities, as liberal enclaves, as un-American in their ethnicities and their ideologies. New Orleans, like Detroit, is feared and loathed as a black city by some of its surrounding white communities.

New York was (and is) regarded as the capital of American Jews, and in another presidential campaign, in 1984, candidate Jesse Jackson notoriously referred to the metropolis as Hymietown (the city now has about a million Jews, down from two million in 1950). Other people hated the city for being black, of course, and yet others for being ethnic, back when the Irish, then the Poles and the Italians, along with the Jews, were regarded as not quite white by the people who considered themselves in charge of defining whiteness. Jews and blacks have both clashed and collaborated—the demigods of Tin Pan Alley credited the cross-pollination of the two cultures for the golden age of songwriting in the city. New York is human rights activist Abel Meeropol (who's on the map "What Is a Jew?") writing Billie Holiday's signature song "Strange Fruit." It's also the 1991 Crown Heights Riot (on the map "Riot!"), which arose after a driver lost control of his car in a motorcade for Lubavitcher leader, rabbi, and scholar (and Nazi refugee) Menachem Mendel Schneerson, striking and killing a Guyanese child and injuring another. And it's the black Jews of Harlem, very present on the maps "What Is a Jew?" and "Black Star Lines." A city is not one or the other of these things but all of them, contradictions and collaborations and conflicts together, forever churning and spitting out new possibilities.

New York has long been the gateway for immigrants, many of whom stayed in the city. A great wave came in the late nineteenth and early twentieth century, until the restrictions of 1921, and a second wave began when the 1965 Immigration and Nationality Act reopened the gates. Contemporary New York is a city where more than a third of the population is foreign-born, and only a third is white. Half the population speaks a language other than English at home, and there is no majority population. In its own chaotic way, New York is a triumph of coexistence interrupted by people yelling at each other. The protagonist in Martin Scorsese's 1976 *Taxi Driver* hated it for being dirty in both the sexual and the literal sense, and then like most Puritans he went hunting for filth. "Dirt is matter out of place," anthropologist Mary Douglas once said, and dirt can mean mingling, impurity, hybridity—in that sense it's the fertile soil from which new things grow. It's what makes cities so generative.

. . .

There are ways the three cities of our trilogy are profoundly different. New York is nearly 100 years older than New Orleans, 225 years older than San Francisco, and vast in size and in population, once one of the largest cities on earth and, since the late eighteenth century, the largest city in the United States. New Orleans has half the population of San Francisco; San Francisco has a tenth of the population of New York City. They are far apart in many senses.

Their differences and distance from each other are also reminders that the USA is best thought of as an empire, not a nation. It was made, as historian Roxanne Dunbar-Ortiz reminded me long ago, by invading and cobbling together hundreds of native nations, and its scale means that even the lower forty-eight states extend through areas whose ecological, cultural, economic, and historical differences are so huge that they've never been fully bridged. The Revolutionary War was a northeastern event that unfolded when only thirteen colonies had been carved out of the indigenous continent; the Indian Wars that began in the seventeenth century in New England weren't really in full swing in California until the mid-nineteenth-century gold rush. The Golden State had just, along with the rest of the Southwest, been seized from Mexico in the 1846–48 war, fought in an expanse that was still Mexico in name and mostly indigenous homeland in fact. The North-South dialectic of the Civil War had mostly indirect effects in the Far West.

Mediterranean San Francisco faces Asia in a region that, thanks to immigration, is being reunited with Latin America. Steamy New Orleans lives in relationship to the Caribbean and the Gulf of Mexico, musically and economically. Temperate—by which is meant really hot and really cold—New York never quite stopped looking across the Atlantic to Europe, though it is now the most diverse city on earth, a quarter black (based on

U.S. census data lumping African and Caribbean emigrés with African Americans whose ancestors arrived in North America centuries ago), more than a quarter Latino (ditto the lumping), still nearly an eighth Jewish, hugely Caribbean, another eighth Asian, with ethnic whites—old-immigrant Irish and Italian Catholics, new Russian and eastern European arrivals, and a residual WASP aristocracy that won't go away but whose sway is withering into irrelevance. Our map "Mother Tongues and Queens" pays homage to that borough as the most linguistically diverse area of that scale on earth, a place where obscure and nearly extinct languages are spoken and dreamed in, along with Punjabi, Patwa, and Polish.

But the similarities also matter. They are all port cities, cities built on trade and commerce, and not only facing water, but defined and surrounded by rivers and seas, estuaries and deltas and islands. San Francisco's port faded and the traffic went to Oakland and Long Beach; New York's is now mostly in Jersey. But to be founded as a port city is to be a wide-open town, a place of intermingling and exchange of goods, of bodies, of cultures and ideas and diseases and tongues. In old maps of San Francisco and Lower Manhattan, so many docks fringe the shoreline that they look like a three-day stubble or even a beard. (You can see them in our map "Harper's and Harpooners.") The sailors are largely gone, but they too made these cities, as maritime capitals and as shore-leave sites catering to the nautical thirst for drink and for debauchery.

They are all sexual cities, New Orleans in particular a sort of erogenous zone below the Bible Belt of the South, a sultry place whose reputation for mingling and Dionysian excess was well earned. Each was a sanctuary for queer people long before the liberation movements of the 1960s and after. Harlem had cross-dressing and drag balls in the 1920s; New Orleans's French Quarter queer community was going strong in the 1930s; and San Francisco was so queer that lesbian bars were all over North Beach in the 1920s, and some of the heroic early efforts for rights for gays and lesbians were centered there. But New York City is the nation's capital in all but name and seating of the three branches of government (and it was even that for a brief period after the Revolutionary War). What happens in New York is magnified by the (largely New York–based) media into a national discourse. Thus the lesbian rights group the Daughters of Bilitis founded in 1955 in San Francisco and that city's 1966 Compton's Cafeteria Riot are all but unknown; the Stonewall Riot of 1969, a celebrated event considered a watershed. If a tree falls, or riots, in New York, everyone hears it in the mainstream media. And yet the city still has secrets.

Louisiana, New York, and even California are each more conservative than these cities that are often at odds with their states (as even voting records will show, but of course the common voting pattern of the United States in recent decades makes most cities islands of blue in the red seas of the more conservative hinterlands). These three cities are refuges to which people have come to be free, to be weird, to be radical, to be creative—whether in the most traditional sense of making art or music or books, or in the modern sense of self-invention—and to find communities of people who are like them if they are not like the mainstream. They come for liberation, including liberation from death and persecution, beginning with the Quakers and Jews who came near the dawn of New York City's history, to the refugees from African and Middle East wars today, as well as all the refugees from dead-end poverty who've been coming steadily the whole time and all the queer kids who have come from hateful families and homicidal communities. It's important to remember, however, that one person's refuge is another's gulag: when Ellis Island was Little Oyster Island, Africans were brought against their will as slaves to New Orleans and to New York City. Much later, many African Americans escaped the economic and social brutalities of the South in the great northern migration that turned Harlem into a cultural capital.

New Orleans is a place of origin whose native sons and daughters have a hard time leaving and to which they struggle, even after the devastation of Katrina, to come back. San

Francisco is something of an incubator, to which people come to come out of the closet or learn Chinese medicine or explore experimental dance and then often take their new skills and sense of self off to a new place or back to where they came from. New York is a place of origin, a training ground rich in colleges, but it is most celebrated as a destination. So there are cities of origin, cities of incubation, and, as E. B. White once wrote, cities "of final destination, the city that is a goal." New York is often imagined as a culmination, an endpoint, rather than a way station. As the center.

THE CENTER

The opera diva from the rustic West at the center of Willa Cather's novel *The Song of the Lark* leaves small-town Colorado for Chicago for her first round of education as a musician, but she triumphs by becoming a successful artist in New York, as Cather did herself for the last forty-one years of her life. There she wrote vividly about the West, while living with her partner, editor Edith Lewis, in the East, where a publishing job had brought her and where privacy, tolerance, sophistication, maybe access to Europe and editors, seem to have kept her.

It's a reverse of the old mythic westward migration for freedom—though it's worth remembering that other New Yorkers left the city in search of liberation, whether it was the patrician Edith Wharton checking out of the closed upper-class society she continued to write about or James Baldwin escaping American racism for a while. Then there's Djuna Barnes, who had a lively early career with the New York newspapers, including the *Brooklyn Daily Eagle* Walt Whitman once edited, moved on to a legendary era in lesbian Paris, and then spent the reclusive last half of her life on Patchin Place in Greenwich Village. You could come to New York to appear or to disappear; the city accommodated all kinds of wishes.

New Orleans and San Francisco are edges and know it, but New York, dangling like a pendant off the bottom of New York State, bumping up against New Jersey and Connecticut, on the rim of the continent and the country, has always imagined itself as a center and aspired to be the most, the biggest, the greatest, the center and the capital. (As early as 1837, notes the monumental tome *Gotham,* a writer "gently mocked New Yorkers for their insatiable need to proclaim their city biggest and best.") Even the best-known history of Dutch New York, that little settlement at the southern tip of Manhattan, is called *The Island at the Center of the World.*

The financial collapse of 2008 pointed to Wall Street's centrality as a curse; Occupy turned that centrality into an inspiration as the protest became a near-global movement, with Occupy Kyoto and Occupy Melbourne and more than 100 documented Occupys in California alone, some of which are still doing good work under other names. The sheer density of Lower Manhattan and its global reach is the subject of a map in this atlas called "Crash"—it explores 9/11, the crash of 2008, Occupy Wall Street in 2011, and Hurricane Sandy in 2012. With the last, there may not seem to be global consequences for what goes on in Lower Manhattan, until you count Wall Street's role in preventing meaningful action on climate change, as well as the portent of climate change to come as the storm surges retook the landfilled edges of the city. Which in this book we do.

What does it mean to be a center? Years ago a student of mine told me of her distress that her husband's job had taken her away from what she regarded as the centrality of New York City, questioning the value of my region. Students teach by questions, and trying to contemplate that one made me come to prize edges more consciously. Back then it was possible to imagine San Francisco as what it had always been, an edge, a place of alternatives and innovations and subversions. Since then the metastasizing of Silicon Valley has made it the global center of the new technologies, including surveillance and military technologies and information corporations that wield enormous and unchecked power.

In this way it's become more akin to New York. As my atlas co-director Joshua Jelly-Schapiro explores in his essay for the map "Capital of Capital," New York City is still a, if not the, global capital of finance, though the Internet has decentralized trading to some extent. It's also the center of fashion, publishing, theater, dance, visual art, and mainstream media for the country, though perhaps not quite as central as it used to be, since the rise of electronic communications and representations and the increased mobility of the artistic population have made it easier to be a participant from the outskirts and backwaters—while housing costs have made centers harder to inhabit for anyone chasing idealistic dreams. The idea of it as the crucial proving ground was expressed in ideas like that old adage "if you can make it in New York you can make it anywhere," which really meant that if you flourished there, you'd conquered the center of the world and the edges didn't matter.

Being a center means that millions know a place, a Paris or London or New York, even if they've never been; people look toward these places from across the country and around the world, and the place comes to them in the news and in entertainment and culture—as in our map "Singing the City." Cather wrote in her story about a Pittsburgh misfit, "Paul's Case," "Not once, but a hundred times, Paul had planned this entry into New York . . . and in his scrap-book at home there were pages of description about New York hotels, cut from the Sunday papers." He's a predecessor of the Texas dishwasher turned New York hustler in the 1969 film *Midnight Cowboy*, a dreamer looking to appear, to become, to fully emerge from his cocoon and spread his wings. (And, as with many stories about fragile young newcomers in New York, the wings get crushed.)

What happens locally in the capital is treated as national or international news, as significant, as something that happened onstage, while the rest of the country or world is regarded as a sort of backstage or maybe an audience for the show. The lights are bright onstage; everyone can see you; you can't see the audience; you have visibility but perhaps not as much vision. The theatrical construct is made and reinforced in various ways. These places control representation, and they are well represented, maybe overrepresented. And marketed, for they are the marketplace itself. People read the *New York Times* and the *New Yorker* in what is cruel but accurate to call, in this context, the provinces. So the provinces know at least some versions of the capital well, while those in the capital may know little about the provinces, which is how capitals can be provincial in their own way (and then, as people around the USA have come to rely increasingly on the *Times* for their news, they too have come to be ignorant about where they live).

Growing up on the West Coast meant growing up with edicts from New York about our barbarian lack of culture, including scorn for our bagels by people who thought that bagels and not, say, tortillas were the currency of the land. Of course other New Yorkers were more concerned about cannoli or fufu, but the New York that seemed to dominate from afar was a very specific version of New York. To dominate in the colonial sense. The enormous worldwide impact of hip-hop and rap as youth culture and channel for outspoken expression offers up another New York and entirely other New Yorkers, what you could call the South Bronx gone global (which we celebrate in the map "Burning Down and Rising Up").

Mostly, when New York imagines itself as a center, it's only some of New York, demographically and geographically: Staten Island is the center's edge, the limelight's shadow, the place where the rest of the city sent its garbage for several decades (mapped in "Trash in the City"). Maybe edges are freer; maybe it's the marginality of Staten Island that allowed the members of the hip-hop band the Wu-Tang Clan, who grew up there, to imagine it as Shaolin, as they shuttled between the 42nd Street movie houses, where Hong Kong action films filled their imaginations, and the quieter island to the south (mapped in "Mysterious Land of Shaolin").

Alexandra Momin, *Hell's Kitchen #1*, 2008

There are other ways to imagine New York as a center. Some are common to most cities: the surrounding network of production that keeps the city going, the convergence of water, food, and energy on a population center. Two maps in this atlas attend to this: "Water and Power" (which shows only part of the electrical grid reaching all the way up to James Bay in northern Quebec) and "Trash in the City," looking at a dysfunctional disposal system that, since the other boroughs stopped dumping, literally, on Staten Island, pushes New York's copious trash upstate and to other states.

The people come and go, constantly, incessantly, in streams and rivers and flood tides. New York native and Cooper Union graduate Milton Glaser designed the famous "I ❤ NY" graphic in 1977, still selling on tourist souvenirs, its three letters and a heart a riff on pop artist Robert Indiana's 1960s *LOVE* sculpture (and print and postage stamp and more). Adriana Krasniansky redesigned Glaser's icon with a heart that looks a lot more like the fist of muscle that thumps inside the chest of each of us, and her design is on the map "Love and Rage" and was an inspiration for our cover icon by atlas chief artist Alison Pebworth.

New York, as we talked to David van der Leer and Sarah Farwell at Van Alen Institute, an architectural forum in Manhattan, came to seem like a huge heart forever pumping an exceptionally fluid population in and out of the city. When your heart stops, you die; the city never stops; and New York in particular is a nonstop metropolis, throbbing and rushing at all times of day and night. Major thoroughfares are sometimes called arteries, but if New York is a heart, all the modes of transit are veins and arteries and capillaries, and its population the lifeblood. This is the subject of the map "Oscillating City," which tracks the daily influx and outflow of Manhattan in particular, a place whose population shifts and swings around the clock more dramatically than in almost any place on earth, with millions pouring in and out by train, ferry, subway, and private car, including daytime workers and students and nighttime revelers, as well as one-time visitors—tourists, patients, and people coming for professional purposes.

In addition to the daily cycle are out-migrations of the well-heeled to their country places every weekend or to summer houses on Fire Island or Cape Cod or in the Hamptons or any of those other places whose names one knows whether one's visited them or not. Summer camp is a more iconic, widespread activity in the Northeast than elsewhere in the country, so that another far-flung circulatory system is particular to children (and spins off into crazy only-in-New-York, like the professional packers who put together camp luggage for the children of the wealthy).

And then there are the poor and not-so-poor who emigrate from around the world and stay (and whose children mostly do not go to camp and who tend not to own country homes). The next generation often moves out to the suburbs, or used to. Housing economics now push poor and even working people to the periphery; one of the complicating factors for many cities is that the people who keep them running can't afford to live in them, and so they serve a city that does not serve them.

New York is a center that pulls people in and a centrifuge that spins them out into the world.

THE CHANGES

What we call New York City has been many things in its four centuries. It was a little Dutch outpost in Lower Manhattan that became a compact British city and then the official capital of the newly liberated United States as it kept growing in scale (with an expanding footprint geographer Richard Campanella mapped for us in "Capital of Capital"), spreading northward on the tall island and then annexing the other boroughs in 1898. The city was almost 90 percent white at the beginning of the nineteenth century and even more than 90 percent at the end. In 1860 one out of every four New Yorkers was an Irish immigrant, mostly Catholics fleeing starvation and persecution in British-controlled Ireland.

It was the shining capital of the world in the postwar era, the city that emerged into its full glory as much of Europe and some of Asia lay in ruins from World War II, becoming a capital for visual art and intellectual culture with the rise of abstract expressionism and the legions of prodigal refugees in nearly all media and scholarly fields, during an era that was also perhaps the golden age of Broadway theater. It was a center of radical politics from the great union movements of the nineteenth century through the utopian socialism whose trace lies in many housing sites, murals, and less locatable phenomena like rights and practices to contemporary organizing around a host of issues.

Knowledge of New York built up in me in successive waves, even during my total absence from the place between ages eight and twenty-eight. But although I was far from New York, New York in the form of my mother was never far from me. She had left, eagerly, but it never left her. She always recalled with a glow her New York City of the late 1940s and 1950s, when she had a series of clerical jobs in Manhattan.

One day in New York I realized I'd been raised by someone who walked through suburbs and along trails like a New Yorker, fast and confident, with a stride all about getting places. She had trained me to be that kind of walker and even a jaywalker, to never stop if you could manage to keep going, and to make your stride mean something, to go places, not dawdle. My mother, born in Brooklyn, raised in Queens, never stopped being a New Yorker even though she spent the last two-thirds of her life elsewhere. She recited show tunes instead of nursery rhymes to her children. Her New York was the shining city of possibility and musicality, of Broadway musicals and Brill Building tunes, of Times Square as a glittering enchantment, tall buildings as emblems of aspiration.

And then the central city became, by imperceptible stages, a turbulent ruin notorious for its violent crime, beginning in the 1960s. The old blue-collar industrial city died, and New York teetered on the brink of bankruptcy. In 1975 the *Daily News* carried the famous headline: "FORD TO CITY: DROP DEAD," describing the president's disinterest in bailing out the city. The decaying and ruinous urban spaces of New York were emblematic in the 1980s, when many anticipated a nuclear Armageddon between superpowers that would target cities first, when the old order was a disintegrating corpse and the birth of the new was not foreseen. In 1987–88 Spanish artist Francesc Torres presented a photographic suite comparing the South Bronx to a city destroyed by bombing in the Spanish Civil War; the point seemed to be that this too was war, economic war.

While a museum and monuments make sure no one forgets 9/11, few remember the far vaster destruction that charred and erased more than 90 percent of the buildings in some precincts of the South Bronx (as the original research by Jonathan Tarleton in the map "Burning Down and Rising Up" documents and as Bronx son Marshall Berman describes movingly in his essay in this book). A RAND report urging closing of firehouses even as fires escalated was part of what brought it all down; conservatives were engaged in an attack on social services that was in effect an attack on the city itself. "Hoodlums did not burn The Bronx," as Joe Flood wrote. "The bureaucrats did." But today we have largely forgotten that city full of ruins, because a glossy new metropolis rooted in finance and information and tourism was born in the rubble. Is it the same city or an entirely different city occupying the same space? Both, perhaps, since there has been both continuity and rupture.

One of the great mysteries of recent cultural history is how hip-hop could emerge from a place undergoing such extreme destruction. The Bronx gave birth to cultural forms still vibrant globally four decades later; poetry, photography, painting, punk rock all flourished in the ruinous city of the 1970s and the slowly reviving city of the 1980s. These emergences raise questions about the conditions in which cities are generative, creative, fertile, and when they stagnate or go somnolent. And beyond that inquiry lie even larger questions about the future of cities, for which New York, London, and San Francisco can serve as case studies. All three are in the grip of real estate booms that have made the central city unaffordable to ordinary people and that seem to be driving diversity and complexity out of these cities. What are cities when the qualities that have defined them are drowned in rising tides of what we call wealth—that increase in holdings for some that increases scarcity, desperation, and exclusion for others?

The old notion of the central city as a place where bohemia and dissent thrive has been withering away as cities become enclaves of the affluent and the corporate—or empty zones. Many of the condominiums and luxury apartments are often unoccupied, either because they're not primary residences, or because they're places to park money for the transnational super-wealthy or their corporations. In the thicket of super-high-rises going up near Central Park South, it's anything but rare to read of apartment sales like the $95 million recently fetched by the penthouse at 432 Park Avenue, a ninety-six-story needle in the sky. That particular building, with over 400,000 square feet of usable interior space, contains only 104 units for people to live in. But as *Fortune* magazine reported of those units' owners—oil magnates from the Middle East, Chinese and Russian oligarchs, billionaires from Latin America—they "all have one thing in common: More money than they know what to do with and a desperation to get as much of it out of their home countries as possible." The tower casts a shadow on Central Park, making it all too perfect an emblem of the sacrifice of the public to the private in the neoliberal age.

In 2015 an NYU professor observed to this atlas's editors that his children, who are being raised in faculty housing in Greenwich Village, don't see much of the middle class in Manhattan; instead, they coexist with the desperate and the elite. This augurs a grim future for the cities, now that postwar white flight turns out to have been a boomerang, and the affluent are finding urban life so desirable they're ousting the less well-off in waves of hyper-gentrification. This is happening in other cities around the world. In New York, the Bronx, Queens, and Staten Island remain reasonably affordable, but Brooklyn has become an increasingly expensive borough as those priced out of Manhattan have turned neighborhood after neighborhood into housing for the upper crust. Long ago, native New

Philip Bell, *Under the El*, 2008

Yorker Grace Paley said of the Village, "I don't think there's as much energy in Greenwich Village any more. Not in these nice neighborhoods. . . . They've become too 'single class.'"

One notable aspect of this phenomenon, in areas like SoHo and Times Square, is that the new affluence is a suburbanizing force; retail outlets in places like this are the same kind of national and international chain stores and restaurants you'd see in a shopping mall. So many urban places, from the Chelsea piers to SoHo, have passed from being centers of industrial production and blue-collar labor through a subversive phase—as ruins for the former, as often-illegal artist housing for the latter—into managed spaces of consumption and leisure, from the golf-teeing center at the piers to the boutiques south of Houston Street in what was once a district of sweatshops from the later nineteenth century until well into the twentieth (on what was long, long before land farmed by freed slaves who were located there as a buffer against the Native Americans to the north). What we call a city is a succession of wildly different places in the same location.

Housing too, in this city and others, is now often built according to suburban templates: block-size fortresses you can drive your car into and stay inside, exercising in the gym, swimming in the pool, sending out for provisions, walled up against the contact that used to be so central to urbanism. As cities change in these ways, the density and infrastructure remain urban, but the culture and activities are what we used to think of as suburban. The poor are pushed to the periphery, to the old suburbs, which fall into their own kind of decay. In the inner city the poor had access to shared resources like public pools and parks, to public transit, and to the possibility of a collective power and civil-society engagement that the suburbs do not offer. There they become literally marginal.

What might make New York notable in this context is that it is, as a global center of capital, a place where the new economic inequality has been engineered, with the rise of the super-rich and the fall of the once-secure into penury and debt. In that sense, New York can be imagined as the city that is destroying cities and a belt of wealth engineering the rise of global poverty—but still hosting some of the rebels against it all, from scholarly analysts to street protesters. This ability to produce the antithesis to capitalism as well as its thesis—to have Karl Marx toiling away on *Das Kapital* in the British Library as Parliament oversaw the British Empire, to give rise to revolutions in ideas and regimes—is part of why cities have mattered. It's why our map about Jews in New York is subtitled "From Emma Goldman to Goldman Sachs."

Cities are not over. But it's hard not to fear that the great cities of the North are never going to be what they were. Just as most have ceased to be centers of industrial production, so they may cease to be centers of cultural production, at least with the intensity they once possessed. Now they're menaced by climate change, too. New York City's coastline will be pummeled with hurricanes and blizzards; hotter, wetter weather will bring the kind of heat waves that tend to kill seniors; food prices will likely rise, and climate refugees will become a new subpopulation. It's impossible to say exactly what this city, like other great cities ceasing to be what they were, will become.

The *New York Times* reported in the spring of 2016 that the West Antarctic ice sheet is melting far faster than previously believed, fast enough, according to current data, to raise the sea level possibly five or six feet by 2100, and many times that by 2500. Which means that New York City is a city with a long past but possibly a short future, and that any map of New York or any other coastal area will soon be out of date, and so we can envision a succession of future atlases showing different coastlines and disappearing cities. When they tell of the crucial era when climate change was understood but too little was being done to limit its impact, New York as the nation's media capital will have a central place in the stories, of how the American media caved in to the pretense there were two equal sides to the discourse on climate change, rather than one scientific consensus and a minority propaganda effort against that consensus supported by the likes of the Koch brothers, also of New York, and of how much the refusal to respond adequately was driven to a significant degree by Wall Street's refusal to let go of short-term profits for long-term well-being. These forces are marked on our map "Carboniferous," but the intrusion of Hurricane Sandy's floodwaters onto the territory of Wall Street in 2012, which we show in another map—"Crash"—suggests how shortsighted this version of self-interest can be. Maps of New York and other coastal areas will become maps of a lost world. We can envision a succession of future atlases showing different coastlines and disappearing cities as the melting continues.

MAP STORIES

As Joshua Jelly-Schapiro said one day, every map is a story, and by implication every story contains a map. I loved maps for a long time, but it wasn't until I made them and put them out in the world that I discovered how not alone I was. People love maps. There is a special incandescent joy to how they respond to a good map that is different from the way I've seen people respond to any other art form. They light up. They get greedily engrossed. They start tracing possibilities, thinking, interpreting, measuring: maps demand work, and this kind of cerebral work can be exhilarating.

By a good map I mean an aesthetic one, a map that is an invitation to the imagination, a map that offers a fresh view of the familiar or an introduction to the unfamiliar or finds the latter in the former. If every map is a story, most of them are mysteries that invite you to solve them while remaining forever unresolved, in that they indicate more—more past, more future, more adventure, more travelers. They have an openness, indicating more than they depict.

"There are eight million stories in the naked city. This has been one of them," declares the famous voice-over for the 1948 documentary-style feature film *The Naked City,* which interrupts its murder story with vignettes of New Yorkers—janitresses, wealthy diners, disk jockeys, blue-collar ladies. It's an unusual film because it digresses intentionally to try to evoke the coexistence of many stories in the same place, weaving and tangling, overlapping and undermining each other. A narrative is one of those stories, and though the film digresses to indicate the existence of others, it follows one story.

A map can trace one story, though it often portrays the coexistence of many stories in relation to each other. It can show how the physical, economic, visual, and social landscape can shape those stories, letting some bloom, grinding out others. Multiple stories in spatial relation become the geosocial constellations of our lives. The seventy maps in this atlas trilogy are maps about relationship, about which species thrive, about how two phenomena inflect each other, about the registers of change, about what remains invisible in the cities people think they know.

A map is a proposition: here is what this place is, or was, or will be. Most contemporary maps are predictable propositions: here are streets and freeways and also parking and maybe shopping or subway lines. But imagination can always go beyond what even the most quotidian map shows. You know that when you exit the Columbus Circle subway stop, Central Park will be there, and that may evoke majestic trees or strolls or memories of crimes or performances; or the Mets–Willets Point subway stop in Queens on the 7 may make you think about the Unisphere or Venus and Serena Williams at the U.S. Open or when the ash heaps described in *The Great Gatsby* were nearby.

We furnish maps with imagination; they offer us rooms to furnish thus. Even the most straightforward map is an invitation, because you can look at a subway map, a gas-station road map, and say what the child who grows up to be the narrator of Conrad's *Heart of Darkness* said to the blank spots on a map of Africa: "I will go there." Because every map has blank spots, because mapping can be used against colonialism and invasion as much as it was used for it. And because you know that every map indicates more than it can show, offering data and offering you the possibilities that hover beyond it.

These atlases were made as an adventure in what else maps can say about cities. And they were made because even conventional maps are falling by the wayside as people just consult their phones about where to go. With that, the map as a work of art vanishes, and so does some key part of learning the lay of the land; most digital devices just teach obedience to listed or audio instructions. Digital devices tend to offload knowledge from brains to machines, promise us that our ignorance will be adequate because machines will augment us. All recording technologies do this, but paper maps have a way of transferring their data to your mind, so that you become the map. You don't become the phone. Expertise about place never becomes yours with the digital devices, but it often does with paper, which, paradoxically enough, makes paper a more fluid and interactive technology. Mapping can also mean the spatial learning, the process whereby the map is no longer on paper or in pixels but within us.

The digital method may be adequate to get from here to there in the most literal sense, but it isn't adequate for knowing where we really are, either in the literal or in the metaphysical sense. Not only do the batteries and the signals sometimes fail, but orientation goes deeper than practical knowledge: until you know where you are, you can't think about it with any depth. Or breadth, because breadth is what maps give us, the indication of all eight and a half million stories, of this in relation to that, of the options for getting from here to there. Paper maps, on the other hand, have long been objects of contemplation, even daydreaming, ornaments on schoolroom walls, equipment for treasure hunts and idyllic plans and adventures (a prisoner tells me that he may not receive any book with a map of the vicinity in it, lest it aid him in planning an escape). They provide both practical guidance and space for dreaming, and exploring can be a waking dream.

In the maps created for our trilogy of atlases, we have experimented with what maps can do. Many have celebrated the coexistence of two or more forces and by implication the way that cities have always been places of difference and intersection. We have looked at how prisons and levees seek to control and repress underclasses and rivers in Louisiana, how death and beauty coexist in San Francisco, how the publishing and seafaring industries all but defined Lower Manhattan in the middle of the nineteenth century. Some of our maps have sought to challenge conventional wisdom. In the first atlas, for example, "Right Wing of the Dove" looked at the corporate-military complex that makes the San Francisco Bay Area more complicated than the clichés about it as being all peace, love, and left-wing politics. In the second, "Repercussions" offered an alternative story to the famous Triangular Trade map of the slave industry, tracing and celebrating what enslaved Africans brought with them and how this culture grew and morphed and became ubiquitous, even returning to Africa as a liberatory music and framework for speaking up and out. In "The Suburban Theory of the Avant-Garde" in this volume, we celebrate the overlooked avant-garde history of New Jersey and reverse the usual foreground-background relationships that tend to include Jersey in the frame of a New York City map but blank it out or cover it over.

Some have sought to honor overlooked cultures or to show the diversity of cultures more precisely, none more so than "Mother Tongues and Queens," our map of the greatest concentration of linguistic diversity on earth, created with the help of the Endangered Language Alliance. We have explored the spatiality of stories, whether it's Garnette Cadogan's grand loop around New York City in the course of a twenty-four-hour walk or the lives of centenarians who lived their long lives within San Francisco, in a map called "400 Years and 500 Evictions." That map seemed overly sunny when it just traced the lives of four ancients; pairing them with people who were not given a chance to spend their whole lives in one place, because eviction shoved them onward, gave it balance. (Had we made the San Francisco atlas a few years later, it would have addressed the depredations of Silicon Valley's expansion on that city.) With maps of the way the banana trade connected New Orleans to Central America and the Caribbean—and gave rise to "banana republics"—and of water and power in this book, we've looked at what reaches beyond city limits to define or sustain the place.

These are only a few of the variety of things we've asked maps to do, but as the titles of all three books—*Infinite, Unfathomable, Nonstop*—indicate, every map, each volume, is meant to celebrate the complexity, the layers and tangles, the cross-pollinations and conflicts, the hidden and overlooked, the ugly and beautiful aspects of the city in question. They are meant to suggest how much there is to discover in these places and by implication in any town or city or village, how it can all be connected and traced. They are made with the hope that you will be inspired to go beyond these books on your own voyages of discovery.

SINGING THE CITY
THE NEW YORK OF DREAMS

BRONX
MANHATTAN
QUEENS
BROOKLYN

NEW JERSEY

STATEN ISLAND

River

Hudson

"Take the 'A' Train" Billy Strayhorn and Joya Sherrill

"I Love the New York Yankees" Paula Lindstrom

"Déjà Vu (Uptown Baby)" Lord Tariq and Peter Gun

"212" Azealia Banks

"1 Train" A$AP Rocky

"Alfie from the Bronx" Toy Dolls

"Harlem Air Shaft" Duke Ellington

"Harlem Camp Meeting" Cab Calloway

"80 Blocks from Tiffany" Pete Rock and Camp

"Harlem Drive" Quincy Jones

"El Número Seis" Rubén Blades

"Tom's Diner" Suzanne Vega "Small Talk at 125th and Lenox" Gil Scott-Heron

"I'm Waiting for the Man" Velvet Underground

"Uptown Funk" Mark Ronson and Bruno Mars

"Harlem" Bill Withe

"Way Out West (On West End Avenue)" Richard Rodgers and Lorenz Hart

"Across 110th Street" Bobby Womac

"East Harlem" Beirut

"Broadway Blues" Ornette Coleman

"110th Street and 5th Avenue" Tito Puente

"Spanish Harlem" Ben E. King

"Central Park Blues" Nina Simone

"Central Park West" John Coltrane

"Broadway" The Clash

"Panic in Central Park" Yo La Tengo

"Strawberry Fields Forever" The Beatles

"West Side Story Overture" Leonard Bernstein "Empire State of Mind" Jay-Z with Alicia Keys

"Tavern on the Green" Chic

"Tenth Avenue Freeze-Out" Bruce Springsteen "Madison Avenue" Bachman Turner Overdrive

"Studio 54" "Window Shopping on 5th Avenue" Harry Geller and His Orchestra

Blondie "Carnegie Blues" Duke Ellington

"So Long, Astoria" The Ataris

"52nd Street Theme" Bud Powell "Copacabana" Barry Manilow

"The Treat of 42nd Street" Gary Glitter

"Best of Queens (It's Us)" Mobb Deep

"Midtown" Tom Waits "Three Minutes on 52nd Street" Lionel Hampton

"To Birdland and Hurry" Herbie Mann "53rd & 3rd" Ramones "Queensboro Bridge" David Mead

"Times Square" Marianne Faithfull "The 59th Street Bridge Song (Feelin' Groovy)" Simon and Garfunke

"The Boxer" "On Broadway" "Mambo at the Waldorf" Xavier Cugat and His Orchestra

Paul Simon The Drifters "Rhapsody in Blue" George Gershwin "The Bridge" MC Shan / Juice Cr

"When the Lights Go Out on Broadway" Whistle "(Castles in Spain) On a Roof in Manhattan" Irving Berlin

"Off Broadway" George Benson "U.N. Building" Harry Geller and His Orchestra "N.Y. State of Mind" Na

"Chelsea Morning" Joni Mitchell "Tin Pan Alley" Jimmy Wilson "Go Queensbridge" Super Kids

"The Chelsea Hotel" "Fuego en el 23" La Sonora Ponceña "A Queens Story" Na

Graham Nash "When the Moon Comes over Madison Square" Bing Crosby

"Sunnyside Queens" John Leguizamo

"14th Street" Rufus Wainwright "Gramercy Park" Grover Washington Jr.

"Y.M.C.A." Village People

"Positively 4th Street" Bob Dylan "Union Square" Tom Waits

"West 4th Street" Valerie and Bobby Capers

"First We Take Manhattan" Leonard Cohen

"Rose of Washington Square" Alice Faye

"Zen Koans Gonna Rise Again" Dave Van Ronk

"Great Jones Street" Luna "St. Mark's Place" Kirsty McGee

"Bridge and Tunnel" The Honorary Title "The Village in the Morning" The Magnetic Fields

"Daughters of the Soho Riots" The National "Avenue B" Iggy Pop

"Piss Factory" Patti Smith "La Vie Bohème" Jonathan Larson

"Tribeca" Kenny G "Venus of Avenue D" Mink DeVille

"Scenes from an Italian Restaurant" Billy Joel

"You Said Something" PJ Harvey

"Chinatown, My Chinatown" Al Jolson

"The Luckiest Guy on the Lower East Side" The Magnetic Fields

"Great Police Fight (Riot at City Hall)" June Lazare

"L.E.S. Artistes" Santigold

"L.E.S." Childish Gambino "The Bridge" Sonny Rollins

"She's a Latin from Manhattan" Al Jolson "Train Underwater" Bright Eyes

"Wall Street Shuffle" The Melodians "Subway Train" New York Dolls

"Brooklyn Bridge" Carla Bley

"Yeah! New York" Yeah Yeah Yeahs

"Brooklyn-Queens" 3rd Bass

"Ellis Island" Mary Black

"Brooklyn We Go Hard" Jay-Z

"Lady in the Harbor" Waylon Jennings

"No Sleep till Brooklyn" Beastie Boys

"Quincy Street Stomp" Sidney Bechet

"Do or Die Bed Sty" Divine Sounds

"Statue of Liberty" Laurie Anderson

"GG Train" Charles Mingus

"Flyin' High in the Brooklyn Sky" Digable Planets

"Staten Island Baby" Black 47

"Mizz Bed-Stuy" Brooklyn Funk Essentials

"Shaolin Worldwide" Wu-Tang Clan

"Flatbush Avenue" Weird Al Yankovic

"Drones over BKLYN" El-P

"Thank You, Lord, for Sending Me the F Train" Mike Doughty

"Crooklyn" Crooklyn Dodgers

"Coney Island" Mel Tormé

"Coney Island Baby" Lou Reed

"Albee Square Mall" Biz Markie

"My My Metrocard" Le Tigre

"Coney Island Whitefish" Joan Jett and the Blackhearts

"B.K. Anthem" Foxy Brown

"Bucktown" Smif-N-Wessun

"Under the Boardwalk" The Drifters

"Let's Keep the Dodgers in Brooklyn" Phil Foster

"Crown Heights Justice" Mighty Sparrow

Upper Bay

"Ocean Parkway" Spirogyra

"Brooklyn Zoo" Ol' Dirty Bastard

Fordham Road" Lana Del Rey   **"Boogie Down Bronx"** Man Parrish

"The Zoo" Scorpions   "The Bronx" Regina Spektor

"The Bronx" Kurtis Blow   **"The Traveling Song (Bronx Is Beautiful)"** Robert Klein

The Tremont Avenue Cruise Wear Fashion Show"
erry Livingston, Leonard Adelson   "Back to the Bronx" Home Team

"Our Lady of the Bronx" Black 47   "Bronx (Point Du Jour)" Five Letters

"Cross Bronx Expressway" Lord Tariq and Peter Gunz   **"Bronx Blues"**

ake It to the Bronx" Tony Touch   Stan Getz and the Oscar Peterson Trio

"Zulu Bronx River" Afrika Bambaataa

"Streets of the Bronx" The Moonglows

'Bronx Nigga" Tim Dog   "On the Banks of the Bronx" Viktor Jacobi,
Fritz Kreisler, William LeBaron

"Bronx Express" Creamer and Layton

"My Ass Is in the Bronx" Soul Coughing   "Bronx Tale" Fat Joe

Nueva York" Willie Colón   "Jenny from the Block"
Jennifer Lopez

"Planet Rock" Afrika Bambaataa & the Soulsonic Force

"South Bronx"   **"Joyce from the Bronx"**
Boogie Down Productions   David Matthews Big Band

"You Never Seen a City Like (the Bronx)"
Pete Rock and Camp Lo

Bronx Bombers" Grandmaster Flash

"Whitestone Bridge"
Tir na nOg

"Rikers Island"
Cocoa Tea

"Way Up Here" Fleshtones

Can You Tell Me
How to Get to
esame Street?"
Joe Raposo

**"Heading Back
to New York City"**
Joan Armatrading

"Montauk" Bayside

"Get Bronx" Sick of It All

"Laiyan Laiyan" Saad Sultan
and Rizwan Anwer, *Jackson
Heights* theme song

"Alley Pond Park"
Culver Street Playground

"Let's Go Mets" New York Mets

Queens Get
the Money"
Nas   "Me and Julio
Down by the Schoolyard"
Paul Simon   "See You at the Fair" Ben Webster

"What a Wonderful World" Louis Armstrong

"Know the Ledge" Eric B and Rakim   "At the World's Fair"
Les Cooper and the Soul Rockers

"Jimbrowski" Jungle Brothers

"T.O.N.Y. (Top of New York)" Capone-N-Noreaga

"The Sun Will Rise in Queens"
The Exit

"Going to Queens" The Mountain Goats

"California Dreamin' "
The Mamas and the Papas

"Christmas in Hollis"
Run-D.M.C.

"Queens Is" LL Cool J featuring Prodigy

"Those Were the Days" *All in the Family* theme song   **"Queens, NY"** 50 Cent

"Funkin' for Jamaica" Tom Browne

"Don't Stop (Funkin' 4 Jamaica)" Mariah Carey

"Only in America"
Jay and the Americans   "P.S. 48" Organized Konfusion   **"Doin' It"**
LL Cool J

"The Rough Side of Town" Organized Konfusion

"Check the Rhime" A Tribe Called Quest

"Moment 4 Life" Nicki Minaj

"Hillside Avenue" Simply Red   **"Straight Outta Southside"** G-Unit

"Queens" Pharoahe Monch

"Girls Just Want to Have Fun" Cyndi Lauper

"Rockaway Beach"
Ramones

"East NY Theory" Group Home

**"Slow Bus Movin'
(Howard Beach Party)"**

'Welcome to Brownsville" M.O.P.

"Howard Beach" Biohazard   Fishbone   "JFK 2 LAX" Gang Starr

Long Island Sound

1 SINGING THE CITY

Maybe what it means to be a capital is to be a seat not of government but of imagination, the place that the rest of the country focuses on. Think of the places you know without ever going there, the places so celebrated in books, paintings, films, and songs that you think you've been there, whether it's the Paris of Honoré de Balzac and Eugène Atget or the London detailed by everyone from Charles Dickens to the Clash to Zadie Smith. New York has shown up over and over, disproportionately, in the arts, but it would be impossible for reasons of crowding to put all the arts that have described the city on a map, so we left out books and films and paintings and focused on the ways that what starts as a particular place can end up as the tune that you hum, a song line with no guidance other than to the human heart. The sheer range of songs celebrating New York, from Broadway musicals to hip-hop and every possible kind of ballad and rant in between, makes it rich. So many who came from afar were introduced to the city through song that it seemed like the way to introduce *Nonstop Metropolis*'s versions of the city. So here, in songs about parks and corners and subway lines and neighborhoods: New York. CARTOGRAPHY: MOLLY ROY; ARTWORK: GENT STURGEON   MAP APPEARS ON PAGES 14–15.

OUR CITY OF SONGS

WEST SIDE STORY BY JOSHUA JELLY-SCHAPIRO

When you're growing up amid cows and streams and the dancing bears that Vermont's Grateful Dead fans love sticking on their Saabs, New York City sounds like the world. Monk and Mingus and Billie Holiday, in the LP libraries of mountain parents, are jazzy staples. So is every album by that other Jew from the sticks, Bob Dylan, whose songs conjured both familiar barns and that urbane dude and his lady love striding down Bleecker Street on the cover of *Freewheelin'.* My friends and I also reveled, like all kids turned on by words and rhythm in the 1990s, in Nas's *Illmatic.* But no songs shaped my own image of the city as possibility, when I was a kid, as much as those on my mom's worn copy of the score to *West Side Story.*

By the time I learned tunes like "Tonight" and "Maria" by heart, it had already been some decades since Stephen Sondheim's lyrics helped make this musical postwar America's best-loved show (it opened on Broadway in 1957 and then conquered the provinces with its Oscar-winning film version in 1961). But those tunes' bounding melodies, with their tonal leaps precisely mimicking the sound of a subway leaving its station, still evoked immigrants' kids hymning erotic combat. These New York songs were orchestral-mambo mashups fit for dancing on a fire escape. They didn't merely figure the city as a place whose streets forced different people to "deal with" each other. They acknowledged how cultural mixing is American culture. And they also suggested how all of that culture's makers, within their own communities, waged the conflicts parsed by Anita, the queen of the Puerto Ricans. In "America," she extolled the hard freedoms of a new island where her girls could forgo becoming tropical housewives, and instead be working women. Anita acknowledged that Manhattan's streets could be hostile (when she exclaims, "Life is all right in America!" Bernardo replies, "If you are *white* in America!"), but she also insisted on their promise.

West Side Story's progressivism, like its handling of difference, came with more than a smidge of fifties-era exoticism: it wasn't until the show's 2009 Broadway revival that its "Latins" got to speak Spanish. But if *West Side Story* presents New York as a place where encounters with difference can end in a switchblade rumble's needless death, it also figures the city as the site, par excellence, where meeting with difference can birth something else: love.

GIL SCOTT-HERON, "NEW YORK CITY (I DON'T KNOW WHY I LOVE YOU)" BY GARNETTE CADOGAN

There was no shortage of great homegrown music in 1970s Jamaica, where I grew up. But that didn't prevent me from moving along to the confident beats of New York City as if they were mine. I was John Travolta strutting through the opening scene of *Saturday Night Fever*. Later, I was Joan Jett declaring "I Love Rock n' Roll." Setting my sights northward was a yearning for the person I imagined myself to be, could be: energetic until dawn, receptive to myriad experiences, vibrant. And no Pied Piper was as evocative as Gil Scott-Heron in his 1976 song "New York City." His soothing bass-baritone sauntered over a polyglot lattice of jazz and bossa nova to tell of a city at once open and mysterious, charming and frustrating—a place that's home to underdog and aspirant.

When he asserted that the city's musical variety helped bring its residents together, I couldn't help but believe him. The song's groove and rhythmic energy—rattling timbales, delicate piano, funky horn—left me no choice: the city's pulse beat into mine. Moving there felt inevitable. And when I did, Gil Scott-Heron's rhapsody became my refrain. "I don't know why I love you / Maybe it's because you're mine." Here was an attachment born of, well, attachment, but no less real for that. Indeed, lovers of this taxing, beautiful city often find their love ineffable, even unreasonable, and coupled with wonder.

BELLE AND SEBASTIAN, "PIAZZA, NEW YORK CATCHER" BY VALERIA LUISELLI

When I arrived in New York I was twenty-five: young enough to still believe in the prophetic power of certain songs and old enough to elope. I heard "Piazza, New York Catcher" over and over again during my first winter in Harlem. I had been a Belle and Sebastian fan when I was in high school, and maybe I was still holding on to the last embers of my teenage enthusiasm for nerdy Scottish bands from the 1990s. The winter that I arrived in New York from Mexico I heard "Piazza, New York Catcher" so many times and listened to it so intently that I somehow, maybe subconsciously, played part of its story out. That is how prophecies work. Even when you don't know exactly what a prophecy means, some deeper and darker strand of you feels compelled to enact it.

I certainly didn't understand then, and don't now, what this song is really about. I guess it's a song about Mike Piazza, the New York Mets catcher, a song about choosing to leave one life for another, about sleeping in many borrowed bedrooms, about being a kind of ghost in your own life, and about looking for the last rays of sunlight hitting rooftops in winter. For me it was a song about deciding to elope with someone when you're twenty-five and have just arrived in New York.

But good songs, like good books, are never really about anything. And sometimes, the minute we know what something is about, its radiance fades. Cities and relationships often suffer the same fortune. Maybe a key to saving things from their inevitable erosion through routine and repetition lies in knowing the lyrics by heart—as you might learn the names and order of the streets in a city by heart, or as you may come to perceive the many different faces your loved one has in a single day—but never being able to really decipher their meanings or predict the effect they will have on you at a given instant. The songs we like, as the cities and people we come to love, are always sung in a kind of foreign language.

THE CHANTELS, "EVERY NIGHT" BY JOE BOYD

For a New Jersey kid, Little Richard and Elvis were great, but their Southern sound was almost as exotic for us as it was for the Brits; doo-wop, on the other hand, was *our* music, a distillation of the air we breathed. Or at least the wisps of New York fumes that wafted across the Hudson River. And my favorite sound of the doo-wop era was the astonishing cry of Arlene Smith of the Chantels in "Every Night."

According to legend, doo-wop grew on Bronx and Harlem street corners, mainly a boy thing until the Chantels broke through that glass echo chamber. Smith's agonized repentence on "Every Night," delivered over perfectly clichéd descending piano chords in 1958, crowned her queen of the barely pubescent girl-group leads. She combined innocent Holiness Church ecstasies with shockingly knowing adult sexuality.

I was too young for the Alan Freed extravaganzas at the Brooklyn Paramount, where the Chantels and others helped rebrand "race music" as rock 'n' roll. But by 1964, records from only a few years earlier were being celebrated by that advance outpost of postmodernism, the "oldies" industry. Oldies shows came regularly to the Apollo Theater. And it was there I finally heard Arlene Smith in person.

Getting off at the 125th Street IRT station, we walked past a street full of hostile, wary, or welcoming eyes to enter the temple of American music, where the most demanding audiences in the world made stars of Ella Fitzgerald, Billie Holiday, James Brown, Jackie Wilson, and so many others. Each oldies act got two songs: Screamin' Jay Hawkins took dry-ice-filled ages climbing out of his coffin with a skull on the end of a mop handle to sing "I Put a Spell on You," the Five Keys crooned "The Glory of Love," and the Cleftones finger-popped "Little Girl of Mine." But for me, the show belonged to the Chantels. The night before I had been in a Village coffee house listening to long-forgotten folk singers. The Apollo provided an unforgettable antidote.

BILLY STRAYHORN, "TAKE THE 'A' TRAIN" BY WILL BUTLER

"Take the 'A' Train" taught me both the importance and the unimportance of lyrics. On the one hand, "If you miss the 'A' train / you'll find you've missed the quickest way to Harlem" is pretty damn prosaic. On the other hand, the evocation of Harlem and the modernity of the music and mood of the arrangement make the song one of the most poetic descriptions of twentieth-century America I know.

The music is propulsive and complex and optimistic. Life isn't a meditative journey—life is about getting to where the action is in the most efficient way possible. You're not trying to get to Sugar Hill in Harlem because that's where the office is. You're going there because that's where the future is—where there are sophisticated people dancing to music that you want to dance to.

"Take the 'A' Train" was the signature tune of the Duke Ellington band in the 1940s. It was composed by Billy Strayhorn; Ellington's singer, Joya Sherrill, made up the lyrics. But growing up in suburban Texas, I first heard it on a live recording made by my Mormon grandparents. They were jazz musicians, and the album was from a show at a casino in Lake Tahoe in the 1960s. I had a vague knowledge of Harlem as a center of black culture in the early twentieth century. I certainly didn't think of the A train as connecting Bed-Stuy and Upper Manhattan. But even ungrounded in history or geography, the song had a real effect on me— New York is where culture happens, it said, and Harlem is the heart of that culture. And now that I live in the city, it's actually had a terrible subliminal effect on how I get around—I keep accidentally getting on the A train, when I really want the C or the D or the F.

SIMON AND GARFUNKEL, "59TH STREET BRIDGE SONG (FEELIN' GROOVY)"
BY MIRISSA NEFF

I grew up on *Sesame Street*. My West Indian mum worked at the show, and I spent a lot of time on its set. But that's not all I mean. In the late 1970s the Upper East Side, where my family moved when New York went bankrupt, felt like an extension of the show's Technicolor set: a colorful bubble of brownstones and stoops where eccentrics like David Bowie stumbled into our building to hang with a friend downstairs. But I had a notion that things in the city weren't quite right, and that not-rightness entered my world—like when Jackie O's mum, who lived across 75th Street, would affix her icy gaze upon my family's brown skin. On weekends, though, when my brown mum wasn't battling white men to make sure kids of all colors were featured in *Sesame Street* ads, our home's open spaces were filled with the sounds of her favorite record. For a woman who grew up in Harlem's housing projects, after arriving at age eleven from Barbados, the city was about aspiration. And aspiration was Simon and Garfunkel, those two Jewish guys from Forest Hills. Their songs evoked hope for what the city might deliver to people like her—and to my own Jewish dad from Queens. Even after our apartment started getting broken into, that hope—and the playful patter of "The 59th Street Bridge Song"—remained. Its hummable lines were the soundtrack to a city where Sesame Street and 75th Street were paved with the same cobblestones, and where a five-year-old girl could greet lampposts and feel groovy.

BLACK STAR (MOS DEF AND TALIB KWELI), "RESPIRATION" BY TEJU COLE

Black Star, the self-titled first album by the Brooklyn hip-hop duo, formed by Mos Def and Talib Kweli in the late 1990s and named for the 1920s shipping line Marcus Garvey dedicated to the global African economy, has as its main theme black identity in a time of hip-hop's paradoxical success. It is also about the pleasures of words, friendship, creative achievement, and love. The production, done by various musicians but primarily by DJ Hi-Tek, manages to be both minimalist and lush, with hints of soul, funk, and acid jazz.

Black Star is superb from start to finish, but "Respiration"—a celebration of nighttime in the city featuring Mos Def, Talib Kweli, and guest emcee Common—has been a kind of personal anthem for me for a long time now. It is the song that best encapsulates my experience of America: that of being young, black, and sensitive to New York City's stories, visible and otherwise. The voices on "Respiration" have become part of my mental weather. They have been as steady to me as the night and the air; we know a song has hit a special mark when it can bear such incessant repetition. Mos Def, aware of his role as a poet of the city, closes out his verse with this: "My narrative rose to explain this existence / amidst the harbor lights which remain in the distance."

Talib Kweli—his voice a measure higher-pitched than Mos Def's, his rapping style faster—interlocks puns and rhymes at worrisome and exhilarating speed. He goes deeper into the question of the night and its deceptions. Countless times in the past decade, as I set out into the city on my night walks or returned home on the late train or sat on a rooftop watching the lights of Brooklyn or Manhattan or Queens, this was the music in my ear. It has taught me something about how to love a city's complicated dreams.

NEW YORK SONG CYCLE BY MARGO JEFFERSON

When we were young, our parents would leave my sister and me in the care of some compliant relative and go off to New York City for a nightlife of jazz clubs and Broadway shows. When they came home, they'd buy records, and these relics of their expeditions became my Manhattan treasure trove, a sonic vision of the New York I ached to join.

Guys and Dolls: The louche gambler Sky Masterson's city is "a couple of deals before dawn / ... When the smell of the rain-washed pavement / Comes up clean and fresh and cold."

The Late Late Show: With a white fur stole framing her shoulders on the album cover, Dakota Staton curls her suavely girlish voice around "Broadway," where "the night is brighter than day."

Each "Live" album is a station on the pilgrimage to art, glamour, and glory. Bud Powell at Birdland. Lena Horne at the Waldorf. Thelonious Monk at the Five Spot.

I sit at the piano with my songbooks (Jerome Kern, Duke Ellington, the Gershwins), playing, singing, and trying out my own embellishments. Imitations, every one. But imitation is aspiration.

And then my generation's Manhattan arrives. It's 1963. I'm in high school and we're all dancing—do we cha-cha?—to the Drifters as they soul-croon "On Broadway." With its Spanish tinge and aspirational chord changes the song edges toward despair in the second and third verse, then rights itself for those final lines. Rudy Lewis is self-possessed now, and hell-bent for stardom. Just where I want to be.

THE DRIFTERS, "UP ON THE ROOF" BY BARRY LOPEZ

My boyhood unfolded in an agricultural valley in Southern California in the early 1950s and that was the boyhood I brought to New York City, to a brownstone in the Murray Hill neighborhood of Manhattan. When I left California I left behind a flock of eighty tumbler pigeons, birds that thrilled me to speechlessness with their aerial grace and maneuvering. They were hard to let go of, as were the experiences of my regular encounters with rural wild animals, coyotes and alligator lizards and feral honeybees. When I entered the seventh grade that first fall in New York, I learned my classmates saw more shabbiness than grace in pigeons, though I discovered later that up in the Bronx and over in Brooklyn and out on Staten Island men built pigeon coops on the rooftops of buildings they lived in, and that flying their birds over the boroughs restored something that the grid of streets down below took away.

I didn't miss my pigeons for long. Eleven seemed the perfect age to be swept up in another kind of wildness, which I found in Vermeers hanging in the Frick Collection on 70th Street, in the imposing sight of the prow of the Flatiron Building, and in learning the labyrinth of the IRT, the BMT, and the IND. The strongest shift in my appreciations, however, came with my discovery of Manhattan's rooftops. When I visited the homes of my new friends in school I always asked to be taken up to the roofs, for the endlessly vast and engaging views they provided—the sight of human intimacy in the window of an apartment two blocks away, the obdurate façade of the Palisades across the river in Jersey, and once, from a friend's rooftop on East 29th, the way the architecture of Manhattan bellied out between Midtown and Wall Street, the glacial till overlaying the bedrock there being too deep to safely foot a building. On my own block I clambered from rooftop to rooftop, studying the foot traffic on Lexington, so distinctly different from human traffic on Park Avenue. And I came to understand how different deference to someone else's privacy was in the city from what it had been in rural California. I also came to understand a type of freedom that had not occurred to me in California, as I entered the volumes of raw space apparent from up there and felt the expansion, the release that came from the absence of crowding, from the tedious queues at the headline museums or at theaters where the most popular plays were running.

The day in 1962 I entered the record store on East 34th Street where I bought all of my 45s, having that afternoon heard "Up on the Roof" by the Drifters for the first time on 1010 WINS, I no longer felt I was just living in an apartment in New York; I was now *of* New York. I was starting to fall in love with girls, and the Drifters' lyrics in that song spoke directly to the soaring and deflation I was experiencing in my heart. Up on the roof now, I was a city boy, entering that landscape of dreams, floating above the hustling streets.

2 CAPITAL OF CAPITAL

New York is thought of, and likes to think of itself, as the capital of many things—fashion and finance, publishing and art, walking, even the world. (Nowhere else was seriously considered when, in the late 1940s, after a catastropic world war, the United Nations searched for a home.) But the story of how New York became a capital of human culture, and the most outlandishly wealthy city the world has ever seen, is above all a story about *capital*. It's a story about the role a tiny Dutch trading post that became a small English town in the seventeenth century played in the rise of the political-economic system we know as capitalism, and all the ways New York persists as a world center of that system (and a showcase for its economic injustice). The economy of this birthplace of American banking, which became the continent's greatest center of manufacturing in the nineteenth century, has changed a great deal—its most vexingly important products, these days, are strings of computer code and dodgy bits of make-believe "paper" traded by financiers. But through the years, two of its products of capital have remained constant. One is the extraordinary dynamism and stunning capacity for growth that thrust the Empire State Building skyward at the depth of the Depression; the other is the corruption and exploitation, and the violence of inequality, which has only grown with its wealth. Roaming the streets of Lower Manhattan, we all become Melville's Pierre—we can't help but marvel at what capital creates, even as we sense an "utter pauperism of the spirit."

CARTOGRAPHY: MOLLY ROY AND RICHARD CAMPANELLA; ARTWORK: THOMAS NAST, PORTRAIT OF CORRUPT POWERBROKER BOSS TWEED, *HARPER'S WEEKLY*, OCTOBER 12, 1871   MAP APPEARS ON PAGES 22–23.

THE BEST CITY MONEY CAN BUY

BY JOSHUA JELLY-SCHAPIRO

When you look at a map, stripped of human traces, of what became North America's "eastern seaboard"—that vast conurbation of highways and homes and addled commuters stretching down I-95 from Maine to the Carolinas—there are a few spots on the continent's shore that look super-primed for city building. One site is Boston, sheltered behind Cape Cod's beckoning finger. Another includes the Chesapeake's inviting mandible of inlets, one of which became Baltimore. Then there's the spot by the Delaware's mouth where colonial Philadelphia thrived. But one site in this region—a great sheltered harbor, at the base of a great river, with a long island jutting out to sea and angling the eye toward its heart—looks like the slam-dunk Giovanni da Verrazzano had no clue it would prove to be when he floated through its harbor's narrow entrance in 1524. There, hailing the Lenape who paddled from its woods to say hello, he judged that their home was "not without things of value."

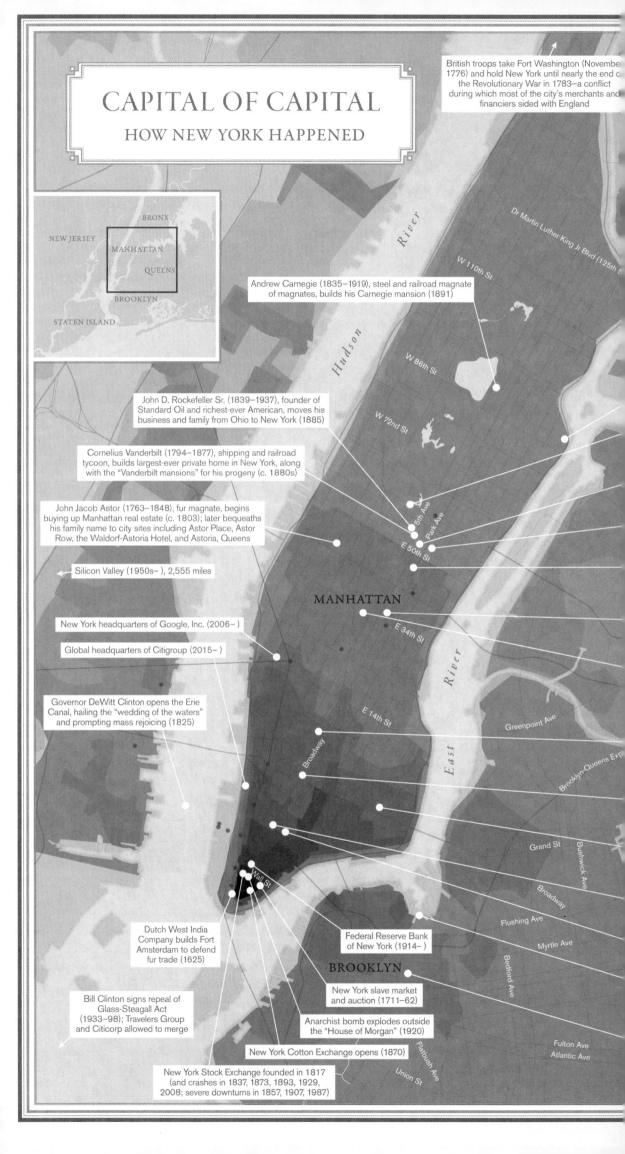

CAPITAL OF CAPITAL
HOW NEW YORK HAPPENED

British troops take Fort Washington (November 1776) and hold New York until nearly the end of the Revolutionary War in 1783—a conflict during which most of the city's merchants and financiers sided with England

Andrew Carnegie (1835–1919), steel and railroad magnate of magnates, builds his Carnegie mansion (1891)

John D. Rockefeller Sr. (1839–1937), founder of Standard Oil and richest-ever American, moves his business and family from Ohio to New York (1885)

Cornelius Vanderbilt (1794–1877), shipping and railroad tycoon, builds largest-ever private home in New York, along with the "Vanderbilt mansions" for his progeny (c. 1880s)

John Jacob Astor (1763–1848), fur magnate, begins buying up Manhattan real estate (c. 1803); later bequeaths his family name to city sites including Astor Place, Astor Row, the Waldorf-Astoria Hotel, and Astoria, Queens

Silicon Valley (1950s–), 2,555 miles

New York headquarters of Google, Inc. (2006–)

Global headquarters of Citigroup (2015–)

Governor DeWitt Clinton opens the Erie Canal, hailing the "wedding of the waters" and prompting mass rejoicing (1825)

Dutch West India Company builds Fort Amsterdam to defend fur trade (1625)

Bill Clinton signs repeal of Glass-Steagall Act (1933–98); Travelers Group and Citicorp allowed to merge

Federal Reserve Bank of New York (1914–)

New York slave market and auction (1711–62)

Anarchist bomb explodes outside the "House of Morgan" (1920)

New York Cotton Exchange opens (1870)

New York Stock Exchange founded in 1817 (and crashes in 1837, 1873, 1893, 1929, 2008; severe downturns in 1857, 1907, 1987)

BRONX

NEW JERSEY

MANHATTAN

QUEENS

BROOKLYN

STATEN ISLAND

Hudson River

East River

MANHATTAN

BROOKLYN

Dr Martin Luther King Jr Blvd (125th St)

W 110th St

W 86th St

W 72nd St

5th Ave

Park Ave

E 50th St

E 34th St

E 14th St

Broadway

Greenpoint Ave

Brooklyn-Queens Exp

Grand St

Bushwick Ave

Broadway

Flushing Ave

Myrtle Ave

Bedford Ave

Wall St

Flatbush Ave

Union St

Fulton Ave

Atlantic Ave

Concourse

Cross Bronx Expy

E Tremont Ave

E 163rd St

E 149th St

Bruckner Expy

Area urbanized by

- 1640s
- 1680s
- 1700s
- 1720s
- 1750s
- 1780s
- 1800s
- 1820s
- 1840s
- 1860s
- 1880s
- 1900s
- 1920s
- 1930s
- 2000s

NY Stock
Exchange
data servers

*(Note: all roadways
shown are modern
thoroughfares)*

Billionaire Michael Bloomberg, founder and majority owner of "the world's leading financial information company," serves as mayor of New York (2002–13)

Onetime site of Hogtown and the "Piggery War" (1859); now home to priciest real estate on earth

Madison Avenue becomes center of American advertising "industry" (c. 1920s)

Astoria Blvd

Global headquarters of Citigroup (1961–2014)

Global headquarters of JPMorgan Chase (2000–)

Northern Blvd

Main St

Broadway

Longtime home of J. P. Morgan (1837–1913), king of finance, creator of US Steel, begetter of US capitalism's "corporate age"

Roosevelt Ave

QUEENS

Grand Central Pkwy

Queens Blvd

Businessman Frank McNamara forgets his wallet while dining out (1949) and invents Diner's Club and the modern credit card

Triangle Shirtwaist Factory fire kills 146 people, mostly low-wage seamstresses in a locked workshop, spurring the formation of the International Ladies' Garment Workers' Union (1911)

Aaron Burr founds his Manhattan Company (later Chase Manhattan Bank) to "bring water to New York" (1799)

Metropolitan Ave

Samuel Gompers, future founder of the American Federation of Labor (AFL), immigrates to the Lower East Side from England and joins Local 15 of the United Cigar Makers (1864)

15,000 slaves and others interred at the "African Burial Ground" (1690s–1794)

Alexander Hamilton creates the Bank of New York (1784) and the First Bank of the United States (1791)

Massive public "jubilee" to hail the laying of the transatlantic telegraph cable and the return of the *USS Niagara* to the Brooklyn Navy Yard (1858)

At Fort Greene, George Washington's Continental Army is defeated by the British in 1776 and retreats to Manhattan

Chemical Bank installs first networked ATM cash machine in the world, at Rockville Centre, Long Island (1969) →

Geography, *pace* Herodotus and a hoary saying oft-repeated in the *New York Times,* isn't destiny. But it can count for a lot, especially in a human epoch defined by waterborne trade. It helped shape how a scraggly colony managed to grow, within three brief centuries, into the most populous and powerful and richest city on earth. Founded by Dutchmen at a time when their little nation of windmills was Europe's great mercantile power, this outpost called New Amsterdam had the luck to be taken over, fifty years later, by another damp North Sea nation—a nation that was fated to become the seedbed, after James Watt made his steam engine tweet, of the Industrial Revolution. That revolution's spark created a new need for hard metal and raw materials and fertile soil—all available to an unthinkable degree in the vast Americas. And New York became the port, par excellence, for joining the riches of its continent's hinterlands to a new age of industrial production and growth.

But why did New York's harbor, rather than that of Buenos Aires or Rio or New Orleans, become not merely the Americas' biggest port in the early nineteenth century, but perhaps *the* central node in the political economic motor—capitalism—that made Watt's revolution whir? What, in the decades after our Revolutionary War, made newly free New York such an exemplar of what Karl Marx described as capitalism's stunning power to create a "world after its own image"? The simplest answer lies in how New York's owners were able to build on history's contingencies, and their profits from farming and furs, to *transform* New York's geography for a new industrial age. In the early nineteenth century they financed and built a new watery highway—the Erie Canal—that joined New York to the Great Lakes and made the vast resources of America's back country available, from New York's frenetic wharfs, to the world (and to local industrialists too).

But we're getting ahead of ourselves. One place to begin tracing the city's rise is on the May day in 1626 when Peter Minuit, an agent of the Dutch West India Company, allegedly hoodwinked the Indians into accepting the equivalent of $24 to sell him Manhattan. The dodgy merits of this tale, about the steal of a deal that saw the Dutch take possession of this twelve-mile island fated to become the most valuable bit of bedrock on earth, are many. First of all, the band of Canarsees with whom Minuit dealt probably resided on Long Island; they were just passing through a place mostly controlled by their Weckquaesgeek cousins. Moreover, in accepting Minuit's tools and trinkets, they certainly didn't think they were offering him control of this island in perpetuity. However, like many myths that become accepted as historical truth, this story suggests much about our current obsessions—"real estate regret," perhaps most of all. It's a tale whose popularity, like its elisions of the truth, offers its own lessons.

Commerce didn't arrive at this place—called Mannahatta, or the "island of hills," by Lenape-speakers like the Canarsees—with Europeans. Sited at the drainage of the region's biggest river, it was a spot to and from which Lenapes and Raritans, to say nothing of Mohicans and Algonquins and many others, toted shell beads and deer hides along forest trails extending as far as what's now Cleveland. To them, long-distance trade, unlike the notion of "owning" or selling ineffables like sky or land, was nothing new. But that fact aside, there's another core detail of Minuit's bargain that's even fishier—the $24 he is supposed to have paid. It comes from a nineteenth-century historian's rough attempt to convert 60 Dutch guilders, the approximate worth of the harmonicas and awls that Minuit recounted giving the Indians, into their rough equivalent in U.S. dollars circa 1846. None of this, though, is any match for the power with which the $24 story—a tale of commerce that turns on an encounter with difference and delights in one party "getting over" at the expense of some un-urbane bumpkins—has resonated, for generations of New Yorkers, as a fitting origin myth. Their city was allegedly founded not as a seat of learning or government, but as a monument to what that well-known apostle of city bombast and avarice, Donald Trump, termed "the art of the deal."

· · ·

At first most of the deals in New Amsterdam were completed by agents of the Dutch West India Company. Chartered by Holland's Estates-General in 1621, the company held a monopoly on all Dutch trade west of Africa's Cape of Good Hope (the older East India Company maintained the same monopoly to the Cape's east). With its boats moving between West Africa and the Americas, protected by its own armed forces, the company thrilled its investors in Amsterdam by soon securing a dominant position in the world market for both African slaves and Brazilian sugar. Its "factory" by the Hudson's mouth was built to lock up this bit of North America for Dutch traders, at Spain's expense, and to wring profit from the surrounding forests by trading for prized beaver pelts. (Later, bulk sales of beaver pelts would help New York's first real plutocrat, John Jacob Astor, buy up much of Manhattan.)

New York's Dutch roots, according to easy-chair historians and devoted fans of Washington Irving, shaped the city in lasting ways. But when New Netherland's last Dutch governor, Peter Stuyvesant, signed the colony over to England in 1664, it contained scarcely 5,000 people. By the time Irving published his super-popular yarns about charming old Knickerbockers and Sleepy Hollow in the early 1800s—tales forged with the express aim of furnishing for American readers rough equivalents of the tales "which live like charms and spells about the cities of the old world"—New York's actual Dutch tinge was far less than Rip Van Winkle may have claimed. Still, this was a town founded by liberal traders, not religious zealots. Compared with their European contemporaries, the seventeenth-century Dutch were much less given to discriminating against anyone with coins to pay. And that ethos remained key to a town whose first permanent foreign trader was a Hispaniola-born mulatto called Rodrigues, whom the Dutch left to set up shop by the Battery in 1614, and where in 1654 twenty-three Sephardic bankers fleeing Catholic Brazil came to forge the first Jewish community in the northern Americas. The English, who took over the colony and renamed it New York in 1664, were less tolerant. But plenty of Dutch and other traders remained, and so too did something of their willingness in 1657 to hear a "remonstrance" concerning local Quakers, insisting not merely that they should be allowed to worship as they pleased, but that all followers of all faiths be allowed the same freedom. New York remained a market town uniquely open to people of all lands for commerce—unless, of course, they *were* commerce. For enslaved Africans were present from the start. When Peter Stuyvesant decreed that a high spiked fence be built along New Amsterdam's northern edge in 1653, it was the "Company's Negroes" who built the rampart giving Wall Street its name. Where Wall Street abutted the East River, the English built an auction block, from which thousands of slaves were bought or loaded onto boats in the 1700s, bound for southern slave ports or for the Caribbean.

The wealth that accrued to Europe from the West Indies dwarfed what came to England from its North American colonies. The most important and lucrative bits of New World real estate in the eighteenth century lay on the old French sugar juggernaut of Sainte Domingue (whose slaves would revolt and rename it Haiti) and on England's prized plantation colonies like Barbados and Jamaica. Those little islands were far more important to the English crown than their northern colonies. This fact would be key to how the American Revolution unfolded. But it was also key to the large role in building Britain's maritime network that New York played—as a port closer to Britain than Kingston or St. Kitts were, but also far enough south that its harbor, unlike Halifax's or Boston's, didn't freeze over in winter. New York didn't merely help bind the Antilles' sugar trade to London; it was where sugar was traded for North American codfish and goods imported from far-off China, like tea and porcelain (to say nothing of opium, which made fortunes for august New Yorkers like Franklin Delano Roosevelt's grandpa).

When, in 1773, some mischievous rebels in Boston boarded one of those China boats to toss its dried leaves overboard, to express their weariness at paying tax to George III, replies in New York were mixed. This town was more imbricated within England's seaborne empire than Boston was. New York's merchants were ambivalent about snipping their London ties. George Washington, at the Revolutionary War's start, advocated burning this Loyalist stronghold to the ground, before he then lost it to General Howe. Throughout the war, New York served as a supply depot and staging ground for England's redcoats, much to the satisfaction of city merchants. The tension bred between those wholesalers' wants and the new republic's national interest would endure. And before that, in the years when the United States was born amid heady rhetoric from Boston and Monticello about inalienable rights, New York's main role was to host debates over how the country—whose commerce was then conducted with a motley assortment of coins and bank notes and IOUs—was going to mediate and grow its volume of trade.

The key figure in those debates had ties, like many New Yorkers then and today, to the West Indies. Alexander Hamilton was born on the English sugar island of Nevis. He became Washington's key aide in running the Continental Army, and then a driven young lawyer centrally involved, after the army's victory, in ratifying the Constitution of the new United States. But Hamilton's larger legacy was born of his convincing his moneyed friends in Manhattan to provide seed funds for the nation's first bank, the Bank of New York—and then by his determination, once Washington appointed him the first secretary of the treasury, to found the First Bank of the United States: an organ purposed to extend loans both to businesspeople and to their government, and funded by selling shares denoted in paper "scrips," for which holders could pay in installments. Thomas Jefferson rejected this scheme, along with Hamilton's larger love for banks, as fed by the immoral "rage of getting rich in one day." He voiced a rural republic's skepticism of a financial system run by urban elites whose manipulations of the nation's wealth would, he warned, amount to "an infinity of felonious larcenies."

The fact that Jefferson didn't see the use for credit among yeoman farmers less privileged than himself, whatever his feelings about banks, perhaps bespoke the aristocratic assumptions of a freedom-loving slave owner whose contradictions were as legion as his gifts. But in any case, Jefferson lost the argument. The centrality of banking was enshrined, right next to the Bill of Rights, at the heart of the American Experiment—but not before disagreements over the banks' proper role in it helped birth two dueling political parties whose animus, if not their specific names and policies, remain key to American democracy. Banking helped foster the split between Hamilton's Federalists and Jefferson's Democratic-Republicans. But the latter party's aversion to the "money power" didn't stop the Democratic-Republicans from realizing that a bank, as Hamilton observed, could be "a very convenient instrument of profit and influence." New York welcomed the birth of its third such financial organ in 1799, after a spate of yellow fever hit the growing city and Aaron Burr, Hamilton's great nemesis, introduced a bill in the state legislature to charter the Manhattan Company, whose project was to safeguard New York's public health by piping fresh water to Lower Manhattan from the Bronx. Thanks to Burr's sneakily including a proviso that authorized the company to handle its own financing, this bill's passage also created a new bank, the Manhattan Company Bank. (This bank would later merge with the Chase Bank to become a lasting behemoth—Chase Manhattan—whose blue logo still depicts the interlocking water pipes it was founded to build.) At its start, Burr's bank backed the projects and aims of Democratic-Republican partisans—heralding a corrupt financial age, wherein hundreds of new banks and bond brokerages would be born by founders pulling the right levers or schmoozing the right people in Albany or later in Washington, DC.

* * *

Hamilton's relationship with Burr devolved, after that subterfuge, until the pair crossed the Hudson by ferry for their famous final meeting, in July 1804, by the Palisades in Weehawken. Burr, who was then serving as Jefferson's vice president, drew his pistol more quickly than Hamilton and shot him dead. By then, Hamilton's conviction that well-funded banks would provide, for the young United States, "a new spring to agriculture, manufactures, and commerce," had been proved. But so had the risk inherent to finance and to placing faith in the banks' bosses to manage it.

When the Bank of the United States first began issuing shares, in 1791, both practiced investors and simple shopkeepers scrambled to obtain them. They were convinced their scrips would skyrocket in price (and they could easily afford the scrips thanks to Hamilton's policy of buying on credit). This demand caused the shares' price to rise. The result was a big speculative bubble, gassy with imagined wealth. Its inevitable burst arrived after the share price peaked, the next spring, and then dived earthward as investors flooded the market with their worry and shares. The Panic of 1792 plunged into debt those who'd borrowed cash or sold belongings to buy their shares. It also prompted the semiprofessional punters at the Tontine Coffee House on Wall Street to strike an agreement that they'd trade such shares, henceforth, only among themselves. Those caffeinated traders' fraternity would soon evolve into the New York Stock Exchange. But the kind of periodic dip that birthed their society would become as inbuilt a feature of American capitalism as the government's vacillating will to regulate the determination of those characters circling Lower Manhattan to "get rich in a day"—or at least find ever new and better ways to bulge their purses.

Where Hamilton's Bank of the United States, chaotic first IPO aside, was largely modeled on the sober Bank of England, it was perhaps predictable that his American progeny would invent novel ways to leverage what the flamboyant private banker Jacob Barker—who made a fortune bundling the federal bonds that paid for the War of 1812—described as Americans' "inordinate appetite for gain." Barker and colleagues like Nathaniel Prime, the felicitously named financier who sold the securities that paid for building the Erie Canal, pioneered what came to be called investment banking. By buying and selling large blocks of bonds issued by states and municipalities to fund their governments' work, or by big public-private companies raising money to lay railroads and dig canals, such banks became crucial to financing large infrastructure projects like the all-important "Big Ditch" that Governor Dewitt Clinton opened in 1821. Investment banks were also crucial to helping New York City fill in the great grid of streets that was laid out, along more aspirational than rational lines, by Manhattan's "master plan" in 1811. And they were key to turning New York into what Oliver Wendell Holmes would term "the tongue that is lapping up the cream of commerce and finance of a continent."

Such was the volume of goods passing through city wharves, by the late 1820s, that the duties collected in New York's customs house were sufficient to fund the entire federal budget. Profits from Great Lakes pelts and Pennsylvania pig iron were now also being funneled into city factories that made hats and shovels and nails and dresses for America's farmers. They also employed the masses of new immigrants, from Ireland or the German Rhineland, who during the 1830s—the decade when New York passed Mexico City as the hemisphere's most populous city—hunted new lives in the brothel-lined streets of the Five Points. No less chaotic than the Bowery's streets was the scene in a stock exchange now run by professional "operators" who were also professional liars. Perhaps the most notorious of these characters, Jacob Little, invented the "manipulated short sale": a bit of financial chicanery that found him promising to sell someone shares of a stock he didn't yet own, but that he would in, say, sixty days. Once a deal was in place, the "Napoleon of Wall Street" would launch a whisper campaign to drive down the stock's price, spreading rumors about the company's debilities or coming collapse. Once the stock's perceived

Map of original grants and farms on Manhattan Island, c. 1928. Courtesy New York Public Library.

worth had fallen suitably low, he would purchase the shares and sell them to his buyer at the old agreed-upon price. Such was Little's great "bear" tactic. But he also flourished as a bull. Drawing on inside information or employing plain old graft to shape the moves of politicians backing new railroads or utilities, he mastered the tactic of "cornering" the market on a given stock—buying up all available shares to drive the price skyward and then forcing would-be "bears," who lacked his inside knowledge, to buy the stock at its new inflated price. Over time and as the exchange's rules evolved to push such manipulations into the shadows, if not into oblivion, these forms of "liar's poker" would evolve. But what has never varied—between Little's day and the junk-bond apogee of Michael Milken and our era's hedge funds (for which what used to be called "insider trading" is a basic raison d'être)—is the excess of cash that its cannier players can make. These riches were poured not only into new investments, but into ever tonier townhomes, whose building by and for the city's financier class prompted ex-mayor Philip Hone to note in his diary, way back in 1836, that "living in New York is exorbitantly dear, and it falls pretty hard upon persons like me, who live upon their income."

Since then, such concerns about the cost of living in New York have been ever-present. They've gripped people both during good times, when the spending of the rich raised prices for everyone, and during moments like the crash of 1837—an event set off by Andrew Jackson's decree, as a leader even more hostile to "fictitious" bits of paper than Jefferson was, that the city's banks stop allowing the purchase of western lands and other property with securitized "soft money" unless it was backed, in their vaults, by actual gold. The resultant scarcity of money in the system ground New York's economy nearly to a halt for several months. But luckily for the banks and their patrons, it rebounded on the strength of the "white gold" that comprised fully 40 percent of East River exports in the 1840s—the cotton picked by slaves down south and sent to New York for shipping to England's mills by slave owners who deposited their profits in city banks. Not only did cotton money constitute a big portion of New York's economy, but those who picked it—the four million slaves whose very bodies could be securitized, insured, or borrowed against in city banks—represented a sum of capital comparable to the entire combined value, before Emancipation, of all the nation's real estate.

It's hardly surprising, given those truths, that during the Civil War many of New York's bankers and brokers advocated for their old friends from Britain to enter the conflict on the side of the South. That didn't happen. But the enduring ties of New York finance to slave finance are perhaps distilled in the story of one of the era's signal firms.

Founded in Montgomery, Alabama, in 1850 by three German Jewish brothers from Bavaria, Lehman Brothers began life as a cotton brokerage. Soon enough, though, the Lehmans moved their firm to New York and turned it into a major investment bank. By the time it went belly up in 2008, their company was synonymous with novel kinds of fictitious wealth whose levels of remove from any real asset, let alone actual precious metal, would have made Andrew Jackson's shaggy head explode.

. . .

The most crucial aftereffect of the Civil War, both political and economic, was the end of racial slavery. But another impact of the war, which had greatly expanded the power and role of the federal government, was the overdue birth of a national currency. The new uniform greenbacks (printed at first by engravers tied to New York banks) helped New York solidify its stature as not merely the nation's financial center, but its capitalist one as well. The city poured its wealth not simply into buying new securities or trading goods but into growing its own capacity to produce commodities. As the great iron works and smoke-stacked dynamos that Marx called "fixed capital" came to cover large parts of Brooklyn and the Bronx, Queens and northern New Jersey, they were surrounded by new housing for workers arriving in a ceaseless stream from Europe, through Ellis Island, or from southern states, whose "smoked Irish" (as New York's factory owners called the kids of freed slaves) streamed north, to become wage slaves instead. New York could claim, by the century's turn, to be the greatest manufacturing center on the planet. That productive capacity joined with the outsized financial muscle of investment houses like J. P. Morgan's, helping many of the country's main industries consolidate into new beasts known as "corporations." Many jazz age investors grew convinced that those corporations' profits and their stocks' prices would climb forever—until the foundations of American capitalism, built as it was with capitalist bricks prone to crisis, crumbled one dark Tuesday in 1929.

With rag-clad families camping in Central Park and breadlines snaking past shuttered factories whose "fixed capital" was now worthless, the country's leaders and citizenry alike placed blame at the bankers' feet: at their willingness to speculate and gamble with the assets of the people and companies whose deposits filled their vaults. Franklin Delano Roosevelt's new regulatory laws, passed after the crash, included the launch of the Securities and Exchange Commission to monitor the banks and brokerages, and a set of new rules for them to follow, the Glass-Steagall Act. The new laws aimed to dampen volatility and to attenuate risk in the financial system by enforcing strict limits on rates of interest the banks could offer on deposits and collect on loans, and by mandating that every financial firm in the country choose between being a commercial bank, devoted to safeguarding assets and issuing loans, or being an investment bank trading in securities. The swashbuckling J. P. Morgan and Company, for example, now morphed into the staid investment house Morgan Stanley. These rules remained in force throughout the staidly prosperous decades after World War II, when New York's banks didn't merely stake the globe's only intact industrial economy, but also financed the rebuilding of Europe and funded development plans and infrastructure projects across industrializing Asia and Latin America, making the United States "the creditor to the world."

But as a new downturn gripped global capitalism in the 1970s and city factories began shipping jobs to the newly industrialized nations, New York hobbled into its "postindustrial" age. The city, like the closed-again factories ringing its edges, became a debt-ridden shell of its former self. Yet as the factories closed, the resurgent banks rose under powerful chiefs, led by David Rockefeller Jr. at Chase Manhattan and Walter Wriston at Citibank.

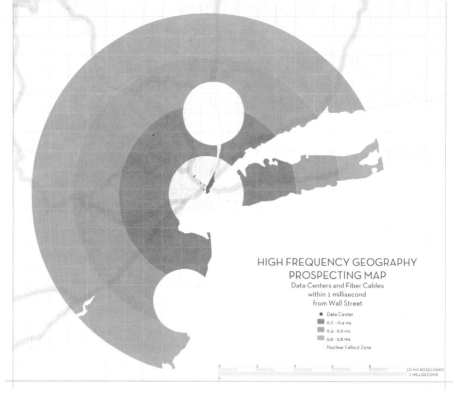

HIGH FREQUENCY GEOGRAPHY
PROSPECTING MAP
Data Centers and Fiber Cables
within 1 millisecond
from Wall Street

● Data Center
■ 0.2 - 0.4 ms
■ 0.4 - 0.6 ms
■ 0.6 - 0.8 ms
Nuclear Fallout Zone

Genevieve Hoffman, *High Frequency Geography–Prospecting Map*, 2012

They solidified New York's central role in the ever more global financial system by open-ing branches abroad and extending loans to the struggling governments of the world's younger, poorer nations, from Jamaica to Zaire, who swelled the UN's ranks by 100 new members after World War II. Closer to home, during the painful years when New York was forced to shutter schools and lay off 50,000 public employees, Citibank's Wriston spearheaded the banks' insistence that they wouldn't underwrite further bonds for city hall. As New York's banks gained increasing power in shaping city life, they revolutionized the quotidian financial lives of people everywhere with made-in-New-York inventions like plastic credit cards and the networked ATM. They also modeled a new role for powerful lending institutions in the global economy: when the International Monetary Fund and the World Bank began issuing punitive loans and enforcing "austerity measures" across much of the Third World in the 1980s, they found their blueprint in New York's banks' demands that the city suborn its citizens' needs to their dogma's bottom line.

Since then, the size and clout of the financial sector have only grown. With the city's "new economy" producing not nails or dresses but fashion ads and information and bits of code, New York's wealth rests not on its stature as a great capitalist city but on its role, ever tenuous, as the "command and control" center for global finance that David Rockefeller Jr. envisioned when he urged and oversaw the building of the World Trade Center. The twin towers that loomed over Manhattan's southern tip until their destruction on 9/11, along with the lives of thousands working inside, may be gone. But Rockefeller's vision persists in a city where the longest-serving modern mayor, Michael Bloomberg, became a billion-aire by selling information to bond traders, and where the larger financier class succeeded in convincing President Bill Clinton, in the late 1990s, to lift most of the last remaining strictures of Glass-Steagall. This new deregulated age saw the nation's commercial banks and investment banks and insurance issuers and credit-card sellers combine and recom-bine into colossal companies with vast assets, and few checks on their will to invest them in ever more abstract forms of securitized "paper"—which actually wasn't paper at all but slices of computerized debt attached to dodgy mortgages. These, in many cases, were owned by borrowers in Nevada or New Zealand, whose loans would have been illegal just a few decades ago. As the old investment banks like Goldman Sachs became publicly traded companies, run by executives whose pay packets were tied to the performance of company stock, short-term gain was incentivized to a degree that would have prompted

Alexander Hamilton to gag. His love of banks was less about creating frothy wealth than augmenting the greater good.

That the fumes from this toxic brew would not merely inflate a bubble ready to burst, but also lead to the federal government's realization that the country had only four "mega banks," which couldn't be allowed to fail, is perhaps in hindsight plain. The miseries and upset of 2008 prompted some new safeguards and oversight—but not the actual reinstatement of Glass-Steagall, or anything like it. Instead, the new regime resembles what came before: the bosses of Wall Street, shuttling between New York's board rooms and Washington's halls of power, are still calling the shots—and still shaping the city's built environment. They may not be growing its productive capacity or industrial base, but they are helping to finance and construct ever-pricier condominium towers. These new duplexes and triplexes are often bought up by Russian oligarchs or Saudi princes whose fortunes derive from the same sort of "primary resource abstraction" that once enriched the Astors and Rockefellers, and who now rub shoulders, on their rare visits to town, with city traders shuffling oil futures at Cipriani. Many of these $100 million units serve more as parking places for speculative capital, hidden behind shell companies and LLCs, than as homes. But their net effect is still to drive up prices and make the city ever less livable for those who "live upon their income," or try to, in a city whose geography of finance has itself in a way, been emptied of its center. Today you might walk from the old seat of the Dutch West India Company, near the leafy Battery, and past the two great aqueous holes in the ground where the World Trade Center once stood, to reach the New York Stock Exchange. Its imposing Greek Revival façade still guards the great hall, once abuzz with shouting traders, that remains the hallowed heart of American capitalism—though nowadays all the NYSE's trades actually occur in an air-conditioned "data center" in Mahwah, New Jersey.

But the island on which the exchange sits remains at the heart of a metropolis where the world's people still come to find fortune—a place desired, and desirable, for offering up all the best that money can buy in food and clothes and culture and art, which, at its finest, can still peel back the city's layers to excavate its past and illuminate its present. In 2014, the artist Kara Walker erected a giant "subtlety," which was anything but, in the cloyingly sweet air of a rusting fixture of the industrial waterfront—at the old Domino sugar factory, on Brooklyn's edge and right across from Lower Manhattan. Built by the Havermeyer family in 1871, this factory was once responsible for refining fully half of America's sugarcane, unloaded here from the West Indies, into a sweet white powder. From the same white powder, Walker crafted a great "sugar sphinx," shaped like a leonine black woman and dedicated to "the unpaid and overworked Artisans who have refined our Sweet tastes from the cane fields to the Kitchens of the New World." This brilliant work was built to bake in the factory hall's warm air during the city summer. It called thousands to feel the ghosts of those upon whose toil, and selves, New York was built. But what spoke as plainly to where the city is heading came in the form of an announcement from the developer who'd bought the Domino factory. He was all set, as soon as the art was gone, to begin filling its ghostly halls with construction crews converting this old monument to industry (and exploitation) into more condos for the wealthy. As a condition of being allowed to build a pair of fifty-five-story apartment towers on the surrounding site, the developer struck a deal with the city to provide several hundred affordable units for local residents. But the full plan for the site, say its initial estimates, will cost $1.5 billion to build. For the 80 percent of its 2,000 units that will be "market rate," they'll be looking, one can be sure, to get at least a couple of million apiece.

September 11, 2001

2008 Financial Crash

Occupy Wall Street, 2011

Hurricane Sandy, 2012

200 million gallons of the Hudson River flood World Trade Center construction site during Hurricane Sandy

Goldman Sachs

Merrill Lynch

Irish Hunger Memorial

"We, the 99%, call for an open general assembly" –resolved at organizing meeting for Occupy Wall Street, August 9, 2011, Irish Hunger Memorial site

Nexus of finance migrates from Wall Street to World Trade Center with towers' completion (1973)

September 11, 2001

2,603 immediate deaths in NYC (including 341 firefighters, 10 hijackers, 8 children, and citizens of more than 90 countries); 1,400+ subsequent deaths of first responders from toxins and poor protection; 30,000 responders and survivors with 9/11-related illnesses, including 2,500+ responders with cancer

American Airlines Flight 11, collided 9:03 am, September 11, 2001

North Tower, World Trade Center (1973–2001)

South Tower, World Trade Center (1973–2001)

United Airlines Flight 175, collided 8:46 am, September 11, 2001

Occupy Wall Street

Founded in Liberty Square on September 17, 2011, and broken up by police on November 16, it inspired Occupy encampments and economy-focused insurrections worldwide

Zuccotti Park/Liberty Square

Brown Brothers Harriman

Federal Reserve Bank of New York

Chase Manhattan Plaza

Trinity Church (founded 1697)

Bank of New York Mellon

Rector Street subway flooded

New York Stock Exchange

Broad Street subway flooded

Charging Bull Statue

Bowling Green subway flooded

September 22, 2014: Flood Wall Street action occupies Broadway from the Charging Bull to Wall Street

500,000 evacuated by boat on 9/11 (largest maritime evacuation in history)

Financial Colla[pse]
October 2008: Wa[ll] Street bankers, trad[ers] and financiers caus[ed] global economic cr[ash;] $22 trillion disappea[red] from US economy

US Bankruptcy Court

Standard & Poor's

Whitehall Street subway flooded

South Ferry subway flooded

Wall Street

North End Ave
Vesey St
Greenwich St
W Broadway
Warren
Murray St
Park Pl
Church St
Barclay St
West St
Liberty St
Broadway
Maiden L[n]
Liberty Pl
Nassau St
William [St]
Pine St
South End Ave
Albany St
Rector Pl
W Thames St
Battery Pl
3rd Pl
2nd Pl
1st Pl
Little W St
Morris St
New St
Cedar St
Thames St
Beaver St
Broad St
S William St
Pearl St
Old Slip
Stone St
Bridge St
Water St
Whitehall St
State St
Battery Park Underpass
Hugh L Carey Tunnel

Hudson River

East River

NEW JERSEY
BRONX
MANHATTAN
QUEENS
BROOKLYN
STATEN ISLAND

Chambers Street subway flooded

Citigroup (until 2015)
Morgan Stanley
Lehman Brothers
Bear Stearns
JPMorgan Chase

Duane St
Reade St
Chambers St
Elk St
Broadway
Park Row
Nassau St
Spruce St
Beekman St
Ann St
John St
Gold St
Cliff St
Fulton St
Platt St

Extent of Hurricane Sandy Flooding

AIG Risk Management

Slave market (1711–62)

AIG

Water St
Front St
Maiden Ln
Fletcher St
John St
South St
FDR Dr

October 29, 2012: Sandy hits New York and surrounding states killing 117, damaging 200,000 homes, and cutting power to 8 million; ranks as second costliest hurricane in US history, after Katrina. Recovery ongoing.

CRASH
CRISES AND COLLISIONS IN 21ST-CENTURY LOWER MANHATTAN

3 CRASH

New York can be a pressure cooker, a world stage, a target, a catalyst, and a think tank, and in one small area of Manhattan it's often been all these at the same time. In the twenty-first century, four collisions marked the southern tip of the island. First came the two airplanes that brought down the two towers of the World Trade Center on September 11, 2001, and gave the Bush administration justifications for two wars abroad and a third against civil liberties, including privacy, at home. As Astra Taylor reminds us in her essay, that administration insisted that democracy and the free market were the same thing, and so an unregulated Wall Street brought down the global economy with the crash that began in the spring of 2008 and peaked in October of that year. Occupy Wall Street responded on September 17, 2011, to the destructiveness of the financial system, and that response became global as well. That destructiveness has ecological as well as social and financial impacts, and all three were felt with the $100 billion disaster that was Hurricane Sandy on October 29, 2012. That storm devastated the Jersey shore, coastal Brooklyn, Staten Island, and other parts of the region, but the floods and blackout in Lower Manhattan meant something else as part of a climate-change-enhanced superstorm that briefly shut down the place that had refused to address climate change. In a sense this is a map of wildly varied reactions to Wall Street, by violent fundamentalists, nonviolent social justice activists, the global economy, and nature itself.

CARTOGRAPHY: MOLLY ROY; ARTWORK: ALEX FRADKIN, FROM *DARK MONOLITHS*, PHOTOGRAPHS OF LOWER MANHATTAN AFTER HURRICANE SANDY 🌀 MAP APPEARS ON PAGES 32–33.

FALLING AND RISING IN LOWER MANHATTAN

BY ASTRA TAYLOR

SEPTEMBER 11, 2001

A lot can change in a decade, even if your proximate location doesn't change much. On September 17, 2011, I assembled with hundreds of others who had answered the call to come "Occupy Wall Street" in Lower Manhattan's Zuccotti Park. Ten years and six days prior, I was not quite a mile and a half uptown when the World Trade Center buildings collapsed. Ground Zero was nearly as close to the fledgling occupation as it was to Wall Street, and the unfinished "Freedom Tower" loomed over us to the northwest.

9/11 began as a beautiful, clear autumn morning. I was en route to SoHo with my seventeen-year-old brother Alexander, who was living with me in Brooklyn at the time, along with my sister Sunaura, age nineteen, and a gaggle of roommates. I was twenty-one, in graduate school yet utterly ignorant about geopolitics. As we emerged from the subway to see gray smoke snaking across the sky, I was overcome not just by confusion but by shame at my own cluelessness about what was happening and why. My brother and I gathered with others around car stereos to hear the news while my brain stumbled over a term that would soon be ubiquitous: terrorism.

Most people on the street were calm, but some were weeping, quietly or hysterically. The weepers seemed attuned to the gravity of the situation, while I felt disassociated, unable, or maybe unwilling, to fully grasp the unbearable truth that people were dying nearby. My own emotions broke through only when I found a landline and called my mother in Georgia, the full weight of the responsibility for my siblings hitting me as I tried to explain the depth of the tragedy unfolding—"buildings are falling," I said, choking on words that were pathetically inadequate, however unnervingly true.

Alexander and I began our walk home after the authorities opened up the Williamsburg Bridge to pedestrians in the early evening. Thousands of us filled the lower lanes usually dedicated to vehicular traffic and were welcomed by dozens of Hasidic Jews on the other side, who offered us bottles of water. By the time we arrived at my apartment in Greenpoint, talking heads were already instructing fearful citizens to tape the windows shut; soon we were told that terrorists were plotting to put arsenic in the public water supply and that anthrax might arrive by mail. (It was later revealed that the anthrax-containing letters that killed five people and sickened seventeen more were likely the work of a government biodefense lab employee—not, as the media and politicians implied, Al Qaeda.) The fearmongering struck us as particularly hypocritical given our family history: my sister is disabled and uses a power chair because of toxic waste related to the U.S. military, the world's largest polluter. One of the many compounds that seeped into the aquifers of the Tucson, Arizona, neighborhood where we lived while my mother was pregnant with her was arsenic. Who were we supposed to be afraid of exactly?

SEPTEMBER 17, 2011

It wasn't until I became a regular at Zuccotti Park, the little plaza in which Occupy Wall Street held a round-the-clock encampment with a kitchen, library, and endless discussions and forums from September 17 to November 15, 2011, that I began to realize the inebriating fear of the prior decade was finally wearing off. Occupy was a rebuke of sorts to the dread-filled aughts, one I ultimately found far more hopeful than the valedictory election of Barack Obama. Instead of imagining that a single politician could magically set things right, the thousands of occupations that popped up not just in the United States but worldwide—from Nigeria to Slovenia—were an expression of faith in collective action.

I didn't realize this on day one, though the demonstration was different from any I had ever attended. Instead of marching and chanting, we sat in small groups and discussed the issues that brought us together: the foreclosure crisis, the burden of unpayable student loans, the bogus concept of corporate personhood, the problem of money in politics, and our deep discontent at living in a society caught in the death grip of an economic system fueled by greed and guided by the delusional idea that endless growth is possible.

That grip had tightened in the wake of 9/11. "I ask your continued participation and confidence in the American economy," President George W. Bush said in an address on September 20, 2001. "Terrorists attacked a symbol of American prosperity. They did not touch its source." A few days later he recommended to Americans: "Get down to Disney World in Florida. Take your families and enjoy life, the way we want it to be enjoyed." For Bush and his minions, 9/11 was an attack on capitalism and democracy, the terms inseparable and fundamentally synonymous. That's how his administration justified "bringing democracy to Iraq" by using military force to impose a new constitution reflecting neoliberal market ideology in its purest form.

The burgeoning global justice movement was dealt a blow by 9/11, though its trenchant criticisms of the World Trade Organization, the World Bank and International Monetary

Fund, and free trade agreements such as NAFTA would still prove to be transformative over time. The hysterical fervor that took hold after the turn of the millennium could not countenance a highly visible public campaign based on the insight that deregulation and austerity make societies more inequitable and undemocratic, not the other way round. Today the idea that the massive gulf between rich and poor erodes democracy is not particularly controversial, in good part thanks to the twin legacies of the global justice and Occupy movements. It isn't simply that things have gotten worse, or that we know more about inequality than we once did (like the shocking statistic that eighty-five people control half of the world's wealth and all the power that wealth can buy); it's that people have come to recognize that capitalism is more than willing to circumvent democracy—which is time-consuming and inefficient by design—as an unacceptable impediment to maximizing profit.

Of course the financial collapse helped provoke this collective epiphany. In pursuit of maximum profit, the "confidence" in the economy Bush asked for morphed into the destructive hubris of credit default swaps, toxic assets, and subprime mortgages, triggering a recession many members of what we in Occupy called "the 99 percent" have not recovered from and one that wiped out half of the wealth held by black families nationwide. But it wasn't just the banks that became calamitously bloated on deregulation. Investigative reporter James Risen argues that the so-called "war on terror" effectively deregulated national security, allowing hundreds of billions of dollars to flood into the defense industry without any checks or balances, establishing what he has dubbed a permanent "mercenary class that feeds off unending war" and precipitating a crisis on par with the one that shook the financial sector. This expanding disaster was essentially invisible to the average American until Edward Snowden appeared on the scene, aided by journalists Laura Poitras and Glenn Greenwald. When the courageous whistleblower was asked in 2014 when the last time civil disobedience brought about change, he was quick to answer: Occupy Wall Street.

SEPTEMBER 17, 2012

By the time Occupy's first anniversary came around, the encampment was long gone but I was back in Lower Manhattan. I stood with a small group at 180 Maiden Lane, a block from Wall Street, picketing outside American International Group Incorporated (AIG), a firm pivotal to the 2008 meltdown. "They're crooks! They're crooks! They cooked their fucking books!" we shouted. "And they taste good too," responded a man in a suit as he scuttled past us into the building.

Wall Street is everywhere and nowhere, invisible yet omnipresent, which makes opposing it difficult. How can regular citizens fight high finance? Occupy found a creative way to break through this dilemma. The tent city concretized a problem (inequality) that is so pervasive it can appear inevitable or natural; it pointed a finger at the nameless financiers who propagate and profit from our economy's fundamental unfairness; and it simultaneously embodied both a political critique and a possible alternative. It's true that most banks have their main headquarters in midtown now, and of course they have offices in many other major cities around the globe as well. In some sense, then, Wall Street—meaning the place, the actual street—was always a symbolic target (not unlike the charging bull statue, which was assigned round-the-clock police protection after it was featured in the original Occupy poster, a ballerina perched atop its back). But it was also a strategic target, because it gave people a new way to comprehend class politics, firmly grounding the still-popular concept of "the 1 percent" in the financial sector.

Today, though the tents have been packed up, the battle against economic exploitation continues in many forms and places. Along with a growing group of collaborators,

Occupy Wall Street protesters head uptown for a demonstration, November 15, 2011. Photo by Rebecca Solnit.

I have channeled my post-Occupy political energies into organizing around indebtedness through Occupy offshoots: the Rolling Jubilee, a surprisingly successful debt-abolishing campaign, and the Debt Collective, a sort of twenty-first-century debtors' union. Financiers seek to wrap debt around and collect fees and interest from every product, asset, and income stream, including our housing payments, the educational "aid" we receive in the form of student loans, and the groceries and other necessities we put on credit cards. Debt is one of the means through which Wall Street occupies our lives and thus a site of potential solidarity and resistance.

In many ways, the Black Lives Matter movement can also be seen as a struggle against Wall Street and economic inequity more broadly. The destructive handiwork of financial predators is visible in all the cities that have been sites of recent protests for racial justice. While the mainstream media chastised "rioters" and "looters," little was said about the economic pillagers whose actions during the lead-up to the financial crash exacerbated poverty and desperation in Baltimore. Wells Fargo employees in that city pushed subprime mortgages known as "ghetto loans" on clients they called "mud people," forcing hundreds of homeowners into foreclosure and costing the city tens of millions of dollars in the process. "We just went right after them," a bank employee told the *New York Times.* "Wells Fargo mortgage had an emerging-markets unit that specifically targeted black churches, because it figured church leaders had a lot of influence and could convince congregants to take out subprime loans." What's more, in many of the communities where black people have died at the hands of police, officers of the law effectively serve as mercenary tax collectors, punishing the poor with fines and fees for petty infractions. Starved of revenue by the kinds of regressive tax codes championed by Wall Street hedge fund managers, local governments are increasingly turning to the courts to raise revenue, pushing already-struggling people further into poverty and too often into jail.

Capitalism is not only not synonymous with democracy, the movement for black lives reminds us—its development is intertwined with white supremacist domination. On June 27, 2015, this troubled history became the subject of an official memorial sign in a small park at the intersection of Water Street and Wall Street; it points to the site of an open-air slave market that operated for half a century, from 1711 to 1762, one block away, at Wall and Pearl, a spot that is now inland but was then right on the East River waterfront. Wall Street was named for a wall built by African slaves in 1653 (to guard Dutch settlers against Native American raids), and later well-known firms such as Aetna and J. P. Morgan profited from slavery by insuring slaves as property and lending to plantation owners, who could use slaves as collateral. Artist and activist Christopher Cobb initially conceived the idea for the sign during the early days of Occupy Wall Street, when he began to research the area. "Within months of the market's construction, New York's first slave uprising occurred a few blocks away on Maiden Lane," the marker concludes.

OCTOBER 29, 2012

On September 17, 1920—ninety-one years to the day before the occupation of Zuccotti Park began—thousands gathered on Wall Street to mark Constitution Day. The Sons of the American Revolution, a patriotic organization that still exists, demonstrated defiantly, resisting the temptation to stay home out of fear that another gruesome attack might take place.

The previous day, at 12:01 p.m., a bomb made of dynamite and 500 pounds of iron weights was delivered by horse-drawn wagon and detonated across the street from the headquarters of J. P. Morgan at 23 Wall Street, killing thirty-eight people and injuring hundreds of others. The New York Stock Exchange suspended trading for the day, petrified of a panic, but was open and running the next morning. In the rush to clean up and get back to business, much of the evidence needed to solve the case was destroyed, but a consensus emerged that the explosion was the work of Italian anarchists, a merciless act of terrorism that helped fuel the Red Scare. 23 Wall Street, a striking triangular building in the neoclassical style at the corner of Broad Street, still bears the shrapnel's pockmarks, some holes as big as hands, in its limestone façade. Today this landmark of American capitalism sits empty and mostly unused, owned by an elusive Chinese billionaire named Sam Pa, who has not yet decided its fate.

Over the years, activists have tried and failed to effectively shut down or occupy Wall Street nonviolently. It took a natural disaster—or, arguably, an unnatural one—to succeed in doing so. "Frankenstorm" Sandy, as it was sometimes called, caused the New York Stock Exchange to cease operations for two days, the first time a weather event had imposed such a dramatic response since 1888. When Sandy hit New York City on October 29, 2012, water coursed up Wall Street to Pearl Street, flooding subways, parking lots, and buildings, doing substantial damage to the AIG offices on Maiden Lane where I had picketed the previous month.

Faced with the wreckage of Sandy, Occupy Wall Street kicked into high gear, utilizing the skills and networks developed in Zuccotti Park to set up multiple distribution centers and mobilize thousands of volunteers, who fanned out over the region and provided everything from evacuation assistance, food, shelter, and medical services to cleanup and carpentry crews. Occupy Sandy challenged the top-down model of charity promoted by organizations such as the Red Cross, which notoriously mismanaged its own aid efforts. (A government-commissioned study eventually dubbed Occupy Sandy "one of the leading humanitarian groups providing relief to survivors across New York City and New Jersey," yet investigative reporters revealed in late 2014 that senior Red Cross officials instructed staffers not to collaborate with Occupy Sandy volunteers for political reasons.) The system of mutual aid at the heart of Occupy Sandy also served as an admonishment to the avarice that pushes the financial and fossil fuel industries to pursue our collective destruction, as well as the smaller-scale opportunism of real estate developers. A month after the storm I visited one of Occupy's impromptu hubs in Staten Island. "The vultures are circling our community," one woman despaired. "They see valuable beachfront property, not a place where families live."

Sandy may have temporarily halted stock trading, but the storm was less an antagonist to capitalism than a product of it, a contradiction best conveyed by the ghoulish image of Goldman Sachs lit up by the company's private generator while the rest of Lower Manhattan lay drenched in darkness. (Its ability to keep the lights on during the worst of the storm was, of course, publicly subsidized—in the wake of 9/11 the investment bank had received $1.6 billion in special Ground Zero area loans to rebuild its headquarters.) That Sandy was the result of climate change was accepted even by most mainstream sources. "It's Global Warming, Stupid," a *Businessweek* cover blared, though the magazine failed to connect the dots between global warming, its own championing of market growth and deregulation, and the enormous power of oil corporations to prevent a sane response to the climate change threat.

SEPTEMBER 22, 2014

The last time I saw Zuccotti Park the plaza was empty, barricaded, and surrounded by cops. It was a little after dawn on September 22, 2014, the day after the massive People's Climate March, and I was heading to Battery Park, where over a thousand of us gathered for speeches and quick civil disobedience training. We were dressed in blue and would soon parade uptown to symbolize the rising tide and to protest the financial sector's profiteering from an antiquated energy policy at the expense of the public good. By then construction on the Freedom Tower, officially called One World Trade Center, was almost complete.

Flood Wall Street was described in the media as a "family reunion" for Occupiers, but it wasn't just an occasion for old friends to reconnect; individuals who had cut their teeth in Occupy's Direct Action Working Group were able to put the lessons they had learned to good use. Protesters held their ground, obstructing the main thoroughfare of Broadway and steadily streaming northward. Hindered by a mass of bodies and enormous bouncing balloons representing atmosphere-poisoning CO_2, traffic came to a standstill, including numerous sightseeing buses. (Tourists, for the record, didn't seem to mind the delay, and I saw one driver invite protesters onboard and up to the bus's second level to take photos of the sea of people below.)

Among those willing to risk arrest was my sister, Sunaura. She and a few other disabled activists had united during the march and were determined to make a statement. When the protest reached its literal eleventh hour, the NYPD finally had enough, and instructed us to clear the intersection or be taken into custody. My sister and her friends stayed put. In the end, 102 people were arrested, including a man dressed in a hyper-realistic polar bear costume, who became a viral media sensation when he was photographed in handcuffs.

Soon the group of civil disobedients dwindled down to just Sunaura and her comrades in their heavy wheelchairs, including an individual who also uses a respirator. They represented a broader community of disabled people who are especially vulnerable—to terrorism, yes, but also to climate chaos—a population often stranded on high floors for days or weeks after Sandy due to broken elevators, a population put in an exceptionally perilous position by power outages, given their dependence on electricity to survive, to move, to breathe. Sitting in the East Village, I watched the protest's final moments unfold over Twitter and cried tears of gratitude and pride. My sister, whom I had been so concerned about protecting after 9/11, had just been arrested as part of a movement aiming to protect not just me, but all human and nonhuman creatures who call earth home. ✺

RIOT!
PERIODIC ERUPTIONS IN VOLCANIC NEW YORK

A larger label indicates a larger riot, either by size or impact. When a rioting group traveled, this map indicates its starting point.

Attica Prison Riot of 1971

Columbia University Police Riots of 1968

Straw Hat Riot of 192[?]

Riverside Park

Orange Riot of 1870

Jewish Student Riots of 191[?]

Anti-Nazi Riot of 1934

Central Park

Rocking Chair Riot of 1901

Puerto Rican Day Parade Riot of 2000

Roosevelt Island

Piggery War of 1859

Race Riot of 1900

Times Square Riot of 2010

Draft Riots of 1863

LOWER MANHATTAN

QUEENS

Orange Riot of 1871

Hog Riots of 1825, 1826, 1830, 1832

Beginning of the citywide Draft Riots of 1863

Rocking Chair Riot of 1901

May Day Riots of 1919

Draft Riots of 1863

BROOKLYN

Stonewall Riot of 1969

Stonecutters' Riot of 1834

Astor Place Theater Riot of 1849

Tompkins Square Police Riot of 1988

Tompkins Square Riot of 1874

Draft Riots of 1863

Holland Tunnel

Fugitive Slave Riot of 1832

Callithumpian Riot of 1828

Doctors Riot of 1788

Anti-Abolitionist Riots of 1834

Eagle Street Riot of 1801

Riverside Park

Election Riot of 1834

Dead Rabbits vs. Bowery Boys Riot of 1857

New York School Riots of 1906

Brothel Riot of 1793

Police Riots of 1857

Fugitive Slave Riot of 1826

Five Points Riot of 1835

Augustus Street Riot of 1806

John Street Theater Riot of 1766

Flour Riot of 1837

Golden Hill Riot of 1770

Fugitive Slave Riot of 1819

Negro Riot of 1712

Negro Plot of 1741

Occupy Wall Street Police Riot of 2011

Stamp Act Riot of 1765

Hard Hat Riot of 1970

Mariners Harbor Riot of 2011

Flushing Ave

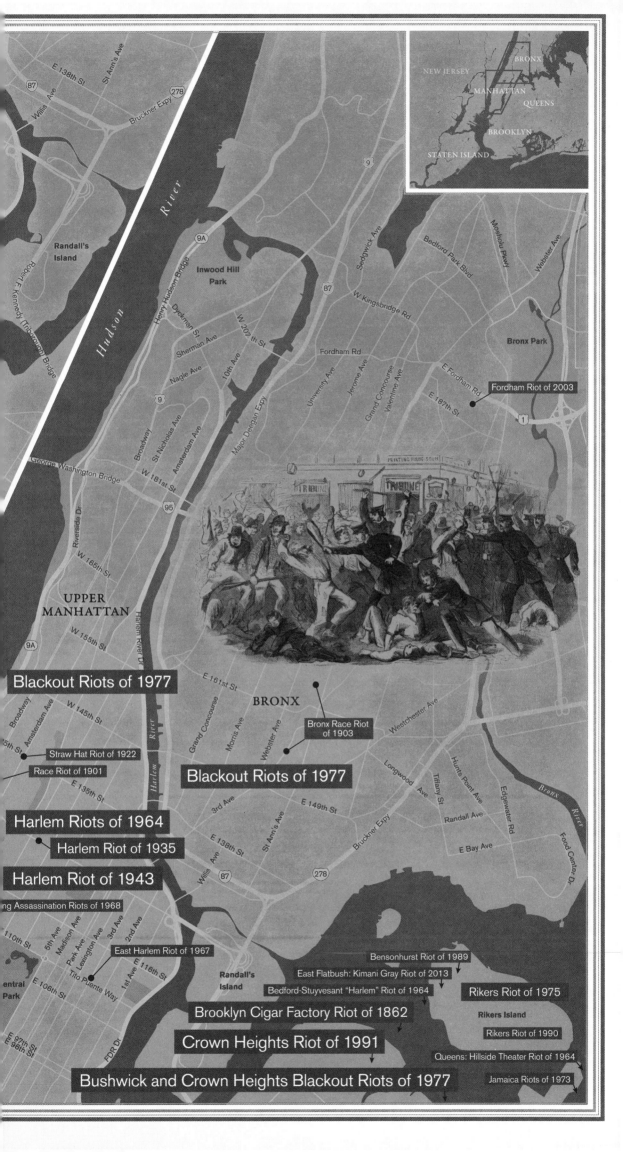

NEW JERSEY

BRONX

MANHATTAN

QUEENS

BROOKLYN

STATEN ISLAND

Randall's
Island

Inwood Hill
Park

Bronx Park

Fordham Riot of 2003

UPPER
MANHATTAN

Blackout Riots of 1977

BRONX

Straw Hat Riot of 1922

Race Riot of 1901

Bronx Race Riot
of 1903

Blackout Riots of 1977

Harlem Riots of 1964

Harlem Riot of 1935

Harlem Riot of 1943

ng Assassination Riots of 1968

East Harlem Riot of 1967

Randall's
Island

Bensonhurst Riot of 1989

East Flatbush: Kimani Gray Riot of 2013

Bedford-Stuyvesant "Harlem" Riot of 1964

Rikers Riot of 1975

Brooklyn Cigar Factory Riot of 1862

Rikers Island

Crown Heights Riot of 1991

Rikers Riot of 1990

Queens: Hillside Theater Riot of 1964

Bushwick and Crown Heights Blackout Riots of 1977

Jamaica Riots of 1973

4 RIOT!

Naples is a city overshadowed by a volcano; New York is a city that at times is a volcano. Riots erupt when two constituencies come into conflict or one group protests against the status quo and it gets turbulent, or when the status quo decides to quash an insurgent group. Sometimes an urban uprising is dismissed as a riot, sometimes a police riot is whitewashed as maintaining law and order, but however you classify riots, New York City has been good at them, or at least good at having them. It's a city at a simmer that boils over readily and did so especially in the nineteenth century, when the immigrant underclass hurled itself at the establishment and rival groups smashed into each other with abandon—over everything from gang turf to interpretations of *Hamlet* in the theater riots. As Luc Sante's essay points out, many of the riots have been about race, from the Draft Riots of 1863, which cut a swath of carnage and conflagration across Lower Manhattan, to the Crown Heights Riot of 1991. And what went around came around: Tompkins Square had riots in 1874 and 1988, both about the poor refusing to disappear. Other riots, picturesque for their names—from the Rocking Chair Riot, which overthrew an attempt to impose pay-to-sit policies, to the Straw Hat Riot, about gangs and haberdashery—were nevertheless horrendous for their violence. New York City's energy can be celebrated, as it often was by Walt Whitman, or feared, as it sometimes was by Herman Melville, and many of the city's laws are constructed to tame and control that seemingly boundless energy. Riots happen when those in charge can contain that energy no more—or fail to give it proper release.

CARTOGRAPHY: MOLLY ROY; ARTWORK: THOMAS NAST, ILLUSTRATION OF DRAFT RIOTS, *HARPER'S WEEKLY*, AUGUST 1, 1863. MAP APPEARS ON PAGES 40–41.

THE VIOLENCE OF INEQUALITY BY LUC SANTE

Twice I've wandered into riots in New York City. On the evening of July 13, 1977, I was having dinner with friends on the Upper West Side when the lights suddenly went out. After we determined that the cause wasn't a fuse and that the problem wasn't limited to their building, I left for my apartment, three blocks away. When I got to Broadway I found a river of humans, urgently pressing in the dimming light of dusk. I knew right away that, whatever was up, I had no business being there. The people in the street lived with few resources in the neighborhood's many decrepit single-room-occupancy hotels; I lived comfortably in a big place on a bookstore clerk's salary. I gingerly threaded my way across, walked eleven flights up, and spent the evening with my roommates, hanging out the window and listening to a battery-powered radio. We watched as cars pulled up onto the sidewalk below and men ran chains from them to the grates on the storefronts. We watched an endless stream of people running into and out of the supermarket across the street. We watched a family of Yemeni immigrants guarding their bodega on the corner opposite. We watched low-flying helicopters raking the rooftops with searchlights. We watched many hours of amorphous chaos. The next morning, empty buildings to the east were still smoking.

On the evening of August 6, 1988, I was walking my dog along First Avenue near 9th Street when I saw eight cop cars tear up the avenue and turn onto St. Mark's Place. I had an idea of what might be happening, so I took the dog home to 12th Street and headed south on Avenue A. Along the front of Tompkins Square Park stood a bewildering array of police vehicles: Hazardous Materials Squad, DWI Task Force, Emergency Services, each bigger than the next. Milling around were hundreds of cops, from beat patrolmen (who, ominously, wore their caps turned around and had their badge numbers obscured) to the rigged-out Tac Squad to easily identifiable plainclothesmen. Helicopters flew so low the backwash from their rotors drew trash from corner trash cans upward in spirals. This massive presence was occasioned by a homeless encampment in the park, which had apparently drawn complaints from more fortunate local residents. The neighborhood then was swiftly transitioning in a manner that has since become familiar: tenements bought, flipped, cosmetically improved; apartment rents grossly multiplied; new residents' expectations fully suburban.

I spent the rest of the night moving up and down the avenue, witnessing sporadic confrontations. There would be a face-off between a few dozen locals and a dozen cops, with insults flung, which might last five or ten minutes—then someone would throw a bottle and the cops would charge, bloodying heads. The locals had no plan and no organization, only emotions. The police, having accomplished the task of emptying the park, were now also guided only by emotions. Occasionally, priests and other neighborhood figures would attempt to mediate, but to no avail; there was no middle ground to reach. Ambulances carried away the more seriously injured of the locals. Fire trucks arrived in response to spurious reports of fires. Cops went around ostensibly securing businesses that had already been secured. Around four in the morning I had finally had enough and started walking home, but was caught in a police charge and dragged a few yards, my clothes destroyed in the process.

What both these riots had in common was property, which is to say, class. The first was a riot by the poor, who in thoroughly American fashion took advantage of a disruption to avail themselves of goods, hard and soft. The second was a riot by police, who in thoroughly American fashion took advantage of a disruption to break the heads of random citizens. Nevertheless, money and property lay at the root of the disruption, beginning with the fact that many of Tompkins Square's homeless had previously lived in SRO hotels but had been turned out when those buildings were sold to speculators. The 1977 riot—whose unrest marked the nadir of New York's wary "summer of Sam," and which was as citywide as the blackout occasioning it—resulted in 1,616 damaged stores, 1,037 fires, 4,500 arrests, and 550 injured cops, not to mention such details as the 50 new Pontiacs driven away from a Bronx dealership and the many mixing boards and other electronic equipment lifted from stores, which directly contributed to the birth of hip-hop. The Tompkins Square Riot, as the second fray was soon dubbed on a t-shirt, resulted in no significant property damage but over a hundred complaints of police brutality, which were answered with a few, mostly temporary, shufflings of jobs and two officers charged with excessive force.

There weren't direct or immediate predecessors to either of these events, which is not to say that they arose in a vacuum. At a cursory glance, riots over property in New York would seem to have been rare over the centuries. The 1837 Flour, or Bread, Riot, when scarcity and high prices saw the city's un- and underemployed destroy, paradoxically,

"Mr Andrews" of "Virginia" speechifying to the rioters, from the roof of a butcher's shop in Forty-Sixth Street, engraving of Draft Riots, *New York Illustrated News*, 1863

more than 500 barrels of flour and 1,000 bushels of wheat, is the only real commodity riot, although those were numerous in other places then. And police riots had long been limited to the 1857 clash between the city's two competing departments, the Municipals and the Metropolitans (the Municipals lost and were dissolved). That was the case, at least, until the Columbia University student strike of 1968, when the NYPD responded to peaceful protest with outsized violence, prefiguring its response to the encampment and marches of the Occupy Wall Street movement in 2011. The latter set of events, like the Tompkins Square Park affray, involved police concealing their names and badge numbers.

Although it became associated with protests against the Vietnam War, the Columbia strike was initially sparked by the university's plan to build a private gym in Morningside Park in Harlem, denying admission to locals. In other words, beneath the ostensible causes of the riot lay a serpent's nest of intertwined issues: property, class, and, overwhelmingly, race. Every major riot in the city's history has involved these ingredients, including the very largest and most destructive, the Draft Riots of 1863. Those riots, which raged for three days in the summer of 1863, were nominally caused by working-class resentment of the fact that the well-to-do could buy their way out of military conscription. Another ingredient was the sympathy for the South that lingered, along with old commercial and industrial ties, among many city-dwellers. But it was a resentment of black laborers—in March, white longshoremen had revolted against the hiring of blacks, with whom they had worked peaceably for years—that surfaced most destructively. Mobs, mostly composed of working-class Irish and Germans, lynched eleven black men, burned the Colored Orphan Asylum, destroyed the homes of African Americans and businesses that catered to black people, and attacked armories, police stations, two churches, the mayor's residence, and the homes of interracial couples and abolitionists. At least 120 people died. Order was restored only when the military was finally brought in on the third day. A large percentage of the black population of Manhattan left as a consequence, many moving to Brooklyn.

Nearly half of all the city's riots—and nearly all the most serious ones—have hinged, directly or indirectly, on race relations. The Negro Riot of 1712 was New York's very first social upheaval. Its facts are scant—between twenty and seventy African slaves allegedly set fire to a building on Maiden Lane, then the city's northern boundary, and attacked whites attempting to douse the flames, killing nine. Of the forty-three slaves arraigned, eighteen were acquitted, twenty hanged, and three burned at the stake. In 1741 the facts are even murkier—a ship was seized, possibly for piracy, and its African crew were sold as slaves, but they managed to break free and burn down a number of houses, including the governor's mansion. The Doctors Riot of 1788 was sparked by medical students digging up cadavers for dissection from the Negroes Burial Ground. A petition from African American citizens was ignored by the authorities, but when a newspaper article alleged that the body of a white woman had been dug up, citizens attacked the hospital and the violence resulted in some twenty deaths.

The Eagle Street Riot of 1801 began as an attempt to free the twenty slaves held by Jeanne Volunbrun, a French émigrée from Haiti—slaves who had already been freed by the French Revolutionary Convention of 1794 but whose status she attempted to alter by sending them south. Twenty persons of color were imprisoned for their part in the fray. Other small riots in 1819, 1826, and 1832 resulted from interventions to prevent the reenslavement of runaways from the South—gradual abolition began in New York State in 1799 and slavery ended altogether in 1827. The white abolitionists of the period tended to be well-educated members of the upper classes; their activities were resented by many in the white working class—mostly Irish Catholic immigrants—who saw free blacks as competing for their jobs and accepting lower wages. Tempers rose to the point of violence in the Anti-Abolitionist Riots of 1834, when a mob ransacked the Rose Street home of the abolitionist Lewis Tappan and attacked the Bowery Theater, whose stage manager was a British-born abolitionist—he appeased them by sending out an actor in blackface to sing "Zip Coon." The Brooklyn Cigar Factory Riot of 1862 was the work of local Irish and German unskilled laborers who resented the fact that African Americans, who commuted from other parts of the city, were employed as skilled cigar rollers and made more money. The agitators relied on what was to become a sadly common race-baiting tactic—an alleged assault on a white woman—but the violence was muted by their ineptitude and by the factory's prescient decision to send its black workers home.

The turn of the twentieth century saw race riots in many American cities, and New York was no exception. Riots in 1900 (in Hell's Kitchen, which then had a large African American population), in 1901 (in Harlem, which was still predominantly white), and in 1903 (in a mixed-race part of the Bronx) all had flimsy pretexts—rumors, mistaken identity—and all were flare-ups of sudden and contagious violence, albeit without fatalities. The Harlem Riot of 1935 began when a sixteen-year-old boy was caught stealing a penknife from a dime store. The store owner told the cops to let him go, and they took him out via the back door, but onlookers thought he was being taken for a beating and later thought he had died. The ensuing violence resulted in three dead black men, seventy-five arrests, and looted stores. The Harlem Riot of 1943 had an even murkier origin—an African American veteran may have been disrespected by a hotel clerk, but the facts were never established. Its harvest, however, was worse: five dead, 400 injured, 500 arrested, and $5 million in damages.

In the 1964 version, a fifteen-year-old black youth, who may or may not have brandished a knife, was shot dead by an off-duty cop. Rioting spread throughout Harlem and across the river to Bedford-Stuyvesant. The 1973 riots in Jamaica, Queens, began when plainclothes cops stopped a ten-year-old boy and his stepfather on suspicion of having robbed a taxi driver (although the perpetrators were described as both being around six feet tall and in their mid-twenties). The pair, who thought they were the ones being robbed (the stepfather had just been paid), tried to flee; the boy was shot dead. Rioting followed the incident and, again, a year later, with the acquittal of the cop, who previously had been charged with pistol-whipping a fourteen-year-old.

The so-called Bensonhurst Riot of 1989 was something of a misnomer. On August 23, a sixteen-year-old black youth was shot and killed by members of a large group of white teenagers in the predominantly Italian American neighborhood, where he had gone to buy a car. A protest march in Bensonhurst the next day was met with hostility but no outright violence. The ultimate cause of the 1991 Crown Heights Riot was the deep-seated misunderstanding between the Jewish Lubavitcher community on one side of Eastern Parkway and the African American community on the other. The immediate cause was a car accident: a driver in Chief Rabbi Menachem Schneerson's motorcade swerved onto the sidewalk and killed the seven-year-old son of Guyanese immigrants. Rumors circulated that the boy was refused aid by a Lubavitcher ambulance, and in the ensuing three-day fracas, Jewish homes and cars were attacked and a rabbinical student from Australia was stabbed to death by a black teenager.

There is one New York City riot that had a long-lasting effect and is now commemorated around the world. In June 1969, when police raided the Stonewall Inn, a Mafia-run gay bar on Christopher Street in the Village, they unexpectedly met with resistance, and rioting ensued over several days. The events galvanized the gay community, and the city's first Gay Pride March, a year later, began at the Stonewall's site.

The death of Eric Garner in the summer of 2014—from the effects of a chokehold, a prohibited tactic, applied by an NYPD officer who was taking him into custody for selling untaxed individual cigarettes on the street—didn't prompt a riot, for a list of reasons ranging from the intelligence of the Black Lives Matter movement to changing demographics to the increasingly military disposition and equipment of the police. But that hardly indicates that things have changed much since the end of slavery, in a city where many may now revel, most days, in "coexisting" with difference, but where the violence of inequality, inevitably, can still be made very real.

5 CARBONIFEROUS

Cities are contradictions. There's an argument that living densely with public transit and public amenities is inherently green, the way to have the smallest carbon footprint. But people's ecological impact includes the full global footprint of their consumption, which isn't counted by prevailing urban studies. Those miss the fact that affluent New Yorkers fly more, own more homes, consume more imported goods. There's a directly political dimension too. Take David Koch, the richest man in New York and among the top ten on earth. He's one of the country's most devoted climate deniers. He also lives near the headquarters of 350.org, the heroic and effective climate action group. On September 21, 2014, New York hosted the world's biggest-ever climate march (the green zigzag on this map). Protestors walked down Central Park West, past millionaires' homes and Fox News's climate-denial studios. New York is a global stage for the battle between unchecked capitalism and climate justice. Our map gives a sample of some key protagonists. Housing and labor groups are also low-carbon champions, even if they say little about it. Indeed, our map shows that many of the greenest people in New York City live in public housing. The data, which estimates zip-code-specific, per-capita global carbon footprints using a range of sources and modeling techniques, was kindly provided by the researcher Kevin Ummel, based on his 2014 study "Who Pollutes?" published by the Center for Global Development.

CARTOGRAPHY: MOLLY ROY; ARTWORK: BETTE BURGOYNE　　MAP APPEARS ON PAGES 48–49.

PETRO GOTHAM, PEOPLE'S GOTHAM

BY DANIEL ALDANA COHEN

Climate change is an uneasy topic. Good news is welcome. For those lucky enough to live well in Manhattan, it's comforting to imagine that at least as far as carbon is concerned, the borough's density is right and good. Sure, the streets of midtown are clogged with cars. But walking, subways, and tall buildings with their cozy apartments and offices—all are exemplars of energy efficiency. Low-carbon virtuous, by default. This is the story told by the *New Yorker* writer David Owen in his classic essay "Green Manhattan." It's the story that's been repeated a thousand more times by Michael Bloomberg.

But the story is incomplete. And the implications are global. Manhattan isn't a snow globe, and neither is New York City. It just pretends to be one in its annual carbon-accounting reports, the city's official tallies of the greenhouse gases that cause global warming and of those gases' attribution to local activities. The unfortunate norm, which New York follows, is to use a method that ignores the emissions caused by growing and raising the city's food, ignores the carbon emitted to power the factories that assemble

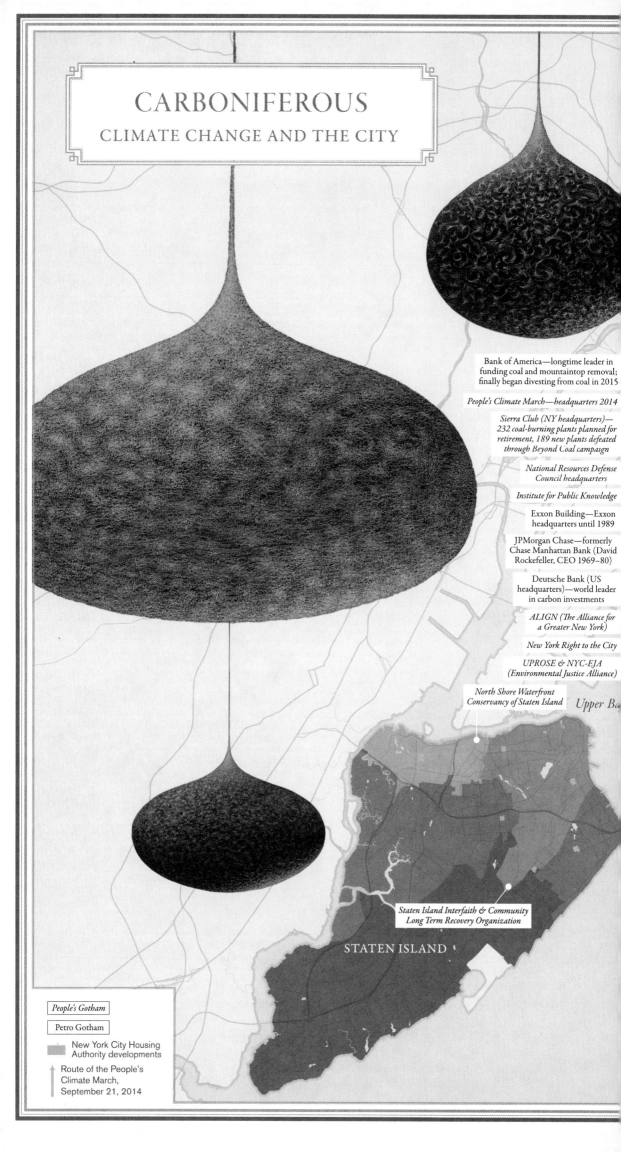

CARBONIFEROUS
CLIMATE CHANGE AND THE CITY

Bank of America—longtime leader in funding coal and mountaintop removal; finally began divesting from coal in 2015

People's Climate March—headquarters 2014

Sierra Club (NY headquarters)—232 coal-burning plants planned for retirement, 189 new plants defeated through Beyond Coal campaign

National Resources Defense Council headquarters

Institute for Public Knowledge

Exxon Building—Exxon headquarters until 1989

JPMorgan Chase—formerly Chase Manhattan Bank (David Rockefeller, CEO 1969–80)

Deutsche Bank (US headquarters)—world leader in carbon investments

ALIGN (The Alliance for a Greater New York)

New York Right to the City

UPROSE & NYC-EJA (Environmental Justice Alliance)

North Shore Waterfront Conservancy of Staten Island

Upper Ba

Staten Island Interfaith & Community Long Term Recovery Organization

STATEN ISLAND

People's Gotham

Petro Gotham

New York City Housing Authority developments

Route of the People's Climate March, September 21, 2014

Sustainable South Bronx

WE ACT for Environmental
Justice (West Harlem
Environmental Action, Inc.)

Rockefeller Brothers Fund
(divested from fossil fuels, 2014)

Mike Bloomberg (climate
contradictions aplenty)

David Koch's NY lair

Fox News
headquarters

350.org

St. Jacobi Lutheran
Church, Occupy
Sandy relief hub

St. John's Episcopal Church,
Occupy Sandy Distribution Center

Worker's Justice Project

BRONX

Green Worker Cooperatives

(There Be Monsters)

Rockefeller Center

United Nations—organizer
of Intergovernmental Panel
on Climate Change

MANHATTAN

El Puente

Food and Water Watch

Fracking and fossil fuel filmmaker Josh Fox

Mayday Community Space—home
to People's Climate Arts, 2014

Crown Heights Tenant Union

QUEENS

BROOKLYN

(There Be Monsters)

You Are Never Alone
(YANA) Community Center

Hudson River

East River

Long Island Sound

Lower Bay

Global Carbon Footprint
(tons CO$_2$ equivalent emitted per person per year)

No resident
data for NYC

10   15   20   25   30   35 tons

New Yorkers' smart phones and weave their clothes, and ignores the fumes spewed by planes that ferry New Yorkers around the world.

There are, however, more sophisticated methods for calculating the global carbon footprint of everything that a person (or organization) in a given area is responsible for. This consumption count paints a whole other picture.

Levels of density shape a person's carbon footprint; so do income and lifestyle. When it comes to the carbon emissions of New York's individual residents, as calculated in terms of consumption, Manhattan is the worst borough. Because it's the richest. Crowded but well-to-do West Villagers' carbon footprints are comparable to sprawling suburbanites' all over the country. It is only residents of Manhattan's less-gentrified neighborhoods who have really low carbon footprints. They reside by the island's northwest and southeast tips, in zip codes anchored by public housing.

And so, the image of New York City that should inspire the world's would-be low-carbon urbanists is the combination of towers run by the New York City Housing Authority (NYCHA) and the outer boroughs' mosaic of mixed-income, mixed-use neighborhoods. Sometimes beautiful, sometimes plain, from Woodside to Clinton Hill, a still-democratic New York teems with life and ecological promise. This isn't to suggest celebrating the poorest New Yorkers' lack of income, their inability to consume. On the contrary, the thing to celebrate is what the radical urbanist Mike Davis in his essay "Who Will Build the Ark?" calls the "cornerstone of the low-carbon city . . . the priority given to public affluence over private wealth." Public housing, well-stocked libraries, accessible transit, gorgeous parks: these are democratic low-carbon amenities. And they're the political achievements of working-class New York.

Still, your eyes are narrowing. Surely New York City has more to offer the politics of global warming than a stack of individuals', even neighborhoods', moral balance sheets, with pounds of carbon standing in for sins. And you're right. New York isn't a political snow globe either. Woven into the city's local geographies of consumption are global geographies of power. From the United Nations Security Council to Citibank boardrooms to Fox News studios to the underventilated activist meeting room on Beaver Street, New York is a city where global political networks are knotted together. Here, people combine resources and symbols; they create stories, projects, and policies. All of this influences the ways that other cities try to organize themselves. And it helps shape the global debate about who matters to the climate and how. What happens here literally remakes the atmosphere—in direct and indirect, obvious and subtle ways.

The stakes are high. The carbon dioxide emissions of the world's cities make up about half of the world's total. Between now and 2030, argues a thorough report from the London School of Economics' Cities Centre, smart pro-density planning by just 724 of the world's largest cities could save 14.4 gigatons of carbon. That's over half of the currently recoverable carbon stored in Canada's tar sands. A lot of carbon. So the question is: What counts as smart? And what can New York contribute to that conversation? Greenwich Village is minuscule. But thanks to the activist and writer Jane Jacobs, the neighborhood became a global template for living well. Then again, Jacobs wasn't the only New Yorker working to reshape the world all those years ago.

. . .

On May 20, 1960, in the New York Plaza Hotel, the petroleum heir and vice chairman of Chase Manhattan Bank, David Rockefeller, gave a speech called "New York: Economic Center of the World." It was prophetic. With the global economy becoming more complex, Rockefeller said, "there is a growing need for a headquarters city, a focal point for decision-making." He urged the construction of a downtown World Trade Center to enable the expansion of the city's already "marvelously varied and skilled facilities." In other words, an agglomeration of lawyers, advertisers, public relations experts, management consultants, and other professionals—an ecology of skills and talent in support of globe-wrangling financiers.

Rockefeller also insisted that money ruled most effectively when joined to beauty and wisdom. New York's centrality, he said, required that "cultural and educational facilities [be] so developed that the city would exercise leadership in the arts." The city needed "new museums and theaters." For particular praise, he singled out the forthcoming Lincoln Center for the Performing Arts.

We don't need to give Rockefeller undue credit for what came next. Still, something of his vision was realized. The city that, as he pointed out, was then the world's largest manufacturing center, has since outsourced most physical production. Rockefeller's proposed World Trade Center revitalized Wall Street.

#FLOOD WALL STREET
STOP CAPITALISM!
END THE CLIMATE CRISIS!

NYC SEPT 22ND

FLOODWALLSTREET.NET

Postcard for Flood Wall Street demonstration, 2014

New York's capitalists traded mechanical levers for remote controls. The economic elite turned to finance, real estate, knowledge, and culture. In the age of globalization, New York became a machine for converting far-off greenhouse gas emissions—in the form of smokestacks, factory farms, and sprawling suburban development—into local money and glamour. Manhattan's glitz laundered the distant, dirty combustion of fossil fuels, just as local laundromats and hair salons recycled the moneys of the Mob. And Manhattan did it in style.

Lincoln Center's main theater opened four years after Rockefeller's speech, becoming home to the city's ballet. Today, it bears the name of another oilman, David Koch, who pledged $100 million for its restoration. Koch also gave $65 million to the Metropolitan Museum of Art, to rebuild its four-block public plaza. And thanks to Koch's donation of $20 million to the American Museum of Natural History, his name adorns two great halls of dinosaur bones. Sometimes you have to look over your shoulder. As climate change hastens the next Great Extinction, there's an eerie, retrospective futurism to spending oil profits on the veneration of vanished giants.

David Koch is Charles Koch's brother. Together, they own the second largest privately held corporation in the United States. They fund a vast network of right-wing causes, of which the Tea Party is the most famous outcome. They've destroyed one attempt by American senators to put a price on carbon, and they're determined to block the next. Meanwhile, on each side of Central Park, they gild the museums and theaters that are prosperous, cultured, and carbon-rich Manhattan's most attractive alibis.

But there is more to Manhattan's moneyed interests than the Kochs. Wall Street as a whole has poured untold billions into oil and coal. The borough's 1% isn't exclusively invested in carbon, however. In the summer of 2015, the Street soured on King Coal, slashing direct investments into the sector. Just as interesting is the way that the Street is multiplying its twenty-first-century bets. The Street is directing more money and prestige to all manner of low-carbon and resiliency companies. Gotham isn't determined to drown

51

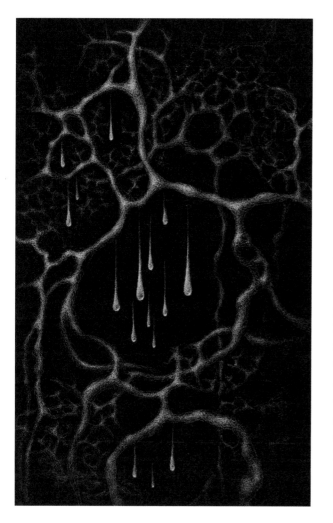

Bette Burgoyne, *Inside*, 2010

Manhattan in seawater, only to drown itself in dollars. Problem is, the difference between the two goals is slight.

Take Deutsche Bank, an early adopter. Its New York headquarters are at 60 Wall Street—the building whose atrium served as a meeting hall for Occupy Wall Street protestors during that movement's heyday. By 2008 Deutsche Bank's innovative "Green Climate Fund" was already worth $2.9 billion. In the main, Deutsche's investments have been ploughed into green tech, like solar panels. But the fund also balanced its optimism by investing in the prospects of climate catastrophe. It took stocks in Veolia, which builds desalination plants for increasingly scarce water. It invested in Monsanto and Syngenta, agro-business companies trying to engineer drought-resistant crops for a warming world. It put money into the giant fertilizer multinationals Yara and Agrium, as increasing carbon in the atmosphere is expected to drive down grain yields. And it invested in Royal Boskalis, a Dutch dredging company that rebuilt an island in 2004 in the Maldives—a country that rising seas are swallowing.

Other Wall Street investors are plowing money into water treatment companies, foreign farmland at the frost line, even a mosquito genetic engineering company, whose business is booming as global warming expands the sting zone of dengue-bearing bugs. Former New York mayor Michael Bloomberg donates to the Sierra Club's anti-coal campaigns but is a vocal supporter of fracking. Goldman Sachs and other Wall Street banks are big proponents of pricing carbon; in fact, they're eager to sell their expertise. Hope for the best, hedge for the worst. Profit either way.

After all, there will always be islands of privilege to which the winners of all these bets can retreat. Maybe Manhattan will be one of them. Maybe not. Maybe one laundromat must close so that another can open. Thankfully, it is not just Petro Gotham that is taking advantage of the city's "marvelously varied and skilled facilities." The thing with skill and talent is that it's wielded by all kinds of people. Infrastructures of capital, densities of intelligence, and creativity and purpose—they don't belong to the Street alone. Capitalism is a system of contradictions. People don't always do what they're told.

· · ·

And some smart people are stubborn. Occupy Wall Street, even at the peak of its 2012 American Autumn, probably never managed to put over 50,000 people in one spot. On September 21, 2014, the People's Climate March managed over eight times that number: more than 400,000 marchers assembled above Columbus Circle, streamed past Central Park, cut through midtown, and finally spilled through Hell's Kitchen, fronted by colorful banners, giant yellow flowers, bright orange life preservers, and tents perched on poles. Is marching bigger and better than occupying? Patient planning better than spontaneous outburst? Or is that like asking if cakes are better than flour?

"There are so many ways you can look at the People's Climate March and see Occupy infrastructure throughout it," said my friend Tammy Shapiro, who was deeply active in both. The march was largely organized through a networked hub system inspired by the cross-country InterOccupy network. Most of the march's art pieces were built in the Mayday space housed on Starr Street in Bushwick, which is mostly run by former Occupiers. The march's exclamation point was the next morning's "Flood Wall Street," a defiant denunciation of the Street's global climate-change complicity. Thousands strutted past Zuccotti Park in exuberant rage, then piled up and roiled at the edge of Wall Street. It was a show of confrontation that the march had been polite enough to only whisper.

In a sense, Flood Wall Street realized a concern for climate change long dormant in the Occupy movement. After Hurricane Sandy in 2012, a network of Occupiers sparked the 60,000-strong relief network called Occupy Sandy. Seizing on the instincts of some of the original Occupiers, the network made the atmosphere a central concern. Still—as I learned at a postmortem summit at a waterside bar in Bay Ridge months later—many key activists wished they had done even more to connect local inequalities laid bare by the storm with the imperative to slow global warming everywhere.

Meanwhile, if the People's Climate March owed a lot to Occupy, it also drew on groups that never flocked to Lower Manhattan to wiggle their fingers. The march started as a partnership—proposed by the climate activist group 350.org and the broader online activist group Avaaz—with the Climate Justice Alliance, a national network of organizations, based in poor communities of color, which have borne the greatest brunt of urban regions' toxic pollution and are now most vulnerable to climate-linked extreme weather.

This was no trivial coalition. "We live in a very segregated society, by class, color, and communities," Luis Garden Acosta told me after Hurricane Sandy. Acosta is a founding leader of El Puente, an environmental justice group based in Williamsburg, Brooklyn. He continued, "Nowhere is [that segregation] more starkly apparent than in the environmental activist community." Bridging that gulf, even for the march, took long and painful meetings. Likewise for building partnerships with the city's powerful big unions. "To change everything, we need everyone," ran the climate march's unofficial kicker. It was easier said than done.

Through the summer of 2014, the march's organizers gathered in midtown, in a grim office near Grand Central. The tall, gray neighborhood that helps coordinate carbon capitalism served the same purpose to that system's enemies. By day the growing ranks of staffers, seconded by green groups, planned the family-friendly march. By night they combined with the veterans of Occupy to plot the more confrontational Flood Wall Street.

There were immediate results. New York mayor Bill de Blasio, who was elected with rhetoric and political supporters borrowed from Occupy, saw what was coming. He polished up a plan to slash the city's greenhouse gas emissions by 80 percent by 2050, building on and accelerating the prior administration's commitments, but this time with more emphasis on affordable housing. De Blasio announced the plan on the eve of the march. Months later, he reframed the city's "sustainability vision" in terms of social justice.

Will those emissions cuts actually happen, showing the world that urban climate politics can be turbocharged by long-standing social justice campaigners? Can New York divest itself of Petro Gotham, instead prioritizing democratic, low-carbon communities? Can the Occupiers' irreverent networks build lasting power with the more stable, rooted community groups of the climate justice movement? What sound like local questions are also global questions. Will a red-green coalition transform New York into a democratic mural that shows other cities how to slash all those gigatons of carbon in an effective, democratic, and egalitarian way? What will it look like if it does?

* * *

When I close my eyes and picture a low-carbon People's Gotham, I don't start with gleaming office towers certified by cheesy acronyms. I don't picture broad green bike lanes lining Manhattan's avenues. At the edge of my mind, kale grows on a rooftop. But that image is out of focus.

Sharper is my vision of the 7 train, just as it is, packed and multicolored. I imagine the boroughs crisscrossed by comfy buses running express. They leave the G train in their dust. I see red-brick NYCHA towers, the city's venerable affordable housing. Wrapped in new exterior skins and patched up inside, NYCHA's buildings could undergo what experts call a "deep energy retrofit," which would massively reduce their energy expenditure. Such a program wouldn't only create thousands of local jobs. It would serve as a kind of regional innovation and industrial policy, training technicians and improving techniques to apply to other buildings in and beyond New York. An urban green new deal, anchored in working-class New York.

Envision NYCHA as a whole, which houses 400,000 people, cutting energy use by three-quarters (or more) while using the renovation process to clean out mold, seal the cracks and crevices where pests now thrive, and increase leaf canopy. With these and other measures, NYCHA could become the world's largest—albeit decentralized—green city, an outpost of a far-off future in tomorrow's New York. I can hear—I can *smell*—the packed, endless meetings at which residents and designers hash out the specifics.

This vision, with its contrast of detail and grandeur, reminds me of other spaces that I've seen, other moments I've spent in this emerging People's Gotham. I recall the haunting, yellow-tinged beauty of the City University of New York's Lehman College campus in the Bronx, with its carved stones and winter trees, framed by a third-floor classroom's window as curious undergrads debate the meaning of the urban environment. I recall the great interior hollow of Judson Memorial Church, where in the fall of 2012 the Indian writer and activist Arundhati Roy told Occupiers that they numbered less than a hundredth of the crowds mustered in her home country, but since the world media was watching, it was worth it, so long as the local Occupiers maintained a healthy sense of perspective. I recall the yet vaster interior of a warehouse by the water in Sunset Park in Brooklyn, the site of a youth climate justice summit hosted by the environmental justice organization UPROSE. By the time I get there, late and sweating on my bike, the program is wrapping up, the teenagers eating and jostling each other, flirting.

You can recite a thousand objections to this vision. First and foremost, you can point out that the core of the People's Gotham, its dense, low-carbon, working-class neighborhoods of color, is under assault—from finance-backed developers and "creative economy" gentrifiers and from the cops who follow them. But those neighborhoods are also fighting back. When I think of a frontline struggle in New York's climate politics, of accidental low-carbon protagonists, I also think of the Crown Heights Tenant Union—a multiracial, multiclass alliance defending affordable density. Their neighborhood may not be threatened by a hurricane. But it's on the front lines of New York's battle to defend, even to expand, the shared character of its affluence.

Here is the bright line linking struggles to defend the democratic fabric of the city, the rights of workers and of the poor who live there, and the possibility of defeating Petro Gotham. The threads that weave everyday consumption and global warming, that weave localized battles for a decent urban life and the great planetary effort to decarbonize prosperity, these are the threads of politics. And a great global city's politics are more open-ended, more awe-inspiring than the swirl of carbon in the atmosphere. While Wall Street hedges its bet, the People's Gotham musters to go all in.

6 WATER AND POWER

Officially New York City is a little more than 300 square miles, but what allows nearly eight and a half million people to live here is what lies far beyond and all around the city: the global network that delivers food, clothing, building materials, and—daily, hourly, incessantly—the water and power that keep the place going. These outside forces are often invisible and overlooked by inhabitants, who assume that a light switch turns on a light, a faucet turns on water, and don't ask where the juice begins. It's important to see the larger networks, as well as not to imagine the city as merely a parasite siphoning vitality off the countryside; people in the countryside rely on work done in the city—notably the production of research, education, information, media, medical care, and culture—to thrive, though those products are rarely as tangible as apples or eggs.

CARTOGRAPHY: MOLLY ROY; ARTWORK: DUKE RILEY, DETAIL FROM *THAT'S WHAT SHE SAID*, 2016   MAP APPEARS ON PAGES 56–57.

THIRSTS AND GHOSTS BY HEATHER SMITH

The Temple of Dendur at the Metropolitan Museum of Art is one of the most New York places for many reasons, but one of them is because if you sit there long enough, everyone in New York will pass by, from dowagers to schoolkids to tourists to locals to the young woman I once saw spend several minutes unsuccessfully trying to vomit in front of the temple, on the grounds that it was imperialist.

A lot of things are imperialist. When you're a temple built by an emperor, you're kind of imperial by definition. But New York itself also gets called imperial, despite what, in Roman terms, would be considered an emperor shortage. The Temple of Dendur was a gift, donated to the Met in the 1960s because Egypt had figured out a new way to approach a project that it had been scheming about since the tenth century—building a dam across the Nile and turning it into a controllable supply of energy and water. Control has its casualties, and the temple would have been one of them: once the Aswan Dam was built, the temple would have been underwater.

The Temple of Dendur is older than any known plans to engineer the habits of the water flowing next to it, though it could be seen as a form of social engineering. It is dedicated to Osiris, a god who died often, and to his wife, Isis, who flooded the Nile with her tears over those deaths, which made the crops grow—but also sometimes drowned them completely. The temple is also dedicated to their son, Horus, and to two guys who just happened to be sons of a local chieftain. This last bit is very New York, even if it went down 1,700 years before Manhattan began to exist as a city. The Temple of Dendur is about gods and rich guys, and, at its core, it's about something much older—the desire to control the movement of water by any means possible, including flattery.

In front of the temple are two sleek rectangular pools, set into the floor of the Met. The water they are filled with is still and tame—there to reflect the sky and the architecture to best advantage—but it is carried by aqueducts that extend into the city from 100 miles outside. On its journey the water slides around the underwater remnants of other, less

8 WHAT IS A JEW?

Stereotypes and generalizations generally precede discrimination. Often they depend on the belief that all members of the hated group have common characteristics, so much so that you can punish any member for the sins all members share. Except that they don't. Categories are leaky, anomalies often occur, and differences within groups can matter as much or more than similarities. You could make this map, pointing up diversity, of any ethnic group, but we made it of Jews because New York has the greatest concentration of Jews on earth outside Israel, and because the word *Jew* contains a host of internal contradictions, from positions on Israel and capitalism and religion to race and class. What can you say of a group that, even within New York, ranges from Bugsy Siegel to Sammy Davis Jr. to Ruth Bader Ginsburg to the Beastie Boys? Whether Judaism is a culture, an ethnicity, or a religion is an unresolved question for people who are good at questions, and even Judaism the religion runs from the progressive inclusiveness of Chelsea's queer-friendly Congregation Beit Simchat Torah to the mysticism and strictures of the Hasidic ranks of Williamsburg. What is a Jew? This is an exploration without an answer, or with as many answers as there are Jews. CARTOGRAPHY: MOLLY ROY ✺ MAP APPEARS ON PAGES 70–71.

MY YIDDISHE PAPA BY SHEERLY AVNI

Welcome to America from "who knows where"
Put your past behind you son and leave it there.
Keep yourself clean, don't make a scene,
No one's gonna love you if they know that you're green!
—J. M. Rumshinsky, "Watch Your Step" (1922), *Great Songs of the Yiddish Stage,* vol. 3

If you live in New York . . . you are Jewish. It doesn't matter if you're Catholic, you're Jewish . . . Jewish means pumpernickel bread, black cherry soda and macaroons. Goyish means Kool-Aid, Drake's cakes, and lime jello.
—Lenny Bruce, 1957

"Don't worry about all those Jews with their kosher and their synagogues. You have more Judaism in your pinky than an American does in his entire body." This is what my father's bosses at the Israeli cultural organization told him when they were preparing him for his working visit to the United States.

Dad's assignment: to "share Israeli culture abroad" and help his employers get closer to deep-pocketed U.S. Zionists. It was 1969, and at twenty-seven, six years older than his own country, my father was the perfect sabra: a paratrooper, a strapping, suntanned kibbutznik who played the accordion and danced the hora—and a model candidate for shaking down the old diaspora to finance the new Jewish paradise.

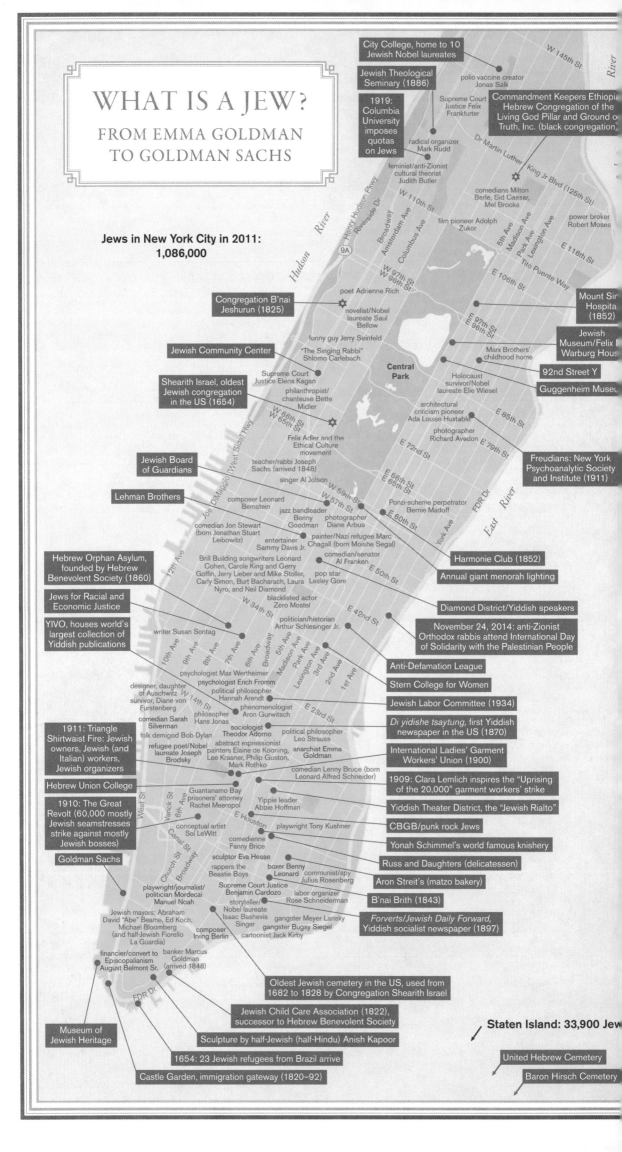

WHAT IS A JEW?
FROM EMMA GOLDMAN TO GOLDMAN SACHS

Jews in New York City in 2011: 1,086,000

City College, home to 10 Jewish Nobel laureates

Jewish Theological Seminary (1886)

1919: Columbia University imposes quotas on Jews

polio vaccine creator Jonas Salk

Supreme Court Justice Felix Frankfurter

Commandment Keepers Ethiopi[an] Hebrew Congregation of the Living God Pillar and Ground o[f] Truth, Inc. (black congregation)

radical organizer Mark Rudd

feminist/anti-Zionist cultural theorist Judith Butler

comedians Milton Berle, Sid Caesar, Mel Brooks

film pioneer Adolph Zukor

power broker Robert Moses

poet Adrienne Rich

Congregation B'nai Jeshurun (1825)

novelist/Nobel laureate Saul Bellow

Mount Sin[ai] Hospita[l] (1852)

Jewish Museum/Felix [M.] Warburg Hous[e]

funny guy Jerry Seinfeld

Jewish Community Center

"The Singing Rabbi" Shlomo Carlebach

Central Park

Marx Brothers' childhood home

Holocaust survivor/Nobel laureate Elie Wiesel

92nd Street Y

Guggenheim Museu[m]

Shearith Israel, oldest Jewish congregation in the US (1654)

Supreme Court Justice Elena Kagan

philanthropist/chanteuse Bette Midler

architectural criticism pioneer Ada Louise Huxtable

photographer Richard Avedon

Felix Adler and the Ethical Culture movement

Jewish Board of Guardians

teacher/rabbi Joseph Sachs (arrived 1848)

singer Al Jolson

Freudians: New York Psychoanalytic Society and Institute (1911)

Lehman Brothers

composer Leonard Bernstein

jazz bandleader Benny Goodman

photographer Diane Arbus

Ponzi-scheme perpetrator Bernie Madoff

comedian Jon Stewart (born Jonathan Stuart Leibowitz)

entertainer Sammy Davis Jr.

painter/Nazi refugee Marc Chagall (born Moishe Segal)

comedian/senator Al Franken

Harmonie Club (1852)

Annual giant menorah lighting

Hebrew Orphan Asylum, founded by Hebrew Benevolent Society (1860)

Brill Building songwriters Leonard Cohen, Carole King and Gerry Goffin, Jerry Lieber and Mike Stoller, Carly Simon, Burt Bacharach, Laura Nyro, and Neil Diamond

pop star Lesley Gore

blacklisted actor Zero Mostel

Diamond District/Yiddish speakers

Jews for Racial and Economic Justice

writer Susan Sontag

politician/historian Arthur Schlesinger Jr.

November 24, 2014: anti-Zionist Orthodox rabbis attend International Day of Solidarity with the Palestinian People

YIVO, houses world's largest collection of Yiddish publications

psychologist Max Wertheimer

psychologist Erich Fromm

political philosopher Hannah Arendt

Anti-Defamation League

Stern College for Women

designer, daughter of Auschwitz survivor, Diane von Furstenberg

phenomenologist Aron Gurwitsch

Jewish Labor Committee (1934)

comedian Sarah Silverman

philosopher Hans Jonas

Di yidishe tsaytung, first Yiddish newspaper in the US (1870)

folk demigod Bob Dylan

sociologist Theodor Adorno

political philosopher Leo Strauss

1911: Triangle Shirtwaist Fire: Jewish owners, Jewish (and Italian) workers, Jewish organizers

refugee poet/Nobel laureate Joseph Brodsky

abstract expressionist painters Elaine de Kooning, Lee Krasner, Philip Guston, Mark Rothko

anarchist Emma Goldman

International Ladies' Garment Workers' Union (1900)

comedian Lenny Bruce (born Leonard Alfred Schneider)

1909: Clara Lemlich inspires the "Uprising of the 20,000" garment workers' strike

Hebrew Union College

Guantanamo Bay prisoners' attorney Rachel Meeropol

Yippie leader Abbie Hoffman

Yiddish Theater District, the "Jewish Rialto"

1910: The Great Revolt (60,000 mostly Jewish seamstresses strike against mostly Jewish bosses)

conceptual artist Sol LeWitt

playwright Tony Kushner

CBGB/punk rock Jews

comedienne Fanny Brice

Yonah Schimmel's world famous knishery

Goldman Sachs

sculptor Eva Hesse

rappers the Beastie Boys

boxer Benny Leonard

communist/spy Julius Rosenberg

Russ and Daughters (delicatessen)

playwright/journalist/politician Mordecai Manuel Noah

Supreme Court Justice Benjamin Cardozo

labor organizer Rose Schneiderman

Aron Streit's (matzo bakery)

Jewish mayors: Abraham David "Abe" Beame, Ed Koch, Michael Bloomberg (and half-Jewish Fiorello La Guardia)

storyteller/Nobel laureate Isaac Bashevis Singer

gangster Meyer Lansky

gangster Bugsy Siegel

cartoonist Jack Kirby

B'nai Brith (1843)

Forverts/Jewish Daily Forward, Yiddish socialist newspaper (1897)

composer Irving Berlin

financier/convert to Episcopalianism August Belmont Sr.

banker Marcus Goldman (arrived 1848)

Oldest Jewish cemetery in the US, used from 1682 to 1828 by Congregation Shearith Israel

Museum of Jewish Heritage

Jewish Child Care Association (1822), successor to Hebrew Benevolent Society

Sculpture by half-Jewish (half-Hindu) Anish Kapoor

Staten Island: 33,900 Jew[s]

1654: 23 Jewish refugees from Brazil arrive

United Hebrew Cemetery

Castle Garden, immigration gateway (1820–92)

Baron Hirsch Cemetery

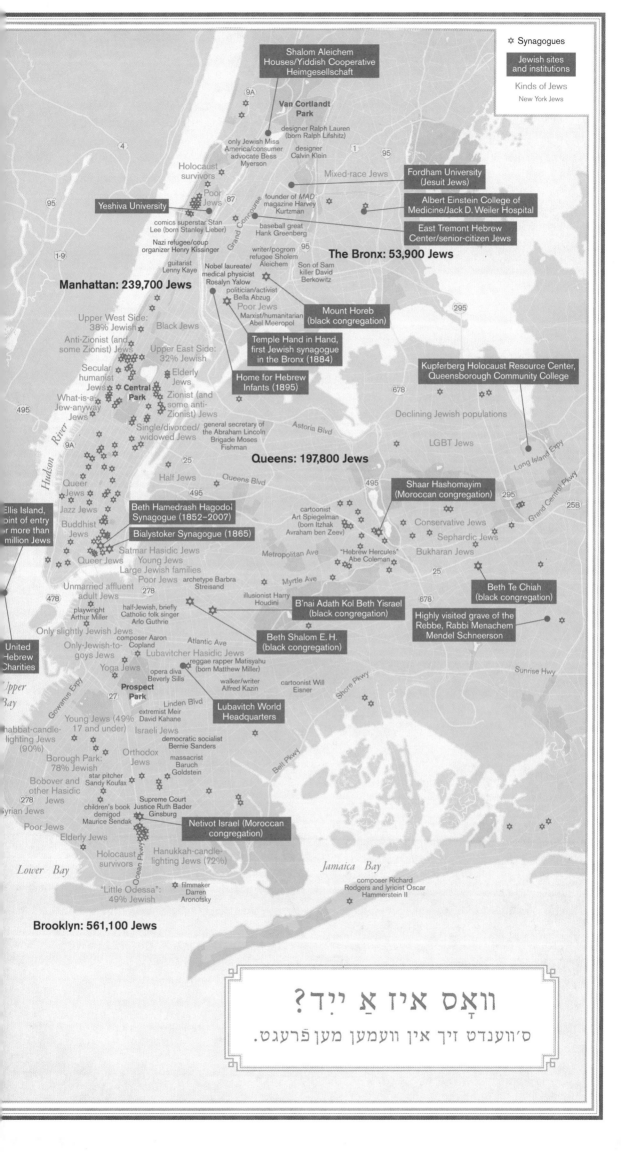

Legend (top right):
✿ Synagogues
Jewish sites and institutions
Kinds of Jews
New York Jews

Shalom Aleichem Houses/Yiddish Cooperative Heimgesellschaft

Van Cortlandt Park

9A

designer Ralph Lauren (born Ralph Lifshitz)
designer Calvin Klein

only Jewish Miss America/consumer advocate Bess Myerson

Mixed-race Jews

Fordham University (Jesuit Jews)

Holocaust survivors

Albert Einstein College of Medicine/Jack D. Weiler Hospital

East Tremont Hebrew Center/senior-citizen Jews

Yeshiva University

Poor Jews

founder of MAD magazine Harvey Kurtzman

comics superstar Stan Lee (born Stanley Lieber)

baseball great Hank Greenberg

Nazi refugee/coup organizer Henry Kissinger

The Bronx: 53,900 Jews

writer/pogrom refugee Sholem Aleichem

Son of Sam killer David Berkowitz

guitarist Lenny Kaye

Nobel laureate/medical physicist Rosalyn Yalow

Manhattan: 239,700 Jews

politician/activist Bella Abzug

Poor Jews

Mount Horeb (black congregation)

Marxist/humanitarian Abel Meeropol

Upper West Side: 38% Jewish

Black Jews

Anti-Zionist (and some Zionist) Jews

Upper East Side: 32% Jewish

Temple Hand in Hand, first Jewish synagogue in the Bronx (1884)

Kupferberg Holocaust Resource Center, Queensborough Community College

Secular humanist Jews

Elderly Jews

Central Park

Home for Hebrew Infants (1895)

678

What-is-a-Jew-anyway Jews

Zionist (and some anti-Zionist) Jews

Astoria Blvd

Declining Jewish populations

495

Single/divorced/widowed Jews

general secretary of the Abraham Lincoln Brigade Moses Fishman

LGBT Jews

Hudson River

9A

Queens: 197,800 Jews

25

Half Jews

Queens Blvd

Shaar Hashomayim (Moroccan congregation)

295

25B

495

495

Grand Central Pkwy

Queer Jews

cartoonist Art Spiegelman (born Itzhak Avraham ben Zeev)

Conservative Jews

Jazz Jews

Beth Hamedrash Hagodol Synagogue (1852–2007)

Sephardic Jews

Ellis Island, point of entry for more than million Jews

Buddhist Jews

Bialystoker Synagogue (1865)

Metropolitan Ave

"Hebrew Hercules" Abe Coleman

Bukharan Jews

25

Satmar Hasidic Jews

Young Jews

Queer Jews

Large Jewish families

archetype Barbra Streisand

Myrtle Ave

Beth Te Chiah (black congregation)

Poor Jews

Unmarried affluent adult Jews

278

illusionist Harry Houdini

B'nai Adath Kol Beth Yisrael (black congregation)

678

Highly visited grave of the Rebbe, Rabbi Menachem Mendel Schneerson

478

playwright Arthur Miller

half-Jewish, briefly Catholic folk singer Arlo Guthrie

composer Aaron Copland

Atlantic Ave

Beth Shalom E. H. (black congregation)

United Hebrew Charities

Only slightly Jewish Jews

Only-Jewish-to-goys Jews

Lubavitcher Hasidic Jews

reggae rapper Matisyahu (born Matthew Miller)

Yoga Jews

opera diva Beverly Sills

walker/writer Alfred Kazin

cartoonist Will Eisner

Sunrise Hwy

Upper Bay

Gowanus Expy

27

Prospect Park

Linden Blvd

Lubavitch World Headquarters

Shore Pkwy

Young Jews (49% 17 and under)

extremist Meir David Kahane

Israeli Jews

Shabbat-candle-lighting Jews (90%)

democratic socialist Bernie Sanders

Belt Pkwy

Borough Park: 78% Jewish

Orthodox Jews

massacrist Baruch Goldstein

star pitcher Sandy Koufax

Bobover and other Hasidic Jews

278

Supreme Court Justice Ruth Bader Ginsburg

children's book demigod Maurice Sendak

Syrian Jews

Netivot Israel (Moroccan congregation)

Poor Jews

Elderly Jews

Holocaust survivors

Hanukkah-candle-lighting Jews (72%)

Jamaica Bay

Lower Bay

"Little Odessa": 49% Jewish

filmmaker Darren Aronofsky

composer Richard Rodgers and lyricist Oscar Hammerstein II

Brooklyn: 561,100 Jews

וואָס איז אַ ייד?
ס׳וועגדט זיך אין וועמען מען פֿרעגט.

But this model candidate was also an aspiring actor, a boy who'd grown up secretly listening to decadent, capitalist rock 'n' roll on a homemade transistor radio. He'd picked potatoes in the fields every morning, but while performing his duties he was more likely to hum along to the Platters than to the Hebrew folk songs he dutifully sang at kibbutz festivals. And paradise or no, Israel was a poor country then—his childhood memories were of hunger, hard labor, and of course the ever-present fear of attack from furious neighbors (and recent exiles, since one man's *aliya* is another's *nakba*).

So in the years that followed that first assignment, Dad went astray in the United States, at least in the eyes of the country that first sent him here. He had a daughter who would never learn more than a few words of Hebrew. He got an MFA in directing. He and his wife learned the English word for divorce and promptly applied it while I, the daughter, was still in diapers. My father found himself on Staten Island, teaching accordion lessons at a Jewish Community Center and dreaming of starting a theater of his own in a city now being run by its first of three Jewish mayors. (Three and a half if you count La Guardia, who was mostly Italian but had grown up in a mixed neighborhood and once held a debate in Yiddish to appeal to Jewish voters.)

Israel was not quite the tribal paradise it appeared, but then neither was New York City. Or at least—not anymore. It had been our people's land of opportunity for hundreds of years before, starting with the first Jewish Dutch settlement of six families in 1654—drawn to New Amsterdam's promise of more open commercial rules for the people. And since then, home to wave after wave of Jews seeking economic freedom, political opportunity, escape from persecution, and finally, in the twentieth century, escape from physical extermination under the Nazis. From generation to generation, those Jews both shaped the city and were shaped by it, and the Jewish presence was as far from a monolith as the city itself. My atheist, straight-talking Israeli father, raised with what can only be called a healthy contempt for those diasporic Jews who hadn't seized their destiny in Zion, would become part of that tradition himself—as the founding director of a tiny repertory theater whose mission was to showcase the Jewish experience. In New York, "What is a Jew?" wasn't merely an abiding question of daily life; for some, like my father, it became a nonprofit mission statement.

New York has always been a city of immigrants within a country of immigrants, and Jews hold a particular place in its history, not only because of numbers. It is impossible to separate the history of the city from the history of its Jews. There are the great German banking families—the Lehman brothers, Goldman and Sachs. Then there are the singer-songwriters of Tin Pan Alley, the founders of Macy's, Gimbels, Bloomingdale's, and Barneys. Jews dressed, decorated, financed, and, once you add Robert Moses, literally built the city. During one eighteen-year span in the 1930s and '40s, City College graduated nine Nobel Prize winners, all Jewish.

By 1972 urban flight had taken over the now-floundering, blight-ridden metropolis, and a city that had once been 25 percent Jewish was now losing its Jews, along with many of its most affluent citizens. The upward mobility of the country's most economically and culturally successful immigrant group meant that many were in a position to leave a New York that was now entering one of its darkest economic eras. For the first time in history, Jews were fleeing en masse the city they'd helped build—lost, as Rabbi Solomon I. Berl would complain of his waning Bronx congregation in 1970, "to the three M's: mortality, move-outs and Miami Beach."

But if my father was a "failure" as an Israeli, he found success as a purveyor of Jewish nostalgia, catering to these second- and third-generation Jews' deep longing for an older New York, with its pumpernickel bread and black cherry sodas. He found space on the second floor of the Emmanuel Midtown Y on 14th Street, at the northern border of what had once been the fabled Yiddish theater district, now almost entirely occupied by Puerto Rican discount stores. The room itself was not a theater but a dance studio, with broken paneling, poor acoustics, an astonishingly loud air conditioner, and a bevy of maintenance men, who were more likely to steal equipment than repair it. But it was home.

. . .

The real miracle was that it existed at all. It may now seem redundant to think that there could ever have been a need for a Jewish theater in a city known as "Hymietown." But just as the brash pioneers in Los Angeles amassed fortunes and built an industry by helping to forge a new American ideal that looked nothing like them—pale, patrician, and blond— the Broadway producers regularly rejected shows they deemed "too Jewish." A few blocks away from the Second Avenue Deli, which would for years send over a complimentary plate of meats and liver every opening night, Dad put on plays about the history of Jewish separation—greenhorns on Canarsie, victims of anti-Semitism in Germany, outsiders in Brooklyn. This when the biggest threat facing the future of the Jewish people was not annihilation but integration, as Jews confronted the triple threat of intermarriage, secularization, and the gradual disappearance of both Yiddish and Ladino.

In 1976, the year I learned to roller-skate in front of Dad's $150-a-month walk-up on East 62nd Street (current monthly estimate, according to Zillow: $9,000), City College ended its 129-year tradition of free tuition, removing the first rung on the upward ladder climbed by so many determined Jews. That year one of the theater's productions got reviewed for the first time in the *New York Times*. It was also the year that Yitzhak Rabin called people like my father "weaklings and traitors" because they'd abandoned their country. But its director's presumed moral failure aside, the Jewish Repertory Theater emerged as a modest but recognized success, winning awards, increasing its audience, and earning a reputation as a place to which playwrights could turn when Broadway producers said their plays were "too Jewish." You were never too Jewish for the JRT.

My father became a workaholic, reviews-obsessed New Yorker's New Yorker, largely through his role at the theater and his new position as provider of Jewish experiences for his audience. And for me, weekend visits to the city usually meant sitting in on rehearsals and watching Dad direct actors—some of our tribe, some not (my father's rule for casting was "he doesn't have to be Jewish as long as he looks Italian"). He coaxed out performances of a Jewish nostalgia almost entirely outside his own personal experience, mostly based on the history of the Jews who came through Ellis Island decades before him. A simulacrum of a vanishing Jewish cultural experience: *Crossing Delancey,* a play about a romance on the Lower East Side; *Vagabond Stars,* a musical review that translated Yiddish songs from the golden age of Yiddish theater, songs full of longing for home and loneliness in a strange new world; *After the Fall,* Arthur Miller's play about being married to the ultimate shikse, Marilyn Monroe; and of course the inevitable *Merchant of Venice* revival, which recast Shylock as the play's tortured hero and moral conscience.

My father had settled down, and his ex-wife and daughter became the wandering Jews. I followed my academic mother from New England college town to New England college town in her search for tenure, never staying in one place longer than a year or two. On weekends I rode Metro-North, New Jersey Transit, and Amtrak into Manhattan. At those lines' end, out in New Haven, in Princeton, in Mount Holyoke, lay the lacrosse players, Izod shirts, and ski weekends to which I was never invited. But those were the edges of my life, temporary way stations . . . my center was fixed: the ninety-nine-seat theater on 14th Street where I heard my first Yiddish lullaby, saw my first Neil Simon play, and first learned the difference between a *schlemiel* and a *schlemazel.* In short, it was where I learned how to be a Jew.

THE LOST WORLD OF JEWISH FLATBUSH

BY JOEL DINERSTEIN

It's just before 8:00 p.m. on a Tuesday night in 1973 and I'm standing outside on the corner of Ocean and Church Avenues, waiting for the night's truck driver to throw down a wire-bound sheaf of tomorrow's *Daily News,* the so-called bulldog edition. I work at Spike's candy store and newsstand, where a group of old horse-betting Jewish men with names like Lefty and Chootch leaf through *Penthouse* and *Playboy,* mock each other for what they can't do anymore, tell me to cut my long hair, then buy the *News* and head off for coffee and a smoke at the diner. This is a nightly ritual at Spike's—which Spike hasn't owned for years—and Lefty's crew is the last rush of customers before the late-night stragglers. I am fourteen and working from 5:00 to 10:00 p.m. on Tuesday through Friday nights, for two dollars an hour under the counter. I keep the newspapers stacked and the magazines neat, restock candy and ice cream, sweep and lock up, and make sure "the colored kids" don't steal. That last part is the most important aspect of my job as far as my boss Bernie is concerned. At night's end, I bring the *News* back to my family.

I am about as young as it is possible to be first generation to the Ellis Island migration of Ashkenazi Jews. Both my grandfathers were born in the 1880s, a cantor and tailor on my mother's side, a Hebrew teacher on my father's. When I was born in 1958, my parents were forty-five and forty-eight—neither one born here and both native Yiddish speakers. My mother, Gertrude, was from *Minsk-a-Pinsk*—a Yiddish colloquialism meaning "some one-horse *shtetl* near Minsk." She arrived in the United States at nine years of age with her twin sister and my tiny *bubbe,* the culmination of a daring two-year end-run out of newly Soviet Russia through Poland. My father, Irving, immigrated here from Lithuania two years later at the age of thirteen with his father and older brother. Both of my parents lived on the Lower East Side and later moved to the East New York section of Brooklyn, following a common-enough Jewish migration that then led to Crown Heights (where I was born) and soon after to Flatbush, where I grew up a working-class kid on the streets.

We grew up in a period when the Holocaust did not define Jewish identity. I was raised in a kosher home within a critical mass of conservative Jewry, and we all had an ingrained ethno-religious identity: New York street-cred, *Yiddishkeit,* Mel Brooks, summer camp, Paul Simon, Carole King, Bugs Bunny (he's from Flatbush). I went to Hebrew school three times a week—*wayyyy* too much—and yet found the Jewish past compelling enough to read my history books cover to cover the first week of class. On Yom Kippur, even the most religious of men walked out of services and stood three-deep outside the Zenith TV shop on Flatbush and Albemarle to watch the World Series. The military strength of Israel and high-profile American Jewish successes obviated any need to play the victim. Neither my parents nor cousins nor Hebrew school teachers ever discussed the camps: for one thing, it wasn't relevant for American children living through the 1960s and 1970s; for another, they were too

Meanwhile, my father was learning how to be an American on a much bigger stage— and by "American," I mean that very specific version of American that is the New York Jew. Lenny Bruce's holy triptych of black cherry soda, macaroons, and pumpernickel bread was replaced by Philip Roth, Woody Allen, and a love for the Yankees. Then there was his half-hearted flirtation—blessedly short-lived—with the casual racism through which so busy living the American dream or striving for it. The first Holocaust book I read was William Styron's *Sophie's Choice,* in lesser part because he was a *goy* author (an outside perspective), and in greater part because it was set in Flatbush, literally in the house across from my grade school (PS 249).

Most of my friends from college and camp grew up in the suburbs with a dual ethnic and racial identity—both Jewish and white—and never knew the cultural comfort of the urban critical mass of postwar Flatbush Jewishness. A generation removed from Philip Roth and Woody Allen, I remain more at home in their artistic worlds than in the *shtickiness* of Seinfeld, Jon Stewart's confident self-deprecation, or Ben Stiller's twice-removed *putzdom.* In fact I've wanted to kick Stiller's ass ever since seeing *Meet the Parents* in 1999—he was still playing the clumsy, needy Jewish guy desperate for WASP approval. My Jewish friends and I were nearly all solid playground athletes—at baseball, football, and basketball—and did not doubt our own worth. Our streetwise Jewishness remains both richer than these proud nerd caricatures and more complex than the mythologized literary Judaica of Jonathan Lethem, Michael Chabon, or Jonathan Safran Foer. Those authors sidestep the main schism of Brooklyn Jewry—the social flux caused by white flight in the 1960s and '70s due to racial conflict in the schools.

In the midst of white flight I attended the fabled Erasmus Hall High School, one of the oldest (founded 1786), largest (5,000 students), and most Jewish public high schools in America. Of its fabled alumni, we knew of Barbra Streisand and Neil Diamond, and that Bobby Fischer, the world chess champion, had dropped out. (Hey, he was a genius and didn't need high school, so why did we?) I only later learned of Mae West, Barbara Stanwyck, Bernard Malamud, Mickey Spillane, Joseph Barbera (of Hanna-Barbera), and Marky Ramone. In 1968 Erasmus was 70 percent white (mostly Jewish), but five years later it was 75 percent African American and Afro-Caribbean, with 10 percent Latino and Asian American. What happened? Race riots at Erasmus in 1969 and black-Jewish tensions during the 1968 teachers' strike led to a Flatbush Jewish diaspora to Queens and Long Island, Westchester and New Jersey. The neighborhood had become a bit more dangerous, but that danger certainly didn't feel commensurate, to me anyway, with the fear that emptied the neighborhood of Jews. At Erasmus the racial bullying from junior high had tapered off—the tough guys now had way better things to do (girlfriends, drugs, cutting class to watch kung fu movies). By my senior year I was familiar with the hostilities between the Haitians and black Americans, and I was the token Jew on a math team with this resonant starting five: *Wong, Chong, Lim, Li, and Dinerstein.* In effect, Erasmus did not survive the ethnic transformation of the neighborhood. In the 1980s the board of education broke up its block-square rectangular campus into a set of magnet schools; by 1994 the name was removed during a second restructuring of smaller units. Now only the old white clapboard building in the center is called Erasmus Hall Academy, a museum to the dream of public education going back to the American Revolution.

many immigrant ethnics, as Toni Morrison has pointed out, "become white." And finally, there was the sentimental education he received from a succession of Jewish American women, starting with a frizzy-haired actress who may or may not have dumped him for Al Pacino, another who convinced him to go into psychoanalysis (Dr. Sachs at the New York Hospital on 68th Street, four times a week, five dollars a session, for seven years), and later a social worker from the boroughs. She would teach him table manners and make him read Paul Fussell's *Class,* only to be replaced by a green-eyed Sarah Lawrence graduate who fought a losing battle against his nightly ritual of eating bowls of sunflower seeds during Johnny Carson. Then, finally, a fantastic lighting designer, whom he married and with whom he had a second daughter, my sister Sonia.

. . .

The historical experience of Jews in the United States, and always in New York, was one long battle with the paradox of assimilation and the putative promise of the American dream. And the history of that paradox is as old as the city itself. The first Jewish country club, started in 1852 by a group of German Jews excluded from its WASP equivalents, is perhaps best known today for the fact that Michael Bloomberg had to quit it before running for mayor because it is not only 90 percent Jewish, but also 100 percent white.

Ultimately, the seventies may have been the last great era of Jewish influence in New York (it was also the last era of mass Jewish migration, as Russian-born Jews settled in Orthodox enclaves in Brooklyn). If Dad's theater were still open, he'd most likely be staging plays about Larry David, Richard Lewis, Jerry Seinfeld, and all the other Jewish comics who got their start at Budd Friedman's legendary Improv. Or putting on a musical review based on the songs of Hilly Kristal's now-shuttered CBGB, home to the Beastie Boys and the Ramones. Or maybe a one-man show (always the cheapest and best option) based on the life of the late Lou Reed, today lovingly referred to as the *zeide* of Second Avenue. Far from being a swan song for New York Jews, the seventies were a foul-mouthed, foul-smelling triumph of Judaism's influence as a culture rather than a religion.

What did that mean for the tribe? According to a 2011 study, one in six New York households is Jewish. But religious observance is at an all-time low, while intermarriage is at an all-time high. The *Jewish Daily Forward,* America's first Yiddish newspaper, once dedicated to preserving the soul and specialness of its readership, now has a column dedicated to helping interfaith couples navigate Hanukkah and Christmas, Passover and Easter. At our annual family seder, my father, as devout an atheist as a child of communism can be, likes to announce that he's taken all the "God" out of the Hagaddah and left only the "haha." Goyische partners and friends regularly turn us into a minority at our own holiday—by our own invitation.

The theater is gone. My father retired, now part of yet another great New York tradition—the successful third marriage. My little sister, Sonia, like me, regularly marched up to the second floor on 14th Street; but to attend the private children's day care that now occupies the space where I first heard Yiddish songs. The closest she came there to the teachings of the Old Testament was through her favorite teacher, a God-fearing Christian Trinidadian with wondrous curled purple fingernails.

Sonia's mom is half-Jewish, on her paternal grandfather's side, which means that Sonia herself is 75 percent Jewish by blood but 0 percent by doctrine. Blond, boisterous, and curiously angst-free, Sonia surfs and skis and attends a Quaker school. She doesn't have the theater, and she wasn't bat-mitzvahed. She thinks of Israel as a place where the beaches are fun—but not as fun as the ones in the Dominican Republic. She may be as much of an emblem of the supposed demise of the Jewish people as the JRT's success was once an emblem of their thirst for a usable past. But Lenny Bruce wouldn't have worried: she's a New Yorker. ✡

9 ARCHIPELAGO

Your deepest relationships are not always to the people next to you. New York City is not far from Connecticut, Long Island, and New Jersey, but a huge portion of its population actually comes from the Caribbean, bringing the Caribbean to many city places, practices, festivities—two of the biggest parades in Manhattan, for example, are the Puerto Rican Day and the West Indian Day parades—and professions, from civil service to childcare. New York City is also, except for that tip of the North American continent known as the Bronx, an archipelago of big and little islands, of Ellis and Rikers and Roosevelt Islands, of the marvelous uninhabited marshy isles in Jamaica Bay, and so it has a natural relationship to the island nations of the Caribbean, where many of the poor of New York come from and the rich vacation in. This map is, in other words, a lie that tells the truth, the truth that New York's archipelago nature is an important part of its character, as are its deep and complex relationships with Cuba, Haiti, the Dominican Republic, Puerto Rico, Jamaica, Trinidad, and the rest. Scale is another convention of maps that deceives us: Cuba and Iceland are about the same size, but the former has more than thirty times the population of the latter; New York City in its few hundred square miles has a larger population than all but three of the Caribbean nations, Cuba and the two countries that were once one on the island of Hispaniola. Chinese immigrants may finally be edging out Dominicans as the city's largest immigrant group, and as of 2013, Jamaicans and Guyanese were the city's fourth and fifth largest immigrant populations. Los Angeles is sometimes called the capital of Central America; this map reminds us of the ways that New York can be imagined as the northern capital of the Caribbean. And also a pan-Caribbean capital: many interactions not possible or frequent in the islands themselves occur here abundantly, and people refer to themselves as Caribbean here in a way they never would back home; in New York they develop relationships with and attachments to the people once next to them.

CARTOGRAPHY: MOLLY ROY; ARTWORK: DETAILS FROM THE TITLE PAGE OF THOMAS JEFFREYS, *WEST-INDIA ATLAS* (1788), COURTESY OF DAVID RUMSEY.   MAP APPEARS ON PAGES 78–79.

OF ISLANDS AND OTHER MOTHERS   BY GAIUTRA BAHADUR

Guyana, my birthplace, might as well be an island. It sits in South America but belongs less to the mainland than to water. Anyone who has been there when it rains can testify to that. So did the dozens who died in floods there a decade ago, or the many thousands who, enslaved two centuries ago, had to manually excavate 100 million tons of earth to carve the drainage canals indispensable to growing sugar along the often-submerged Atlantic coast. Rainforests and an absence of interior highways separate the country from the rest of the continent, as

ARCHIPELAGO
THE CARIBBEAN'S FAR NORTH

Gulf of Mexico

THE BAHAMAS

CUBA

COZUMEL

CAYMAN ISLANDS

JAMAICA

ROATÁN AND UTILA

ISLA DE TIERRA
BOMBA

*Islands not to scale

NORTH
AMERICA

HUNTER ISLAND
(until 1937)

Long Island
Sound

PELHAM
ISLANDS

BRONX
PENINSULA

HART
ISLAND

CITY
ISLAND

NORTH
BROTHER
ISLAND
(Bronx)

SOUTH
BROTHER
ISLAND
(Queens)

RIKERS
ISLAND

MANHATTAN
ISLAND

RANDALL'S
AND WARDS
ISLANDS

MILL ROCK
ISLAND

LONG ISLAND

ROOSEVELT
ISLAND

ELLIS
ISLAND

U THANT
(BELMONT)
ISLAND

•Jamaica, Queens

LIBERTY
ISLAND

GOVERNORS
ISLAND

Route of West
Indian Labor Day
Carnival, Brooklyn

RULERS BAR
HASSOCK

SHOOTERS
ISLAND

CANARSIE
POL

PRALL'S
ISLAND

STATEN
ISLAND

BARREN/DEAD HORSE
ISLAND (until 1926)

Jamaica
Bay

SUBWAY
ISLAND

ISLE OF
MEADOWS

HOFFMAN
ISLAND

MAU MAU
(WHITE)
ISLAND

SWINBURNE
ISLAND

CONEY
ISLAND
(actually an island
until 1962)

RUFFLE
BAR

LITTLE
EGG ISLAND

ROCKAWAY
PENINSULA
(almost an island)

HOG ISLAND
(1861–93)

TURKS AND CAICOS

HISPANIOLA

Atlantic   Ocean

HAITI

DOMINICAN
REPUBLIC

ANGUILLA

PUERTO RICO

VIRGIN
ISLANDS

BARBUDA

ST KITTS

NEVIS

ANTIGUA

MONTSERRAT

GUADELOUPE

Caribbean   Sea

DOMINICA

MARTINIQUE

ST LUCIA

ST VINCENT

ARUBA

THE GRENADINES

BARBADOS

BONAIRE

CURAÇAO

GRENADA

TOBAGO

ISLA MARGARITA

TRINIDAD

THE GUYANAS (GUYANA, SURINAME,
FRENCH GUIANA [CAYENNE]) →

does history. Guyana's colonial masters were British, not Spanish or Portuguese. The English it speaks, creolized on its plantations with the vocabulary and grammar of India and Africa, connects it to the Anglophone Caribbean. Culturally, it floats out on its deserted own. If the archipelago of the West Indies didn't claim my home country, who would?

Guyana, a swamp the size of New Jersey with less than a million people, is a blip in the geopolitical ocean. It ranks in two things: suicides (the world's highest rate) and exodus (aside from two minuscule islands in the South Pacific, it has the world's highest out-migration rate). Its people choose to leave it in droves, whether by quitting existence or quitting its borders.

Which brings us to another archipelago. Despite Guyana's tiny population, it accounts for the fifth-largest group of immigrants in New York City. About 140,000 New Yorkers were born in Guyana. They have settled in separate enclaves, as ethnically divided here as they are "back home." About a third, overwhelmingly of African origin, have settled in a few Brooklyn neighborhoods: East New York, Crown Heights, and Flatbush. Twice as many, overwhelmingly of Indian origin, have settled in Queens, mainly in Richmond Hill and Ozone Park. There, at the last stop on the A train, as I descend from the elevated subway tracks, the aromas of the street tell me where I am. Curry is in the air, and so is the devotee's incense, and together both plunge into my lungs, instantly intoxicating.

Two features distinguish the modest, close-set houses here: arabesque chrome fences polished to an aspirant's shine and Hindu prayer flags in an array of colors—the white of Saraswati (goddess of learning), the pink of Lakshmi (goddess of prosperity), and the red of the monkey god Hanuman (which British troops in Guyana in the 1960s mistook for a communist signal). The pennants point to a Caribbean reality far more complex than one might imagine, in this city where a million people trace their roots to the region. The flags suggest a world unseen, beyond the street.

When Derek Walcott accepted the Nobel Prize for Literature in 1992, the great poet from St. Lucia described the Antilles as "our archipelago becoming a synonym for pieces broken off from the original continent." This was no lament but a shout of joy for our parallel attempts to reassemble the shards of language, of religion, of epic from separate homelands in Africa and Asia. What others mourned as mere parody, Walcott celebrated as poignant gestures toward reconstituted identity. His hope was that the descendants of the enslaved and the indentured might see how our fragments actually form a chain that connects us. We are all heir to rupture, from whichever continent.

The organizers of Brooklyn's annual West Indian Day Parade also trumpet unity. In this city where revelers from disparate nations come together each Labor Day to celebrate carnival, Caribbean people have forged ties often impossible to imagine on isolated islands. New York is the place where we have become "West Indian." But the limits of that unity lie close to the skin. For as much as the West Indian parade is touted as a symbol of federation, it's a gathering still dominated by English-speakers from major islands like Jamaica and Trinidad, home of the Antilles' biggest carnival. Dominicans and Puerto Ricans, who have their own parades, largely stay away, and the historical exclusion of Haitians has long marred its claims of inclusivity. Caribbean New Yorkers with roots in India, who number more than 100,000, barely participate.

Where, amid these fractures and our failures to see our fragments side by side, might "Caribbean unity" lie? Some look to Labor Day's revelers, crowding Eastern Parkway during carnival. Others look to those other highly visible icons of Caribbean New York: the backgammon and domino players who line Church Avenue in Flatbush, and so many New York sidewalks, on warm summer evenings. They slap dominoes onto folding tables in a rhythm (brap-brap-brap!) that keeps time with back-home dialects. But overwhelmingly, it is men who perch out under grocery store awnings or in the shelter of the odd oak tree. And the streets mislead. What is fundamental about Caribbean New York is hidden inside. In a sea of difference, the one demographic factor that might make an archipelago of Caribbean immigrants in New York is the number and role of women.

Among this city's immigrants from the Caribbean, there are far more women than men. There are 91 males per 100 females in New York as a whole, but among both Guyanese and Haitian immigrants, the male/female ratio is 79 per 100; for Jamaicans and Dominicans, it's 69 per 100; and for Trinidadians, it's 65 per 100. Mexican, Indian, Pakistani, and Bangladeshi immigrants, by contrast, are disproportionately male. What's more, Caribbean women participate in the labor force at higher rates than women from the other groups. On average they earn less than their countrymen, and they may be less visible, because they work inside homes, as nannies or housekeepers or health care aides. For many countries, the migration out was led by women, who then sponsored family members, including husbands and sons, to come to America. Often, these women were nurses, allowed to enter during a nursing shortage in the United States.

That's how my family came to America. The Jersey City Medical Center hired a nurse aunt in the 1970s—and she brought a husband, who brought a sister, who brought my parents, my baby sister, and me in 1981. We lived five miles from the World Trade Center, just across the Hudson River. From the fire escape of our apartment on the Palisades, we could see the Twin Towers. Outside that view loomed large, but inside our apartment the geography was defined by a linen closet. Behind its white shuttered doors perched the gods my mother had brought from our village: framed pictures of Lakshmi, Saraswati, and Hanuman.

The image of my mother praying dominates my memories of our first years in America. With a white lace ohrni covering her head, eyes shut, nostrils flared in demure steeliness, she stood in front of the closeted altar singing devotee's songs with an intensity that made me quiet. Any reader of Jamaica Kincaid, the Antiguan American novelist, will know this terrain, this point at which mother and motherland meet, a juncture charged with too much love, too many expectations, and subtle accusations of abandonment. Both mother and motherland give you a hard time for leaving; neither quite lets go of you. Both, too, are sacred.

And in the hidden Caribbean, the worship of Mother is everywhere. Indians brought their faith in the goddess Kali to the Caribbean and also transformed it. At the Shri Maha Kali Devi Mandir in Brooklyn, worshippers call her Kali Mai or simply "Mother." Its website attempts to explain her duality—fiercely dark, yet nurturing—with a nineteenth-century mystic's words: "She is like the ocean under the moonlight, from far it is black and scary, but up close, the water is clear and pure." Orthodox Hindus view Kali's followers as transgressive because fealty to her can involve spirit possession, animal sacrifice, and fire walking. But Kali's Brooklyn temple is a place where Caribbean women come to inhabit their full humanity and embrace identities as believers and mothers, not just immigrants and laborers.

On a recent visit I met a Guyanese American woman chosen to speak for the goddess. Tisha Morrison's very body—hazel eyes, hair marked as African, skin the same color as mine—joined the fragments from Asia and Africa that Walcott invoked. She told me how her father, half-black and half-Indian, practiced Hinduism offhandedly, and how some of her mother's ancestors were Kali worshippers from South India. Kali temples were in the backdrop of Tisha's childhood, but she practiced Catholicism. In Brooklyn she attended Pentecostal churches until she and her mother fell on hard times about five years ago, when Tisha started to receive visions. Once, while brushing her teeth, the pungent smell of fish and the sea filled her bedroom. A lady wearing white suddenly floated past. Panicked and bewildered, Tisha Googled "fish-smelling lady in white." The search engine deciphered the vision: it was Kali's sister, an incarnation of the Ganges River. "The Mother," Tisha said, was

Ruddy Roye, *J'ouvert: At the Devil's Playground,* 2004. For the "dutty mas" (dirty masquerade) that opens Brooklyn's West Indian Carnival, revelers follow the J'ouvert tradition from Trinidad, coating themselves in mud, paint, and oil to emphasize the play of gender and color and the "turnabout" of daily life at carnival's start.

telling her that she "needed to come home." More Googling ultimately led to the Shri Maha Kali Devi Mandir, where women are allowed to be priests, breaking Hindu orthodoxy, and worship lasts all day.

Tisha told me that envisioning the divine as maternal is a way of acknowledging her own mother, who brought her out of Guyana to deliver her from violence. When the pair emigrated, they were fleeing her father, a boxer with political connections who physically abused her mother. "Everyone's mother is part of Mother Kali because Mother has . . . that unconditional love," Tisha explained. "When you want to give up, you just look at her . . . and you feel defended in the physical and the spiritual—and protected."

Some worshippers at the Kali temple also follow Spiritual Baptism, which allows for spiritual possession too. This syncretic religion was started in Trinidad by former American slaves resettled there in reward for fighting on the British side during the War of 1812. In Spiritual Baptism the orishas, who act through healers and mediums, are from West Africa, but its rites are inflected with Hindu fragments, as it developed in a corner of Trinidad with a large Indian population. Mothers also figure prominently in its churches.

Spiritual Baptist churches are scattered all across Brooklyn, in storefronts or, in the case of St. John's Spiritual Baptist Church, in the basement of a Flatbush apartment building. With its brick back facing the street, St. John's barred windows are painted over like ever-lidded eyes. Its recessed doorway retreats behind a metal gate. At an adult baptism I attended there, feet stamped and hips moved for many hours. Congregants cried out and danced as if entranced, the way they had at the Kali temple. And their ceremonies were just as intense with incense and drumming—and just as taboo. (Until 1951 Spiritual Baptism was an underground faith, banned by the colonial government in Trinidad, its followers derided as "shouters.") On the day of the baptism I witnessed, the abbess who heads St. John's sat enthroned, wearing sunglasses, near an altar. Occasionally, she tended it, rearranging ritual objects I know as Hindu. She was dressed the way all the female parishioners were: in a long skirt with an apron, a belt around her waist, her head wrapped in a kerchief. The outfit brought to mind the Aunt Jemima of pancake mixes—a mammy image burdened, for many of us, by racist stereotype. For some Spiritual Baptists, however,

Aunt Jemima is one of a long line of ancestral mothers, including Jesus's grandmother, who communicate with them, visiting them in dreams and visions.

"Other-mothering," as the Spiritual Baptists call it, beckons all mothers except biological ones: grandmothers, godmothers, and even the stereotypical plantation mammy who nursed the master's children. For the many Caribbean women who have migrated to New York as domestic workers, the role of other-mother mirrors how they make their living: taking care of other people's children, while in some cases leaving their own behind. Those far from their families sometimes need to be mothered too. During the baptism ceremony, I witnessed elder women in the church standing behind younger candidates for the faith (all but one of them young women), adjusting their white robes from time to time, setting a lazy foot straight, fixing a posture, or whispering encouragement or rebuke into their ears. Mother is an actual title in the Spiritual Baptist hierarchy, earned through devotion.

But if their attire marks Spiritual Baptist women everywhere, it also links them to Muslim women who wear the veil. The clothing their religion requires gives women of both faiths joy, but it also opens them up to ridicule on the everyday street. Fazie Farouk, a Guyanese immigrant in her early fifties who worships at Masjid al-Abidin in Richmond Hill, shared how she started to wear the headscarf after going on the pilgrimage to Mecca a decade ago. When she first "covered," it was a hardship. People wouldn't sit next to her on the subway; white boys riding by on bicycles would tug it off. Worst of all, when she went to work, she was forced to remove it. Fazie, who has no children of her own, was a nanny for a couple in an upscale Manhattan neighborhood. "It was after 9/11. People were scared of me," she told me, as we sipped cane juice at a halal eatery in Queens' Little Guyana. "Because I needed the money, I put up with it." In 2008 Fazie stopped working as a nanny to take care of her own mother, who—before suffering a stroke—had also been a nanny and who had sponsored Fazie to come to America.

America's conflicts become the province of Caribbean women once they arrive on its shores. New York's deepest wound has, certainly. Fazie Farouk wasn't the sole one caught as collateral in 9/11. It was mid-September 2015 when another victim, a Spiritual Baptist I had met at a Flatbush church a week earlier, returned my call. Mother Myrtle declined lunch, a little gruffly, explaining that every year around September 11, she would lose her temper at the slightest provocation, and even her own family left her alone. Fourteen years after the terror attacks, this time of year still found her a recluse. I apologized for disturbing her. The sixty-eight-year-old great-grandmother repeated that she did not want to talk. I told her that I respected that and prepared to say goodbye. But she didn't hang up. Instead, for the next ninety minutes, she talked and I listened, in silent awe at the size of her grief. I held the phone to my ear gingerly, poised on the edge with her as she told me, with careening momentum, about her daughter Shevonne. Shevonne, who was left behind in Guyana when Myrtle came to America. Shevonne, who had nonetheless managed, running a grocery and taxi service by herself at seventeen. Shevonne, who ultimately made her way to New York too. Shevonne, who studied evenings at the Borough of Manhattan Community College. Shevonne, who was at her job in the World Trade Center when the planes hit on September 11, 2001.

That morning, mother and daughter had ridden the subway to work together. Three times, Myrtle heard a voice say: "Admire your daughter." At first, Myrtle thought it was the person sitting next to her. From girlhood, she had had visions, and spirits spoke to her, but there, in that everyday commuter crush to Manhattan, she thought the source of the command more earthbound. When she realized it wasn't, she was confused. Why should she admire Shevonne? She saw her every day. The third time the spirit spoke, it was roughly, admonishingly. So Myrtle obeyed. She registered every detail of her twenty-five-year-old daughter: neat office clothes, hair pulled back tight, glasses on her nose, reading her Daily Word prayer book. Mother Myrtle tapped Shevonne on the knee, smiled goodbye, and got off to change trains.

An hour later at Beth Israel Hospital, where she worked as a nurse's aide, she fainted when she saw the towers collapse on television. A fifth of the casualties were foreign-born, and Guyanese suffered one of the highest losses, with twenty-five dead. Shevonne was among them. For Mother Myrtle, the months that followed were a blur of her own near-madness. She stopped eating and had to be put on an intravenous drip. Her hair went completely gray. She heard voices, which told her to strip and run down the street or jump out the window. She would wander in a trance and end up at the World Trade Center site and not know her way home. When ultimately she reclaimed her senses, it was through prayer and her church. "If I didn't know God," she told me, "I'd be one of the crazy ones."

She has found her God at St. Gabriel's for almost two decades. The day I met Mother Myrtle, about fifty congregants were there, almost all of them middle-aged or elderly black women from Guyana. I knew their accents. I could easily place their villages on a map. I was clearly an outsider, the only one there visibly Indian, but they acted like reproving mothers to me. Several shot me disapproving looks as my veil dropped; one, in a gold pontiff's hat, a bishop in the church hierarchy, snapped at me for taking notes on my phone. Another reached back repeatedly to uncross my legs: "Why you lock yourself up so?" she asked. I had come before the Lord, and I needed to open to Him.

St. Gabriel's allows its followers to approach Jesus through different lineages. Mother Myrtle approached through Hinduism. And as our phone call ended, she grunted, then cried out, apparently as a medium for the Mother—that is to say, Kali. The goddess had possessed her. Speaking in Guyanese creole, she prophesied for me a Hindu wedding and a child in white. Then this matriarch from my home country told me that she also saw "flag work." (By this, she meant the involved worship rituals that the prismatic flags in Little Guyana commemorate.) I would not be the one to perform the prayer ceremony; my mother would, she said. There seemed, in all this, a certain pattern. My mother would pray for me, as Myrtle still grieves in memory of Shevonne, as Tisha's mother had engineered her exodus to New York City. From one woman acting on behalf of a daughter to the next, had maternal fierceness somehow forged a chain to connect us across the divisive waters of race and religion and history? Was this then, at last, our Caribbean archipelago?

10 CITY OF WOMEN

There is one map nearly everyone in New York City consults constantly, the subway map posted at nearly every station entry and on every platform and subway car (or at least it used to be posted everywhere). It's an odd map, distorting the sizes and shapes of the five boroughs, tilting Manhattan upright, off its southeast-northwest axis, and still not achieving the user-friendly clarity of the famous London Tube map. We call it the subway system, but it was built piecemeal by private developers, with stations that didn't quite connect and redundant lines and areas that don't get served; it is in other words unsystematic. It's still one of the marvels of urbanism, by some measurements the largest such transit system on earth, with more than 400 stations and 233 miles of routes, and one of the seven most heavily used transit systems anywhere. It had more than 1.75 billion riders in 2014 alone, several million a day, and it has hardly ever been closed in more than a century of existence. It has its own major standing in New York City culture, as a dangerous, an unpleasant, or a magical place, and just to say "the A train" or "the 7" is to invoke realms of experience. In the 1970s graffiti on the outside of subway cars marked the creative power of young people of color working with spray cans in the train yards at night (including Lady Pink, whose art appears on our map of the Bronx) and the lack of control over the city by the authorities. The cars covered in "wildstyle" writing sped by like illuminated manuscripts gone manic. But the station names remained the same, a network of numbers and mostly men's names and descriptives. It's an informational scaffolding on which other things can be built, so on it we have built a feminist city of sorts, or a map to a renamed city of women. Ours is a counter to the familiar subway map and maybe to the map generated by Hollaback!—a global movement founded in New York in 2005 to combat sexual harassment on the street. On the Hollaback! map (reproduced on page 90), so many reported incidents of harassment appear that they obliterate the city. In contrast, ours is a map of recovery and possibility.

CARTOGRAPHY: MOLLY ROY MAP APPEARS ON PAGES 86–87.

THE POWER OF NAMES BY REBECCA SOLNIT

"It's a Man's Man's Man's World" is a song James Brown recorded in a New York City studio in 1966, and whether you like it or not, you can make the case that he's right. Walking down the city streets, young women get harassed in ways that tell them that this is not their world, their city, their street; that their freedom of movement and association is liable to be undermined at any time; and that a lot of strangers expect obedience and attention from

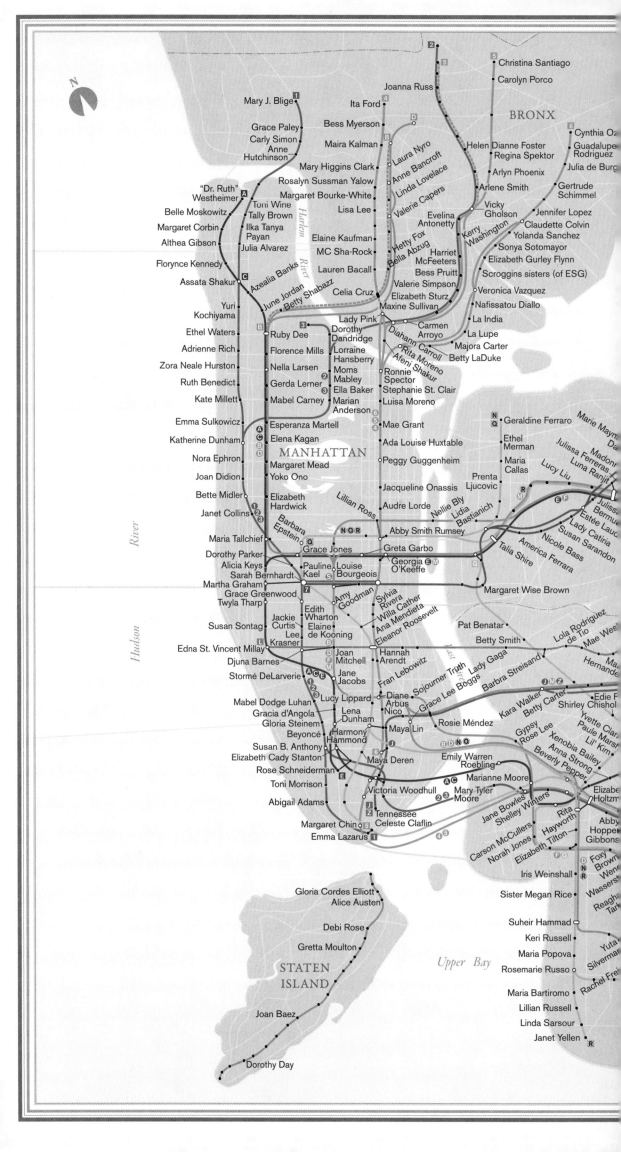

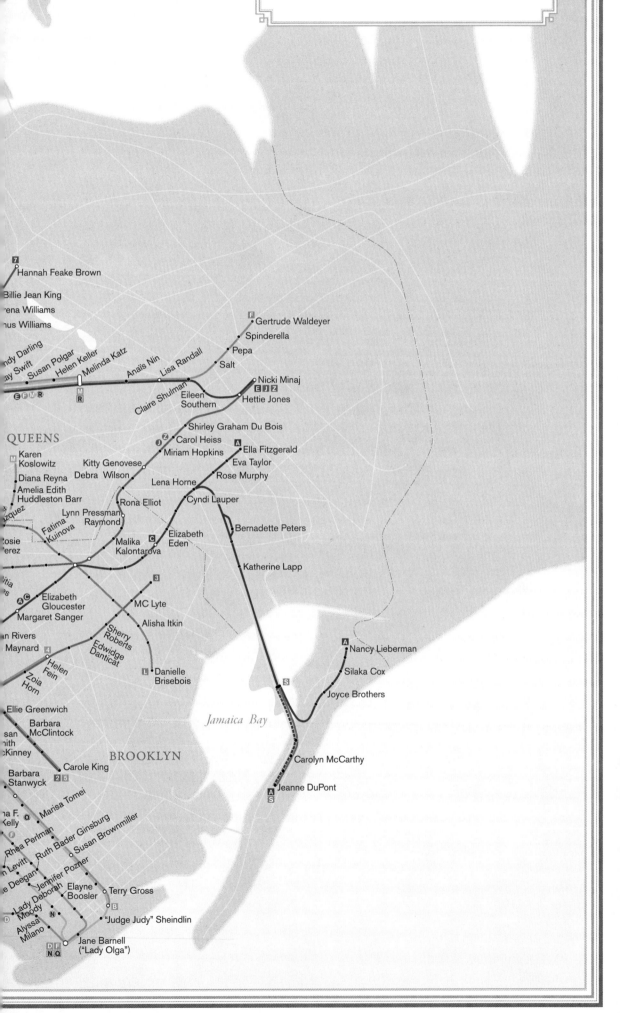

CITY OF WOMEN

7 Hannah Feake Brown

Billie Jean King
rena Williams
nus Williams

dy Darling
ay Swift   Susan Polgar   Helen Keller   Melinda Katz   Anaïs Nin   Lisa Randall

E F M R   M R   Claire Shulman   Eileen Southern   Hettie Jones

F   Gertrude Waldeyer
Spinderella
Pepa
Salt
Nicki Minaj
E J Z
M R

QUEENS
Karen Koslowitz
W
Diana Reyna
Amelia Edith Huddleston Barr
azquez
Fatima Kuinova
Rosie Perez

Kitty Genovese
Debra Wilson
Rona Elliot
Lynn Pressman Raymond
Malika Kalontarova
C

Shirley Graham Du Bois
J Z   Carol Heiss
Miriam Hopkins
Lena Horne
Cyndi Lauper
Elizabeth Eden

A   Ella Fitzgerald
Eva Taylor
Rose Murphy

Bernadette Peters

Katherine Lapp

itia
s
4 C   Elizabeth Gloucester
Margaret Sanger
n Rivers
Maynard
4
Helen Fein
Zoia Horn

3
MC Lyte
Alisha Itkin
Sherry Roberts
Edwidge Danticat
L   Danielle Brisebois

A   Nancy Lieberman
Silaka Cox
S   Joyce Brothers

Ellie Greenwich
Barbara McClintock
san
ith
cKinney
Barbara Stanwyck
Carole King
2 5

Jamaica Bay

BROOKLYN

Carolyn McCarthy

A   Jeanne DuPont
S

a F.
Kelly   Marisa Tornei
Q
F   Rhea Perlman   Ruth Bader Ginsburg   Susan Brownmiller
n Levitt
e Deegan   Jennifer Pozner
Lady Deborah   Elayne Boosler   Terry Gross
Moody
D   Alyssa   N
Milano   B   "Judge Judy" Sheindlin
D F
N Q   Jane Barnell ("Lady Olga")

them. "Smile," a man orders you, and that's a concise way to say that he owns you; he's the boss; you do as you're told; your face is there to serve his life, not express your own. He's someone; you're no one.

In a subtler way, names perpetuate the gendering of New York City. Almost every city is full of men's names, names that are markers of who wielded power, who made history, who held fortunes, who was remembered; women are anonymous people who changed fathers' for husbands' names as they married, who lived in private and were comparatively forgotten, with few exceptions. This naming stretches across the continent; the peaks of many western mountains have names that make the ranges sound like the board of directors of old corporations, and very little has been named for particular historical women, though Maryland was named after a Queen Mary who never got there.

Just as San Francisco was named after an Italian saint and New Orleans after a French king's brother, the duc d'Orléans, so New York, city and state, were named after King Charles I's brother, the duke of York (later King James II), when the British took over the region from the Dutch. Inside this city and state named for a man, you can board the 6 train at the northern end of the line in Pelham Bay, named after a Mr. Pell, in a borough named for a Swedish man, Jonas Bronck, and ride the train down into Manhattan, which is unusual in the city for retaining an indigenous name (the Bronx was said to be named Rananchqua by the local Lenape, Keskeskeck by other native groups). There the 6 travels down Lexington Avenue, parallel to Madison Avenue, named, of course, after President James Madison.

As the train rumbles south under Manhattan's east side, you might disembark at Hunter College, which, although originally a women's college, was named after Thomas Hunter, or ride further to Astor Place, named after plutocrat John Jacob Astor, near Washington Square, named, of course, after the president. Or you might go even farther to Bleecker Street, named after Anthony Bleecker, who owned farmland there, and emerge on Lafayette Street, named after the Marquis de Lafayette. En route you would have passed the latitudes of Lincoln Center, Columbus Circle, Rockefeller Center, Bryant Park, Penn Station—all on the west side.

A horde of dead men with live identities haunt New York City and almost every city in the western world. Their names are on the streets, the buildings, the parks, squares, colleges, businesses, and banks, and they are the figures on the monuments. For example, at 59th and Grand Army Plaza, right by the Pulitzer Fountain (for newspaper magnate Joseph Pulitzer), is a pair of golden figures, General William Tecumseh Sherman on horseback led by a woman who appears to be Victory, and also a nameless no one in particular. She is someone else's victory.

The biggest statue in the city is a woman, who welcomes everyone and is no one: the Statue of Liberty, with that poem by Emma Lazarus at her feet, the one that few remember calls her "Mother of Exiles." Statues of women are not uncommon, but they're allegories and nobodies, mothers and muses and props but not presidents. There are better temporary memorials, notably *Chalk*, the public art project that commemorates the anniversary of the 1911 Triangle Shirtwaist Factory fire, in which 146 young seamstresses, mostly immigrants, died. Every March 25 since 2004, Ruth Sergel has coordinated volunteers who fan out through the city to chalk the names of the victims in the places where they lived. But those memories are as frail and fleeting as chalk, not as lasting as street names, bronze statues, the Henry Hudson Bridge building, or the Frick mansion.

A recent essay by Allison Meier notes that there are only five statues of named women in New York City: Joan of Arc, Golda Meir, Gertrude Stein, Eleanor Roosevelt, and Harriet Tubman, the last four added in the past third of a century. Until 1984 there was only one, the medieval Joan in Riverside Park, installed in 1915. Before that, only men were commemorated in the statuary of New York City. A few women have been memorialized in relatively recent street names: Cabrini Boulevard after the canonized Italian American nun, Szold Place after Jewish editor and activist Henrietta Szold, Margaret Corbin Drive after the female Revolutionary War hero, Bethune Street after the founder of the orphan asylum, and Margaret Sanger Square after the patron saint of birth control. No woman's name applies to a long boulevard like Nostrand Avenue in Brooklyn or Frederick Douglass Boulevard in northern Manhattan or Webster Avenue in the Bronx (though Fulton

Molly Crabapple, *Monument to the Unknown Straphanger*, 2016

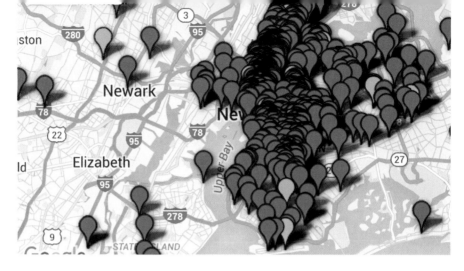

Screenshot of Hollaback!'s crowd-sourced map of incidents of street harassment in the New York region, March 2016. Courtesy of New York City Hollaback!

Street, named after steamboat inventor Robert Fulton, is supposed to be co-named Harriet Ross Tubman Avenue for much of its length, but the name does not appear to be in common usage and is not recognized by Google Maps). No woman is a bridge or a major building, though some may remember that Gertrude Vanderbilt Whitney is the founder for whom the museum is named. New York City is, like most cities, a manscape.

When I watch action movies with female protagonists—from *Crouching Tiger, Hidden Dragon* to *The Hunger Games,* I come out feeling charged-up, superhuman, indomitable. It's like a drug for potency and confidence. Lately I've come to wonder what it would feel like if instead of seeing a dozen or so such films in my lifetime, I had the option at any moment of seeing several new releases lionizing my gender's superpowers, if lady Bonds and Spiderwomen became the ordinary fare of my entertainment and imagination. If you're a man, the theaters are playing dozens of male action-hero films now, and television always has given you a superabundance of champions, from cowboys to detectives, more or less like you, at least when it comes to gender (if not necessarily race and body type and predilection). I can't imagine how I might have conceived of myself and my possibilities if, in my formative years, I had moved through a city where most things were named after women and many or most of the monuments were of powerful, successful, honored women. Of course these sites only commemorate those who were allowed to hold power and live in public; most American cities are, by their nomenclature, mostly white as well as mostly male. Still, you can imagine.

In the map "City of Women," we tried on what it would look like to live in such power by paying homage to some of the great and significant women of New York City in the places where they lived, worked, competed, went to school, danced, painted, wrote, rebelled, organized, philosophized, taught, and made names for themselves. New York City has had a remarkable history of charismatic women from the beginning, such as seventeenth-century Quaker preacher Hannah Feake Bowne, who is routinely written out of history—even the home in Flushing where she held meetings is often called the John Bowne house. Three of the four female Supreme Court justices have come from the city, and quite a bit of the history of American feminism has unfolded here, from Victoria Woodhull to Shirley Chisholm to the Guerrilla Girls. Not all the subway stations are marked, and many of the women who made valuable contributions or might have are forgotten or were never named. Many women were never allowed to be someone; many heroes of any gender live quiet lives. But some rose up; some became visible; and here they are by the hundreds. This map is their memorial and their celebration. 🐝

11 LOVE AND RAGE

If the city is a living organism, then its streets and tunnels are vessels and bones: the physical structure that gives its body shape and keeps it moving. These built systems of concrete or steel aren't hard to map, with the help of the right survey data or satellites. But if the city is a living organism, it also has emotions whose timbre and flow are as key to its health and function as they are to any human. These are harder to chart: not every force shaping our lives can be given discrete visual form or lent the weight of science. This map affirms that that's true. But it also suggests how two emotions in particular animate this city, where the sheer density of humans can give rise to intense feelings of both love and rage. To name one well-known contrast of two of the city's finest sons: Whitman loved the passing hordes in Lower Manhattan, while Melville often found himself annoyed by them. Both love and rage can manifest as an activity often associated with New York in particular.

Complaining is, if not an art form, at least an aria and sometimes a choral achievement in New York City, whose Yiddish-speaking population supplied us with the onomatopoeic word *kvetch* to cover it. Eloquent testimony to the richness and variety of complaints is borne out by the list at 311, the complaint hotline New Yorkers phone to address damaged trees, overgrown trees, streetlights, and toxic lead, as well as a host of other phenomena, including sacred noise, or "noise—house of worship" as it's called, along with noise from helicopters, vehicles, and "street/sidewalk"; myriad animal problems, including "unsanitary pigeon condition," "rodent," "unleashed dog," "animal in a park," and "illegal animal sold"; "panhandling," "poison ivy," and "public assembly." People call in out of empathic concern or annoyance or even fury, articulating a city categorized by concerns—although the less urgent ones, since the more urgent ones go to 911.

These emotions become forces shaping the city and responding to it. Love and rage could be imagined as attractions and repulsions, a set of invisible magnetic fields, of pushes and pulls, that direct our movements through a city, though violence may be the anomaly in this equation, the times when rage brings someone close enough to wreak damage rather than steering them away. We wanted to think big about love, since love of animals, of gardens and community and civil society, of justice, and of the city itself, as well as romantic and erotic love, shape how people act and where they go in the city. Sexual and gender violence might be where what is commonly classified as love warps into rage (though whether there was any love in the perpetrators is another conversation). Sifting through the city's 311 data with Chris Henrick, a cartographer as skilled at "data scraping" as mapmaking, it became clear that some categories of activity were so common they were unmappable at this scale, except as a blur of color. Maps are an art of selection, and so out of the sea of emotions, reactions, and reports in response to the city's everyday life we selected a few to suggest the range of civic-minded and antisocial action that is the everyday warp and weft of urban life.

The fact that the city breeds emotional extremes is also why it's no stranger to romance: to fall in love while bathed in Gotham's bright lights, against its unique backdrop of drama, is its own thrill. But love in the city doesn't just mean romance—it means the love for community, evinced by those who turn vacant lots into gardens; the love for books and the public good, evinced by the city's extraordinary system of libraries; the love for those young men and women who have too often been the targets of state violence, love that was voiced in the Black Lives Matter protests that erupted in 2014. The city makes us intimate in ways we desire and in ways we don't. And with intimacy come all the human complications tied to love and rage, and the vexing place, too, where they twirl around each other and overlap—whether you're on intimate terms with one person or eight and a half million of them.

CARTOGRAPHY: CHRIS HENRICK; ARTWORK: ADRIANA KRASNIANSKY 🜨 MAP APPEARS ON PAGES 92–93.

LOVE AND RAGE

I 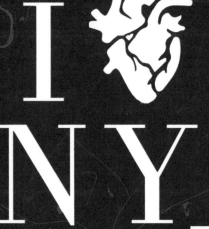 NY

Scoreboard at Yankee Stadium used for marriage proposals upward of 75 times per year

NEW JERSEY

"Central Park Jogger" assaulted and raped (April 1989); five young men, wrongly convicted, spend 7 to 13 years in jail

"Preppy Murderer" Robert Chambers seduces Jennifer Levin, whom he later kills in Central Park, at Dorrian's Red Hand bar (August 1986)

Graphic designer Milton Glaser creates iconic "I♥NY" logo for the New York State Department of Economic Development (1977)

Roberta Flack and Donny Hathaway record "Where Is the Love?" (1971)

Pop artist Robert Indiana's "LOVE" sculpture, based on a Christmas card design for the Museum of Modern Art (c. 1970)

Dominique Strauss-Kahn, head of the IMF, accused of sexually assaulting hotel maid Nafissatou Diallo (May 2011)

Bernhard Goetz, the "Subway Vigilante," shoots four young men from the Bronx on the 2 train (1984)

Central Park

Black Lives Matter protests wind through Manhattan in summer 2014, after the police killings of Michael Brown, an unarmed teen in Missouri, and Eric Garner in Staten Island

Robert DeNiro's mohawk-wearing Travis Bickle, enraged title character in *Taxi Driver* (1976), shoots the pimp and then a client of the teen prostitute Iris, played by Jodie Foster, before trying to shoot himself

MANHATTAN

East River

New York begins issuing marriage licenses to gay couples at City Hall (July 2011)

Rock band Rage Against the Machine disrupts the New York Stock Exchange while shooting a music video with filmmaker Michael Moore (2000)

"Love locks," continually clipped by the department of transportation, affixed to Brooklyn Bridge by loving couples

NYPD officers Wenjian Liu and Rafael Ramos killed in their car by enraged gunman Ismaaiyl Brinsley (December 2014)

Cherry blossoms bloom, with spring romance, in Brooklyn Botanic Garden

"Crown Heights Riot" pits African Americans against Hasidic Jews after Yosef Lifsh, part of a motorcade for the neighborhood's Lubavitcher leader, drives his station wagon into two children, killing one (August 1991)

Prospect Park

Eric Garner is killed by chokehold, for selling cigarettes, by NYPD officers in his Staten Island neighborhood (July 2014)

Upper Bay

BROOKLYN

STATEN ISLAND

Hudson River

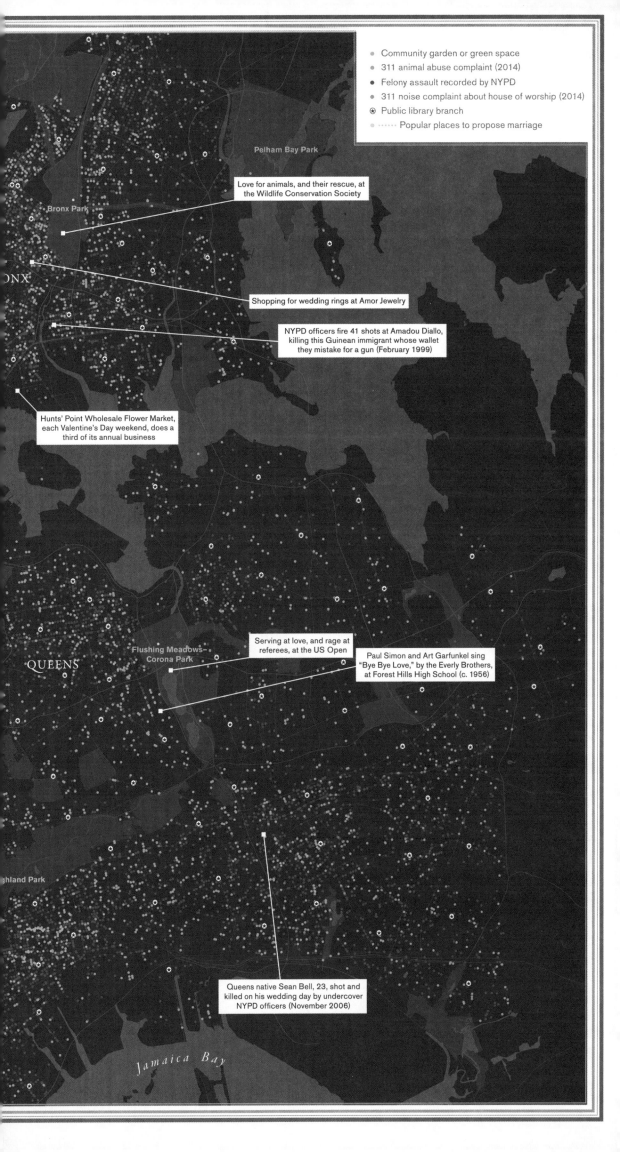

Community garden or green space

311 animal abuse complaint (2014)

Felony assault recorded by NYPD

311 noise complaint about house of worship (2014)

Public library branch

Popular places to propose marriage

Pelham Bay Park

Love for animals, and their rescue, at the Wildlife Conservation Society

Bronx Park

ONX

Shopping for wedding rings at Amor Jewelry

NYPD officers fire 41 shots at Amadou Diallo, killing this Guinean immigrant whose wallet they mistake for a gun (February 1999)

Hunts' Point Wholesale Flower Market, each Valentine's Day weekend, does a third of its annual business

QUEENS

Flushing Meadows–Corona Park

Serving at love, and rage at referees, at the US Open

Paul Simon and Art Garfunkel sing "Bye Bye Love," by the Everly Brothers, at Forest Hills High School (c. 1956)

ghland Park

Queens native Sean Bell, 23, shot and killed on his wedding day by undercover NYPD officers (November 2006)

Jamaica Bay

12 CITY OF WALKERS

New York is a city of walkers. It's a city on the move, whether it be crowds bustling on foot to work and play or lone figures meandering to get relief from the mad rush. To walk in New York is to discover the city's joys and annoyances and complications. Read about New York—its poetry, the fiction and nonfiction—and you find a secret history of walking and walkers: people laying claim to their neighborhoods or ethnicities or professions by way of navigating on foot. Like nowhere else in the United States, New York City is defined by its people walking. Whenever one walks through New York, it quickly becomes clear that it is not one city, but many—and much of it can be found only on foot. This is something our editor-at-large, Garnette Cadogan, knows well. Joining New York's city of walkers, he considers himself part of the latest generation of inhabitants who shape and reshape the city by walking. He's immersed himself in the work of the many walkers who have taken to New York's streets in search of themselves or the people and secrets to be found—from Walt Whitman to Jacob Riis to Alfred Kazin to Vivian Gornick. And he also follows an even longer tradition of immigrants who have left homes where walking is the main mode of transportation, and for whom walking here is a way of finding and connecting with home. One spring afternoon in 2015 he set out from his home in the Bronx to take a twenty-four-hour walk around the city. Guided by the idea that the city is inexhaustible and its stories countless, Cadogan saw no end to his search—or our searching. And so he decided that a circular route was only fitting for New York, a place where mystery, not mastery, is his main entrée to exploration.

CARTOGRAPHY: MOLLY ROY   MAP APPEARS ON PAGES 96–97.

ROUND AND ROUND   BY GARNETTE CADOGAN

> O New York, New York, carousel and carnival of the too-rich, busy, full life, how can one ever do justice to your insane human fullness?
> —Alfred Kazin

> By its nature, the metropolis provides what otherwise could be given only by traveling; namely, the strange.
> —Jane Jacobs

One cold spring night, the promise of summer held back as if in spite, I emerged from a subway station on the edge of Williamsburg, on my way to meet a friend for dinner. I noticed an Orthodox Jew in characteristic all-black attire and *shtreimel* walking swiftly toward me. I assumed that he found me suspicious—a not-rare-enough reaction to the mundane fact of my having black skin—and so was advancing threateningly to ward off the threat I was presumed to be. I began to move away from him, but not too quickly, lest I appear all the more guilty. He altered course to intercept me, like a bullet that wouldn't be denied its target. I zigged, hoping that a quick veer would get me away from him, but somehow he managed to close the distance between us. He didn't walk so much as glide. Perhaps the man was a ninja and I had scanned him wrong. I stopped and flinched, thinking, "Not the face, please," but he leaned in and, with gentle insistence, asked, "Would you like to do a good deed?" There was an undertone of challenge to the question, and also an irresistible strain of pleading. I answered yes, and he made a sharp turn and said, "Follow me."

He took me around a corner, where an older man stood with three young kids huddled beside him. "Follow the rabbi," my chaperone said. So I followed the rabbi, who crossed the road, children in tow, entered a synagogue, and climbed the high stairs that overlooked its majestic hall. There he stopped and entered a modest kitchen. He instructed me to unplug a kettle. When I had done so, the rabbi graciously bid me goodbye, and I stepped out onto the windy sidewalk, ready to rush to my appointment. But my good deed wasn't done, apparently. The friendly ninja said, "There is one more. Come with me."

Off we went, down the road to what turned out to be his own apartment. His wife and two curious children were standing in the living room—they'd been waiting for hours, I was told, for whomever was ready to perform a good deed on a Saturday night (it was the Jewish holiday, Shavuot)—and he had me set his thermostat at a desired temperature and turn on his dryer, which had wet clothes in it. As I was checking appliances, he asked what I did for a living. "I'm a writer," I answered, and he asked me to email him my work. I looked at the email address he scribbled on a paper and tried to repress a smile; it was the kind of address I'd expect from a playful teenager, not from this distinguished-looking Orthodox Jew who was graciously insisting on giving me food for my journey. I explained that I needed nothing—a good deed should be its own reward, after all, plus I was on my way to eat Japanese food—but he insisted that I shouldn't leave empty-handed and gave me a freezie. "Look—it's kosher," he reassured me.

A neighbor was waiting in the hallway. He beckoned me to an apartment one floor below, where I turned on lights to discover about a dozen people standing in the living room, no longer in the dark because I had flipped a switch. I didn't have the heart to ask how long they had congregated there in the darkness. Thermostat and kettle checked, I finally made my way out of this building populated with people who depended on the kindness of strangers.

Out on the quiet sidewalk, I looked around. No one was waiting to accost me. I stared up at the building and the darkness in the windows tugged at me—were people up there waiting for hands willing to work on the Sabbath? Would they shout for assistance if they saw me? The only sound I heard was the whistle of a wind that rushed down to push me along, as if someone had whispered that I was late. Suddenly these sidewalks where I had walked dozens of times before became a place more revealing, and more mysterious.

New York City does that to you—it sneaks up on you. It sneaks up on you and promises that there is always more to see, to hear, to know. It surprises you with its inexhaustibility. At the same time, it reminds you that there is much that is hidden, because of the basic algebra in which knowledge equals identity. Behind what is revealed lie layers of national histories and cultural rituals and religious traditions and family lore. The city is a fossil record, and every layer you peel back exposes another layer whose contours reveal only our limitations in knowing the city.

And yet, New York is as ready to give of itself as it is apt to withhold itself. Nowhere is this tendency to announce its marvels while simultaneously whispering its secrets as interwoven as within its immigrant communities.

. . .

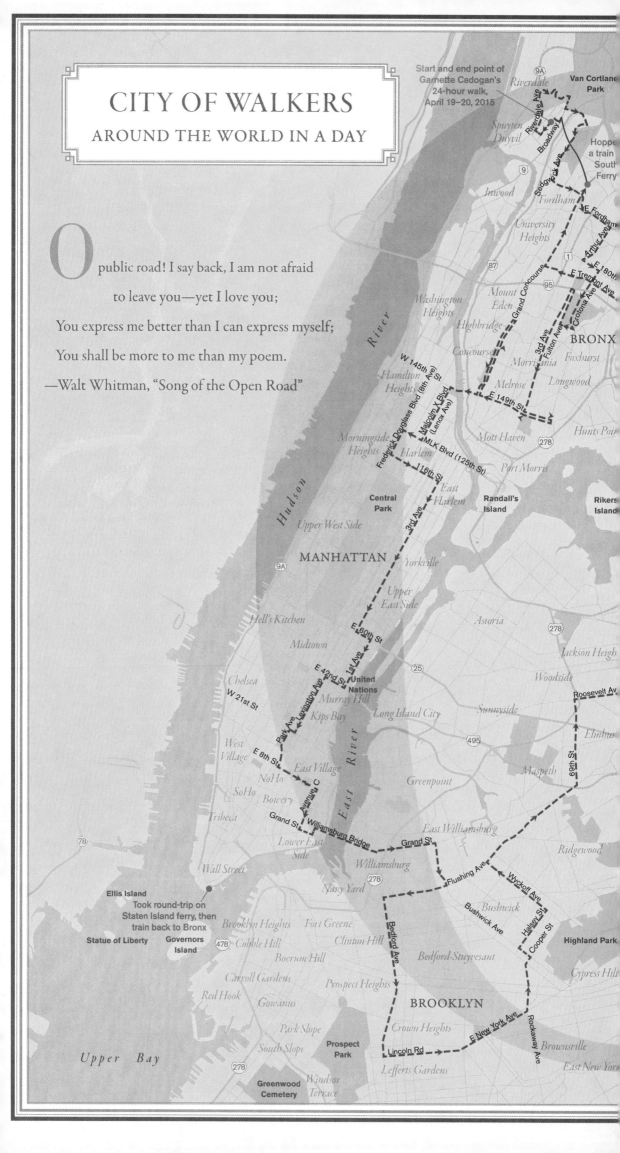

CITY OF WALKERS
AROUND THE WORLD IN A DAY

O public road! I say back, I am not afraid
to leave you—yet I love you;
You express me better than I can express myself;
You shall be more to me than my poem.

—Walt Whitman, "Song of the Open Road"

Start and end point of
Garnette Cadogan's
24-hour walk,
April 19–20, 2015

Hopped
a train
South
Ferry

Ellis Island
Took round-trip on
Staten Island ferry, then
train back to Bronx

Statue of Liberty

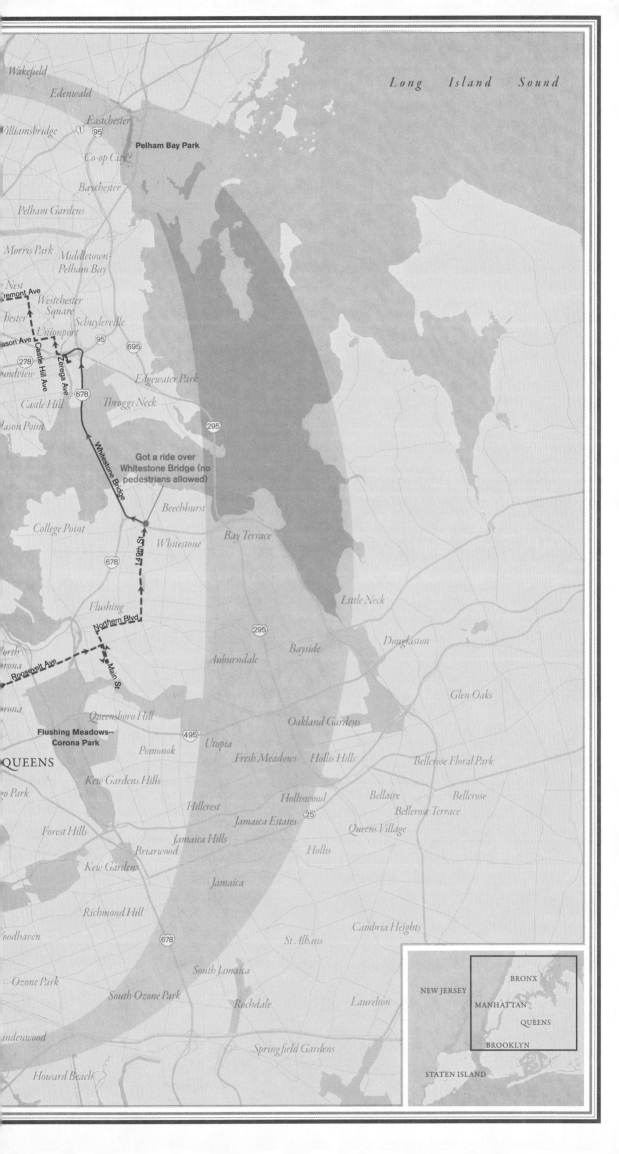

Got a ride over
Whitestone Bridge (no
pedestrians allowed)

Ruddy Roye, *IPK Walk–Jackson Heights*, 2015

Immigrants are central to the allure of the city; it's a truism the city repeats endlessly to itself: immigrants provide a rich diversity and cosmopolitan flavor that awaken one's senses and enliven one's sense of identity. (Though for far too many residents, immigrants are merely wonderful entertainment: "Give us your singers, your dancers, your cooking masses" seems to be the motto for the hordes talking about the coolest new Chinese restaurant or the funkiest new Brazilian band.) The ubiquitous presence of nonnative bodies with foreign tongues is among the reasons people assert that New York has a "low bar of entry": a new immigrant can get off the plane at JFK International Airport and, shortly after, declare status as a New Yorker. So many immigrant groups lay claim to New York—a favor the city, in general, returns by championing itself as a city of immigrants— that a newcomer can feel attached to the city merely by virtue of his or her intense allegiance to a group that already feels at home in the city. Certainly, many who migrate to the city are like the seeker E. B. White described in the middle of the twentieth century in *Here Is New York:* "the person who was born somewhere else and came to New York in quest of something." But for a sizable number of these immigrants, especially those who were forced out of elsewhere to here, home in New York may very well be a facsimile or echo of a home left behind. In some parts of Brooklyn's Crown Heights I am tempted to take photographs, develop them, and playfully write "Kingston, circa 1990" on the back of the prints before I mail them back to Jamaica, where I grew up. In New York one can easily be elsewhere by being here.

New York opens itself up to those willing to explore it, and so the view from elsewhere can be glimpsed—and enjoyed—by wandering the city's streets. I regularly walk those streets, hoping for serendipity and its gift of fascinating encounters. A city is, in part, the sum of its stories, and those stories are best gathered up-close—on foot. So I walk, in this city of walkers, and join its throngs, even in places the locals shun. Many people avoid Times Square because of its aimless tourists walking like drunk goats, erratic in their stop-start-turn anti-rhythms, stubbornly oblivious to anyone around them. But these tourists carry the eyes of the innocent, the refreshing curiosity that asks: Why? Where? How? When? Who? Where? Where again? Creeping crowds of foreigners smiling, laughing, gazing, and grazing, somehow puncture the jaded bubble I surround myself with to block out the high-wattage advertisements glaring down and screaming: want, covet, buy. On some days, as I try to zoom past costumed characters (Elmo and Cookie Monster trying to make the rent) and desnudas (nearly nude women whose costume is mostly the shedding of costume), I catch a glimpse of a face or overhear a voice that expresses surprise at the vibrancy or eccentricity of this city, and my capacity for wonder is refreshed. I'm also reminded that never far from the glamour and gloss of New York are its immigrant workers, the blood and sweat beneath or beside the city's sheen. Most of the performers in Times Square posing for photos in exchange for tips are immigrants. Minnie Mouse might be from Mexico, Cookie Monster from Peru, and the topless woman with the American flag painted on her bare chest from Brazil. The place might feel like Disneyland on meth, but if one pays attention and relinquishes the right to be the hare overtaking the tortoise,

Ruddy Roye, *IPK Walk–Flatbush (Outside Afrika House)*, 2015

I've come to learn, one will see an overture to New York's complex diversity in the many faces gleaming beneath the glare of Times Square.

. . .

All those visitors in Times Square are there to see New York—or a particular dazzling version of it—and I walk around that bustling public space to see past the glitter to "people, endless, streaming, with strong voices, passions, pageants," as Walt Whitman once celebrated. "Manhattan streets, with their powerful throbs . . . Manhattan crowds, with their turbulent musical chorus—with varied chorus / and light of the sparkling eyes." But Manhattan's streets aren't enough for me: I want to witness all across the city how people take their home country with them to New York and adapt easily or uneasily to this challenging metropolis. (E. B. White said that "the city makes up for its hazards and deficiencies by supplying its citizens with massive doses of a supplementary vitamin—the sense of belonging to something unique, cosmopolitan, mighty and unparalleled." Many dreamers in the city—and I count myself among them—will nod to that, but a lot of immigrants press on because of the need and will to survive: they persevere not only for themselves but also for those dependent on them in New York and in the place they left. They trade in the vitamin with its intoxicating vision of the city for a drug that will help them endure the pain this increasingly unequal city inflicts on the poor, the weak, the undocumented.)

I want to see displays that remind me of my old home, like the Jamaicans and Haitians and Bajans and Trinis in jubilant celebration on Eastern Parkway in Brooklyn in the annual West Indian Day Parade, their costumes outshining the most brilliant male Indian peacock you've ever seen. I want to introduce myself, introduce my friends, to the many cultures that call New York home, like the euphoric mix of Colombians and Argentineans and Ecuadorians and Indians and Pakistanis and Bangladeshis and Nepalese and Chinese and Filipinos in Jackson Heights in Queens. I want to see how people long for home; I want to observe how they declare: "This is my home." Cosmopolitan that I am, I'm most at home at the intersection of many homes, so I search for the "turbulent musical chorus" in all five boroughs of New York.

I know of no better way to create a sense of place, a sense of home, than through walking. For as long as I can remember, I've been a walker, one who makes sense of the world by strolling through it. It's no surprise, then, that when I moved to New York I made it my home by walking all over it. Many immigrants, from countries where the walker has not been displaced by the automobile, lay claim to the city by grasping it underfoot. They warm up to it at walking pace. And they reacquaint with it at the same pace. One of the ways they *arrive* in the city is through walking; each step we take, after all, is a movement from departure to arrival. So I walk to connect with the city, but also to connect with other immigrants who pursue home—step by step, encounter by encounter, ambition by ambition—the way I do. And the way I don't. After all, "All day all over the city," Robert Pinsky tells us, "every person / Wanders a different city, sealed intact."

. . .

The city gives itself over—unevenly, but genuinely—to those ready to explore it, and one can catch glimpses of parts of the globe by rambling from neighborhood to neighborhood. The world has come to New York neighborhoods, after all; time and again I've met neighbors who told me they were neighbors in the old country, and their moves were less city to city than neighborhood to neighborhood. One spring afternoon in 2015 I decided to "visit the world in a day" by walking for twenty-four hours through all five boroughs. Though the idea had the whiff of gimmickry, I thought that it would be a good exercise to have the exhaustibility of the body meet the inexhaustibility of the city. I wanted my body to be aware of its limitations (in energy, that is; I'm regularly made aware of the lines of trespass drawn because of my complexion and have inculcated rules for "walking while black"). Moreover, I thought, it'd be fun to walk in a circle around New York to see what it would throw at me—my route was both planned enough and arbitrary enough to make serendipity and vulnerability intersect.

I began near the northwest tip of the Bronx, in Riverdale, walking past its kosher delis and Jewish schools; to neighboring Kingsbridge, with its Irish and Dominican population; over to Arthur Avenue, where the Bronx's Little Italy overflows with Italian American families enjoying culinary delights; across to the Grand Concourse, a thoroughfare modeled on the Champs-Élysées, where the sound of bomba greets me along with its Puerto Rican residents; along to the energetic crossroads in the South Bronx known as the Hub, nicknamed the Times Square of the Bronx, with African and Latino shoppers pouring in and out of the commercial centers; down to Le Petit Sénégal, a stretch on 116th Street in West Harlem where West Africans beckon passersby into shops and restaurants with inviting colors and smells and laughter. I'm greeted with such warmth in a restaurant that I wonder if I've walked into a friend's living room. I linger and observe and chat, as I've done my entire trip. Here in Harlem, as in all the places I've walked, there are signposts of the home being made and reminders of the home left. I remember Jane Jacobs's observation: "Cities have the capability of providing something for everybody, only because, and only when, they are created by everybody."

I make my way down to the headquarters of the United Nations, an institution created to unite high ideals and national interest to promote cooperation; to encourage humanity's best instincts and oppose and temper its worst, you might say. I detect a resonance from abroad in this neighborhood that I don't perceive anywhere else in New York. It has among the city's most diverse mix of people, certainly the most diverse collection of nationalities we can see on a map of sovereign nation-states. There is a whiff of anticolonialism here—or at least the sense that those at the margins get to sit at the table and make their voices heard. (This, in a city where far too often the voices of poor immigrants are muted or ignored.) And to boot, there is the deep affinity that anchors connection: if you come to New York City from, say, Mali and go to the UN headquarters, you know you'll encounter Malians there. Some pleasures that seem trivial—you want Chinese or Filipino or Jamaican or Ghanaian or Colombian food, you can find a lead to it here—run deep for the immigrant new to this city, trying to make it a new home.

The UN complex overlooking the East River is worth a reflective pause, because the clichés about Immigrant New York City—a bouquet of difference, a rich mix, a flavorful stew (that cloying phrase: melting pot)—are tempered here. One is reminded of what we can aspire or even reach to, but we are also shown the depths to which we plunge to degrade ourselves and harm others. And it reminds me why a phenomenally diverse place like Jackson Heights in Queens is such a marvel: people who are at each other's throats in their home countries have found a way to coexist in their new home in New York.

I travel onward, passing through Grand Central's busy mix of travelers; down past "Curry Hill," with its row of Indian restaurants and spice shops; farther down past Loisaida, the Puerto Rican neighborhood on the Lower East Side; on to the Williamsburg Bridge, where I'm led to Hasidic Jewish, Italian American, and Hispanic communities. (Though I've crossed that bridge more times than I can remember, and am aware of the tensions that have arisen between some of those communities, I can't help but feel like the narrator of *The Great Gatsby* when he crosses the Queensboro Bridge: the city I see is "the city seen for the first time, in its first wild promise of all the mystery and the beauty in the world.")

I traverse and linger in neighborhoods—Maspeth, Elmhurst, Jackson Heights, Corona, and Flushing in Queens; Parkchester, East Tremont, Belmont, and Fordham in the Bronx; and Tompkinsville in Staten Island, where I end my journey after jumping on a train from the Bronx all the way down to the tip of Manhattan, where I catch the famously free ferry across the harbor and walk to reward myself with Sri Lankan food. At each stop I encounter familiarity and surprise, continually bumping into the city's mystery and beauty. Block after block, I keep trying to search for what lies *beyond*. *Beyond* my own neighborhood, *beyond* my awareness, *beyond* my self. I am searching for what the city's immigrant communities hold forth and hold back, recognizing that, as Alfred Kazin once said of lights along Jamaica Avenue, "they were searching out so many new things in me."

We carry within us the maps of our wanderings. We inscribe upon our imaginations the routes we have known, and we impose them on new journeys, one map layered on another. So I try to walk against the maps soldered onto my mind, hoping to create fresh, unencumbered ones. (As I move around, though, I never forget that the unremarkable-yet-remarkable fact that because I am black and an immigrant, there are many regions that I have to navigate with caution, and others that are out of bounds to me.) Our maps are our stories, and we leave ourselves open to new stories, new possibilities, new visions of ourselves and the world if we walk to get lost, to admit our ignorance and finitude by encountering the new and different. Something inside of me wants to master this unconquerable metropolis that is New York. But the city is unstoppable, moving on unsentimentally and making my attempts to know it hardly more definitive than snapshots across time. Each pass I make through the city uncovers more of its texture but also reminds me that much is hidden. I'm not seeing the tip of the iceberg—I'm seeing the tip of a wing of a bird on the iceberg. When I walk through the immigrant communities of New York, then, I feel humbled. The city tells me that mastery is beyond my grasp, that the grandest gift of the streets is mystery. New York promises that, in a place where ambition is the treasured watchword, we can more fully find ourselves in each other and learn to be enchanted by the things revealed and the awareness that much is held back, awaiting our gentle curiosity. "And what happens next," to borrow the wisdom of Seamus Heaney, "is a music that you never would have known to listen for." This inexhaustible city need not exhaust us—we can walk into wonder. 🌾

WILDLIFE

Old-growth fores

Pereg
falco

Wildlife painter John James
Audubon (1785–1851)

Three coyotes
attend Columbia
(2010)

Peacocks at
Cathedral of St
John the Divine

Cer
Pa

Eastern
coyotes

Approxima
regularly see
of bird, incl
30 warbler sp
double-cres
cormorants, egret
herons, black-cro
night-herons, Cana
geese, mute swans (w
nest here), ducks, gull
belted kingfishers,
broad-winged hawks,
kestrels, ospreys, bald

American Museum of Natural
History and Hayden Planetarium

Pepper LaBeija, mother of House of LaBeija (1948–2003)

Mambo mania at the Palladium

Latex Ball, organized by Gay Men's Health Crisis (1990–)

Better Days (voguing)

Turtles
(5 species)

eagles, peregrines,
Cooper's hawks,
sharp-shinned hawks,
red-shouldered and
red-tailed hawks, common
loons, canvasbacks,
greater scaup, snow
geese, blue jays, eastern
bluebirds, cedar
waxwings …

Angie Xtravaganza, mother of House of Xtravaganza (1964–1993)

Sally's Hideaway (voguing)

House of Xtravaganza 30th anniversary ball (2012)

Eastern
coyotes

Red-tailed
hawks Pale
Male and
mates
nest

Chelsea piers, a free zone for celebration
and erotic encounter (1970s–90s)

Canada geese
bring down US
Airways Flight
1549 (2009)

Peregrine
falcons

Lenape Edible Estate (opened 2009)

Clit Club/Jackie 60/Mother

Eastern coyotes

Vauxhall Gardens (opened 1767)

Vogue Knights

Latin Quarter

Mattachine Society of New York stages a "sip-in" at
one of New York's first gay bars, Julius (April 21, 1966)

Isadora
Duncan Dance
Foundation

MANHATTAN

Cormorant

Choreographer Merce Cunningham (1919–2009)

Eastern
coyotes

Hindu Holi celebration wit
NYC Bhangra dance grou

Stonewall riot heroines Stormé DeLarverie, Miss Major Griffin-Gracy,
Sylvia Rae Rivera, Marsha P. Johnson (June 28, 1969)

New York City Audubon Socie

Danceteria

Peregrine
falcons

Palace Garden (opened 185

Time Landscape (1978–), artist Alan Sonfist's
re-creation of primordial plant community

Victoria Woodhull advocates fo
free love (November 20, 1871

Paradise Garage (voguing)

Pigeon
central

Eastern
coyotes

Hindu Holi celebratio
with Solar One (201

The New York Earth Room (1977–), artist Walter
De Maria's installation of 280,000 pounds of soil

Eastern
coyotes

Light of Guidance Center fo
Sufi Studies, Inayati Order

Artist Joseph Beuys spends three days in a gallery with a coyote
in the performance *I Like America and America Likes Me* (1974)

Muskrats, pickerel, bass,
pike, ducks, and geese
in Minetta Creek (still
flows under streets)

African Grove Theatre (1821–26

Dergah al-Farah, Nur Ashki Jerrahi Sufi Order

Niblo's Garden (opened 1825)

The Venerable Felix Varela (1788–1853)

Eastern
coyotes

Contoit's Garden (opened 1801)

Artist Agnes Denes plants 2 acres of wheat
and harvests 1,000 pounds of grain (1982)

Ranelagh Gardens
(opened 1767)

St Elizabeth Ann Seton (1774–1821)

Striped bass,
Atlantic
sturgeon, lined
seahorse,
American eel

Black bear
shot (1630)

Hindu-Sikh-Jain
coalition lobbies
for recognition of
Diwali as a school
holiday (2015–)

Finale of classic
hip-hop film *Wild
Style* shot at the
East River
Amphitheater (1981

Members of ACT-UP (AIDS Coalition To Unleash Power)
occupy New York Stock Exchange (September 14, 1989)

Peregrine
falcons

Little Oyster
Island

Peregrine
falcons

Downing's Oyster House (and
Underground Railroad station; 1825–66)

106 humpback whales
spotted (2014)

Great Oyster
Island

BROOKLYN

New York
Aquarium
Coney Islan

Finback whales, dolphins,
porpoises, seals (harbor, harp, and
hooded), longfin inshore squid

Atlantic Coast leopard frog
(*Rana kauffeldi*) discovered on
Staten Island (2014)

Raccoons

Upper Bay

Gowanus oysters,
Brooklyn's first export

Last old-growth forest in the city, replete with coyotes and bald eagle nests

Coyote families

Muskrats

Peregrine falcons

Coyote families

Pelham Bay Park

Spotted salamanders, groundhogs

Bronx Park

Harbor seals, horseshoe crabs, raccoons, snowy egrets, herons, long-eared owls

St Frances Cabrini (1850–1917) and her shrine

Bronx Zoo/Wildlife Conservation Society

NEW JERSEY

BRONX

MANHATTAN

QUEENS

BROOKLYN

STATEN ISLAND

nks

Dusky salamanders

Crotona Park

Rockland Palace, home of annual Hamilton Lodge drag ball (1920s–30s)

Coyote families

Cotton Club, birthplace of jitterbug and Cab Calloway haunt

, the r (c. 1–3)

Savoy Ballroom, birthplace of Lindy hop

Wild minks (up until 1950s)

"Wildstyle" of graffiti writing evolved by TRACY 168 and others

Renaissance Ballroom and Casino

BRONX

Peregrine falcons

arlem, drag balls since 20s, birthplace of voguing

se-dancing at Bethel Gospel Assembly

nrise ceremony and ceremonial dancing at Redhawk Native American Arts Council annual igenous Peoples' Day powwow

Herons

tropolitan Museum of Art: ecstatic art

oreographer Martha Graham (1894–1991)

John Neumann (1811–1860)

e Venerable Pierre Toussaint (1766–1853)

lgin Botanical Garden (1801–c. 1812)

and Central Station's human hive beneath a green night sky painted with backward constellations

UEENS

Red fox →

ubavitcher Hasidim dance in the eets for Simchat Beit Hashoeva

Hindus make offerings to New York's Ganges, Jamaica Bay

Endangered piping plovers at Rockaway Beach

13 WILDLIFE

One inspiration for this map was the art of Tino Rodriguez, a perpetual meta-morphosis in which humans grow wings and breath takes the form of a bird and men's bodies as well as women's can be tender, flower-bedecked, mortal, carnal, spiritual—a world in which nothing is separated by category or species. His paintings are reminders that the natural world comes right into the city and asserts itself in a lover's bouquet, a funeral wreath, in the ways animals furnish our imagination and the animals we catch sight of lift our spirits or break us out of our routine. This is a map about the forces that break the routines of the city, about the dissident forces that are in some ways life itself—life that existed before the orderly city of authority, outside it, despite it, and will live after it—forces that include saints and lovers, humans and animals, birdwatchers and nightclub-bers. CARTOGRAPHY: MOLLY ROY; ARTWORK: TINO RODRIGUEZ 🐦 MAP APPEARS ON PAGES 102–103.

THE OYSTERS IN THE SPIRE BY REBECCA SOLNIT

Has any city tried as hard to be rational and orderly as New York City with its "world's largest private army" police force, much of its central island organized as a grid of numbered streets, its granite outcroppings sanded down like unloved calluses (except in the Bronx), its bankers and brokers convinced that everything can be monetized and money is the measure of all things, its impatient crowds surging forward to meet schedules, its prisons and punishments and panopticon eyes? All cities exist in a daytime version about business and productivity and order, some of which is lovely and necessary, the labor that makes the water flow and the trains run; some of which is not—the forces that put a price on everything and push out whoever and whatever doesn't pay and the authorities who see all wildness and freedom as disorder to eradicate.

All cities also have a dream life and a nightlife and a love life that are the opposite of those things. These can themselves be turned into marketable commodities, and often are, but still at times break free of reason and logic, and the calculated and controlled. Cities not only foment revolution from time to time but contain insurrections as one of the most essential of their infinite ingredients. New York too—maybe New York especially.

New York native son Lou Reed once sang of ecstasy as what cannot be grasped, contained, and quantified, as something that nothing stuck to, not even his arms "dipped in glue." Elusiveness, evanescence, is part of the intrinsic nature of ecstasy and joy and pleasure. One great source of this, even in cities, perhaps especially in cities, comes from observing and coexisting with animals. For though the city was built for people, the non-human remains a huge force in New York with its whale watchers and birdwatchers, its zoo-goers and coyote spotters. The animals never knew the rules, and perhaps one of the pleasures of seeing them is seeing residents who will never pay rent.

Cities produce the kinds of things—shoes, tools, cars—that you can read about in the old geography books and school atlases, objects for sale and export; today, New York's postindustrial economy tends more to produce financial scheming, tourism, and other ineffables. But cities have also always produced glances, fleeting encounters, epiphanies, pleasures, visions, ecstasies. They produce saints, singers, sinners, lovers, dancers, and revolts against the strictures of identity and the rules of productivity. This was the city that Brooklynite Walt Whitman celebrated—the multitudes, the eros of the crowd, the joy of being a stranger among strangers—a city of mystical and erotic connection, a great composite organism:

> City of orgies, walks and joys,
> City whom that I have lived and sung in your midst . . .
> Not those, but as I pass O Manhattan, your frequent and swift flash
> of eyes offering me love . . .

He knew the city of ordinary productivity, working as a printer's devil and typesetter on newspapers, hailing working people on the wharves and in the rail yards. But he was a laborer in that city, a high priest of the other city of passions. Walking was part of his erotic city, the embodied adventure available at no cost to everyone, the endless encounter when "million-footed Manhattan unpent descends to her pavements." He wrote of watching seabirds from the Brooklyn ferry, of love for strangers and passing acquaintances, of casual romances, and of the romance of the crowd; he, more than anyone in his era, embraced and celebrated this other city and its free circulation of desire and pleasure.

This transgression against the everyday, the mundane world, is both erotic and spiritual, and though these are often portrayed as opposites, they are both, at their extremes, ecstasy. There is a spirituality to eros and a sensuality of the spirit as both reach for liberation, for the space in which to flower. Which is another thing that cities produce, and city authorities often fight. New York has always been a place where the struggle to be free is foregrounded.

Sometimes it's political freedom, like the kinds at stake in the Revolutionary War and in the abolitionist movement before the Civil War and now. Among the organizations headquartered in New York, in the present, are the American Civil Liberties Union and the Center for Constitutional Rights. Religious liberty and freedom from persecution have brought Quakers, Jews, and modern refugees, who've flocked to the city to escape everything from female genital mutilation to narcotraficante murder sprees. Freedom exists on all scales of time and space, from the young man of color's right to stroll from 132nd to 110th uninterrupted by the NYPD's Stop and Frisk to the moments of self-discovery found in the arms of a new lover.

Freedom for women has been fought for by the suffragists of the nineteenth century and the feminists of the twentieth and twenty-first, who've done so much of their essential work in this metropolis; freedom lives in what used to be called gay liberation with the Stonewall Riot and in the small everyday riots against closetedness and conformity still going on. Here in New York City, in 1871, revolutionary Victoria Woodhull announced her commitment to free love, her insistence that women have the right not to have sex, even with husbands, as well as the right to have it with whom they wish, and that when eroticism is liberated it is spiritual. "When woman rises from sexual slavery to sexual freedom, into the ownership and control of her sexual organs, and man is obliged to respect this freedom, then will this instinct become pure and holy," she asserted.

The city has produced a few actual canonized Catholic saints: old New York blueblood and Catholic convert Elizabeth Ann Seton, Bohemian immigrant priest John Neumann, and Italian immigrant nun Frances Cabrini. The Lower East Side mystic and radical Dorothy Day, cofounder of the *Catholic Worker*, feeder of the poor, fighter against the authorities, may yet be canonized. Saints are often dissenters—at their most mild mitigating the harms the economic system does by succoring the poor, at their most radical demanding systemic change or realizing it in dissident lives and organizations. And living it in revelations, ecstasies, trances, visions, and thoroughly impractical priorities.

Immigrant, slave, spouse, liberator, hairdresser, spiritual figure—maybe Pierre Toussaint is the most perfect saint for the city, though his canonization has yet to happen. Born into slavery in Hispaniola, he was brought to New York in 1787. When he was freed in 1807, he took the surname of Haiti's liberator but stayed in his profession of society hairdresser and in relationship with the family that once owned him, while also marrying, raising and supporting many orphans, visiting cholera victims, and being a devout Catholic well known in the church. Toussaint moved in many circles, high and low, black and white, moving as though bonds and boundaries did not affect him.

Saints and sinners is an easy opposition, often drawn up, but both camps refuse the rules, serve the impractical, the transcendent, the deeper sense of self. Both pursue freedom and, sometimes, joy and ecstasy. If you go to the Metropolitan Museum of Art you can see the lush, leaky life of the spirit in paintings of the rapture of the saints, of Theresa and Francis and Mary Magdalene; in a twelfth-century manuscript depicting "Green Tara Dispensing Boons to Ecstatic Devotees," with bodhisattvas in bliss; in a bronze sculpture of "Manjuvajra and Vidyadhara in Ecstatic Embrace" from seventeenth- or eighteenth-century Tibet; in the dancing dervishes of the Shah Jahan album from the sixteenth century; in depictions of heavens and paradises and ascents and transfigurations and enlightenments, along with the voluptuously virile Greek and Roman men of marble, the painted odalisques, the bathing women, the lovers, the dances, the kisses, and the caresses.

Dancers broke through in other ways, trying to liberate the body as an expressive means, and the twentieth century saw giants such as Martha Graham and Merce Cunningham center their projects of opening up the possibilities of movement as an art in New York City. Dance parties matter: they are how people travel on their own feet to the other city. They go back at least as far as the Vauxhall and Ranelagh Gardens, opened in Lower Manhattan in 1767, taking their names from London gardens where people promenaded and flirted and orbited each other on the dance floors and watched theater and each other. Black New Yorkers danced in the African Grove Theatre (opened in 1821 on Mercer Street near Bleecker Street), in old pleasure gardens and dance halls of the working class in the nineteenth century, in the kind of shabby dance halls Edmund Wilson described in *Memoirs of Hecate County,* and in the great flourishing nightclubs of Harlem. The Lindy hop and the jitterbug emerged from Harlem's prewar clubs, the former named after aeronautics pioneer Charles Lindbergh, the latter named after a song by that old master of polish and poise and abandon, Cab Calloway. Lindbergh, whatever his later failings, had liberated human beings to fly across oceans with his achievement of the first transcontinental flight; to name a dance after an aviator was a reminder that dancing was sometimes flying.

Voguing became another celebrated dance form, though it was in some ways less like dancing in the sense of the jitterbug or of the great discos of the 1970s, where the city's fancy classes met its working-class heroes, as immortalized in *Saturday Night Fever,* and more like promenading. It was not two people coming together but one person coming into her own with the help of extravagant costuming and makeup, panache and courage. It descended from Harlem drag queen pageants of the 1920s, arriving downtown in the 1980s to make room for more and more subspecies of expression and awards in more and more subspecialties of the art.

Voguing's gender rebels organized, in the 1970s, into houses, less in imitation of aristocracy directly than of fashion houses; just as there was a house of Dior, so there was a House of Xtravaganza and a House of Ninja. Sometimes one person became a mother to others in the house, liberating the definition of mother. When three in the scene purchased a nightclub in the Meatpacking District in 1994, they renamed it Mother. This sense that you could become someone's, many people's, mother through love; that family could be invented along with self; and that love was part of the creative effort made the scene tender in ways that were less often recognized than its ferocious and brilliant sense of style. Watching an after-midnight session of voguing in midtown in 2015, I was struck by how much people seemed liberated from old definitions of gender as they declined to be conventionally male, without embracing the old stereotypes of being female. It felt like a realm in which people set themselves free, another transient capital of the other city. Free in many senses, but not always safe: the volunteer police forces of homophobia and misogny remain a menace to queer and dissident people and women on the streets. Freedom is still fought for and fought against.

In the ruinous Chelsea piers of the 1970s, drag queens and all kinds of gay men found free space to cruise and to copulate, and though the 1970s are remembered mostly as an era of crime and decay, not everything then was falling down. In the South Bronx, hip-hop was rising up as an indigenous expression in music, dance, and art; graffiti art covered innumerable subway cars that sped all over the boroughs; and while burghers and officials mourned that they had lost control of the city, others rejoiced that they had in some way gained it. The 1970s were a period when the uneasy truce between the diurnal and nocturnal city, between commerce and wildness, broke down and the wild side almost won.

Lou Reed's 1972 "Walk on the Wild Side" portrays hustlers and transgender people having arrived in New York to find their home. Luc Sante recollected this era in a gorgeous essay called "My Lost City," a piece celebrating what many mourned, or at least reveling in it:

> On Canal Street stood a five-story building empty of human tenants that had been taken over from top to bottom by pigeons. If you walked east on Houston Street from the Bowery on a summer night, the jungle growth of vacant blocks gave a foretaste of the impending wilderness, when lianas would engird the skyscrapers and mushrooms would cover Times Square. At that time much of Manhattan felt depopulated even in daylight. . . . I spent the summer of 1975 in a top floor apartment on 107th Street, where at night the windows were lit by the glow of fires along Amsterdam Avenue. A sanitation strike was in progress, and mounds of refuse, reeking in the heat, decorated the curbs of every neighborhood, not excepting those whose houses were manned by doormen. Here, though, instead of being double-bagged in plastic, they were simply set on fire every night.

The animals and fires suggest a city gone feral. But both are also emblems of the spirit: the dove that is the Holy Spirit; the angel, winged ox, winged lion, and eagle of Matthew, Mark, Luke, and John; the Hindu elephant-headed Ganesha and monkey god; the good-luck bats, phoenixes, and dragons of Chinatown. The city then was dying and killing off its old industrial, proletarian self, and preparing, like a phoenix, to rise from those ashes. What arose was more orderly than what had come before, but the wildness still found and made its nests in the nocturnal, the dreaming, the marginal, and the overlooked.

Animals populate our imaginations. We have always imagined through them the world and ourselves, a world of owlish, shrewish, dogged, feline, and studly selves. People dress up in feathers, fur, and leather, and preen themselves on being like animals—the bull of Wall Street is a principal example (and one notably amoral opportunist in the world of finance called his memoir *The Wolf of Wall Street*). But people accuse others, especially the poor, the nonwhite, and the nonconforming, of being animals as a way to deny their humanity. During the 1863 Draft Riots, wealthy lawyer George Templeton Strong called the immigrant Irish "biped mammalia . . . that crawl and eat dirt and poison every community they infest."

Animality can mean out-of-control, savage (a word that itself originates in forest), brutal (a term meaning predators and fighters), or bestial. Sometimes the word *wild* has other, uglier connotations. The five teenagers falsely accused and imprisoned for the 1989 horrific rape and near-murder that became famous as the Central Park jogger case were portrayed as a "wolfpack" and other bestial things. A chance remark one of the youths made was seized on and the term *wilding* became an obsession in the press. The attack on the jogger was supposed to have been part of their "wilding" that night. (Some claim that the words *wild thing* were misheard as *wilding;* others that the youth was using a neologism from Ice-T's 1988 song "Radio Suckers.") The real assailant confessed in 2002, the DNA confirmed his guilt, the convictions of the young men were vacated, and the Central Park Five successfully sued the city for millions of dollars.

Celebrating wildlife and wild lives doesn't mean forgetting the full array of ways animals are used to depict the human. But this is not a map or an essay about people as other kinds of animals, but a map about people exploring the full range of being human, the outer limits of the spirit and the flesh—and about the love of animals as epiphanies and as ways the natural world remains present in the human-made realm. It's about breaking free, so to speak, of the bears and bulls of the marketplace and taking wing. We should not surrender the liberatory beauties of wildness or let them morph into slurs.

When bureaucrats insist that they are going to "take the city back," it's from wildness they seek to take it, and from the people on the side of the wild city, the people who in movies such as the much-resented *Fort Apache, the Bronx* are imagined as the Native Americans, the people to be conquered and removed. Times Square was taken back, and so were the Chelsea piers, and much of the city that was once this other kind of place. Even so, New York has remained a place of wildlife but also of wild life and wild lives, of lives lived for other purposes, of merging and reaching out for ecstasy and delight and wonder, for the mystical city. Once you begin to look for it you find it in a thousand places. Here Sufis and Hasids dance sacred dances, uptown Pentecostalists speak in tongues, and drag queens and trans people hold pageants; here music itself has flourished in a thousand ways, not only the formal stuff of symphonies—and the most symphonic music of the nineteenth century was played for workers in informal concert halls—but the songs and moments of release from doo-wop to punk rock to hip-hop.

In the museums, on the streets, in the clubs, and in the parks, eyes devour, people feed upon each other, and the feast generates more appetite. And people watch animals, the whales in the harbor or the birds in the park, seeking a communion beyond the human. Sometimes this craving for otherness takes strange forms, as with animal lover Antoine Yates of Harlem—a man whose "obsession began innocently enough, with the puppies and broken-winged birds every little boy begs to bring home," his neighbors recalled, "[before] his collection came to include reptiles, a monkey or two and . . . even a hyena."

Yates then moved a tiger cub into his mother's five-bedroom apartment, in the Drew Hamilton NYCHA apartment complex. For a while Ming, the tiger, roomed with Yates, Yates's girlfriend, her son, and some other human roommates, the *New York Daily News* reported:

> A woman who shared a Harlem apartment with a 425-pound tiger said yesterday she was terrified at first—but soon got used to living with the man-eater down the hall. Caroline Domingo told the *Daily News* she couldn't believe her eyes when she spotted the big cat roaming free in the apartment where she and her husband rented a room from tiger-owner Antoine Yates. "I walked in the door and [the tiger] was standing there looking at me," recalled Domingo, 49, a seamstress. "I said, 'I know I'm not seeing this. I know that wasn't a tiger.' He turned around and looked at me like I was a damn fool," she said. But eventually, she said, "We all became family."

After Ming mauled Yates, police were alerted, and in 2003 a policeman was lowered on ropes to the apartment window, where he shot the beast with a tranquilizer gun. Ming was dispatched to a wildlife sanctuary in Ohio, his less lucky owner to three months in prison at Rikers Island. Thus ended the reign of the tiger of Harlem, though other tigers live in the Bronx Zoo, and elk and Andean bears in the Queens Zoo, and snow leopards in the Central Park Zoo. Not long ago a coyote was noted on the roof of a Long Island City

Tino Rodriguez and Colette Calascione, *The Lady of the Birds*, 2001

nightclub, one of about eighty estimated to now populate the city (even though they're not indigenous to the region, but moved eastward, canny immigrants good at adapting). The gentrification of Manhattan and Brooklyn often seems to signify that the diurnal city of reason and profit has won, but it has arisen simultaneously with the twenty-first-century proliferation of wildlife, swimming up less-polluted rivers, wandering in from reforested hinterlands, escaping from transnational shipping ports.

Sometimes New York's two cities clash literally, as when migrating songbirds smash into the skyscrapers and die at their feet, or when the police break up a dance party or punish a trans woman for being someone who's broken out of their neat categories, or when another insurrection of the imagination is commodified. And sex is always for sale here, though by the time economic clout gives one person the right to command another's acts and body it often is a very different kind of sex from the love people make for its own sake, as Victoria Woodhull pointed out. But the birds keep flying, the new dances keep emerging, and the other city keeps living and pulsing and embracing, crawling, swimming, swaying, strolling, and soaring.

People reconcile the two versions, find mild versions of the wild city, the city of night and the wild. Dog owners follow their beasts into an exuberant world of smells and immediacy; affluent New Yorkers leave for country properties where they have space, soil, quiet, a genteel kind of wildness. Toward the end of his life, the playwright Arthur Miller wrote a gorgeous memoir of heat waves in New York City in the late 1920s:

> On 111th and farther uptown mattresses were put out as night fell, and whole families lay on those iron balconies in their underwear. . . . With a couple of other kids, I would go across 110th to the Park and walk among the hundreds of people, singles and families, who slept on the grass, next to their big alarm clocks, which set up a mild cacophony of the seconds pass-

109

ing, one clock's ticks syncopating with another's. Babies cried in the darkness, men's deep voices murmured, and a woman let out an occasional high laugh beside the lake.

This trusting, sweating city of stripped-down sleepers and dreamers in public is another New York, not the New York of hurry and suspicion—or air conditioning. Still, even now, every heat wave produces a version of it, when the clothes that signify people's social status wither away to shorts and an undershirt or a sundress, when the air thickens and people swim more slowly through it, the boundaries between them lower than they are in cooler weather. Blizzards also interrupt the city, piling up snow that stops traffic, suspends school, and brings out skis and snowshoes, a hush in the air, and a contemplation of the forces that are still, in some ways, bigger than business, bigger than us.

All this was wilderness once, not a place apart from human beings, but one in which the Lenape were familiar and at ease with the array of species here. The Bowery was a Lenape path, and its Dutch name means farm road, even though its name later became synonymous with "Bowery bums" and gritty urbanism, which is another way to say that it was a refuge for the poor and then the site of CBGB, the mecca of punk in the 1970s. Before those seventeenth-century farms, there were deer, bears, wolves, and smaller mammals, birds, and fish in the streams now buried under the asphalt.

You can mourn that bygone landscape or you can look around for the ways it's still here. The resistance to the rational city is not only human; it's not only mammalian; it's a parade of species insisting on using the city on their own terms. It's the almost 200 bird species that can be regularly found in Central Park; the raccoons and skunks; the red-tailed hawks whose Manhattan nests have been eagerly watched, particularly that of the midtown red-tail dubbed Pale Male, who passed through a series of female partners—First Love, Chocolate, Blue, Ginger, Zena, Octavia—as he nested year after year in the same location. It's the whales who swim around the islands, including the forty-three who were counted in 2013, and the harbor seals who have a colony on Staten Island.

Rats, roaches, and pigeons—with bedbugs a lately heralded fourth—are the undomesticated species New York is famous for. They are unloved pests, weeds, which is another way to say survivors who thrive in the city no matter what, in the tenements and the basements and subways and streets. Undomesticated animals are not here to meet human needs and tastes, though some delight us.

Earlier, New York abounded with wildlife and perhaps no place on earth had more abundant oysters, 350 square miles of oyster reefs in the lower Hudson estuary, until overharvesting and poisoned waters wiped them out. As Mark Kurlansky wrote in *The Big Oyster,* "the history of the New York oyster is a history of New York itself—its wealth, its strength, its excitement, its greed, its thoughtfulness, its destructiveness, its blindness, and—as any New Yorker will tell you—its filth." The Billion Oyster Project aspires to return the abundance to the waters that surround the city and claims to have added 11.5 million oysters to the harbor (which filter trillions of gallons of water). The future of New York may look more like its past when it comes to coexistence with the wild. And the past is still present in some essential and emblematic places.

The stones of Trinity Church, just off Wall Street, were cemented with oyster-shell mortar paste when it arose between 1839 and 1846, the third church to stand on that ground hallowed in 1698. It's a temple of the spirit made out of the mollusks of the waters, and maybe a church, too, is an oyster, designed to filter out impurities as it pumps us in and out of its chambers or to surround our abrasiveness with nacre until we're pearls. Lou Reed sang of an ecstasy that nothing could stick to, nothing could hold on to, but oysters have held together a house of the spirit for centuries. From the depths of the harbor to the height of the steeple that was once the tallest thing in New York City, the spirit and the flesh have never been far apart here.

14 OUR LATIN THING

New York is the great Latin American city. From El Barrrio to Loisaida, Corona to Castle Hill, Los Sures to Sunset Park, Jackson Heights to Washington Heights—nowhere in the Americas, not in Mexico City or Caracas or even in Los Angeles, do so many people from all the regions of Latin America—from the Caribbean to Central and South America—come together to interact and live with such variety and force. Dominicans and Puerto Ricans, Colombians and Ecuadorans and Argentines, Salvadorans and Hondurans and Mexicans— nearly one in four New Yorkers call Spanish their first language. And perhaps nowhere else do these people *together* exert such an outsize cultural influence on the rest of the world. This Latin-tinged influence isn't new for a city whose first permanent resident was a "mulatto trader" from Hispaniola named Rodrigues (he began peddling his wares by the Battery in 1614). In the late 1800s José Martí, the great Cuban writer and patriot, spent years here organizing and funding his nation's liberation—hardly the first or last Latin American revolutionary to do so. In 1917 the passage of the Jones Act allowed Puerto Ricans to come here without either a passport or a visa. This established "Nuyoricans" as a prominent part of New York's ethnic mix—and turned them into central players in the birth of what remains New York's most famed contribution to "Latin music" worldwide: salsa. In 1972 the owners and musicians of Fania Records, borrowing from old Cuban rhythms but giving them a whole new feel, invented this new genre of music and, in a classic concert film, dubbed it "Our Latin Thing." But salsa is hardly the limit of Latino New Yorkers' influence on modern music— they've been central to the evolution of everything from mambo to jazz to hip-hop to reggaeton to rock 'n' roll to bachata (arguably, the most listened-to music in the city today—and, no, not only by Dominicans). Many gringo New Yorkers may be unaware of these stories and sounds—or think they are. But the airwaves don't lie. By far the most listened-to radio stations in the city today broadcast in Spanish. A crucial aspect of this city's public sphere, whether you know it or not, unfolds *en español.* CARTOGRAPHY: MOLLY ROY   MAP APPEARS ON PAGES 112–113.

THE MEGA MEZCLAPOLIS BY ALEXANDRA T. VAZQUEZ

The Bogotá-born, New York–raised and –based DJ Alex Sensation is one of the city's great infrastructural planners. From Monday to Friday between 11:00 a.m. and 3:00 p.m., the city moves to his mega mezclas, or mega mixes (or even better, mega mixxxxxes), which thunderbolt out from 97.9 FM's transmitter at the top of the Empire State Building. The mezcla involves a layering of songs, a mixing together that does not demand unity but an

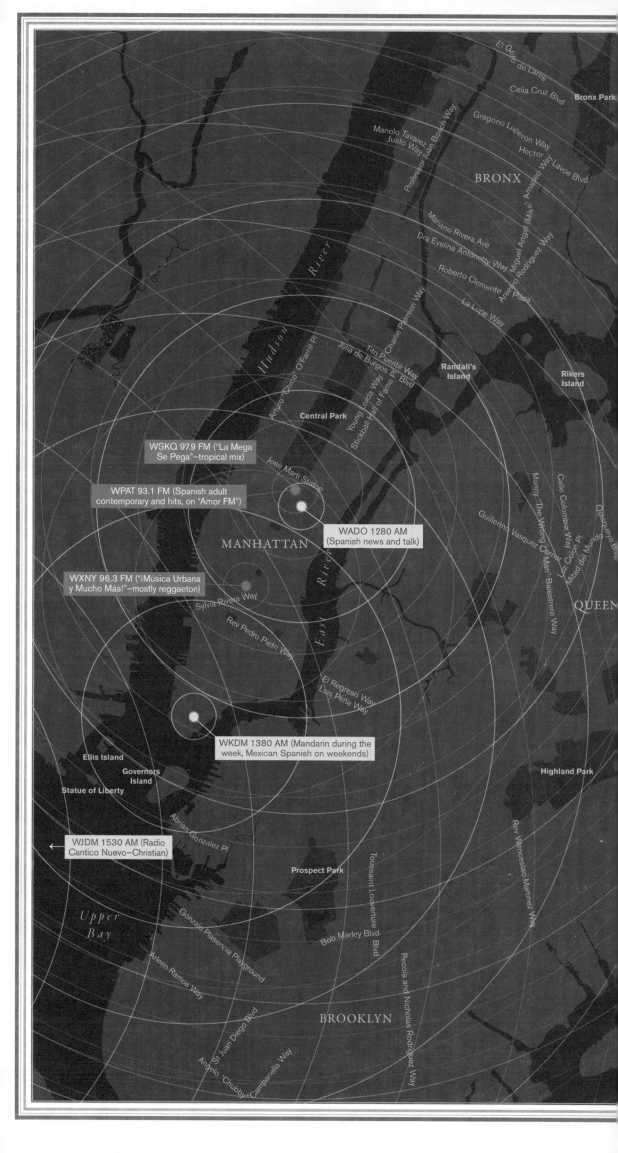

WSKQ 97.9 FM ("La Mega Se Pega"—tropical mix)

WPAT 93.1 FM (Spanish adult contemporary and hits, on "Amor FM")

WADO 1280 AM (Spanish news and talk)

WXNY 96.3 FM ("¡Música Urbana y Mucho Más!"—mostly reggaeton)

WKDM 1380 AM (Mandarin during the week, Mexican Spanish on weekends)

WJDM 1530 AM (Radio Cantico Nuevo—Christian)

BRONX

Bronx Park

El Grito de Lares

Celia Cruz Blvd

Gregorio Luperón Way

Hector Lavoe Blvd

Manolo Tavarez Justo Way

Professor Juan Bosch Way

Mariano Rivera Ave

Dra Evelina Antonetty Way

Arsenio Miguel Angel (Mike Amalbe) Rodriguez Way

Roberto Clemente Way

La Lupe Way

Charlie Palmieri Way

Tito Puente Way

Julia de Burgos Pl Blvd

Young Lords Way

Stickball Hall of Fame Pl

Central Park

Randall's Island

Rikers Island

José Martí Statue

MANHATTAN

Arturo "Chico" O'Farrill Pl

Hudson River

East River

Manny "The Wrong Corner" Balestrero Way

Guillermo Vasquez Way

Calle Colombia Way

Luz Colón Pl

Mitad del Mundo

Quisqueya Bri

QUEEN

Sylvia Rivera Way

Rev Pedro Pietri Way

El Regreso Way

Luis Peña Way

Ellis Island

Governors Island

Statue of Liberty

Highland Park

Abrian Gonzalez Pl

Prospect Park

Toussaint Louverture Blvd

Rev Wenceslao Martinez Way

Upper Bay

Gonzalo Plasencia Playground

Bob Marley Blvd

Pecola and Nicholas Rodriguez Way

Arleen Ramos Way

BROOKLYN

St Juan Diego Blvd

Angelo "Chubby" Campanella Way

OUR LATIN THING
NEW YORK CITY RADIO EN ESPAÑOL

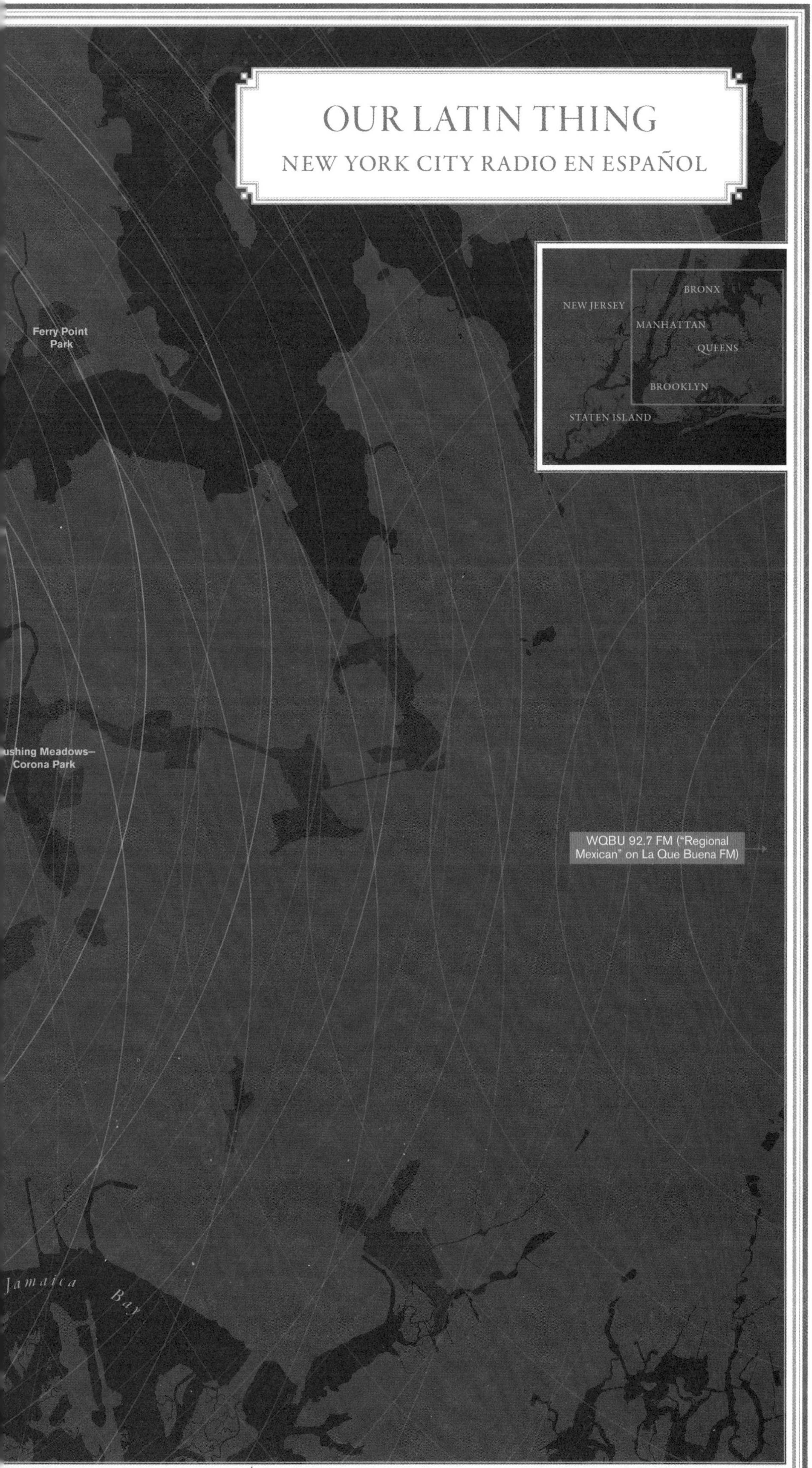

NEW JERSEY

BRONX

MANHATTAN

QUEENS

BROOKLYN

STATEN ISLAND

Ferry Point Park

Flushing Meadows–Corona Park

WQBU 92.7 FM ("Regional Mexican" on La Que Buena FM)

Jamaica Bay

Radio Corporation of America (RCA) building at the 1939–40 world's fair in Flushing Meadows, Queens. Courtesy New York Public Library.

assembly that feels new. Sensation puts together sounds from across genres into a singular horizon and makes much of the intervals that connect them. These intervals are lush gathering spots for the party-life traditions necessary when making New York home. Listening to and becoming part of these radio waves swerves us away from the Landmarks of Hispanic History and toward a more permeating sense of what the village elders and their inter-American progeny have made possible for the New York commons. Alex Sensation is a reviving conduit for all this activity that has molded the city over the centuries. Buoyed by the signature backbeat he plays behind his banter with on-air callers, we hear accents that signal a dizzying range of Spanish-speaking locations in the Americas alongside the resolute imprint of Nuyorican and Dominicanish. DJ Sensation makes music of and with them. And though some might not tune in to his show, all are implicated.

His workaday set will pipe out from a half-open door of a delivery truck, from behind-the-counter speakers at the corner deli, from a tollbooth operator's choked-up radio. In the space of any mega mezcla, Sensation reminds the city of how it functions. He also gives its workers a place to keep functioning. He will tenderly and exuberantly shout out carpenters and bodegueros, day care workers, housekeepers, home health aides, secretaries and bakery employees, body shop garages and car washes; it is a daily education in the various Latino/a populations that make New York possible. He insists upon their various cumbias, multiple independence days, just-yesterday migrations, and the chords they strike, as the city. The mega mezcla testifies to the ordinary and dramatic and forced and chosen ways by which many have come to New York to make it swing. That New York is now Puebla North and that bachata has taken gentle hold of just about everything are not anomalies that can be isolated from the collective grid. They are joyful and difficult materials that mess with anyone who tries hard to lament the city's long-gone unassimilatable energies. This radio show signals New York's real bohemia.

DJ Sensation shapes the week so that we may survive it, while so much of living in the city depends upon the real possibility that we won't. Mondays are a space for "recuperación total," total recuperation from what just went down. Fridays are Viernes Social, social Fridays, a kind of practice cotillion for the weekend, where you can and will encounter him, in a mischievous mood, on Saturday night from 8:00 p.m. to 12:00 a.m. In the midst of all this—the baroque impossibility of *all this*—Sensation will take phone requests for free concert tickets and give married mothers erotic attention. His curiosity about her ("¿qué tú haces, mami?"), his concern for where she is ("¿de dónde me estás llamando, amor?"), the sustained attention he implies by slow-rolling her consonants ("¡Yollllannnda!"), and his insta-diminutive ("mi Yolita"), all give her a place in and on everyone's time. These consensual flirtations are at once charged and safe, and suggest that feeling of dancing with someone who asked your partner's permission before holding you tight on the dance floor. He takes you through bad-weather days, urges you to be careful, be warm, take an umbrella. Through his capacious and round-edged Spanish, Sensation affirms that someone out there cares about how you will get from point A to point B. Sensation inscribes on the radio waves the places of dreamers, the undocumented, and the party supply stores that will be open to them or opened by them on Sunday. He honors all the years you've been alive by making available a birthday mix downloadable direct from his website and depositable straight into your party. His plans reveal a visionary platform that prioritizes Latina health above everything else. This swinging platform untethers health from uplift. It embraces the bad diagnosis and finds in immigrant brokenness, in this music, the beauty of rebellions from several antiquities and continents against undifferentiated masters. DJ Sensation makes a dance floor of their graves.

The mega mezcla is in the bones of New York radio. All of it. Even in its most blatantly infrastructural bones, if we recall that Diego Rivera's 1934 mural *Man at the Crossroads* once stuck hard to the lobby of the Radio Corporation of America building in New York's Rockefeller Center. The mural featured a swirl of bodies operating machines next to a portrait of Vladimir Lenin, a figure snuck into the scene only after Rivera's initial sketches were approved. Because of this—because of the piece's proposal of the brown proletariat and their aesthetics as infrastructural—Rivera's patrons deemed it unfit for this threshold of sonic capital. And so his mural was first draped over, then painted over, and as part of its guaranteed removal, Rivera and all that he brought with him were barred from the site. That work's hidden presence, then as now, models how the radio waves emitting from above carry unruly signals. It suggests how the stations' own pasts are like in-air versions of those creeks that lie buried beneath the city but bubble up now and again to remind us of the dynamic before.

DJ Sensation's show rides the same airwaves that once channeled WEVD-FM, which began its life as the socialist radio station WEVD-AM in 1927. Its call letters were meant to honor the memory of Eugene Victor Debs, and its first studios were built in a space donated by the International Ladies' Garment Workers' Union. The station was a place for broadcasting New York's immigrant blues by featuring news and performances from the recently arrived, whether in Yiddish, Italian, or Japanese. Billed as "the station that speaks your language," its move to the FM dial found WEVD featuring the revelatory shows of two of Latin music's non-Latin DJs, "Symphony Sid" Torin and Dick "Ricardo" Sugar.[1] Later, after being sold again, its waves were used to broadcast Christian meditations and then sports news. In 1989 the frequency was occupied by the Spanish Broadcasting System (SBS) and given the new name WSKQ-FM La Mega 94.9. That its current owner Raúl Alarcón comes from a family prominent in Cuban radio before the revolution of 1959 signals not merely a change in ownership, but the assumption of another island's broadcast history. Despite being created to make market sense, La Mega never conducts itself as "Spanish language radio" among the English-dominant airwaves. It does not ask permission. Because of the radio modulations it rides with—and all the immigrant blues it inherits—it loudly pronounces its fact of brownness ad infinitum: La Mega Se Pega. La Mega Sticks to You.

. . .

The study of radio history can offer another kind of training in how to listen closer to music and to the city. Even a rudimentary tracing of moves in occupation of a station's frequencies expands influence to the unexpected. Such training makes banal fact, and not anomaly, of such collaborations as the one between the Trio Los Panchos and Eydie Gorme in the 1960s. Radio study also helps us to find yet another way, in our interactions with music, of taking in the old and the new at once. It encourages the acceptance of and a reckoning with impossible-to-track audiences and blasts open any demographic sense-making of the city. As one detail in radio's repertoire, the mega mezcla's method of delivery for sounding out Latina/o living and loving in New York far predates Alex Sensation. It has its own well-established history on the radio, including the half century of pioneering work by the

Ponceño DJ Polito Vega that began early on WEVD-AM, and all those greatest hits he worked so hard to make a case for. Those hits, which are stopgaps for a lava flow of non-hit wonders, signaled the many entrances into and exits out of the city, and the fresh sounds that New York's migrants have always made up, and made beautiful, while there.

Hear the wonder of one of those hits made between Mongo Santamaría and La Lupe, one of Cuba's great musical collectives, on their version of Herbie Hancock's "Watermelon Man" recorded for Battle Records and released in 1963. Learn from what they did to the jazz of that moment by reminding us, in that Cuban way of not asking first, that you could dance to it too. It is a hit that retained La Lupe's laugh from the track's outset—a laugh that betrays something that might or might not be funny—and positions her musicianship and her Santiago de Cuba in New York's recorded history. The Queen of Latin Soul continues to have a place in and on everyone's time. The song is often recalled as the record with which Santamaría firmly wedged the tumbadora (the Cuban conga drum) into the top of the American pop charts. But by taking into account the New York airwaves, actual and ephemeral, we can go back, even further, to hear where and how the tumbadora appears—and how so much depended on women musicians as its conduit.

Hear Olga Guillot's work with Machito on José Antonio Mendez's classic "La Gloria Eres Tú," recorded from the Nola Penthouse Studios on 57th Street in 1947. The lineup was a fantasyland of mid-century New York sound artists, including Mario Bauzá on trumpet, Fred Skerritt on clarinet, José "Pin" Madera on sax, and the pianist René Hernández. Tucked inside of this piece is the tumbadora played by Chano Pozo. The recording marks some of his earliest musical establishments in the New York scene, just before his famed encounter with Dizzy Gillespie. The cues call us even further back to how the tumbadora takes shape in the earliest New York recordings by the "first lady of Cuban song," María Teresa Vera. Vera's first imprints on the city were made while performing at the Apollo Theater in 1918, which eventually led to recording contracts with Victor and Columbia. Her troubadouring tested and anticipated New York's capacity for the folk singers packing guitars who would arrive on the scene roughly five decades later. Although Vera's work is described as trova in form, the tumbadoras were deep in her musical substance, including the way she sang into those early raspy microphones and the stories she brought inside of them. Hear her sing Ignacio Piñeiro's anticolonial "Los Cantares de Abacuá," which she recorded for the Columbia label in 1923.

The suggestiveness of hearing the tumbadoras tucked into the New York airwaves does more to quantify how instruments or populations formally register for the U.S. scene. It enables us to tune in across the eras, to get a sense of what's inside the music people bring with them, and to imagine how it emanates out in immeasurable ways. These greatest hits— and all that is at play inside of them—are laboratories that laid the groundwork for DJ Sensation's show. Listening to them helps us to imagine that the mega mezcla has as much to do with a technical dexterity with mixing as it has to do with a willingness to "go there."

· · ·

It was just after 2:00 p.m. and in the front seat of a livery cab, Angel García couldn't find the words to describe the collective draw to Sensation's show. "No se, he just . . . " García scrambled with the words and the way until he took his hands off the wheel and used them to create a pulsating oval. He made a gesture of a gathering together with ample room to breathe. Taking its cue from the mega mezcla, García's gesture does much to intervene in the ways that the city's "Latin Thing" was concretized into a market category in the late 1960s and early 1970s. The story of "salsa," as commonly told, makes a static origin of the Fania Records label founded in 1964 by the Dominican flautist and bandleader Johnny Pacheco and the Italian American Jerry Masucci. Most studies of contemporary Latino/a

Richard Renaldi, *2:16*

music in the city look to Fania to shorthand a dynamic repertoire of musical play into a singular sieve through which all must pass. Perhaps with reason: the label produced and distributed some of New York's most legible hit makers, from Willie Colón to Héctor Lavoe to Celia Cruz. Among the consequences of Fania's success was the actual and discursive blockade of Cuban musicians and their historical networks of production and distribution in the city. Another was (and, given the ample re-releases of the Fania catalog, is) the stamping over of the label's human precedents that helped make but were denied entry in Fania's success—especially the many women musicians made superfluous to the only one it let take the stage. Even if that only one was the almighty Celia Cruz, she deserves to be heard as part of a more resonant cohort.

But the thing about the mega mezcla, as many of its involved already know, is that it has a way of subverting narrow tales of genres—of creating the new sounds it needs for itself and for us. The trajectory of the mega mezcla may be impossible to comprehend; it includes not only the mixing of different recorded objects but all those musicians, those proto-DJs over the centuries, who have made musical spaces that admit all that's not fit to print. Because of this, it has long been useful to making new idioms like house music. Emerging from disco worlds that encouraged connectivity between *all* of the city's parts, the house style gave New York a home for other ways of moving. If disco needed to give people some time—via those long intros and outros—to get on and off the dance floor, house music determined to grow in the soil of those intervals. House had and has a way of spanning the capitals. Its geography takes in Barranquilla and all the Santiagos, San Juan and Quito, Caracas and Havana, and also Detroit, Chicago, Miami, and L.A. You will hear these places in the house sounds often played under and alongside merengue, reggaeton, and salsa on DJ Sensation's show. And you will hear how one of house's greatest hits, beloved to Sensation, comprises a verdant offshoot from one of Fania's wonderfully flawed representatives, Héctor Lavoe. Not the papi-fied version given to us by Marc Anthony, but the beautiful gnarled-up nerd version of Lavoe, the voice, our voice, who we once saw in high-waisted red pants jump into the Kinshasa crowd singing "Mi Gente." He comes to us through Lavoe's nephew, Little

Louie Vega. Vega, the great feminist, music producer, and early house music practitioner, created a new home for his uncle and for a larger return of Fania's repressed.

Vega's work is not the legacy of "salsa" as Fania tried to define it; it instead makes expansive what influenced and was influenced by it. Vega's music takes in all the neighbors and neighboring sounds that have long given mega mezclas vitalizing materials. It is a musical ethos that gives primary space to women's voices and not in the ornamental, tacked-on mode pervading dance music's production protocols. House (especially after Vega) gave us a place to dance, in the bountiful returns of women's full registers, to the airwaves, to records, and to summer block parties infringing on the end time stated on their permits. All this was made especially concrete in 1994, when, under the name "River Ocean," Louie Vega released the exuberant classic "Love and Happiness (Yemaya y Ochun)," co-written with and featuring the heart-expanding vocal by Nuyorico's own La India, aka "Princess of Salsa."

In the "12-inch club mix" version of the song (how many different options of a singular thing house gives us!), the track begins with a jungle-sound sample that once set the mood for Héctor Lavoe and Willie Colón's 1972 hit "Aguanile." You're prepared to move to them as you've been taught to do, but they recede into the triangle thump of house's beat. Out burrows La India's vocal, carrying an oxygenated confidence that refuses the elders' symptoms. Through India's invocations, Yemaya, the mother of the seas, and Ochun, the young orisha of love, gave clubs in New York and across the world new structures of pleasure and pain in the immediate aftermath of the first devastating losses of the AIDS epidemic. Too many of our uncles were taken from us that way, even Lavoe himself, even as he was known as "El Todopoderoso." Later in the track, La India sings a circular sampling of Al Green's anthem that gives this song's love and happiness to those that were left behind. When played on DJ Sensation's show, we are given yet another occasion to let our Latin souls dance with our beloved dead.

. . .

What the call to map the mega mezcla prompts is an exercise thriving in abstraction, a resisting of the singular story. A chart not of the Latina/o, New York, or music, but a sensing out of a collaborative sense of safety and trust and love at their intersection that refuses to stay put. The mega mezcla accompanies us on that daily part of city life—the commute—reminding us of how the human and the humane can be accessed in the Latina/o metropolis. Commuters—those who refuse to work and live in the same place, even if they must—need to keep work and life separate, even if they can't. And that impossible separation offers a space for fantasy and for play—for listening to DJ Sensation's show and to the material histories of Latin music and all it involves in New York. We can see how the collaborative project extends back through the centuries and resounds as we turn some dial or just leave our ears open when walking in this city.

---

1. For this radio history, see Bill Jaker, Frank Sulek, and Peter Kanze, *The Airwaves of New York: Illustrated Histories of 156 AM Stations in the Metropolitan Area, 1921–1996* (Jefferson, NC: McFarland, 1998), 64–67. Many thanks to Bill Jaker for further clarification (personal communication with the author, February 15, 2016).

15 BURNING DOWN AND RISING UP

Langston Hughes, in the last book he wrote, depicts a child hearing grim news about the place where he plays and feels comfortable: "Misery is when you heard on the radio that the neighborhood you live in is a slum but you always thought it was home." For people living in the Bronx, that is too often the experience: the media describe their home as a no man's land or lawless Wild West. A borough of markedly different neighborhoods full of architectural delights, from the quiet waterfront community of City Island with its Victorian homes to the lively Grand Concourse Historic District lined with art deco beauties, the Bronx is too often caricatured as a burned-out wasteland.

The borough's misrepresentation stems partly from an outbreak of fires that ravaged the South Bronx in the 1970s, leaving much of it rubble and many homeless. Residents were blamed for the devastation. But in that mess, kids found a way to achieve some measure of normalcy, remaking the landscape through a culture they would come to call hip-hop, creating beautiful, funky graffiti and sinuous dances, accompanied by infectious beats and catchy lyrics that provided a new soundtrack to the grim times. That culture and its "four elements"—graffiti, break-dancing, DJ-ing, and MC-ing—would quickly grow to become a lingua franca for global youth culture. By deciding to ignore other people's reports about their home, these young innovators revealed how kids at play can burn with a determined fire that inflames the entire world for the better. Drawing on never-before-collated data on housing units lost to the fires, this map features the artwork of iconic graffiti pioneer Lady Pink, yet again hailing the borough through its remarkable story.

CARTOGRAPHY: MOLLY ROY; ARTWORK: LADY PINK; INTERVIEWS WITH VALERIE CAPERS, GRANDMASTER CAZ, GRANDWIZZARD THEODORE, AND MELLE MEL BY MIRISSA NEFF   MAP APPEARS ON PAGES 120–121.

NEW YORK CITY: SEEING THROUGH THE RUINS

BY MARSHALL BERMAN

New York City is vulnerable. To anyone who lived through the attacks of September 11, 2001, the city's vulnerability is so obvious, it seems silly to mention it. But it wasn't obvious to my generation, the kids who grew up in New York after the "good war." We took it for granted that *we* were vulnerable, but we couldn't imagine that *the city* could be vulnerable, too. That was something we had to learn, and we learned it, at least I think we learned it, in the last third of the last century.

I began to see the city's vulnerability when I came back in 1967 after several years away. My neighborhood was the Upper West Side, and somehow I hadn't heard about the heroin epidemic that was tearing up that part of Broadway. The gutters were full of syringes; on the sidewalks, the living casualties lurched at you, though more often they crumbled

BURNING DOWN AND RISING UP

THE BRONX IN THE 1970s

North Riverdale

Woodla

Van Cortlandt
Park

Fieldston

Riverdale

Kingsbridge

Woodlawn

6

Spuyten Duyvil

Marble Hill

10

Norwood

Olin

Bedford Park

4

Fordham

Bronx Park

University Heights

15

13

14

West Bronx

Belmont

BRONX

Mount Heights

20

19

21

7

Mount Hope

Tremont

West Farms

Van Ne

Mount Eden

Crotona Park

MANHATTAN

Highbridge

11

Claremont Village

5

8
9

Boston Road Ballroom

Royal Mansion

McKinley Square (King) Theatre

18

Bronx Music Heritage

Concourse

Center (2010–)

Colgate Gardens

1

Freddie's

Blue Morocco

3

Soundvic

Comet Theatre

Foxhur

Morrisania

Burland Theatre

Tritons Club

17

Tropicana

Alhambra (Black Cat)

Franklin Theatre

16

2

Melrose

Club 845

Hunts Point Palace

12

Club Tropicoro (later 41st Police
Precinct, aka "Fort Apache")

Bronx

Woodstock

Clason Poi

Hunts Point

Mott Haven

Teatro Puerto Rico

Port Morris

River

East

River

Percent housing units lost to fires,
1970–80 (by census tract)

0–20% | 21–40% | 41–60% | 61–80% | 81–100%

Housing remained stable or
increased, 1970–80

Cultural venues lost
to the "War Years"

NEW JERSEY | BRONX
MANHATTAN
QUEENS
BROOKLYN
STATEN
ISLAND

22

THE BIRTH OF HIP-HOP

Stomping grounds of the first influential Bronx graffiti writers: LEE 163D!, SLY II, EL CID, 1968–71

① The Young Lords set up a seized x-ray truck to serve the community, 1970

Plaza Tunnel nightclub: DJ John Brown spins James Brown's "Soul Power" and Rare Earth's "Get Ready," inspiring hip-hop's evolvers, 1971

The "Ghost Yard" subway depot: graffiti pioneers SUPER KOOL 223, AJ 161, STAY HIGH 149, and SILVER TIPS, among others, start painting whole subway cars, 1971. LADY PINK and others grow the art, 1977–82

② Bronx Boys Club: historic truce meeting between the Savage Nomads, Savage Skulls, Black Spades, Seven Immortals, and others after the murder of "Black Benjie" of the Ghetto Brothers, December 8, 1971

⑥ Graffiti artist and b-boy PHASE 2 invents the influential "bubble letter" or "softie" style of aerosol writing, 1972

⑦ Jamaican immigrant Cindy Campbell hosts "first hip-hop party" with her brother, DJ Kool Herc (né Clive Campbell), and their pal Mike-with-the-Lights, August 1973

⑧ Deejay-warrior and "godfather of hip-hop" Afrika Bambaataa founds the Universal Zulu Nation, 1973

⑨ Zulu Kings b-boy crew forms alongside Afrika Bambaataa's Universal Zulu Nation, 1973

⑩ TRACY 168 evolves the "wildstyle" of graffiti, Concourse subway yards, 1973

⑪ Crotona Park: Puerto Rican–led b-boy crews, including SalSoul, Rockwell Association, and Starchild La Rock, hone their moves, 1973–77

⑫ The Writer's Bench: meeting point of the 2 and 5 subway lines: graffiti artists and taggers convene to check new work, 1973–79

⑬ DJ Kool Herc moves his parties to Cedar Park by the tool shed, attracting b-boys and cool kids from across the Bronx, 1974

⑭ Crazy Commandos b-boy crew forms with Spy, "the man with a thousand moves," 1974

⑮ Webster Avenue PAL: DJ Kool Herc's storied sound system bests Afrika Bambaataa's, 1975

⑯ Grandmaster Flash (né Joseph Saddler) masters the turntable and his "Quick-mix" theory of mixing records and extending beats, 1975

⑰ Grandwizzard Theodore, age 13, applies Flash's theories and starts "scratching" records, 1975

⑱ The Black Door nightclub: Grandmaster Flash and the Three Emcees (Keith "Cowboy" Wiggins, Melvin "Melle Mel" Glover, and Nathaniel "The Kidd Creole" Glover)—later part of the Furious Five—start gigging for pay, 1976

⑲ Rock Steady Crew of b-boys founded by Jimmy Lee, Jimmy Dee, and JoJo, 1977; Manhattan chapter later added by Crazy Legs and B-Boy Fresh

⑳ Fifty new Pontiacs driven out of showroom during riots, July 13, 1977

㉑ PS 3 burns beyond Yankee Stadium's right field wall during Game 2 of 1977 World Series. Howard Cosell announces: "The Bronx is burning."

㉒ Sugar Hill Gang records "Rapper's Delight," Englewood, NJ, 1979

VALERIE CAPERS

Eminent jazz pianist and composer, esteemed educator and advocate for the blind, longtime professor at Bronx Community College, and lifelong resident of the borough

DAVID KATZENSTEIN

The fact that the Bronx is the birthplace of hip-hop seems to be all anyone talks about now, but the Bronx is also the borough of jazz. So many of the greats of Latin music and jazz have lived here. When the fires occurred, they affected everything. Even though I can't see, they affected me because of the way [the burned areas] looked. You could feel the degree of deterioration. People talked about it. It was a constant reminder of what was wrong with the city, with the government, and with the people who should be doing something about correcting it. It was an emotional and psychological downer for people who love the Bronx, like I do.

But hip-hop was the most extraordinary thing, because it developed not as a result of the evolution of music I came out of—that history of jazz from ragtime to swing to bebop, bebop into "progressive." They all dovetailed, one into the other. But hip-hop came about in the borough because of the lack of opportunities for work, for education—the lack of opportunities to be heard and to be recognized. Hip-hop came out of very serious economic and social conditions for young people here—a whole new generation that felt they had to find an outlet to express themselves.

into themselves. Exploding with need, they got crazily violent. I had seen plenty of violence already, growing up in the Bronx in the *West Side Story* years, and I had been mugged and robbed and knocked around. But that was stuff teenagers did to each other; the Fordham Baldies and the Savage Skulls had mostly left adults alone. Late-1960s urban violence had no structure, apart from the junkie's one endless need, and no limits. A woman in my building left her key in the front door, and there were two brutal robberies within ten minutes. As a lifelong New Yorker, I couldn't believe there was anything significant about city life that I didn't already know. I was wrong.

It took years to learn how to defend against the next catastrophe: fires. The fires burst out mainly in poor minority neighborhoods all over town, but ethnically and economically mixed neighborhoods like the West Side were afflicted as well. For years, midnight fires ate up not only buildings but whole blocks, often block after block. Then we found out that, even as big parts of the city were burning down, their firehouses were being closed. In fact, all over the city, a collapse of public services was going on. This turned out to be one of the signs of the city's developing fiscal crisis, which led New York to the edge of bankruptcy. After a year-long cliff hang, federal loans helped the city meet its payrolls, the new Emergency Financial Control Board balanced the budget and got the city back into the credit markets. But the cost was crippling layoffs and draconian service cuts. Hundreds of thousands of people lost jobs, homes, pensions. Year after year, streets, subways, bridges, public buildings broke and did not get fixed. One of the EFCB's commissioners confessed that they had balanced the budget "on the backs of the poor." But somehow they got the poor to trust them, to see them as beleaguered honest citizens rather than crooks and hacks of class war. In the poorest neighborhoods more than anywhere, people flaunted t-shirts that proclaimed: I ♥ NY.

Through all these happenings, dozens of ordinary, nice neighborhoods, like the one in the Bronx I grew up in, metamorphosed into gigantic, twisted, grotesque ruins. Diverse

GRANDMASTER CAZ

Founding member of the Cold Crush Brothers, widely regarded as "first simultaneous DJ and MC in hip-hop," writer of classic but uncredited verses for "Rapper's Delight"

JENNY RISHER

I don't remember the fires; I remember the result of the fires. All around our neighborhood were burnt-down buildings, abandoned buildings. There were a lot of empty lots with a lot of junk in them, rubble from buildings. These places were our playgrounds. There were old mattresses piled up, and we would go and play trampoline on the mattresses. If we had had golf courses and tennis courts—who knows, maybe the music wouldn't have happened. But the stars aligned because of the conditions, and us not being able to escape them. When things are at their worst, people start trying to look for alternatives. And I think the music has always been that for our people—for black people, poor people, music has always been that soothing, saving grace that helps us get by. And hip-hop just came at a time when our generation really needed something to occupy us.

The music of the day was disco. But we were *disco-nnected.* We were too young to go to discos or be involved in that movement. So we adopted a kind of youth disco culture, which turned into hip-hop.

The first Kool Herc party I ever went to was at a club called the Heavalo. I was fourteen or fifteen. I snuck in. One of the doormen blinked, and I shot upstairs into the club. I hid behind a speaker and watched everything. It just took me away. When certain records came on the crowd would get hyped; the breaks got everybody dancing. There were certain records, when they came on people would dance together; another record, the girls would move out of the way and the guys would just dance on the floor—it was crazy! It was just a whole new world to me, that I wanted to be a part of.

populations brought up to lead pallid but peaceful lives found themselves engulfed in pathologies, ending in unending early death. The phone's ring late at night became a cry of dread. It was as if disintegration became, not an absence, but a presence, an active force. And yet, and yet, even as this protracted horror show destroyed the city, somehow it energized its citizens; the force that killed New Yorkers made them more alive. As things got worse, more energy was focused on just trying to survive the day and the night; much of the thrill of being here now came to be: *Look! We have come through!*

.   .   .

It wasn't like that when I was a kid. Not that there wasn't plenty of conflict and struggle; but it had a different form. When I was growing up in the Bronx, after the good war, at the start of the cold war, it looked like the basic human conflict was between the magnificent buildings downtown and a lot of yearning, desiring, imagining, questing selves, across some bridge or tunnel, so near but yet so far. I had only a vague idea of what went on inside ("business"?), but the buildings and the skyline seemed magical and eternal, and the greatest bliss I could imagine was to make it there and to be recognized by other people as a man who had made it (my grandmother asked: what was this crude English—"make it"?). The great mass of us would never get anywhere near the towers; or if we did, we could count on getting kicked out before we were ready to go. I knew that was the tragedy of New York, long before I knew the word.

Joe Conzo, *Cold Crush Brothers at South Bronx High School*, 1980, and *River Avenue and 163rd*, 1979

The spring of my first year teaching at the City College of New York, soon after Martin Luther King was killed, buildings around the college started burning down. At first it was only a few, on the side streets of northern Manhattan between Amsterdam and Broadway, where I liked to walk on sunny days on my way home from school. The first fires were small, just an apartment or an upper floor, or one side of a building at a time. Streets that were jammed, with boys playing ball and girls jumping rope and hopscotch, mothers with babies, old men at cards or dominoes, began to thin out. Kids I'd met as part of stickball teams became solitaries throwing rubber balls against walls—and now, suddenly, there were lots of unattended walls and empty lots, great play spaces but hardly any players. When I came back to school in the fall, several densely packed rows of houses were gone, streets suddenly bathed in sunlight. It was ghastly, over the next couple of years, to see crowded streets thin out and noisy ones quiet down. Sometimes I would try to engage people in conversation.

I'd ask, "What happened?" People would point all around and say, "The fires, the fires," and shake their hands to signify they couldn't understand.

Where did people go? Often to nearby housing projects, to double up with family or friends. Without the projects, the neighborhood would have been totally destroyed. It was only thanks to these projects, opened in the early 1960s, that it was continuing to exist at all. And the change in Washington, from the Johnson to the Nixon presidency, marked a great shift in urban policy, which made it pretty clear that cities wouldn't be getting any more money to build housing for people like the people who were being burnt out.

If buildings around CCNY were crashing down around me, many of my kids inside the school were crashing from within. They leaped into crazy love, into deadly drugs—remember, this was heroin's heyday—into bizarre religious and political cults that crushed their members' selves at a point in their lives when their selves weren't yet defined and they were helpless to resist. By 1971 or so, kids I had known as smart, sweet, radical acidheads had morphed into filthy, angry junkies panhandling on St. Mark's Place; others were scuffling "underground" on the mall on upper Broadway, or deep in the bowels of Bellevue, or dead. I couldn't stand it; I became prematurely mature, a kind of hippie square, saying things I never dreamt I'd say, things like: *Stop! Don't do it! Get out! Get clean! Go home!* Eventually, after much *tsuris,* many of these kids came out the other end and became distinguished citizens; a couple are my friends today. But I still miss that brilliant lost generation, so brave as they scaled the towers without stopping to learn to climb, without even knowing for sure which way was down.

. . .

As the 1970s unfolded, it turned out that the troubles I had seen in and around CCNY were just tips of titanic icebergs. Gradually I learned what deep trouble New York was in. It was caught up in a long wave of what economists came to call deindustrialization. In the late 1960s and early 1970s, deindustrializing progress destroyed millions of manufacturing jobs, hundreds of thousands of them in New York, mostly connected with the garment industry. People working themselves to death morphed into people dying for work. The towers downtown still offered plenty of work for *other* people, hypothetical people with education and (increasingly) computer skills, more educated people, but the ground was cut out from under many of the real people who were here. New York's workforce in the 1970s needed federal help more desperately than it had at any time since the Depression; but at just this Nixonian moment, federal help dried up and disappeared.

In the 1970s and 1980s, New York's greatest spectacles were its ruins. Gradually it emerged how they had come to be. All around the town, landlords of old buildings were having more trouble than ever with tenants, who were ever more unemployed. Meanwhile, as many old, shabby buildings began to cave in, the landlords found themselves redlined by banks, so that, if their properties were located on the wrong side of the line, the owners couldn't get loans to fix the buildings up. Somewhere along the line they came to believe that their buildings were worth more dead than alive.

The result was a tremendous, protracted boom in arson, with much destruction of life. All through the 1970s it happened simultaneously in dozens of neighborhoods. But the biggest explosion was in the South Bronx, not far from where I grew up. The building I grew up in was still there and still lived in, but the whole block across the street had burned and crumbled into ruins, and then started to sink into the swamp that the whole neighborhood was built on. In 1979, 1980, 1981, I spent many lonely afternoons wandering through the Bronx's ruins.

I couldn't believe the enormity of these ruins. They went on and on, for block after block, mile after mile. Some blocks seemed almost intact, but look around the corner, and

JENNY RISHER

GRANDWIZZARD THEODORE

Storied Bronx DJ widely credited, after he began scratching records at thirteen, with being the first to perfect the technique to make music

I lived here in the Bronx, so hip-hop was always around me. When I'd go to the train station I'd see the graffiti on the trains. When I'd go to the parks I'd see the b-boys b-boying. As far as the MCs, there were always guys on the corner harmonizing and free-styling. And then once I saw my brother Mean Gene and Grandmaster Flash with two turntables and a mixer—that's when I realized I was born into a culture we call hip-hop.

Back then [the parties we threw] were just called jams. We would go into abandoned buildings and do jams and charge people $1.99 or 99 cents to come in. We were doing "hooky parties"—people would skip school and go to the jams and everybody would throw their book bags to the side and we'd play music until three o'clock.

We were doing breakbeat music—taking Aerosmith and Elton John, Sly and the Family Stone, the Beatles, all of these artists; but taking the breaks in their songs and extending them. That's how the DJ art form was formed. That was what we did in the Bronx. We would take a ten-second break and turn it into a two-minute break. We were taking all kinds of music and chopping it up and slicing it up and putting it together. All the other boroughs were just playing disco music, the stuff that you heard on the radio. We were playing Parliament Funkadelic, Brass Construction, Jimmy Castor Bunch. And once disco died, everybody started to listen to the stuff that we were doing.

there was no corner. The uncanniest part, I thought, was the people who were still there, painting their houses, taking their kids to school, fixing their cars on the street—at least, one man told me, they didn't have to worry about parking spaces anymore. These people were not screaming or foaming at the mouth, as I was sure I would have done, but talking straight and being nice to strangers and working hard to keep life together.

The fire years created a whole new vocabulary and iconography. As all survivors of 9/11 know, urban ruins make great visuals. There were years of tabloid headlines, magazine covers, TV documentaries in many languages entitled something like "THE BRONX IS BURNING!" A new urban picturesque emerged out of horizons lit by lurid flames, montages of buildings in different stages of disintegration, shards of beds, tables, TV sets, debris of real people's lives that might have been our own. For many years the *New York Times* carried a box, always on page 2 or 3 of the Metro Section, that listed "Buildings Destroyed" the previous day or night. I and many people I knew always turned to this box first, even before the baseball scores: was "our" old building still there?

Blaming the victims became the cliché repeated endlessly on the news. The saddest part, I thought, was when the victims—who themselves depended on TV for their news—bought the cliché and blamed themselves. For years, any day or night, on the local news, you could see a tattered family in tears in front of their smoking building, gathering the few possessions not burned up, and asking, like Job, "What did we do wrong?" The man with the mic would say, with great solemnity, "We don't know, Mr. Vargas, we just don't know."

The real ravaging of the Bronx had begun back in the 1950s, when Robert Moses drilled his Cross Bronx Expressway right through its center, destroying some of the most crowded (but intact) neighborhoods in the city, displacing thousands of people from their homes. The CBE was (and still is) a wound in the Bronx's heart, but it made the Bronx very easy to get out of. In the early 1960s, when poor city neighborhoods started getting wrecked, news reports often portrayed residents saying that now the rulers of America would have to rebuild the slums in a better way.

By the end of the decade, it was clear what a delusion—what a touching delusion—this had been. Late in the 1960s the RAND Corporation, the Defense Department's research center, opened up an urban subsidiary. In the early Nixon years, governments at every level were cutting social services, but all of them were uneasy about charges of racism. It then became an intellectual problem to find a formula for service cuts that didn't look blatantly racist. RAND's idea was to base all service policy on gains or losses in population. In neighborhoods that were losing people, cities would have a supposedly color-blind way to cut. In neighborhoods losing lots of people, the cuts could be wholesale. The Bronx seems to have been one place this formula was tested: in the years the South Bronx was burning down, and people were fleeing the fires, the Bronx lost a third of its fire services. *Touché!*

Observers of the Bronx's troubles, including many New Yorkers, developed an elaborate vocabulary of deflection and denial, which very soon would be used against New York itself. "What's wrong with these people? Why are they doing this to themselves?" Magic words like these transform victims of misery and misfortune into perverse perpetrators of malice. Social scientists got millions of dollars in grants, from foundations and federal agencies, to explore the character defects of poor people from the Bronx that led them—here was another dehumanizing cliché of those days—"to foul their own nest."

No one found an answer, maybe because there's really no way to imagine hundreds of thousands of people burning down their homes and getting themselves and their children killed. The mayor's Arson Task Force, probably New York's most thoroughly New Left government agency, and an unlikely ally, the insurance industry, proposed to change the questions and to shift the focus from the tenants to the landlords. The giant insurance companies, which had bought up Bronx insurance pools in the pastoral early 1960s, suffered enormous losses there in the 1970s. Finally, in the early 1980s, the big companies resolved together to stop paying claims on tenement fires. All at once, as if by magic, tenement fires ceased. In the last year of payoffs, the Bronx lost about 1,300 buildings to fire. In the first year without payoffs, it lost 12. In the second year, it lost 3. Isn't it nice when, as happens every now and then, very complex human questions have very simple answers and when the answers keep poor people in their homes, not put out in the street?

· · ·

The defamation of the Bronx helped to create a language for the much more extensive and profound defamation of New York. As the city's finances plummeted and its credit evaporated, it began to seem at least possible that it could go bankrupt. When the crisis was very acute, I had a dream, and I've had it again with minor variations through the years. It's laid out like a television news spot in which "the Colonel," a Southern congressman, is asking the folks in his district what they think about bailing out New York. He gives a long speech about "Jew York's—I mean, New York's" depravity. Then the Colonel says, "So what I want to know, I want you folks to tell me, about New York, about that city, way up there: Should it live or should it die?" As he asks, he smiles (in close-up) in an insinuating way. They jump to their feet, grin obscenely at each other like crowd members in a lynch mob photo, then they clench their fists, bulge out their eyes, and shout in unison: "DIE! DIE! DIE! DIE! DIE!" I know it's (probably) not real, but still I'm terrified, and I wake up screaming.

A number of bailout plans gradually materialized, enabling the city to borrow enough money to pay its bills, at outrageous interest rates, with federal guarantees. But many com-

MELLE MEL

Legendary founding member of the Furious Five, first Bronx rapper to call himself an "MC," lead vocalist and lyricist on "The Message" (1982)

People said that the fires happened because landlords were just burning down their buildings for insurance, but I didn't really grasp that concept when I was younger. I just thought that it was the ghetto and that's how it was supposed to be. One of my cousins lived on Minford Place, right off of Boston Road and 174th Street.

JA'DEE MURPHY

There were maybe six square blocks where everything in that whole radius was burnt down. It looked like somebody dropped a bomb. You wouldn't see anything, except maybe a pack of stray dogs running around. It was the strangest shit.

We were coming out of a gang era at that time. In the Bronx there were the Black Pearls, the Spades, the Roman Kings. But when the music started, it brought everybody out of the gang vibe and into a music vibe. Looking at it now, it was a beautiful thing; it saved a lot of lives.

In those early days it was all about the DJ. When we started MC-ing we didn't have an identity that was separate from the DJ; we were basically the DJ's flunkies. If [Grandmaster] Flash wanted to do a block party ten blocks away, and wanted to have twenty crates of records, we carried all his records. Nobody called it hip-hop then; it was just a party.

We used to do parties in a club called the Black Door on Boston Road. One night there, a guy called Kokomo was going to the army, and Flash's first MC, Cowboy, was on the mic wishing him farewell. Cowboy started to chant, "Hip . . . Hop . . . " He did it that night, and then he did it the next week at the party. By the third or fourth week it caught on. People started telling us, "Y'all better leave that hip-hop shit alone, because it's not gonna last forever!" But that's how it became hip hop. Because you know, [DJ Kool] Herc never used the term *hip-hop,* and neither did Bam [Afrika Bambaataa]. But Cowboy said that chant at the parties, and people started calling it "that hip-hop shit."

mentators and politicians said the plans weren't punitive enough; they aimed to restore New York to some sort of normal life, rather than destroy its capacity for life.

The climax of this animosity was the famous speech in which President Gerald Ford said he was going to veto any congressional bill to bail out New York, because he didn't see how the fate of New York was of any concern to the American people. I heard the speech on a cab radio, coming home from the airport; I remember how Ford's combination of ponderous awkwardness and blasé insensitivity blew my mind. The West Indian driver and I traded obscenities—his were fresher, I thought—but after we'd cursed Ford out, we both felt listless and depressed. My heart leapt up when I saw the *Daily News* front page the next day: "FORD TO CITY: DROP DEAD." I thought, "This is why New York exists: to tell the truth like a wise guy." And I thought, "Whatever those creeps do to us, at least we won't go quietly."

The following day's front page featured Mayor Abe Beame in front of City Hall, looking both wounded and defiant, displaying the page to the world. Ironically, "FORD TO CITY" was not only a great headline, but a superb consciousness-raiser. It helped people everywhere see how New York could be both magnificent and precarious, both a great beast of Babylon and an endangered species. And it helped the city get the help it needed.

We started doing different parties and going downtown to the Mudd Club, the Ritz, the Peppermint Lounge. We were around a whole other different type of people—punk rockers. And we kind of adapted their image to the Bronx. We gave people something to look at when we played. A definite image apart from the DJ. We added our little flair to it, like a hip kind of look. So we had a look, and we also had the music to go with it. When we came uptown and were dressing like the cats from downtown, we were basically accepted. Our people knew what we were trying to do. I guess it would have looked weird, walking around in the Bronx with a long trench coat and boots and spikes and chains. But being from the Bronx you didn't have to fit in a mold. And that's what made it so easy for us to transition from what we were to what we became, when we did "The Message."

All the records before that, we were rhyming about rhyming, rhyming about clubs and dancing, but that record was really the brainchild of Miss Sylvia Robinson [the founder of Sugar Hill Records]. The drummer from the Sugar Hill [Records] Band had two songs, the basic foundation of "The Message" and a record called "Dumb Love." He wanted to do "Dumb Love" and Miss Rob' liked "The Message." She said she would let him do "Dumb Love" if he would let one of the other groups do "The Message." "The Message" was actually supposed to be for the Sugar Hill Gang, but they didn't like it. Nobody liked the record but Miss Rob; she was just obsessed with it. I figured we might as well just do it. I went in and did the vocals and then there was a piece, a rhyme that I had put on the first record that we ever did in '79 or '80, and she put that in the back of the original version of "The Message," and then that's what became the complete song of "The Message." When she put the song out, people just automatically took to it, because a lot of people was going through stuff that was relevant to what the song was about.

We were in a place where we needed an outlet, where we just needed something to make a day normal. And that thing was music.

I never really doubted it. I figured the Babbitts in the GOP could never beat the billionaires; the billionaires might be greedy, but they weren't stupid; they could be counted on to grasp how all markets were integrated and how the act of crushing the biggest city in the country could bring down the whole national economy, including trillions of dollars of their own investment capital. I did my best to help my students see this and maybe relax a little. But emotionally I was racked with pain and helpless rage. I hadn't much respect for the people who hated New York and who, I knew, would hate me if they knew me; still, it hurt to be hated.

And I knew something else, which I'd learned when I'd done that ultra–New York thing, gone into therapy: I learned that the punitive sadists who ran down New York and people like me were not just "out there," in the White House and in the world, but in my head as well, a persistent part of me, and that I was going to have to learn not only to get through their assaults, but to confront my own inner police and to learn to bail out myself.

. . .

As the 1970s ended, there was a sense of relief in the air, a feeling that the city was recovering at last. Ironically, the 1980s brought a whole new wave of disasters: masses of homeless

Ricky Flores, *Carlos and Boogie on the 6 Train,* 1984

people, spread out on the streets and in the subways, filling up every empty public space, and leading the city fathers to rack their brains to find ways to cut public space down; the AIDS epidemic, something completely different, nearly surreal, in the annals of sexual disease; and crack cocaine, the first killer drug to break into the mass market, lift violence to new heights, and jump-start the spiral of horrors all over again.

Meanwhile, inside the walls, the city's high school and college kids—including some of my CCNY kids—were going through an outburst of creative energy and inventing a whole new thing, a thing called hip-hop. Today, hip-hop is the basic idiom of American popular culture. But forty years ago no one could tell how long it would go on, or whether it would be seen or heard or noticed by anybody out of town. Its most distinctive expressions were rap music, break dancing, and graffiti art. The vortex where all these activities converged and whirled together was the subway. The New York subway system in the 1970s was in a state of extreme decay, probably drearier and scarier than at any time in its history. This was the point at which a generation of kids filled its grim cars with dazzling color and its gray spaces with musical structure, dancers' grace, wise-guy irreverence, and life stories. Hip-hop gave New York just the kind of energy we needed to survive the crap that was being dumped on us.

However, there were plenty of New Yorkers who not only couldn't identify with hip-hop in any way, but felt that its graffiti, rap, and dance were themselves the crap that was being dumped on us. It was a moment when thousands of our poor and nonwhite kids, instead of blowing their lives standing on street corners, harassing people, and getting high, had become reflective and active and disciplined and were actually *doing something.* Why couldn't more grown-ups get the message? Maybe this was another symptom of civic collapse: so many people with good heads seemed to lose their heads.

> Don't push me 'cause I'm close to the edge
> I'm trying not to lose my head, *huh-huh-huh-huh.*

This was the opening to "The Message" by Grandmaster Flash and the Furious Five, the first international rap hit, released in 1982. The album cover is set on a South Bronx (or maybe South Bronx-esque) corner. The image evokes the Persuasions' late-1960s album *Street Corner Symphony,* except that, after years of disintegration, the corner has no street.

"The Message" is an instant classic of urban realism, linked in spiritual pathos to older classics like *Maggie: A Girl of the Streets* and *Call It Sleep.* The narrative is a guided tour of the neighborhood-as-horror-show. It features junkies, pushers, pimps, hit men—all sweet homeboys and homegirls just a little while ago.

At the end the survivors are taken away by the cops; only the beat goes on. The rapper Melle Mel confronts a dear friend, now a handsome corpse: How could he get himself killed? He is increasingly desperate to understand: is there any way his friends—is there any way *he*—can keep from dying? New Yorkers (like the rappers themselves) may see a subtext of civic allegory in his question. The prospects look bleak. And yet, and yet, the rapper can't help but see: sometimes, somehow—we don't know how, but somehow—it's possible to emerge from the vortex of horror and violence. You can come from ruins, yet not yourself be ruined. Social disintegration and existential desperation can be sources of life and creative energy. Our first hit rappers know something that Hegel said modern men and women had to learn: they know how to "look the negative in the face and live with it." They have looked the ruins in the face, and they have lived with them, and they have come through. Now they can see and feel their way to new life.

. . .

I can remember when I first heard "The Message" blaring from a West Harlem record shop, in the Reagan summer of 1982. Right away I was thrilled. It wasn't so long ago that I'd lost a kid (*Marc Berman, 1975–1980*); I'd been pretty low. Was I moving my limbs again? Now these kids from the city's most horrendous ruins had created a masterpiece that looked the negative in the face and lived with it, and still dreamt of coming through. I thought, if they could dream this, then damn it, we were going to come through. I knew New York still had plenty of sorrow ahead. There were homeless families all over the streets and in the subways. A dear friend of mine had just died of AIDS—and I don't think it had even been named AIDS. I couldn't even conceive of crack, our 1980s twist of fate. But I knew our Via Dolorosa had a long way to run. Still, of all the forms of suffering, I thought, the worst is where your imagination shuts down. Once you can imagine getting out of the hole you're in, even if you can't imagine how, the worst is past.

I was starting to notice things. I read that New York's population, after dropping sharply for a decade, was growing again. Once more, new immigrants were coming. Many were said to be squatting in the ruins. Was I ready to go up to the Bronx again and look around? All around the town, people from I didn't know where were selling foods I'd never seen from carts and trucks on the street—did I dare to try some? I'd gone to some Mets games, and I was getting to know the number 7, which ran from Times Square through Queens to Shea Stadium and Main Street Flushing. The 7 offered an amazing feeling of connecting to the whole world, a different country or continent opening out at every stop, with breathtaking visions of the skyline bringing it all together. I wondered how I had missed this train all my life; wasn't it there all along? That summer, too, for the first time ever, the subways had air-conditioning that worked and rubber wheels that made it quiet, so you could have a real conversation in a moving car. If New Yorkers could talk, who knew what else might happen? When I heard "The Message," I felt it was post-collapse New York's way of saying "We Shall Overcome," and I believed: *Yes, we can—we will.* 🖂

MAKERS AND BREAKERS
OLMSTED, MOSES, JACOBS SHAPE THE CITY

FREDERICK LAW OLMSTED (1822–1903)

1 August 1840: Arrives in New York at 18, from Connecticut, to clerk for a silk importer; lodges in Brooklyn Heights

2 1848–55: On 125 acres purchased for him by his father, builds Tosomock Farm into a successful nursery between stints traveling

3 February 16, 1853: Publishes first dispatch from the South in nascent *New York Times,* starting a series that transforms him into a staunch abolitionist, respected journalist, and influential public voice

4 Fall 1857–April 1858: Spending nights at architect Calvert Vaux's, collaborates on Greensward Plan for entry into the Central Park design competition

5 June 1859: Marries his brother's widow, Mary Olmsted, by Central Park's Great Hill and then moves into Central Park administration offices with her children

6 1861: Drills park employees at outbreak of Civil War before leaving to head the US Sanitary Commission, precursor to the Red Cross

7 1865: Returns from stormy tenure at a California gold mine and launches Olmsted, Vaux & Company, Landscape Architects; begins planning Brooklyn's Prospect Park

8 1866: Helps found *The Nation* magazine as part-owner and associate editor

9 Mid-1870s: Calls view of Lullwater through the Cleft Ridge Span in completed Prospect Park "one of the most superb and refined park scenes I ever saw"

10 1881: Leaves New York for Brookline, Massachusetts, to live out his days

ROBERT MOSES (1888–1981)

1 1897: Moves to the city from New Haven at 8; grows up in five-story brownstone surrounded by Rembrandts and maids

2 1901–3: Attends elite Ethical Culture School before transferring to even more elite Dwight School and Mohegan Lake Academy

3 1914: Begins work to reform city's corrupt civil service system at the Bureau of Municipal Research, epicenter of Progressivism, where he meets his wife, Mary Louise Sims

4 1918: Living in small apartment with no job, supported by his mother after being drummed out of city government, takes a position running commission to reorganize New York state government

5 1934: Takes helm as the first city parks commissioner, overseeing all boroughs; fires all employees of borough parks departments

6 July 21, 1936: Defying Mayor Fiorello La Guardia, demolishes ferry docks to make way for approaches to the Triborough Bridge; later builds his permanent office under its toll plaza

7 1936: Reportedly orders that Thomas Jefferson Pool, one of 11 massive pools funded by the New Deal, go unheated to discourage use by "coloreds"

8 December 11, 1946: Pulls together last-minute deal with money from the Rockefellers to build permanent UN headquarters

9 1950–53: From his apartment down the street from Gracie Mansion, exercises virtual control over city government, through daily consultations with "accidental" mayor Vincent Impellitteri

10 Early 1950s: Rents penthouse of Marguerite Hotel to watch excavation for Brooklyn-Queens Expressway

11 1952: Refuses alternate Cross-Bronx Expressway route through East Tremont; 1,530 apartments, home to over 5,000, are demolished

12 April 24, 1956: Orders park employees to destroy glen beloved to mothers and children of Upper West Side under cover of night

13 November 21, 1964: Leads 52-limousine motorcade on first crossing of Verrazano-Narrows Bridge; does not invite bridge workers to celebration

14 1963–65: Presides over transformation of Flushing Meadows for its second world's fair, which flounders in finances and attendance

15 1968: Still swims in Atlantic at age 79 near longtime Babylon, Long Island, home

JANE JACOBS (born Jane Butzner, 1916–2006)

1 1934: Arrives from Scranton, PA, at age 18, intent on breaking into journalism, and with her sister soon moves to the West Village, their "ideal neighborhood"

2 1943: Having dropped out of Columbia's University Extension, rejecting formal education, takes job as writer at the US State Department's Office of War Information; covers urban redevelopment and later faces questions on alleged communist sympathies

3 1944: Meets architect Robert Hyde Jacobs during a party at her apartment and marries him a month later

4 1947: Purchases a former candy store with her husband and begins renovating it into their longtime home

5 1958: While working as an editor at *Architectural Forum,* publishes "Downtown Is for People" in *Fortune,* establishing herself as a major critic of urban renewal

6 1958: Turns two sons and daughter loose with petitions in campaign to defeat Moses's plan for avenue bisecting Washington Square Park (Jacobs's daughter, Mary, appears at center in front of the park's arch on the opposite page)

7 1961: Frequents Lion's Head pub, hub for West Villagers' successful fight against urban renewal plan for neighborhood

8 1961: Working with editor Jason Epstein of Random House, publishes *The Death and Life of Great American Cities*

9 1962: Pickets in protest of planned demolition of Pennsylvania Station and then joins Joint Committee to Stop the Lower Manhattan Expressway (LOMEX) as its co-chair

10 December 6, 1967: Arrested for blocking entrance to a military induction center in protest of Vietnam War

11 April 10, 1968: Arrested for disrupting public meeting on LOMEX and charged with inciting a riot; LOMEX, by 1971, is officially killed

12 Summer 1968: Moves to Toronto to keep sons out of the draft

12

Van
Cortlandt
Park

10

Van
Cortlandt
Village

Co-op
City

Pelham Bay
Park

*Long
Island
Sound*

BRONX

Cross Bronx ⑪ Expy

Hudson

River

Riverside
Park 4

⑤ ⑦ ⑥

Triborough
Bridge

⑨

Central Park

12
2 ⑥
2
1

⑤
⑧

Flushing
Meadows–
Corona
Park

5

1

⑭

9

⑧

Jacobs Way 4

MANHATTAN

QUEENS

Expy

4

7 3 6

Stuyvesant
Town

1

Brooklyn-Queens

LOMEX 11

East River

3

7 3 8

10

10
1

Fort Greene
Park

Prospect Park

⑨ Eastern Pkwy

*pper
Bay*

BROOKLYN

Ocean Pkwy

15

13

*zano-
ws
e*

Jamaica Bay

Belt Pkwy

Lower Bay

16 MAKERS AND BREAKERS

Cities are accretions—of lives, structures, landscapes, histories, and plans. While marks of the millions who've touched New York over time can be identified within its layers, those wrought by three central figures in the making of the modern metropolis are nearly impossible to avoid. Frederick Law Olmsted was the "father of landscape architecture": he designed the city's greatest parks and the world's first parkways, pleasure grounds celebrated by the masses today. Robert Moses was the "master builder" of New York in the twentieth century: he drew a new city by sprinkling even more parks across the boroughs but also by erasing neighborhoods to make way for monumental highways, bridges, cultural centers, and housing projects. Jane Jacobs was Moses's nemesis: the celebrated writer and activist rallied fellow citizens to reject his wholesale and undemocratic reworking of their communities, helping to birth the preservation movement. This is a map of three lives and their remnants—the plans each giant made and thwarted; the places they birthed, destroyed, and saved; the New Yorks they dreamed of and brought into being. As Jonathan Tarleton's essay here reminds us, the line between a maker and breaker of the city can be a fine one. But whether through enduring ideas or those embedded in the city's very structure, the legacies and values of these three titanic urbanists continue to clash and combine in the ever-evolving framework organizing New Yorkers' lives.

CARTOGRAPHY: MOLLY ROY   MAP APPEARS ON PAGES 132–133.

WAYS AND MEANS   BY JONATHAN TARLETON

Walking among the original elms of Brooklyn's Eastern Parkway, I find it hard to conceive that this grand boulevard lined with benches and trees—one of Frederick Law Olmsted and Calvert Vaux's many masterpieces—didn't always course through Brooklyn. Completed in 1874, the world's first parkway serves as a boundary between neighborhoods, a place to sit and stroll, and a concourse ferrying all kinds to the sylvan woods and meadows of Prospect Park—another much-loved Olmsted and Vaux creation. But of course this thoroughfare and the seemingly timeless patchwork of buildings along it weren't always here. Grand plans and speculative aims conspired to build them. And the prerequisite for these plans' fruition, as with all such designs in a place defined by density, was tearing down some of what came before.

    The building of Eastern Parkway, like that of Olmsted and Vaux's Central Park before it, entailed what would a century later be known as slum clearance. Much of the proposed route for the parkway, running east toward Queens, was undeveloped. But Carrville, a thriving middle-class community established by free black families in what's now Crown Heights, stood in the way. Eastern Parkway didn't just tear down many of Carrville's homes; it paved over the only official burial ground open to black Brooklynites—a loss necessary to gain the new boulevard and pleasure ground lined with homes that Olmsted pitched for prosperous "city-bred country boys." Today, Carrville is remembered only for no longer existing, not for what it once was.

This kind of destruction is rarely associated with "the father of landscape architecture," who also midwifed modern regional planning and suburban design. Olmsted's name calls to mind the urbane wilderness of his best-known masterpiece. He's the genius who forged Central Park—its Ramble of wooded paths encased in the city's grandeur—from a part of Manhattan that engineer Egbert Viele described as "a pestilential spot, where rank vegetation and miasmatic odors taint every breath of air." Which is why, perhaps, the site was also home to Seneca Village, another refuge for free black New Yorkers. As with Eastern Parkway, Olmsted and Vaux's first slum clearance project wasn't admired exclusively for the park it brought to life; its removal of the black community provided another cause for celebration among city elites.

The name most New Yorkers would associate with such demolition of low-income, minority neighborhoods in the name of a greater good is Robert Moses: the planner-cum-power broker and so-called master builder of the city who, for a key stretch of decades in the mid-twentieth century, simultaneously held twelve appointed positions in city and state government, among them parks commissioner, chairman of the Triborough Bridge and Tunnel Authority, and, perhaps most fittingly, a sui generis omnibus designation as "construction coordinator of the City of New York." For over forty years, he wielded a not-so-invisible power over New York's ruling establishment, bending mayors, the press, and Wall Street to his vision. Thirteen bridges, 416 miles of parkways, 658 playgrounds, and 150,000 housing units are attributed to Moses's monomaniacal, arrogant leadership—and that's a partial accounting. The synonymy of Moses and large-scale displacement of the city's marginalized is appropriate: under slum clearance and related urban renewal programs, he flattened 300 acres of city land and displaced, by one estimate, at least half a million people. He was fond of saying, "To make an omelet you need to break a few eggs." Break many he did.

Olmsted and Moses are typically regarded as antitheses—the maker and the breaker of ideal urban life. But there's also a lineage connecting the two. Commonalities of privilege, manipulation, and deft administration infuse their realized visions—just as their crucial differences, and contrasting regard for "the public" and individuals' lives, shape their divergent legacies.

. . .

Olmsted was born in Connecticut in 1822. As a restless youth living off his father's largesse, he had trial runs as a clerk, sailor, and surveyor before taking up scientific farming on a Staten Island plot bought by Dad. After a pair of walks around Europe piqued his eye for park design and supplied fodder for early writings, Olmsted launched the journalism career that first made his name.

Devoted to social reform, Olmsted reported from the antebellum South for the city paper that became the *New York Times*. Exhibiting an unusually nuanced account of slavery's effects on society, he turned from a gradualist on the "slavery question" to a committed abolitionist, whose dispatches, according to some accounts, swayed Britain from entering the Civil War on the side of the Confederacy.

Olmsted soon parlayed his growing notoriety as a journalist into work as an editor, playing a role in the founding of *Putnam's Magazine,* long defunct, and *The Nation,* still at it after 150 years. Those labors, though, didn't pay the bills. So Olmsted took on the role of Central Park superintendent, overseeing the clearance of land to make way for whatever as-yet-undesigned park took shape. He soon joined with Calvert Vaux, an old acquain-

Triborough Bridge span over Hell Gate, connecting Queens to Randall's Island. Courtesy Library of Congress.

tance and an ascendant architect, to create his own vision for the park, which not only came to pass, but revolutionized urban park-making everywhere.

Bringing their design to fruition was fraught with challenges both technical and bureaucratic. In 1859 Central Park comptroller Andrew Green—the man who would one day unify five boroughs into one city—was put in charge of bringing down the project's costs. Olmsted, full of fervent belief in his cause and chafing at the comptroller's "cross-examination" over each expense, submitted his resignation. The Central Park Commission, though, asked him to stay on. He did, in exchange for increased power and a general acquiescence to the Olmsted mode of unilateral leadership that prompted a friend to describe him as a "little monarch."

Moses's similarly overbearing self-confidence grew with each degree, first from top prep schools and then from Yale, Oxford, and Columbia. Recognized for his academic prowess in the realm of public policy, Moses dedicated himself to civil service reform. Right out of school, he sought and won a job with the city's Progressive establishment, for which he was able to forgo payment thanks to a doting mother. The young Moses preached a staunch adherence to a meritocracy that could dismantle the patronage and corruption epitomized by New York's Tammany Hall political machine. But after Moses's entrée into city politics evaporated alongside such reforms' possibility, a pragmatic thirst for power overrode his idealism.

Moses climbed the political ladder alongside a Tammany politician and in 1924 became president of the State Council on Parks. In that position, he greatly expanded parkland across New York, and then used his resulting popularity, in an early deployment of his trademark tantrum, to threaten Governor Franklin Delano Roosevelt with his resignation unless cuts to his budget request were reversed. Roosevelt gave in, as many other governors and mayors would after him. When Mayor Robert F. Wagner, for one, took office in 1954, he was intent on constraining Moses's power. But his attempt to block the master builder's advance, by halting his reappointment to the City Planning Commission, crumbled in much the same way Roosevelt's had when Moses marched into Wagner's office with a completed appointment form and dared the mayor to forget who held power in the relationship. Wagner signed.

Moses was an authoritarian at heart; the tag *monarch* would certainly have fit if *master builder* had been taken. His career is littered with the productive suggestions of colleagues and peers tossed by the wayside because they weren't his own. In a tragic inversion of his namesake's exodus, Moses parted a human sea to make way for a flood of cars into the heart of New York's northernmost borough along his Cross Bronx Expressway. Rather than

Triborough Bridge exchange plaza on Randall's Island. Courtesy Library of Congress.

swing a one-mile stretch of the route a few blocks south to save 1,530 apartments, home to 5,000 people, he carved up the dense and thriving community of Tremont with his "scythe of progress." All people or parties who stood in his way could count on being ridiculed and smeared as "commies," "radicals," or—his favorite slur—a mere "bunch of mothers."

But however alike Olmsted and Moses may have been in bearing and approach, their regard for the publics they structured—with steel and trees, concrete and streams—did diverge sharply.

Olmsted's humanist commitment to the well-being of the individual is evinced, at each turn, in the exceptional design of his parks. The public's love for his creations, generation after generation, proves their success. In Prospect Park, the Long Meadow—a study in expansive, grassy views crafted to heal the greenery-starved urban dweller—leads one gently toward the Ravine, Brooklyn's only extant forest and a ready provider of quiet solitude along dirt paths in the city's heart. Olmsted made spaces not only with an abstract public in mind, but for actual people. While his strict, often paternalistic views on what kind of behavior belonged in his parks tended toward those espoused by his privileged class (no baseball allowed), they were commons open to all, in theory and in practice.

Moses did not share such a progressive view of all New Yorkers' "right to the city." He was, among other things, a well-documented racist. Apologists characterize Moses as a man of his age. But any reverence for his unrivaled brilliance in getting things done is skewed without acknowledging his projects' human costs. In Moses's New York, neighborhoods supposedly blighted enough to necessitate their wholesale demolition were often those with black or Latino residents: "urban renewal" grew synonymous with "Negro removal." Though Moses built 658 playgrounds, far fewer were placed in neighborhoods most in need of investment than in wealthier zones. The community benefits of his monumental West Side Project, which expanded Riverside Park over a buried, busy commercial freight line and brought a new parkway to the Hudson shore, stopped at Harlem's start.

Certain of Moses's public pools—the ones in or near black neighborhoods—were, by some accounts, kept colder than comfortable for swimmers. Covenants barred blacks from the massive Stuyvesant Town housing development he made possible. Disinvestment in public transportation, relied upon by poor New Yorkers, was official policy. "Dirty" and "colored" individuals were steered away from the best parks. Through it all, systemic segregation, instituted from on high by one of the most powerful nonelected public officials in U.S. history, is as enduring a legacy as his great Verrazano-Narrows Bridge.

Moses did not reserve his contempt exclusively for New Yorkers of color. "He doesn't love the people," his friend Frances Perkins told Moses's legendary biographer Robert

Caro in an interview for his opus *The Power Broker*. "He loves the public, but not as people. . . . It's a great amorphous mass to him; it needs to be bathed, it needs to be aired, it needs recreation." Even some of Moses's grander successes at the Bronx's Orchard Beach and in his New Deal pools exhibit a monumental scale that speaks to his view of the public as a mass, rather than a collection of individuals needful of quiet or beauty.

Moses painted the city by numbers—dollars, units, blocks, jobs, and cars, preferably ones traveling the lattice crust of highways he baked into the city. Individuals didn't serve as beneficiaries or co-creators of Moses's vision, only as boundaries. The most famous of these, Jane Jacobs, proved remarkably successful in that role, and many others. The writer and activist employed grassroots organizing to block Moses's plans to extend Fifth Avenue through Washington Square Park, demolish part of the West Village in the name of urban renewal, and ram an eight-lane elevated highway across Manhattan. The human costs of such projects, to Jacobs, were paramount; to Moses, the cost to the "city as system" was of primary concern.

Such was the pique he felt at any and all opposition that his ideal neighborhood might be the one that arose along his Cross Bronx Expressway in the 1980s. The city covered the windows of adjacent, abandoned apartment buildings with decals of potted plants and Venetian blinds, a Potemkin village without complaints, or people, to consider.

. . .

For a pivotal block of years in the 1960s and after, Jacobs played Moses's foil in the streets and in her books, refuting his theories of city-making with examples and inspiration drawn from her beloved Manhattan neighborhood. The West Village served as the observational lab for *The Death and Life of Great American Cities*, the enduring classic that began her influential investigations on the intersections of design, economics, and urban social life. Where Moses found aging, dense structures filled with an undesirable mix of families, businesses, and industry, Jacobs saw communities built by neighbors invested in their streets and one another.

Resident uprisings against Moses's plans, fanned by Jacobs and her fellow community activists, preserved the charm of many Lower Manhattan neighborhoods. But Moses-style destruction and Jacobs's drive to protect extant neighborhoods and their built environments are another pair of curious cousins. When "preservation" is perverted by the privileged into not-in-my-backyard politics, it can breed exclusions just as pernicious as displacement. The city's designation of many blocks and buildings in Jacobs's West Village as historic landmarks, in conjunction with altered zoning, spared the area out-of-context high-rises. But it also starved the neighborhood of more middle- and low-income units, which might have stopped, or at least stalled, the neighborhoods' contemporary gutting by the wealthy.

Jacobs, for her part, was not averse to new housing in the neighborhood, nor unaware of the perils of rising unaffordability. She pushed for the development of the subsidized West Village Houses, an idea born from the community, after Moses's urban renewal plan was defeated. But the development ended up a small, dull, low-rise Band-Aid—an insufficient counterweight to the prevailing winds of gentrification. Elsewhere, the public housing and middle-income co-ops, built alongside luxury towers and cultural complexes on Moses's "renewal" sites, stand as islands of affordability in ever-gentrifying seas. Those units, though born out of destruction and displacement, do function as Moses intended: they provide housing to New Yorkers who, without them, would have long ago been swept from town by affluence into unglamorous Jersey or the growing ranks of the suburban poor.

History's plans, like the long-term results and effects of designs for the city, are unpredictable. But while the less desirable results of Jacobs's vision are not always visible, Moses's shortcomings are embedded in the concrete that New Yorkers traverse every day. His love for the car is felt not just in the shadows of overpasses or dizzy footbridges over his highways, but on their edges. Along parts of the Cross Bronx Expressway, agglomerations of driving schools, auto shops, and car washes thrive, and for good reason—this is a realm made more for chassis and tires than for people.

To Moses's champions, he's a visionary who brought unprecedented investment into the city, updated its infrastructure for the future, and gave parks to its people—all of this is true. But he only earned the moniker *master builder* because he was a master bureaucrat who broke the public contract with loathing for both the laws and the people he was supposed to serve. Moses's New York is one based on a doctrine of rationality and efficiency, where communities are fungible and a scale model is a reliable stand-in for the messy intricacy of life as lived. Olmsted's New York may have also been created by destroying presents and pasts to sculpt parkways and parks. But what separates his vision from Moses's, and joins him to Jacobs, is that the inhabitants of his parks, like the residents of her West Village, were also meant to determine the ultimate shape of their surroundings through use. The New Yorks of Olmsted and Jacobs are still fraught with unforeseen consequences and collateral damage; but moored by humanist ideals, they're also far kinder.

. . .

I often tread the pavers of Olmsted's Eastern Parkway—sometimes on my way to the Long Meadow, Botanic Garden, or library. On a June Sunday afternoon, I sat on a bench across from the First Baptist Church of Crown Heights as a jazz quartet jammed out front in the open air. This is the kind of pleasant happenstance that I can no longer separate from the setting, or its designer. The ghost of Olmsted sits beneath those pavers along with his legacy's quiet contradictions—the buried histories, like that of forgotten Carrville here—which for most never infringe on the splendor of New York's cherished public spaces.

Olmsted's realms are scattered throughout the city, but Moses haunts almost everywhere. He hovers over the ball courts crafted from leftover land next to the Brooklyn-Queens Expressway, over his triumphant Triborough Bridge and the cool waters of Astoria Pool, over the abandoned beachside blocks of the Rockaways and the gleaming marble and glamour of Lincoln Center—beautiful places all, but spaces in which you feel like just another cell in the arteries of the city, an expendable element that will eventually go its way and leave scant hints of its existence. And there's little chance of escape from Moses's New York. Leaving the city one summer weekend to hike in the Ramapo Mountains, I met him in the dull whir of traffic on his Palisades Interstate Parkway. There in wild New Jersey, I stepped over a brook strewn with litter to follow the trail across the highway.

Specters of what was also inhabit the irony-rich West Village. The same old buildings and crooked streets with which Jacobs fell in love still define its air. But much of what she championed here—the street culture of looking after your neighbor, the complex ecosystem of businesses supporting one another, the diversity of uses and people—has been devoured by aspirants of a *Sex and the City* ideal made at home by speculative capital. Jacobs's former home at 555 Hudson Street, a candy store she and her husband renovated into their home of twenty-one years, now houses Next Step Realty—a firm that touts "complimentary transportation in our luxury SUVs" and its own "docu-series," bringing the stories of moneyed house hunters to the masses on ABC Family. Storefronts sit empty, not because of a lack of demand, but because the rent is too high for anything but the most expensive boutiques or national chains. Like the neighborhood's deviance from Manhattan's grid, here where West 4th is allowed to intersect West 10th, the place most synonymous with Jacobs's vision meets the locus of its starkest erosion. The grip that even the city's giants can exert on its shape and psyche is tenuous.

New York City's household garbage, dumped on the curb in plastic bags, ends up in landfills far out of sight. From 1947 to 2001, the city dispatched its refuse to Fresh Kills, a Staten Island wetlands turned municipal dump, which at its peak received 29,000 tons of trash per day, ranking as the largest human-made structure on earth. Now New York's residential garbage, close to 4 million tons of it a year, is shipped by barge and truck to distant landfills, from Niagara Falls to South Carolina.

Waste destination

Metal/glass/plastic recycling

- Paper recycling
- Municipal and commercial waste transfer stations
- Carting services for commercial refuse

Unions   Strikes   Lawsuits

NEW JERSEY

Trash to Waterloo, NY
Trash to Fairport, NY
Trash to Niagara Falls, NY
Trash to Dunmore, PA
Trash to Lowellville, OH
Trash to Steubenville, OH
Trash to Bethlehem, PA
Trash to Ashland, KY
Trash to Morrisville, PA

Trash to Newark, NJ

North Mound
140 ft above
sea level

East Mound
120 ft above
sea level

Springville Creek

Fresh Kills

Richmond Creek

Richmond Ave

Plastics shipped to Chinese markets

West Mound
195 ft above
sea level

Burial mound for
1.2 million tons
of debris from the
World Trade Center

South Mound
130 ft above
sea level

W Shore Expy

Arthur Kill Rd

Port Richmond

Travis-Chelsea

New Springville

Heartland Village

STATEN ISLAND

Fresh Kills

Pratt Industries' Visy Paper Mill receives over half the paper recycled in New York, 1,200 tons a day, much of it turned into corrugated cardboard, especially pizza boxes

Fresh Kills received its last waste from Manhattan when it absorbed the rubble from the destruction of the World Trade Center on September 11, 2001. Holding approximately 108 million tons of New Yorkers' trash, it covers 2,200 acres and is being turned into a park, which, when complete, will be almost three times the size of Central Park.

Arden Heights

Rossville

Arthur Kill

Trash to Bishopville, SC
Trash to Chester, VA
Trash to Waverly, VA

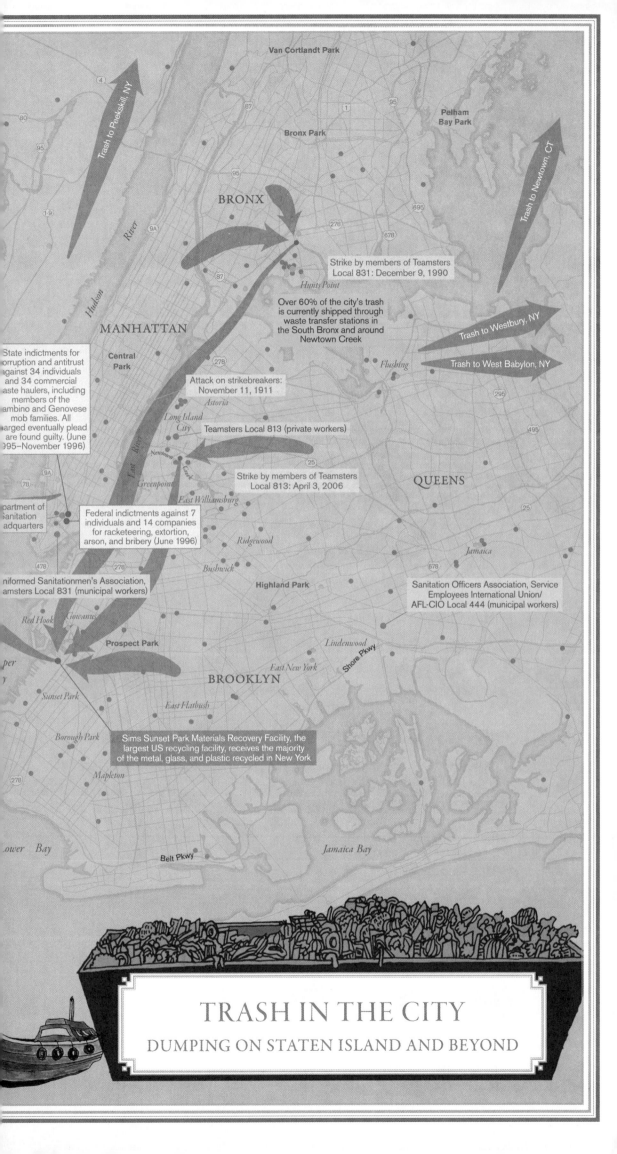

Trash to Peekskill, NY

Trash to Newtown, CT

Van Cortlandt Park

Pelham Bay Park

Bronx Park

BRONX

Hunts Point

Strike by members of Teamsters Local 831: December 9, 1990

Over 60% of the city's trash is currently shipped through waste transfer stations in the South Bronx and around Newtown Creek

Trash to Westbury, NY

Trash to West Babylon, NY

MANHATTAN

Central Park

Flushing

State indictments for corruption and antitrust against 34 individuals and 34 commercial waste haulers, including members of the Gambino and Genovese mob families. All charged eventually plead and are found guilty. (June 1995–November 1996)

Attack on strikebreakers: November 11, 1911

Astoria

Long Island City

Teamsters Local 813 (private workers)

Newtown Creek

Strike by members of Teamsters Local 813: April 3, 2006

Greenpoint

QUEENS

East Williamsburg

Department of Sanitation Headquarters

Federal indictments against 7 individuals and 14 companies for racketeering, extortion, arson, and bribery (June 1996)

Ridgewood

Jamaica

Bushwick

Red Hook   Gowanus

Uniformed Sanitationmen's Association, Teamsters Local 831 (municipal workers)

Highland Park

Sanitation Officers Association, Service Employees International Union/ AFL-CIO Local 444 (municipal workers)

Prospect Park

Lindenwood

Shore Pkwy

per y

Sunset Park

East New York

BROOKLYN

East Flatbush

Borough Park

Sims Sunset Park Materials Recovery Facility, the largest US recycling facility, receives the majority of the metal, glass, and plastic recycled in New York

Mapleton

Lower Bay

Jamaica Bay

Belt Pkwy

TRASH IN THE CITY
DUMPING ON STATEN ISLAND AND BEYOND

17 TRASH IN THE CITY

Throwing things away proposes that there is a place we can label as *away* and then overlook and ignore, and so the "age of garbage" is the age of disposability, and that disposability has a geography, the place where things are disposed of. And what is disposed of resembles other things from the age of garbage, which was also the age of Freud and psychoanalysis, the unconscious, the repressed, the denied, maybe what later critics would call the other or the outcast. New York's repressed other was the landfill on Staten Island, where all the whiskey bottles and cigarette butts, the hot-dog wrappers and newspapers and broken things went, where everything no longer desired or all used up or beginning to spoil found its final resting spot. The stuff turned into towering mounds, imperial middens that overshadowed the Staten Island community next to them. Fresh Kills closed in 2000 but was reopened after 9/11 to receive the rubble that had been the World Trade Center, then closed again and converted to a park that seems to belie this history, to literally smooth it over with a surfacing of earth and greenery. Meanwhile New York City, so good at so many things, notably public transit, remains terrible at garbage. Some West Coast cities have radically reduced their landfill with intensive recycling and curbside composting; New York has not caught up with these programs. The household stuff is bagged up in brand-new bags and set out on display on the curbs, like some misbegotten installation or involuntary self-revelation. There is corruption and redundancy and inefficiency in the private contracting and a huge climate footprint in the current policy of sending the stuff far, far away, as far as Ohio and South Carolina. Somewhere before the age of garbage was an era in which very little was thrown away—chickens and hogs ate food scraps, manure and "night soil" were composted back into the earth, disposable packaging was rare, and even worn-out linen and cotton clothing became paper; somewhere after this era is where we should be headed—and cities with more vigorous recycling and composting programs are already on the way.

CARTOGRAPHY: MOLLY ROY; ARTWORK: LINNEA RUSSELL   MAP APPEARS ON PAGES 140–141.

COMING CLEAN BY LUCY R. LIPPARD

> After the revolution, who's going to pick up the garbage on Monday morning?
> —Mierle Laderman Ukeles, 1971

"It stinks!" This was Staten Islanders' first response when asked about Fresh Kills—their dubious civic landmark. For many years it was the largest landfill in the world, although it has been exhaustively remediated and now reportedly smells like "open meadows." Many residents still bear the scars of their role in New York City's digestive system—the receptacle of almost all of its garbage for almost seventy years. (It was opened in 1947 as a temporary dump on salt marsh and agricultural land.) The landfill has long contributed to Islanders' sense of being a backwater, the forgotten borough, confirmed by slow official response to the devastation wrought by Superstorm Sandy in 2012. Then there was Eric Garner, strangled by a cop on Staten Island in 2014 for selling loose cigarettes. That stank too.

I was born in New York City and spent nine years of childhood and thirty-five years of adult life there. Now and then I went to Staten Island for the ferry ride, art, friends, the Buddhist center, but I've never seen Fresh Kills. *Kill* is a Dutch word for stream. Long an apparent geographical misnomer, the name suddenly made tragic sense in 2001 when the landfill became a sorting ground and then burial site for personal effects and human micro remains from Ground Zero. Some thought that mingling human bodies with garbage would cross a line, defy a social taboo. But expediency won out, and what is now known as West Mound holds the remains, human and architectural, almost a million and a quarter tons of them. A memorial is planned.

I never considered the fate of my trash until artist Mierle Laderman Ukeles brought it to public attention in the 1970s. By the end of the decade, she was appointed Official Unsalaried Artist in Residence with the New York Department of Sanitation and later Honorary Deputy Commissioner of Sanitation. Her ever-expanding Maintenance Art began in 1969 with her own small-scale, underappreciated domestic work as the mother of three small children and progressed to the large-scale, underappreciated work done by the city's sanitation workers. For eleven months in 1979–80, in a "performance" piece called *Touch Sanitation,* she shook hands with all 8,500 of them, on all shifts, choreographing her visits in a geographic spiral of ten "sweeps." She thanked every Sanman for "keeping New York alive," reminding residents that it was their own garbage that stank, not those "housekeepers" who did them the service of hauling it away. Ukeles's now iconic *Social Mirror* (1983), a garbage truck with mirror-lined sides, made the point still clearer. She also choreographed a public Ballet Mécanique of street sweepers and then another with barges. The rest is solid waste history. Ukeles has made public sculpture and performances on a massive scale with municipal sanitation departments all over the world, as well as in museum and gallery installations. (In one of her first Maintenance Art performances, in 1974, she scrubbed the floors of the Wadsworth Atheneum in Hartford, Connecticut— one of fourteen pieces performed in association with my traveling women's conceptual art show, titled *c.7500.*)

Ukeles's preoccupation with "the back half of life" took her from diapers to the 150 million tons of "un-differentiated, un-named, no-value garbage" at Fresh Kills. She has become a role model for ecofeminists and for the increasing number of artists who aspire to rendering legible the land uses and invisible infrastructures on which our lives are built. But where so many such projects consist of documentation or temporary interventions, networked out rather than focused in, and more significant in the art world than the real world, her art has always been based in long-term thinking about the *flow* of materials defining this society. As artist/geographer Trevor Paglen observed in a 2009 article for the *Brooklyn Rail,* "The task of experimental geography . . . is to seize the opportunities that present themselves in the spatial practice of culture. To move beyond critical reflection, critique alone, and political 'attitudes,' into the realm of practice." In 1983 *Flow City,* one of Ukeles's most ambitious works, was proposed for the city's West 59th Street Marine Transfer Facility. Its Passage Ramp, Glass Bridge, and Media Flow Wall were to demonstrate the circulation (and occasional constipation) of our detritus, as a "metaphor for urban vitality." Although the Department of Sanitation spent over a million dollars on the piece, it was never completed due to the decision to close Fresh Kills, and it was never opened to the public.

Ukeles calls landfills "extraordinary urban sites composed of all the things we want to forget . . . a social sculpture we have all produced," and "sort of inner-city-outer-space." Garbage out offers a way of looking in. What goes in must come out. (Sexual innuendoes are appropriate, given how the environment is routinely screwed.) No public place is a better gauge of a society's values than a landfill. After the consumption of global goodies *in* the privacy of our homes, city-dwellers take *out* the garbage. The scale of this disgorging/excretion process is noticeable only during garbage strikes, when the stench of the bursting, plastic-bagged mountains on every street corner permeates daily life. Capitalism thrives on unsustainable growth and expansion while its by-products, its waste, also grow and expand exponentially. In the United States we toss 15 to 25 percent of the food we buy. We throw away stuff coveted by the rest of the world, exposing our social values as we dispose of its use value. All over the poorer world, children scavenge in the dumps where their families are forced to live. (I'm from the *dump* generation, preferring that colloquial term to the sanitized euphemisms of *landfills* and *transfer stations*. The British term is *tips,* presumably referring to the actions of trucks depositing their loads or plates being scraped into plastic bags. More recently we have to factor in *tipping points.*) Commercial waste, which makes up two-thirds of the city's 36,000-ton daily total, did not go to Fresh Kills, and its circuitous journeys are another story, involving intensely competitive private carters, which were sometimes controlled by Mafia groups—including the Gambino and Lucchese families—and other organized crime syndicates. Still, Fresh Kills at its height received about 10 million tons of garbage annually, transferred from barges by cranes and dump trucks to create trash mountains that towered over the neighboring communities.

What fills a landfill? Garbage archaeologist William Rathje says it's not the Styrofoam and disposable diapers we imagine, but paper—which biodegrades very, very slowly, after hundreds and maybe thousands of years. As an aging writer and hard-copy freak, living virtuously off the grid on solar power, owner of far too many books, which may, in this electronic age, end up in landfills, I represent a sizable percentage of the garbage-producing demographic. I shudder to think of my banished personal trash archive.

Although it was estimated that Fresh Kills still had twenty more years of capacity, the landfill was abruptly closed by three Republican officeholders who owed their victories to the people of Staten Island. By 2000 all five New York boroughs had found out-of-state sites to replace it, leading to more transportation by trucks, more climate-changing emissions. The 13,000 tons of residential waste generated by eight million people every day have been diverted into a new "urban waste stream" (another kind of kill). The 2008 bill for collecting and "disposing" of New York's residential trash was around a quarter of a

Linnea Russell, *Untitled,* 2016

billion dollars. The insidious inequalities built into contemporary capitalism still make it easy to tell if you're in a less visible neighborhood that generates little clout or respect by the amount of trash in the streets. Residents tend to internalize neglect until some really heavy community organizing gets under way and pressure is applied to the most effective power points. Artist Lize Mogel, in her *Sludge Economy* (2010), addresses New York's racially unjust sanitation geographies by exploring the stench (workers called the worst of it "maggot juice"), performing picnics in parks built over wastewater treatment plants and other unsavory sites.

According to waste pundit Steve Cohen, the incineration of trash, which can also generate electricity, pollutes less than transporting waste in diesel-fueled trucks to leaking out-of-state landfills; he recommends smaller-scale, community-based waste management facilities that would share the blessings and the burden of this most necessary public service. The Department of Sanitation is currently involved in a long-term process to rebuild its marine transfer stations to export residential waste in containers, by rail and barge—still expensive but not as bad as trucks hauling it out of state and then coming home empty. And then there's recycling, which, even into the twenty-first century, has never been fully enforced in New York; it doesn't pay well enough, so the stuff often ends up in the landfill. Each new mayor makes a resolution to amend this situation. Each new mayor fails.

Ukeles has been waiting to get her hands on Fresh Kills for some forty years. In 1989 it looked as though her time had come. She was designated the "Percent for Art artist of the Fresh Kills landfill" to participate in its eventual closure and end use, which came about in March 2001. She made *Penetration and Transparency Morphed,* a collaborative six-channel video on alternative visions for the site, with the Twin Towers still looming in the distance. Fourteen years later, *Landing,* her Percent for Art project, received final design approval, to become the first permanent artwork at the emerging Freshkills Park. It has three components: two earthworks, *Earth Bench* and *Earth Triangle,* and a soaring, cantilevered *Overlook,* surveying two paths. One offers a long view of the future (vast engineering projects in process, as the urban park landscape slowly reveals itself), and the other looks toward the past (the "ecological theater" of the original wetlands and tidal inlet just below). "This has been my whole professional life!" Ukeles explains. It's been a long haul, and it's not over yet.

If Fresh Kills had stayed open it would soon have become the highest point on the East Coast, another marker of human triumph over nature, dubious heir to the great mounds of the pre-European Mississippian cultures. In 1983 Ukeles ended a formal letter to the commissioner of sanitation with a reference to "the mother of Fresh Kills"—Silbury Hill, the human-made, probably ceremonial mound built in England around 2660 BC. Thirty years later the comparison makes sense. After a tangled bureaucratic history, Fresh Kills' 2,200 acres is now moving toward its reincarnation as a public park almost three times the size of Manhattan's Central Park. The New York Sanitation and Parks and Recreation Departments will be collaborating on its development for decades. Field Operations, the firm of James Corner (architect of the extremely successful High Line on old elevated tracks in Lower Manhattan), won the International Design Competition for the master plan of Fresh Kills in 2001 and has suffered ever since from the frustration of trying to work creatively with forty-five city agencies.

The park plan has been viewed skeptically by some Staten Islanders, but certain aspects of the never-ending purification process are truly green. Methane is harvested on the site, providing energy to heat 20,000 local homes. Tree planting and other beautification efforts began in the 1980s and accelerated in 2008. The mounds of refuse are being capped with an impermeable plastic liner and eight additional layers of barrier material to separate the ground we touch and walk on from the landfill below, where an extensive network of piping and drainage channels works away unseen, emerging here and there in the white stacks of the flare stations, bringing news from the underworld. Reclamation includes a system for the capture of leachate (also known as garbage juice), containment and delivery for treatment, and a slurry wall around the site's perimeter. As sea levels rise with climate change, a rehabilitated Fresh Kills will offer human-made wetland buffers for neighborhoods threatened in the inevitable future storms.

The official website for the new and improved Fresh Kills features a deliriously positive view of the distant future. Areas of the park will boast networks of paths and waterways, accessible by canoe, kayak, foot, horseback, bike, or car, along with diverse wildlife habitats and research and educational facilities. There are existing precedents in "wildlife refuges" built on toxic sites across the country, like the plutonium production and nuclear waste dumps at the former Rocky Mountain Arsenal and Rocky Flats in Colorado or Patricia Johanson's monumental reclamation of a sewage plant in Petaluma, California. Fresh Kills will offer an ironic sanctuary from the climate effects its inefficient history has helped to produce. (It has been a bird sanctuary of sorts since its inception; historical photos show thousands of gulls circling the unloading barges and Athey wagons.)

So all's well that ends well? Fresh Kills emerges from the muck of death and decay smelling like roses? Green capitalism is good for everybody? The park will become a "post-industrial landmark," as one critic called it? As a more or less communal production of social space, we can all take credit for it. Our garbage is becoming a park. Bully for us. Or not. Given the instability of the globe, the world, the planet, and the fact that New York City's mountains of garbage will rise again in someone else's backyard, we should worry. For most of its life, Fresh Kills may have been invisible to the population of New York City, its absentee landlords, but its undead impacts cannot be forgotten, escaping only as friendly gas. A nice park here, another stinking landfill there. So now we (artists, activists, urban planners, advocates for environmental justice) need to go there. There, where our garbage has found a home, near the homes of others who may have had little to say about it. 🪨

18 MYSTERIOUS LAND OF SHAOLIN

You'd never know that only a bay separates Staten Island from the rest of the city based on how the two sides—and it does feel like only two sides—speak of each other. The rest of New York complains that the island is a sleepy, insular borough that is so not worth the effort of exploring—that when people get off the ferry ride past the Statue of Liberty, they should just turn around, their backs to the borough. Staten Islanders argue that the rest of the city is a bunch of parochial bellyachers who have not taken the time to get to know Staten Island's natural beauty and its increasingly diverse population: Sri Lankans, Liberians, Russians, and Chinese joining those that everyone knows of, the Irish and Italians. What everyone agrees on, however, is that the hip-hop group Wu-Tang Clan is the borough's most well-known entity—and beloved export.

It was in riding the Staten Island Ferry to Manhattan, to frequent the old grindhouse movie theaters around Times Square, that these "project kids" saw the kung fu movies—including *Shaolin* and *Wu Tang*—that came to dominate their imagination. The Wu-Tang Clan "formed like Voltron" around their leader, RZA (which stands for Ruler-Knowledge/Wisdom/Understanding-Allah), and he and his creative cohorts formed a hip-hop dynasty that has been a cultural force since their rise to prominence in the early 1990s. Along with making Staten Island—or, as they called it, "Shaolin"—a destination to visit (at least for a while after their spring to popularity), the Wu-Tang Clan has brought together fans of every imaginable background. Whether singing about Staten Island, or Manhattan ("Mecca," in their nomenclature), or Brooklyn ("Medina"), or New Jersey ("New Jerusalem"), the group has found a way to both celebrate and be critical of their home, bringing their varied personas, ferocious beats, and nimble rhymes to bear on topics that range from poverty to philosophy to violence to video games, and much more. On the way, they have won widespread adoration and given homage to Staten Island's Chinese Americans, whose contributions to that borough have been and continue to be invaluable—well beyond inspiring music that breaks the divides between the borough and elsewhere. (Some of the impact of the borough's Chinese residents is given visual homage by the Beijing-born, Brooklyn-based artist Peach Tao.) The Wu-Tang Clan's "Abbot" and leader RZA, who declared in *The Wu-Tang Manual* that "some old myths and old stories have reality inside them," unpacks the group's myths and stories in conversation with Joshua Jelly-Schapiro to show the Staten Island that lies behind "Shaolin."

CARTOGRAPHY: MOLLY ROY; ARTWORK: PEACH TAO   MAP APPEARS ON PAGES 148–149.

from vernal New Amsterdam—giving us the lasting polarities of *downtown* and *uptown*—Brooklyn began at the East River, inching its way down the map.

By about 1900, most of Brooklyn north of the moraine had hardened into cityscape. Everything to its south, with the exception of Coney Island and a handful of subdivisions and old towns, was still rural countryside. Not until the great building boom of the 1920s did the tide of urbanization roll down to the sea. Brooklyn's built environment thus still cleaves to the ancient dualism of outwash and moraine. Morainal Brooklyn is close to Manhattan and blessed with splendid old buildings. It's the city of gentrification, of the batch-made, fixed-gear, and artisanal. Outwash Brooklyn—basically everything south and east of Prospect Park—is the still-real city of strivers and immigrants, scored along old lines of race and religion. Here you can walk for hours without seeing a hipster. Morainal Brooklyn has undergone convulsive change in recent years; outwash Brooklyn moves to a slower pace. My own neighborhood of Marine Park, where a prewar row house costs less than a studio in Dumbo, is virtually unchanged since I was a child. Across the street this morning, the neighbor sweeping her porch has known me since I was a toddler; this afternoon, teens will dribble basketballs by to the courts around the corner, just as my classmate Chris Mullin did thirty-five years ago.

In an era when Brooklyn has become a global "brand" beloved by British celebrities who name kids for the borough, it is the iconic building type of the moraine—the brownstone—that people think of. Like New Orleans with its shotgun houses or San Francisco with its Victorian "painted ladies," Brooklyn is among a handful of American cities essentialized in the popular imagination by a particular kind of residential architecture. The brownstone townhouse signifies Brooklyn as much as the borough's eponymous bridge or Coney Island's Parachute Jump—perhaps more so. When Absolut Vodka sought a design for the Brooklyn edition of its city series, it passed over both for a brownstone stoop. And though the Brooklyn Bridge may have been sold many times, it's never been the focus of the kind of bidding warfare unleashed nowadays when a good brownstone goes on the market. But the brownstone represents only old Brooklyn, the city of the terminal moraine. Outwash Brooklyn has a signature style of residential architecture all its own—the Tudor-revival home, with its faux half-timbered walls and slate tile roofs. This style may not be popular among creative-class elites who clamor for brownstones—at least not yet. But it too is saturated with significance and speaks to the varied and ever-changing ways that our homes can suggest longing at once for the future and for some imagined past.

·   ·   ·

Most of Brooklyn's brownstones were erected in the second half of the nineteenth century, especially after 1865. During that post–Civil War period of mournful eclecticism in architecture, art, and landscape design that Lewis Mumford memorably described in *The Brown Decades* "the colours of American civilization abruptly changed . . . browns had spread everywhere: mediocre drabs, dingy chocolate browns, sooty browns that merged into black. Autumn had come." The brownstone was the archetypal city dwelling of an era typified by melancholia but also new freedoms and steady economic growth. By 1868, the economy had roared to life. Between 1860 and 1890, New York's population doubled; Kings County's tripled.

Long a rural backwater, Brooklyn began urbanizing after speedy, scheduled ferry service to Manhattan became available in 1814. But it was in the years after the Civil War—which witnessed first the completion of Prospect Park (in 1867) and then the opening of the Brooklyn Bridge (in 1883)—that Brooklyn's development really took off, abetted by the long boom of the railroad age. Touring the city in 1886, a *Washington Post* columnist named Julian Ralph described Brooklyn's growth as "the most amazing thing in this part of the world," dwarfing even "all the tales with which the western borderland has nourished us during the past quarter of a century." Riding the "el," he saw "literally miles of dwellings in course of erection in slender rows, in solid squares, in detached units."

Most of these were brownstones. Known to geologists as arkosic sandstone, brownstone is a sedimentary rock formed in the Late Triassic period—some 200 million years ago—from alluvial grains of silica, quartz, feldspar, and mica. Over time these particles were cemented together, hardened and tinted pink by an iron oxide known as hematite. Brooklyn brownstone came first from quarries in New Jersey, at places like Belleville and Newark, which mined the Passaic Formation, a belt of bedrock that arcs up from Pennsylvania across the tri-state region. Another source was Portland, Connecticut, across from Middletown, where stone was excavated at immense quarries that resembled scenes by Piranesi. There, some 1,500 workers mined, cut, and dressed chocolate rock, which they loaded onto riverboats like the Brownstone for shipment to Red Hook and Gowanus Creek.

Brownstone townhouses came in a variety of flavors that followed the rise and fall of architectural fashion—Italianate, Neoclassical, Second Empire, Romanesque, even Gothic. Developers were mostly small and speculative, building homes in gangs of three or four, sometimes filling an entire block. Brownstones were expensive at first, but mass production soon brought their cost down. Forged metalwork was replaced by cast iron poured into a variety of ornamental molds. Terra-cotta replaced carved stone; hand-worked wood trim was increasingly cut by mechanized planers, routers, and lathes. Even the price of the namesake stone fell, as steam-powered derricks and saws reduced the labor needed to quarry and cut the rock. By the 1880s, a building type long associated with great wealth had moved within reach of a middle-class budget.

One of the ironies of the Brooklyn brownstone is the fact that the celebrated rock is only skin-deep—chocolate frosting on brick-and-timber pound cake. This was hardly meant to be deceptive, at least at first; references in the *Brooklyn Eagle* in the 1850s were mostly to "brown-stone-front houses." But as brownstones slid down the economic food chain, class-fretful buyers required their buildings to make ever-bolder statements of status and upward mobility. By the 1880s, when references to brownstone as mere façade cladding became scarce, and both the *Eagle* and the *New York Times* adopted the shorthand "brownstone," builders began cranking up the aspirational quotient of their product in more overt ways. They used motifs meant to bespeak poshness and exclusivity—mammoth cornices, doors so massive they could crush a skull, elephantine cast-iron railings, windows big enough to let all passersby see the tasteful appointments within. But Brooklyn's long brownstone afternoon was soon to end, and it did so almost in the blink of an eye.

The cause was a change in architectural tastes brought about by the World's Columbian Exposition of 1893. The chief organizer of Chicago's world's fair, Daniel H. Burnham, oversaw the building of a corn-fed Roman Forum so white and brightly lit that its glow—fed by three times the electricity used by the rest of Chicago each night—could be seen 100 miles away. Ending America's long brown days of bereavement, Burnham's radiant White City ushered off Mumford's shades. In Brooklyn hardly a brownstone was built after 1895. All the rage now were bow-fronted Renaissance-revival townhouses dressed in white limestone. Demand for the chocolate rock tumbled. Connecticut's Portland quarries mined $575,000 worth of stone in 1890; by 1908 that figure had fallen to just $56,000.

· · ·

In time, brownstones in neighborhoods like Crown Heights and Bedford-Stuyvesant would be divided and subdivided into apartments—they became housing for striving immigrants from eastern Europe and the American South and, later on, the Caribbean. As brownstone Brooklyn began to fade, the outwash empire came into its own—especially during the 1920s, when Brooklyn underwent a construction boom even more extensive than that of the 1880s. America had changed dramatically by then, and so had architectural tastes. Now even neoclassicism was out of favor, and the Victorian brownstone had become something of an embarrassment. The 1920s were years of great progress. National wealth doubled, women gained the right to vote, automobiles filled the streets, and jazz filled the air. But it was also a conservative, even reactionary, era. The Russian revolution sparked fears of Bolshevism. Temperance radicals forced abstinence on all, creating the Mob overnight. Unprecedented immigration changed the ethnic composition of the nation's cities, spawning a generation of cross-burning yahoos committed to keeping America white, Anglo-Saxon, and Protestant. Well-born racists like Madison Grant helped pass severe limits on immigration from Asia and eastern and southern Europe. Similar fears spurred Congress to establish the Washington Bicentennial Commission in 1924, nominally charged with planning a big 200th birthday bash for George in 1932, but really aimed at assuring that all those immigrants from Sicily and Galicia were washed of unsavory political notions.

All this might seem rather remote from architecture, but it was not. Buildings reify society's yearnings as well as its fears, and the architecture of the 1920s did just that. The dominant styles of the era all harkened back to the colonial era or that putative motherland of America, Olde England. Gothic forms were slapped on everything from dormitories to skyscrapers. The neo-Georgian became a style of choice for civic buildings like the Museum of the City of New York. A national craze for clapboard colonial-revival homes was set off by Colonial Williamsburg, a living monument to a framed set of American values and traditions. Sears Roebuck marketed mail-order houses like the Lexington and Jefferson and was even commissioned by Mayor Jimmy Walker's administration to manufacture a full-scale replica of Mount Vernon for Prospect Park. But the most popular style of residential architecture in New York City in this period reached even further back in time—to a storied age of chivalry and Shakespeare.

Like the colonial and Georgian styles, the Tudor revival was born of fears that America's charter culture was faltering in the face of an influx of millions of eastern and southern European immigrants; it was "a style for the WASP," writes architectural historian Gavin Townsend, "a fortress symbol of established Anglo-American lineage at a time when Poles, Slavs, Italians and other 'undesirables' were seemingly flooding the country." Popular since 1910 for upscale suburban homes, Tudorism was perfectly positioned to take during a building boom that saw New York race ahead of London to become the largest city in the world. As high demand for housing was joined to a robust national economy, New York governor Al Smith signed a 1920 law that eliminated property taxes on new housing for a decade.

This tax holiday, combined with the expansion of the subways and utility infrastructure into long-rural parts of Brooklyn and Queens, unleashed a frenzy of residential construction unlike anything in the city before or since. Gotham's street grid rolled out to the east and south like a mighty carpet of brick and mortar, leaving in its wake a vast new landscape of bedroom communities for a generation of New Yorkers raised in crowded tenements and eager for homes of their own. In nearly all these transit suburbs, the prevailing style was Tudor. But unlike in Westchester or Riverdale, the Tudor style here was an architecture of aspiration more than of yearning for some dewy Anglo past: the biggest consumers, and builders, of outer-borough Tudorism were the very "undesirables"—Jews, Italians, Irish—whose presence helped spawn the revanchist style in the first place.

The architect of the Tudor row house that I grew up in on East 33rd Street was a Jewish immigrant named Philip Freshman, whose family fled Russia first for London and then Brooklyn. Freshman designed over 100 "English Tudor Homes" for Lawrence Rukeyser's Laurye Homes venture in Marine Park. Rukeyser was also the son of Jewish immigrants. He made and lost a fortune in the building industry, with the company he co-founded—Colonial Sand and Stone—supplying concrete to thousands of building projects all over the city in the 1920s, from Brooklyn row houses to the runways of Floyd Bennett Field to Yankee Stadium. The Tudor homes built by Freshman and Rukeyser invoked not Mother

England but resplendent houses erected a decade earlier by and for the patrician elite in Riverdale and Scarsdale and Forest Hills Gardens. By emulating the emulators, they turned a style for the rich into one for the masses. The "banker's Tudor" of Westchester became the "teller's Tudor" of Flatbush, St. Albans, and Marine Park.

By the time Al Smith's tax holiday ended in 1931, most of Brooklyn's vast outwash plain had been transformed into a stage-set Camelot, a wonderland of steep gables and jerkin-head roofs, battlements, turrets, and half-timbered walls. Of course, it was easy to mock this world of strivers and working stiffs, and easier still to poke fun at its make-believe architecture. Critics marveled at how an old-world style could possibly be right for an age of airplanes, skyscrapers, and penicillin. It was all just "a delicious piece of stage scenery," wrote architect Russell Whitehead, no different from "the peasant village Marie Antoinette caused to be erected in the Trianon Gardens." Lewis Mumford worried that whenever "a sophisticated age attempts to reproduce the forms of a simple one . . . the result is bound to be ephemeral."

And yet the Tudor-scapes of Queens and southern Brooklyn have endured. In a city that seems to build today only for the rich, it's worth recalling how much affordable housing was churned out by the profit-hungry speculative builders of the 1920s. The homes they built were neither as resplendent nor as ostentatious as the brownstones of morainal Brooklyn, but they have stood time's tests just as well. And as home prices in "brownstone Brooklyn" continue to skyrocket, the brick row houses of outwash Brooklyn are still largely untouched by gentrification—at least for now. Their owners' taste may run to stainless-steel railings in place of the original wrought iron, peach-pink stucco slapped atop brick, corrugated awnings, and double-hung vinyl windows from China. These renovations may be bungling, but they signal an architecture still suffused with the funk and pulse of life, with an unbroken, unmediated link to the past, unpolished, undiscovered by the merchants of twee.

PRISONERS OF RED HOOK BY FRANCISCO GOLDMAN

An AP story published on Sunday, November 14, 1982, in the inside pages of the *New York Times* under the headline "FOREIGN SEAMEN ABANDONED ON DECREPIT SHIP" began: "Seventeen foreign seamen lived on a rat-infested floating slum on the Brooklyn waterfront for months and endured a lack of plumbing and electricity on a ship that had been abandoned by its anonymous owner. . . . The seamen, Central Americans who speak no English, had been bound to the ship by immigration laws and by their desire to work. On Wednesday, the Seamen's Church [Institute] placed them at a hotel for seafarers." The crewmen had been hired in Costa Rica and Nicaragua by a shipping agency that offered wages of $200 a month to repair the 7,000-ton cargo freighter and to serve as her crew once the ship was fixed and put out to sea.

"When the ship is fixed, the ship will sail" became a kind of exhortatory refrain aboard the *Sea Lift*. From the deck, looking south, the crew could see the lichen–pale green of the Statue of Liberty rising over that fall's low horizon of bare and raggedly brown trees. One day the Nicaraguan hired as a cook, one of the few crewmen with previous shipboard experience, cracked, "When that statue walks, this ship will sail." For all their efforts, the *Times* article reported, the virtually enslaved crewmen were unable to fix the ship. In September the ship's anonymous owner had stopped paying wages and had apparently abandoned ship and crewmen to their fate.

Speaking on behalf of the Seamen's Church Institute, the director of its Center for Seafarers' Rights, the Reverend Paul Chapman, told the AP reporter that the ship "was only good for scrap." Probably the owner had never even intended to run the *Sea Lift*, once she was fixed, as a working ship at sea at all, instead planning to sell her for a handsome profit—a virtual pile of floating scrap that, through the undetected ruse of exploiting a virtually enslaved crew, had been turned into an apparently seaworthy cargo freighter. Now the Seamen's Church Institute had evacuated the crewmen and put them up in its hotel for seafarers at the tip of Manhattan, near the Battery. According to the article, the rescued crewmen would be sent home to Central America on Tuesday.

I telephoned Reverend Chapman and asked to be able to interview the crewmen before they went back. I was in my twenties and had recently temporarily returned to New York from my first sojourn as a freelance magazine reporter in Central America. Fifteen years later I'd finally completed a second novel that began for me with those first news accounts. The novel was inspired as much by a setting as by its original story, the ghostly landscape that the old industrial waterfront of Red Hook, once the vital heart of the country's busiest break-bulk cargo port, had become by the 1980s, forty years or so past its heyday. The neighborhood and its working life were devastated by, among other factors, the rise of containerization in shipping transportation, the partitioning and isolating of the South Brooklyn neighborhood by Robert Moses's Gowanus Expressway (blocks of mostly European immigrant homes and businesses along Third Avenue were demolished to make way for the expressway, which Moses's biographer Robert A. Caro called "a Chinese Wall"), and Moses's influence in the 1962 cancellation of forty-year-old plans to finally build a cross-harbor rail tunnel between Brooklyn and New Jersey, an early indicator of the Port Authority's eventually mostly-realized ambitions to move all of its port operations to New Jersey's burgeoning shipping facilities.

Of course most of that former ghost landscape is also gone now, so much of it vanished without a trace, like the old Todd Shipyards' dry dock, paved over to make way for an IKEA parking lot in gentrifying Red Hook, with its sprouting of wine bars, a handful of destination restaurants, and the like amid the old row houses of Van Brunt Street. So the story of those stranded Central American seamen—urban castaways, Odyssean navigators on a ship that never moves, seamen from impoverished and war-torn tropical latitudes on a journey into a true New York City "Heart of Darkness"—is the story of a landscape that isn't there anymore: the ghostly terrain of long-abandoned ruins and practically marooned still-active shipping piers and business survivors in that stretch of the old industrial waterfront of Red Hook and the isolated, blighted residential area, one of the most extreme loci of the city's 1980s crack epidemic, just outside the old shipping yards but still inside Moses's "Chinese Wall." (The story's co-narrator was the Central America that those seamen believed they had at least for a time honorably escaped from, the places and people that had shaped their lives and that they returned to in memory and desire every night as they lay upon their rotting mattresses in their ship-shaped, rat-infested, garbage-strewn ruin of floating scrap.)

A drive up the Gowanus Expressway provides a now-unobstructed view of the pier where the *Sea Lift* was berthed in 1982. The Grain Terminal, which once had the capacity to hold two million bushels of offloaded grain, now stands isolated and behemoth over what thirty years ago was a cluttered landscape, intimidating and concealed. There what was essentially a criminal slave ship remained hidden for nearly six months without anyone—police, neighbors, port authorities, or institutions responsible for monitoring the port, such as the Seamen's Church Institute with its ship visitation program—discovering or reporting it. You could go inside some of those old terminals and lie in the sand, looking up through the tattered roofs, cargo hooks still hanging from their rafters, and you could hear the warbling of the wood doves that nested inside.

An article in the *Daily News* reported that, "When they ventured off the ship to escape the nightmare situation . . . a number of the men were hit over the head with pipes and beaten up by neighborhood thugs." They had been attacked, badly beaten, robbed of whatever valuables and money they'd been carrying. At night, intrepid youths partied on the pier, threw beer bottles up onto the deck or smashed them against the hull, and shouted taunts at the cowering foreign castaways. Red Hook is a long-stigmatized neighborhood—in such short stories as "The Horror at Red Hook" it inspired some of the most hair-raising xenophobic hyperbole of H. P. Lovecraft, Donald Trump's secret speechwriter and hairstylist; Al Capone got his start as a small-time criminal there in the kind of rough dockworker community portrayed in *On the Waterfront*. But by 1988, when *Life* magazine called it one of the ten worst neighborhoods in the USA and labeled it "the crack capital of America," Red Hook had become an outright urban pariah.

Driving through the neighborhood at night in the 1980s, you'd see how small clusters of figures territorially staked out street corners, like the *halcones,* or lookouts, employed by the drug-dealing gangs that now control certain urban neighborhoods of Mexico City. It was probably because Red Hook was such a marginalized and isolated neighborhood that, in 1972, a small group of Guatemalan immigrants was able to gain official weekend access, which nobody else was petitioning for, to the Red Hook Ball Fields, where they established La Liga de Futbol Guatemala, New York City's pioneering immigrant soccer league. In 1974, when the league's first annual championship was held, the majority of the teams were Guatemalan, the rest Salvadoran, Honduran, Costa Rican, Colombian, and Ecuadorian. The first champion was Livingston FC, made up of Bronx residents from the Afro-Carib town in Guatemala of that name. Now widely known simply as La Liga, its matches are the impetus of the festive weekend food vendor gatherings along the perimeter of the main field.

The *Sea Lift*'s crewmen encountered some of their fellow *centroaméricanos* at those Liga matches; I remember one of them telling me about drinking rum with some of the fans one afternoon. But the league goes into winter hibernation after its September championship march, so that weekend community wasn't around to possibly provide help when the weather turned cold and the situation aboard the ship became desperate. I met with the crewmen more than once before they were sent home. Perhaps the most memorable story told to me was one that was just too incredible to find its way, in any form, into the novel. He was one of the Costa Ricans—I think his name was José—a notably handsome *muchacho,* the only crew member who'd dared to occasionally venture off the ship following the incident of the mass mugging. Somehow, José fell in with the Reverend Moon's "Moonies," who then had headquarters in the New Yorker Hotel, near Penn Station. Like other members of that religious cult, José used to sell roses on the streets. I imagine that he, with permission or not, kept some of the money. At the end of a day of rose-selling, he'd return to the cultists' hotel lair, where, José told me, he was able to take a hot shower, receive some fresh clothes, eat as much as he wanted, get a decent night's sleep, and even have sex. He was constantly proselytized and obediently attended some religious or prayer sessions, though to no effect—whatever they said to him went in one ear and out the other. José was a shipwrecked sailor in New York in search of salvations more tangible than mystical or divine. He took what he wanted from the Moonies and then dutifully returned to the ship, over the Brooklyn Bridge, on foot, bringing back whatever food supplies he could afford.

What happened to the crewmen of the *Sea Lift* over six months in 1982 is only one of infinite stories that belong to Red Hook. But it certainly wasn't the only time something like that happened there. On May 2, 1983, a new story appeared in the *Times* under the headline "17 CREWMEN STRANDED ON SHIP SEIZED AT SOUTH BROOKLYN PIER." This time it was a "rusting oil tanker" that had been abandoned at a Columbia Street pier, and the crew comprised seamen from India, Pakistan, El Salvador, Ghana, and Sri Lanka, some of whom hadn't been paid in sixteen months. Again, it was the Seamen's Church Institute that finally rescued them. The story mentioned the seventeen Central Americans rescued only six months before from their "floating slum" in Red Hook, and it quoted the Reverend Paul Chapman: "They're lovely people. We find so often on these third-world ships simple, honest, articulate people, often brighter than the situation calls for. Your heart really goes out to them."

20 BROOKLYN VILLAGES

It's said so often that it has become a cloying truism: New York City is its neighborhoods. Were this not the case its people would all get swallowed up by scale. The city is only manageable—and appreciable—in slices. Whether native, visitor, or commuter, you can't help but notice that each neighborhood is cordoned not merely by its official municipal borders but also by its character. The easy warmth of Riverdale in the Bronx and the bustling energy of Flushing in Queens and the playful street life of Crown Heights in Brooklyn are among the hundreds, if not thousands, of personalities that characterize swaths of blocks in this maddeningly multitudinous city of 8.5 million residents.

Some neighborhoods feel so self-contained—and are treated as such (a resident proudly declaring, "I haven't passed 14th Street since 1982!")—that they are effectively villages. And, like villages, these neighborhoods provide a place to both connect (with those nearby) and disconnect (from those outside your community) for the sake of making a complex world understandable. This simultaneous push and pull is necessary in a city so large and dynamic and unmasterable as New York. Those who populate it are forever trying to contain and tame it—they are forever trying to convert a metropolis into a village, making new limits in a limitless sea of characters. The city's most populous borough has undergone a lot of changes in recent years, making it the site of fierce battles and new enclaves. The entire city now looks to Brooklyn—a place other boroughs once scorned as not worth the trip over bridges or under tunnels—as a model of what they'd like to become, or a warning of what could befall them.

CARTOGRAPHY: MOLLY ROY; ARTWORK: HANNAH CHALEW MAP APPEARS ON PAGES 166–167.

FREED BUT NOT FREE BY SHARIFA RHODES-PITTS

In 2014 in Brooklyn's Flatbush neighborhood, two women aged thirty and twenty-three knocked on an apartment door to gain entry and then demanded at gunpoint that its current occupants vacate the premises. As reported in the *New York Daily News,* by way of motive one of the women later declared to police that "she didn't like 'that white people were moving into the area.'" The *New York Post* added that one of the women was angry that the apartment had been rented to three white residents instead of to her. The three victims—two men and one woman—fled the apartment upon baroque threats of death. ("If you call the police or management company, I'll pick five people off each of your phones and kill them, and if you're not out of here in 24 hours, five guys will come back and kill you all.") The two women, identified in reports as Precious Parker and Sabrina James, remained in the apartment for two days before being apprehended by the police. Headlines detailing the incident declared the women to have "squatted" in the apartment after the armed

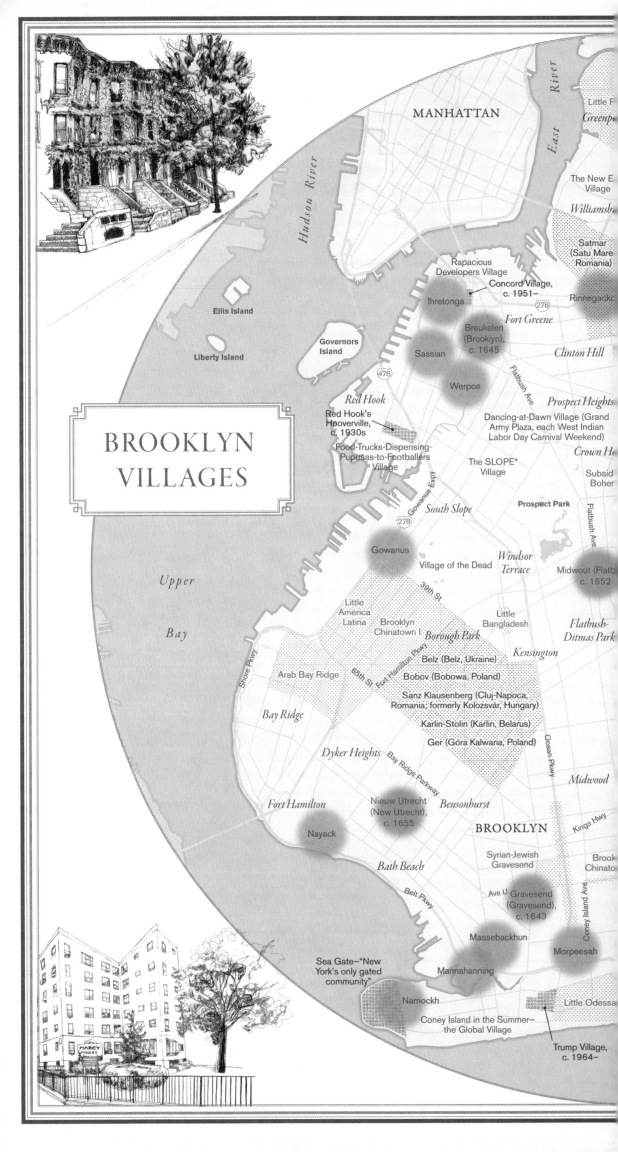

BROOKLYN VILLAGES

MANHATTAN

Hudson River

East River

Little P
Greenp

The New E
Village

Williamsb

Satmar
(Satu Mare
Romania)

Rinnegackc

Ellis Island

Governors
Island

Liberty Island

Rapacious
Developers Village

Concord Village,
c. 1951—

Ihretonga

Fort Greene

Breukelen
(Brooklyn),
c. 1645

Sassian

Clinton Hill

Werpos

Prospect Heights

Red Hook

Red Hook's
Hooverville,
c. 1930s

Flatbush Ave

Dancing-at-Dawn Village (Grand
Army Plaza, each West Indian
Labor Day Carnival Weekend)

Crown He

Food-Trucks-Dispensing-
Pupusas-to-Footballers
Village

The SLOPE*
Village

Subsid
Boher

Prospect Park

Flatbush Ave

Upper

Bay

Gowanus

South Slope

Village of the Dead

Windsor
Terrace

Midwout (Flatb
c. 1652

39th St

Little
América
Latina

Brooklyn
Chinatown I

Little
Bangladesh

Flatbush-
Ditmas Park

Borough Park

Kensington

Belz (Belz, Ukraine)

Bobov (Bobowa, Poland)

Sanz Klausenberg (Cluj-Napoca,
Romania; formerly Kolozsvár, Hungary)

Karlin-Stolin (Karlin, Belarus)

Ger (Góra Kalwaria, Poland)

Shore Pkwy

Arab Bay Ridge

65th St

Fort Hamilton Pkwy

Ocean Pkwy

Bay Ridge

Midwood

Dyker Heights

Bay Ridge Parkway

Fort Hamilton

Nieuw Utrecht
(New Utrecht),
c. 1655

Bensonhurst

BROOKLYN

Kings Hwy

Nayack

Bath Beach

Syrian-Jewish
Gravesend

Brook
Chinato

Belt Pkwy

Ave U Gravesend
(Gravesend),
c. 1643

Coney Island Ave

Massebackhun

Morpeesah

Sea Gate—"New
York's only gated
community"

Mannahanning

Narriockh

Little Odessa

Coney Island in the Summer—
the Global Village

Trump Village,
c. 1964—

MARCY
HOUSES

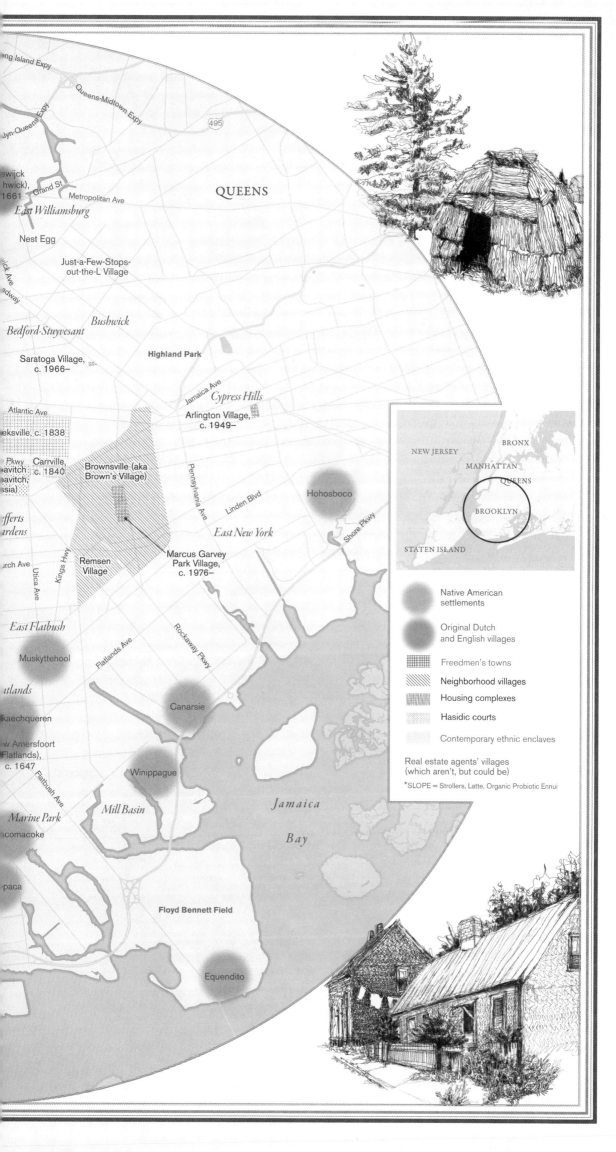

Long Island Expy

Queens-Midtown Expy

Jyn-Queens Expy

Grand St

Metropolitan Ave

495

QUEENS

swijck (hwick), 1661

East Williamsburg

Nest Egg

Just-a-Few-Stops-out-the-L Village

ck Ave

adway

Bushwick

Bedford-Stuyvesant

Saratoga Village, c. 1966–

Highland Park

Jamaica Ave

Cypress Hills

Arlington Village, c. 1949–

Atlantic Ave

eksville, c. 1838

Pkwy
avitch
oavitch
sia)

Carrville, c. 1840

Brownsville (aka Brown's Village)

Pennsylvania Ave

Linden Blvd

Hohosboco

Shore Pkwy

East New York

Marcus Garvey Park Village, c. 1976–

fferts
ardens

Remsen Village

urch Ave

Utica Ave

Kings Hwy

East Flatbush

Flatlands Ave

Rockaway Pkwy

Muskyttehool

atlands

kaechqueren

w Amersfoort
Flatlands),
c. 1647

Canarsie

Flatbush Ave

Winippague

Marine Park

scomacoke

Mill Basin

Jamaica

Bay

paca

Floyd Bennett Field

Equendito

NEW JERSEY

BRONX

MANHATTAN

QUEENS

BROOKLYN

STATEN ISLAND

Native American settlements

Original Dutch and English villages

Freedmen's towns

Neighborhood villages

Housing complexes

Hasidic courts

Contemporary ethnic enclaves

Real estate agents' villages (which aren't, but could be)

*SLOPE = Strollers, Latte, Organic Probiotic Ennui

Philip Bell, *Coney Island*, 2008

encounter. This pointed description, along with the women's alleged racial motivation, transforms the incident from just another bizarre made-for-tabloid Gotham crime to a flashpoint in the protracted struggle black and poor people endure to settle in this city.

The women were arrested for robbery, burglary, unlawful imprisonment, criminal possession of a weapon, and menacing. No mention of hate crime charges was made (except from the army of commenters asking sarcastically why Al Sharpton, Jesse Jackson, and Eric Holder weren't jumping on the case). Something about the headline gave off a dark humor, as if it belonged to the satirical news so beloved by our age. It was a crime resulting more from weariness than malice, one that openly declared something many people think and say without resorting to similar acts of violence. Furnished with only the bare details of newspaper accounts, I hesitate to make the women's actions say more than the women themselves are alleged to have said. Their act cannot be understood in any clear or credible way as political—the race of the victims and the race of the perpetrators do not automatically make the event coherent. It does not conform to any post-civil-rights-era tales we tell about how we are going to bring about a just world.

But can the actions of these two women be understood as a form of resistance? An inherently futile form of resistance, to be sure, for they had literally backed themselves into a corner with no means of escape. Inevitably, they would draw the attention of the state. Perhaps, like many of their peers, they were already under the surveillance of the state. Which is to say, perhaps they were already living in a room with no exit. The attempted theft—apartment-jacking?—sought as its loot the physical space, the lease, the occupancy. But once they had the space, what were they going to do with it? They could not flee. They could not exchange it for money. They were stuck in a worse version of the same situation.

Perhaps what they were stealing was time. I am sending myself into the news reports. Into those two days of squatting. I am sitting with Precious Parker and Sabrina James and their gun and their tiredness—no, I'll say it—*my* tiredness, because I, too, would not be able to afford to move into the neighborhood where I now live, only I don't have a gun or the will to use it. There is nothing to do in this room but wait, so we tell each other stories. I tell them about Fannie Lou Hamer, famously "sick and tired of being sick and tired." Hamer endured beatings and was part of the larger nonviolent movement, but in response to the constant threat of white supremacist terrorism in Mississippi, she said, "I keep a shotgun in every corner of my bedroom and the first cracker even look like he wants to throw some dynamite on my porch won't write his mama again." I am telling them about the occupation of a tent city in Lowndes County, Alabama, erected when black share-

Philip Bell, *Pigeon over Brooklyn,* 2005

croppers were forced off their farms for attempting to vote, in the same place where the first Black Panther Party was founded.

Precious Parker and Sabrina James used the threat of violence to procure—however temporarily—space to live, to be. I am working to understand their actions in light of other happenings in the city that we have agreed are legal and nonviolent. It is supposedly nonviolent when real estate developers secure special privileges for including "affordable" housing in new luxury buildings and then create a second, separate entrance—a "poor door"—for the underclass of residents to use. It is supposedly nonviolent when landlords and brokers in Crown Heights, Brooklyn, systematically dispossess renters by means of paltry lease buyouts and unjustified evictions.

If this act of "apartment-jacking" has any legitimacy, it is borrowed from the very founding of this nation. Here was petty crime as a form of historical reenactment. Without the benefit of Pilgrim-period costumes, Parker and James rehearsed the method by which property was violently transferred from the indigenous people of this land to colonial settlers.

. . .

In my book *Harlem Is Nowhere,* I summarized the problem of Harlem's future as a black place thusly: This is our land that we don't own. Here is a territory to which black people have a spiritual, psychic claim, by dint of having suffered there, having loved there, having stewarded generations in the face of destruction there. The attachment to place across generations is a topic I have spoken about publicly, repeatedly, seeking to assert the value of rootedness in a time when its lived reality is eroding. But I did not in the writing or the speaking realize that I was doing so while sitting in a room with no exit. The violent transfer of land to European settlers created the fiction of property just as it enshrined the legend of the lifeless, worthless, soulless black body that could be turned into a slave. Truly, our land that is not ours.

Consider James Weeks, a Virginia longshoreman who was most probably a former bondsman. Perhaps before he purchased the land that became Weeksville, he had purchased his own freedom. That the purchase of one's own liberty was a pragmatic response to the madness of enslavement is easily understood. But existence within the terms of such freedom requires submission to the idea that you can be bought. Emancipation does not undo this; freedom does not make you wholly free. The freedman who finds himself a piece of property inevitably joins the system that perpetrated his bondage and violently usurped indigenous life. (Note the adjective *freed,* which makes its subject into the object of another man's actions: a freed man is not the same as a free man.) This does not discredit the significance of Weeksville, but helps us properly examine the conditions under which it was built. It was a bastion of the idea of freedom in a land fundamentally unfree. It was a room without an exit—but we could huddle there and protect each other and comfort each other and tell stories.

Weeksville is remembered as a refuge for blacks fleeing Manhattan after the Draft Riots of 1863, but the settlement was built just four years after the Anti-Abolitionist Riots of 1834, when thousands of whites destroyed black churches, homes, businesses, and other locations associated with the abolitionist movement. What kind of house might you build in a time of riots? The preservation experts who worked on the 1983 restoration of the Weeksville houses and who were accustomed to working with "high-style architectural details" noted, with a touch of disdain, that "we're really dealing with low-level vernacular structures." It was "what the average guy would build . . . what the guy who looks at Popular Mechanics would build if he was going to build an airplane. It would look something like a 747, but would have a Volkswagen engine in it." The *New York Times* described the houses as having "no distinct architectural style." But perhaps the effort to preserve and restore the structures—that is, to make them conform to what we understand as a building—erases their most intriguing elements. Perhaps the houses were built in a style beyond vernacular, as yet unrecognized by architectural study. Call it Afro-brutalism, proto-fugitivism, or pre-destructionism. This is the house you would build with meager resources on the unsteady ground of American unfreedom, with the smell of burning black buildings not long on the wind.

Insofar as we yearn to commemorate such efforts, the attempt at sovereignty within the bounds of Fulton Street and Ralph, East New York and Troy Avenues, was a monument already upon its "rediscovery" in 1968 by preservationists hovering in a prop plane. The people who lived near the Hunterfly buildings in the housing projects erected as triumphs of urban renewal did not require their discovery, interpretation, or commemoration. Was not the view of the crumbling shacks as seen from a project apartment window interpretation enough?

· · ·

The city, we're sometimes told, is composed of villages. Fruits of segregation or identification, shaped by the churn of developers' schemes and capital's march, some of the places now called "Villages"—those cubic blocks called projects—evince the city's old will to push those it doesn't wish to see to the margins, where they'll remain (unless of course those projects sit in now-rich neighborhoods and are doomed, too, to be sold off). All sit atop settlements that came before. Most of these—from the Lenape villages of the Canarsee or Nayack to those of the Dutch who chased off the Lenape or the English who came next—are no more commemorated than the other "freedmen's village," Carrville, which once also stood near where Precious Parker and Sabrina James made for themselves a fleeting space in the city, and where Weeksville once stood, too.

Visiting these sites now, we're reminded that when building on unsteady ground and stolen territory, perhaps the most important material is time, and the ability to inhabit an expanded idea of history like the one that Columbia professor Saidiya Hartman offers us when she asserts, "I, too, live in the time of slavery, by which I mean I am living in the future created by it."

An earlier version of this essay was published in *Creative Time Reports,* www.creativetimereports.org, September 17, 2014.

21 PUBLIC/PRIVATE

Public used to be a word that summoned up glory, and homage to the idea of the public was paid by buildings like Grand Central Station, the great cathedrals for everyday populism. The word shifted; the term *public housing* now brings up images of Bauhausian brutalism, danger, and neglect, though the 328 New York City Housing Authority (NYCHA) residential complexes that accommodate 400,000 souls—the equivalent of the whole population of Tulsa or Minneapolis—constitute some of the greenest housing in the city. New Yorkers are exceptional among Americans in their reliance on public transportation and their possession of a great public transit system, in their grace at living in public among strangers while the denizens of many suburbs and sprawling cities cower in car-based and socioeconomically segregated spaces. In New York 1.1 million children are enrolled in one or another of the city's 1,800 schools. You could celebrate New York as a capital of democratic public life, except that it is also the capital of the opposite. As a major world center for the transnational super-wealthy, it is the home of many of the architects of the attacks on the public sphere in recent years, and of course in that narrative Wall Street looms large. The new wealth is sometimes a direct incursion on public space, as when luxury towers on 57th Street put Central Park's lower reaches in the shade. Sunlight literally becomes a private luxury, stolen from the park often seen as one of the nation's greatest democratic spaces. The children of the elite travel in private cars, go to private schools, and have a host of luxuries, privileges, and enrichments thrust upon them, from specialists in packing for camp to SAT tutors to expensive party organizers and entertainers, as well as entrance into private spaces whose fees are steep. To read accounts of their lives is to recognize that their parents regard life as a brutal competition and anxiously try to keep their children ahead in the race with in-utero enrollments in the preschools that set them on the long road to elite success, with rewards all along the way. Equality is often imagined as a flat landscape, a level playing field; this is a map of Manhattan as a place as far from level as high-altitude luxury towers can make it. The public sphere is often magnificent in New York; the private sphere throws shade all over it.

CARTOGRAPHY: MOLLY ROY; ARTWORK: KELSEY GARRITY-RILEY ✺ MAP APPEARS ON PAGES 172–173.

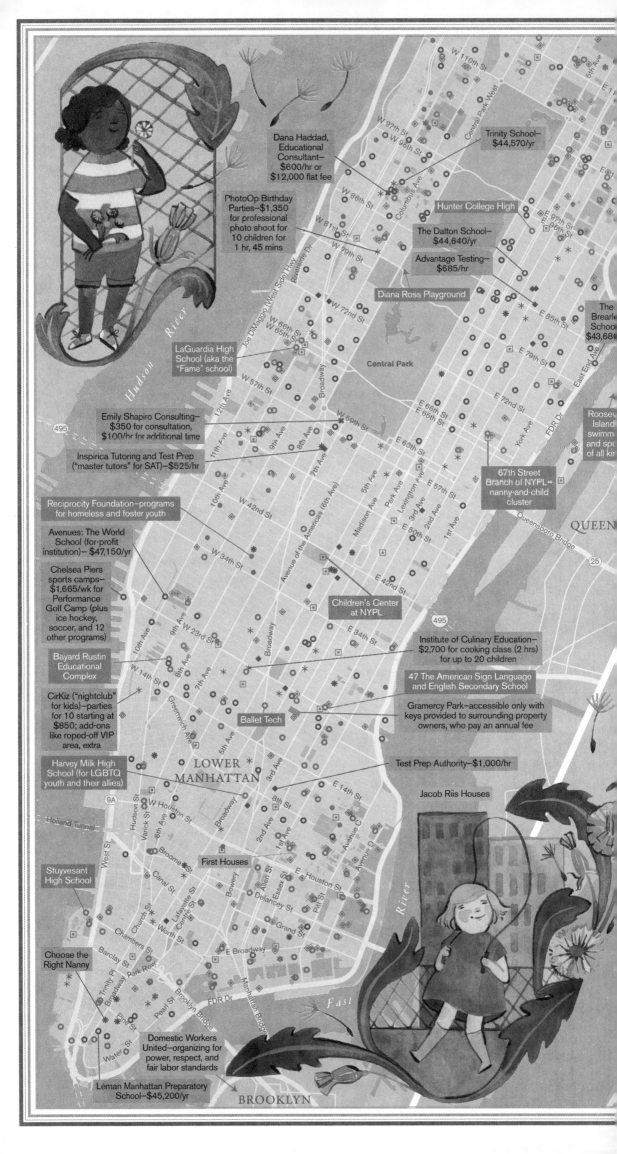

Dana Haddad, Educational Consultant–$600/hr or $12,000 flat fee

PhotoOp Birthday Parties–$1,350 for professional photo shoot for 10 children for 1 hr, 45 mins

Trinity School–$44,570/yr

Hunter College High

The Dalton School–$44,640/yr

Advantage Testing–$685/hr

Diana Ross Playground

The Brearley School–$43,680

LaGuardia High School (aka the "Fame" school)

Central Park

Emily Shapiro Consulting–$350 for consultation, $100/hr for additional time

Inspirica Tutoring and Test Prep ("master tutors" for SAT)–$525/hr

Roosevelt Island swimming and sports of all kinds

67th Street Branch of NYPL–nanny-and-child cluster

QUEENS

Reciprocity Foundation–programs for homeless and foster youth

Avenues: The World School (for-profit institution)– $47,150/yr

Chelsea Piers sports camps– $1,665/wk for Performance Golf Camp (plus ice hockey, soccer, and 12 other programs)

Children's Center at NYPL

Institute of Culinary Education– $2,700 for cooking class (2 hrs) for up to 20 children

Bayard Rustin Educational Complex

47 The American Sign Language and English Secondary School

CirKiz ("nightclub" for kids)–parties for 10 starting at $850; add-ons like roped-off VIP area, extra

Ballet Tech

Gramercy Park–accessible only with keys provided to surrounding property owners, who pay an annual fee

Harvey Milk High School (for LGBTQ youth and their allies)

Test Prep Authority–$1,000/hr

LOWER MANHATTAN

Jacob Riis Houses

Stuyvesant High School

First Houses

Choose the Right Nanny

Holland Tunnel

Domestic Workers United–organizing for power, respect, and fair labor standards

Léman Manhattan Preparatory School–$45,200/yr

BROOKLYN

PUBLIC/PRIVATE
A MAP OF CHILDHOODS

Inwood Hill Park

Professor Juan Bosch School (PS 178)

NEW JERSEY

UPPER MANHATTAN

Duke Ellington School (PS 4)

Polo Grounds Towers

Harlem River Houses

Mahalia Jackson School (PS 123)

Bread and Roses Integrated Arts High School

Car New York ("luxury minivan" service for kids and their caretakers)

Martin Luther King Jr. Towers (previously Stephen Foster Houses)

Choir Academy of Harlem

Marcus Garvey Park

Taino Towers (subsidized)

Alain L. Locke School (PS 208)

Luis Munoz Rivera School (PS 83)

Central Park

Manhattan Center for Science and Mathematics

The Chord Club by Billboard "Hip-Hop Blowout!"—live recording session for 16 kids from $1,895 ("chains, hats, and bling" included)

NEW JERSEY — BRONX — MANHATTAN — QUEENS — BROOKLYN — STATEN ISLAND

Hudson River

Harlem River

Henry Hudson Bridge

Alexander Hamilton Bridge

Legend:

- Public parks and playgrounds
- Public housing
- Public library (NYPL)
- Universal pre-K, Head Start, and early learning child care centers
- Local agencies providing WIC services
- Public schools
- Youth and family shelters

- High-end birthdays
- Luxury buildings
- Preschool admissions consultants
- SAT tutoring centers
- Private schools
- Nanny agencies

Note: All prices are from 2015

PLAYGROUNDS I HAVE KNOWN BY EMILY RABOTEAU

There are countless ways to see in a city of eight million. When my boyfriend left me with a bruised eye, I kicked him out, got a watchdog and a dog's-eye view of New York. I lived in Flatbush, Brooklyn, then. The dog was a stray, a mutt, the best kind of dog, half German shepherd and half something else that made his legs so short he appeared to be sinking in quicksand. He needed walking, so I walked him. I woke early to do it, or what I thought was early at the time. A sacrifice, but worth it for the exercise, the filter of the morning light, the conversations with strangers; worth it for the dew on the grass of Prospect Park when we, the dog owners, were permitted to let our pets off-leash; worth it for the uncomplicated joy of the animals chasing each other, rolling in rotting leaves, chomping at snow, smelling each other's butts.

The park wasn't just a relief from the crush of the city but the city's great equalizer. New York's master builder Robert Moses said of city planning, "As long as you're on the side of parks, you're on the side of the angels." In the park my mutt played on equal turf with highbred wolfhounds and common pit bulls. All of their shit stank the same, and all were uniformly loved. Most of the dogs were pampered. A few wore booties and matching jackets. I tied a red bandana around my dog's scruffy neck. The kids on the block called him a Blood. I liked that he showed his teeth when men came over. He slept in my bed. For a time, we were a couple.

In those days I worked as a secretary in an Episcopal church on Gramercy Park. The private two-acre oasis is only accessible to the rich residents of the buildings that border it. In the *New York Times* journalist Charlotte Devree called Gramercy Park "a Victorian gentleman who has refused to die." Just 383 keys to the park exist. The church where I worked held one of them. On Fridays my job was interrupted by loud protests as a group marched around the square's perimeter wielding handmade signs. "PARKS ARE FOR THE PEOPLE," they yelled. On other days pedestrians searched haplessly for the gate's entrance. Maybe from the key-holder's-eye view, the park looked most paradisiacal when the rabble was cast out. I dreamed of duplicating the key and distributing it like Halloween candy, but the key could not be copied. I never entered Gramercy Park. I had no truck with places that barred the commoners.

I moved to Harlem for a different job at City College, once known as the poor man's Harvard. Because the new building didn't allow pets, I didn't bring my dog. So much for my principles. My address mattered to me more. From the rooftop I could see Yankee Stadium twinkling like a jewelry box and all the zigzagging fire escapes like so many scars. Then I met a good guy and got married. We moved into a co-op on 180th Street in Washington Heights, one block from the George Washington Bridge. In short order I popped out two children and got a parent's-eye view of New York.

Nowadays, I spend my time in playgrounds.

. . .

The playgrounds are everywhere in this city, thank God, or where else would the kids play? But I hadn't seen them before. Or if I had, they were on my periphery—some fenced-off blacktop in a bigger green park, loud and packed with brats in the day, or seedy and dark with shadows at night. There are a half dozen playgrounds within walking distance of our building, each with its own character based on the socioeconomics of the sub-neighborhood, but none equipped with the seesaws, merry-go-rounds, or tether balls of my youth, now considered hazardous. My mother pities her grandkids. She thinks they require a yard attached to a house like the one where I grew up in suburban New Jersey. But my kids spend more time outside than I ever did.

Dolphin Park, on our corner, is so small it doesn't rank on a map, not even as a freckle. It's open only in the summer for the baby and toddler set, with a sandbox full of plastic pails and shovels, a little playhouse, a short slide, and a dolphin statue that spits water from its rostrum. Quisqueya Playground, near the Fort Washington branch of the public library, hangs like a balcony over Harlem River Drive. It's got a swing set, wind chimes, feral cats, empty dime bags, shaved-ice pushcarts, and women hawking pastelitos or bootleg DVDs. Jacob Javits Playground lies at the foot of Fort Tryon Park. It has a peeling rainbow mural, balance beam, basketball courts, sprinklers, and greased-up musclemen doing chin-ups on the monkey bars. And that's just a partial list of the spots I can push a stroller to in under ten minutes.

In the playgrounds with my kids (as in Prospect Park with my dog) I talk with people I would otherwise never have spoken to. A Hasidic mother of six, a decade younger than I. A teenage mom, a decade younger than her. A Trinidadian nanny with a talent for Sudoku puzzles. An out-of-work opera singer, father to twins. A foster parent peddling the *Watchtower*. Back when I owned the dog I relished the public parks for their mixture of high and low. But now that I'm a parent I despair of the divisions the playgrounds make plain. Having children in common, I realize, is not automatic grounds for friendship. Especially when the talk turns to schools, the inequality begins to penetrate.

"You're out of the good zone by one block," another mother tells me on a bench in Bennett Park. Bennett, in the "good" school zone, is the highest point of elevation in the city at 265 feet above sea level. It boasts a $2 million renovation, a spiraling slide, hanging rings, a children's garden, a hand-painted Little Free Library, and a replica of a cannon from the Revolutionary War, in memory of the base of operations General George Washington established at the summit to keep the enemy out.

This mom is a resident of the ritzy Castle Village apartment complex with its river views, doormen, and twenty-four-hour security patrols. Her children attend nearby PS 187 in the area the realtors advertise as Hudson Heights. She suggests that I beg the principal of this elementary school for an exception to admit my son. The school I'm zoned for, PS 173, is failing, she warns: substandard test scores, next-to-no parental involvement, a rotten principal, overstuffed classes. She raises her well-manicured eyebrows and adds: "Ninety-nine percent Hispanic." There's a proposal to de-zone the district, but the parents on the local listserv are up in arms.

Which listserv? Which district?

My son is only three months old. I am sleep-deprived and only getting the knack of feeding him. I haven't yet studied the thirty-two zones of the Department of Education's map, which look an awful lot like gerrymandering, nor discovered that our school district is the most populous in the city, encompassing both Castle Village, on the western promontory over the river, and the Bridge Apartments housing project, whose ugly towers straddle the Trans-Manhattan Expressway, with the noxious fumes of the traffic below rendering the balconies unusable. I've yet to discover that this city has one of the most racially segregated and economically stratified school systems in the country. I merely want my boy to learn to crawl, walk, run, talk, and climb up to the slide over there that spirals like a single strand of the hair he'll eventually sprout.

I'd like to slap this woman, my neighbor, for her entitlement and presumption. Instead, I remark that long before she and I came to squat on this turf holding sippy cups, the Lenape sold this island to the Dutch, and Washington lost this ground to the Redcoats, and eventually the Irish, who settled the hood, were replaced by German Jews, who got scared off by the blacks, who were then outnumbered by the Dominicans. . . . By which I mean: nobody owns bupkis and we're all just passing through. She and I don't become friends.

Cooling down. Courtesy Emily Raboteau.

But later, when my son is ten months old and waking at the ungodly hour of 5:00 a.m., I drag him back to the playground in Bennett to wear him out. There, I meet another woman, a native New Yorker, with a son the same age. Our boys share raisins and bounce together on the squeaky bridge, testing out their legs. When I ask the woman what she hates most about motherhood, she laughs from her diaphragm. A man hollers down at us from his open window to shut the fuck up. We have woken him too early. The playground doesn't open officially until eight. "Come down here and make us, cocksucker!" my new friend shouts back.

.   .   .

One night before we had children my husband and I snorted cocaine with a swizzle stick from Starbucks. The drug seemed not to be working, and we talked for a few hours about its probably being cut with baby powder. Finally, when sitting still grew impossible, we ventured outside. First to the George Washington Bridge Bus Station to watch the heroin addicts nodding off, and the hookers getting lippy with their pimps, and the tired travelers with their entire lives packed up in duffel bags. Then, after the bus station shut down, we headed to Bennett Park, where we slid down the twisting slide and mapped out a terrible short story about two writers in a playground in the middle of the night, high on coke. Ah, the dilettante's-eye view of New York! It's not the recklessness of that memory that surprises me now but the leisure. That we ever had that kind of time to waste or the freedom and energy to roam. The playground in Bennett Park was fun that night precisely because we weren't meant to be in it. The cops could have booked us for trespassing if they hadn't real criminals to bust. Now we go to the playground by default, when the kids start bouncing off the walls of our 800-square-foot apartment.

.   .   .

Sometimes, it's enchanting to play with our kids in the park. I carry bubbles and sidewalk chalk. My husband chases our son on his scooter. It can feel like a second childhood. But just as often it's tedious as hell. We are there as a matter of duty to kill a weekend afternoon.

I injure my wrists from the repetitive stress of pushing the baby "higher, higher," always "higher," on the swing. My husband dislikes the helicopter parents at Bennett Park, the gentry of Hudson Heights who intervene when their children grab a toy or push another child, who hover over the rug rats without letting them duke it out on their own, who wear their newborns like accessories. He prefers the playground in J. Hood Wright Park, which resembles the Queens of his childhood, no parents in sight; where the immigrants' kids play pick-up soccer, scream like ambulances, splash in puddles, scarf junk food, and peg each other in the head with water balloons. I see what he means, even when our second child, a daughter, gets knocked over by a ten-year-old on a bike. This playground has a wild energy. The kids are free.

J. Hood Wright has a dazzling overlook of the George Washington Bridge from a platform up a steep flight of stairs where old men in hats sit reading *El Diario* and young men with diamond earrings sit dealing drugs. Every month or so a film crew arrives to shoot a gritty scene for *Law and Order* or some other projection of rough New York retrofitted to look like the rotten apple of forty years ago, when it was lousy with crack and crime and the population was slumping.

Nobody calls New York the Rotten Apple anymore, except with a kind of nostalgia. More and more, it's referred to as "the playground of the rich," and the population is on the rise. The current baby boom among Manhattan's wealthy class is unique among U.S. cities, with the number of children below age five having grown over 30 percent since the turn of the millennium. My son and daughter are part of this demographic upswing. Their day care borders J. Hood Wright, so we spend a lot of time in its playground. Sometimes a director shouts at us to get out of the movie. But this is our *life,* I want to bark.

The day care is called Bright Beginnings. It costs $12K a year. Per kid. A discount compared to Bright Horizons, the day care at the nearby medical center, which runs closer to 20. I now know about the relative costs from the local parents' listserv, which clutters my inbox with alerts of strange men without children spotted in the playgrounds, referrals for lactation consultants, debates about the dangers of vaccination, opinions on when to stop co-sleeping, dissections of Mayor de Blasio's new policy on universal pre-K, and creative ideas for birthday parties.

When my son's classmate turns two, her parents invite us to her birthday party at Wiggles and Giggles, a playroom on 181st Street and Riverside Drive that rents for $450 an hour. Our son behaves horribly the entire time. "Let's celebrate his birthday at McDonald's," my husband whispers. "Let's not throw him a party at all," I whisper back. While the toddlers eviscerate cupcakes, I look out the window and spot a man in a trench coat holding a revolver. "Is that Liam Neeson?" I ask my husband. Indeed, it is. The actor is playing a hard-boiled detective in a film about seedy New York. When the movie opens the following year, my husband and I want to see it, but not enough to go through the hassle of finding a babysitter. By this time we have the two children. Day care costs $24K. It's been more than a minute since we went on a date.

·   ·   ·

Back when I was single I traded my dog for a used bike and got a bicyclist's-eye view of New York. The bike lanes became a network in my mind, a nervous system. Manhattan was an island whose spine I could navigate in a day, with bridges poking off it like ribs. I got wise to the dangers of car doors opening in my path, the rearview mirrors of city buses at the level of my cranium, and the pleasure of speed on the long thoroughfare of Hudson River Park, with the waterway stretching beside me, my hair whipped back in the wind. I never wore a helmet. My thighs became logs. My rides were epic, and seemingly endless. Then I traded that ride for a stroller.

This is the middle-class, neoliberal parent's-eye view of New York City, beset with anxiety, rumor, distress: we tell ourselves that we didn't choose to live in one of the most diverse cities in the world only to raise our kids in a rarefied bubble. We'd like to send them to a local public school. We believe, as the hallmark of American democracy, that all kids deserve a good education and that private school is not for us. Yet this calculus was far simpler before our own kids arrived. On certain days we ask ourselves: why the hell are we raising our children in this quagmire with its sucky schools and space constraints, its multiple stressors and pollutants, its racing pulse and noise?

My boy is now three, about to turn four, on the brink of entering the public school system. His father and I have toured three preschool programs so far. Our top choice is a well-regarded community school with eighteen seats in its one pre-K classroom, for which several hundred overeager parents will apply. The crammed open house in the cafeteria smelled of spoiled milk and panic. The parents gathered there were furtively trading tips on "gifted and talented" programs, pipelines to the best high schools. There's a booming test-prep market to get into those kindergartens, which are 70 percent white and Asian, though over 70 percent of the city's public school students are Hispanic and black. Ironically, these accelerated programs were meant to promote diversity in urban schools by preventing white flight, but they've effectively resegregated the system. "We're also looking at private schools," one mother confessed. "We're looking at houses in Westchester," a father whispered.

Not since I worked on Gramercy Park has the city seemed more divided. This process is disheartening, to say the least. It has turned me into a version of that lady I despised on the park bench, dismissive of the school we are zoned for and anxious to secure a spot in a high-ranked program. Yet when I grow too cynical or stressed about New York's social caste and our children's place within it, it's the playgrounds that save me from wondering how to get back into the garden. I traded my dog and my bike and my wild nights for this: the little ones at play.

Last spring our boy fell in love with an older girl named Ellia in J. Hood Wright Park. His feeling for Ellia was attached to the poetry of the park with its tot lot, Stegosaurus climber, handball court, dog run, gingko trees, chess tables, outcroppings of schist, picnic area, cigarette butts, sledding hill, ice cream truck, and flagpole, on top of which, on rare occasions at dawn, perches an enormous red-tailed hawk with talons big enough to snatch a squirrel from the rim of a trash can. For my son, who was learning the names of these things, the park contained the spectrum of possibility from menace to joy. The most sparkling of these possibilities was made evident by Ellia's tiara.

Ellia's long black hair fell to her waist. Her school uniform was from PS 173, the school we have tacitly agreed is not good enough for our children, without ever having set foot inside of it. It was easy to see why my three-year-old idolized Ellia. She was pretty and doting, pretending to be his mother, pushing him endlessly on the swing, singing to him in Spanish, and ferrying him on her hip. It was just as easy to see why she cherished my son. He was sweet and adoring, willing to relinquish his snack and follow her commands like a lovesick pup. Their love was mutual and uncomplicated. For a brief spell, they were a couple. One evening at sundown Ellia led my child out of the playground into the vast park, past the dog run, to the place where the boulders drop off onto the shoulder of the road. I checked an impulse to follow after them. She was a third-grader after all, sensible enough to keep hold of his hand and to watch for broken glass. Soon, they had climbed over the rocks and out of my sight. I didn't know what private magic she meant to show my boy at the park's edge. There is a child's-eye view of New York to which I have no key.

"Geronimo!" I heard Ellia holler. And the peal of his laughter was worth it. ✧

22 THE SUBURBAN THEORY OF THE AVANT-GARDE

Mapping San Francisco and New Orleans was easy: each fits nicely onto the rectangle of the page spread of our atlases. New York, on the other hand, is a complex tangle of islands and coastlines that fill only the lower right-hand side of the page spread, with Long Island to the east and New Jersey to the west. New Jersey on so many maps of the city is covered up by art or information, blanked out, or erased altogether, as though it were an utterly separate place or no place at all. Jersey is erased in a larger sense when its cultural riches are discounted or overlooked, and this is a map made to celebrate them and to note that some of the greatest artists of the twentieth century, from William Carlos Williams to Robert Smithson to Patti Smith, are from Jersey, while others, like Dizzy Gillespie, came to live there. This is a map in praise of the suburban avant-garde in music, poetry, art, and other media, of the birth of new forms and styles west of the Hudson, and a map in praise of the need to sometimes turn the background into the foreground and vice versa. It's also a reminder that the state line divided administrations but not culture, because New York City is far closer literally and culturally to the vibrancy of Newark than the vagaries of upstate New York.

CARTOGRAPHY: MOLLY ROY   MAP APPEARS ON PAGES 180–181.

NORTH STARS AND GOSPEL BATTLES
PETER COYOTE'S JERSEY MEMORIES

Peter Coyote spent the first six months of his life on Riverside Drive, facing New Jersey across the Hudson River, and the next seventeen years or so in Englewood, New Jersey, facing the Bronx. There he soaked up the complex mix of cultures and classes postwar New Jersey offered. Sue Howard Nelson, the African American teenager hired to take care of him and his sister, became "the North Star around which my heavens revolved," the connection to a vibrant community and to lives lived to the soundtracks of gospel, jazz, and the other musics flourishing on the Jersey shore. He left, definitively, and has been a Californian for most of the last half century, but something of that experience never left him in his varied career as an insurrectionary, communard, actor, and Zen priest. (And he remains devoted to Nelson.) In his current West Coast home among tangerine and plum trees, he recalled the time and place that was his postwar New Jersey.

—*Rebecca Solnit*

My dad was the president of the Hudson and Manhattan Railroad, which ran between Newark and Lower Manhattan. He went into Rector Street and Wall Street during the

Singer Debbie Harry
(b. 1945) raised

Hawthorne

William Carlos Williams publishes
his epic poem *Paterson*, 1946–58

Paterson

Allen Ginsberg (b. 1926 Newark)
raised (Williams is his pediatrician)

Artist Nancy Holt
(b. 1938 elsewhere) raised

Clifton   *Passaic*

Robert Smithson creates landmark
work *Monuments of Passaic*, 1967

Seminal girl group, The
Shirelles, forms, 1957

Ruther

Poet William Carlos Williams
(b. 1883) raised; returns as
doctor 1912; dies 1963

Artist Robert Smithson
(b. 1938 Passaic) raised

From 1776 to 1807, female
heads of households and
propertied black men are
allowed to vote in New Jersey

NEW JERSEY

Singer/actress Queen Latifah
(b. 1970), raised in East Orange

Vocalist Dionne Warwick
(b. 1940 East Orange) still resides

Writer Stephen Crane (b. 1871)

Stride pianist Willie "the Lion"
Smith (b. 1893 elsewhere) raised

Poet/playwright LeRoi Jones/
Amiri Baraka (b. 1934, d. 2014)

Poet Allen Ginsberg (b. 1926)

Singer Sarah Vaughan (b. 1924) raised

Trumpeter Woody Shaw Jr. (b. 1944 elsewhere) raised

Politician Ras Baraka (b. 1970, son of
Amiri Baraka), elected mayor 2014

Newark

Rapper Ice-T (b. 1958), raised in
Summit, moves to L.A. in teens

Musician George Clinton (b. 1941 elsewhere) raised; forms
doo-wop group The Parliaments here in 1950s, which
evolves into funk group Parliament and later Funkadelic

Plainfield

Elizabeth

Lincoln Hwy

Newark Bay

Bayo

Goethals Bridge

Garden State Pkwy

NJ Turnpike

Inventor Thomas Edison at work
1876–84: invents phonograph
(1877), refines lightbulb (1879),
initiates age of electricity

Princeton: actor/singer/athlete/activist
Paul Robeson (b. 1898) raised

Menlo Park

STATEN ISLAND

Institute for Advanced Study, Princeton:
physicist Albert Einstein in residence
1933–55; anthropologist Clifford
Geertz in residence 1970–2006

Edison

Camden: poet Walt Whitman, resident
from 1873 until his death in 1892

Outerbridge Crossing

Camden/Cherry Hill: feminist
writer/revolutionary Andrea
Dworkin (b. 1946) raised

Raritan River

Red Bank: bandleader Count Basie
(b. 1904), moves to Harlem c. 1924

Deptford Township: poet/singer Patti
Smith (b. 1946 elsewhere) raised

Red Bank: writer/critic
Edmund Wilson (b. 1895),
educated at Princeton

Studio engineer Rudy Van Gelder (b. 1924 Jersey City) records jazz by Miles Davis and others in his parents' living room, 1952–59; Thelonius Monk records "Hackensack" in 1954 as an homage to him

Nancy Holt creates *Sky Mound* earthwork (1988–; unfinished)

Jazzman Dizzy Gillespie in residence, 1965–93

Actor/writer Peter Coyote (b. 1941 elsewhere) raised

Trombonist Tyree Glenn (b. 1912 elsewhere) lives from the 1950s until his death in 1974

The Sugarhill Gang forms 1973; has first rap hit in top-40, with "Rapper's Delight" (1979)

Artist Faith Ringgold (b. 1930 elsewhere) resides

Van Gelder Studio founded 1959; records albums for Verve, Vox, Prestige, and others, including nearly every Blue Note album from 1953 to 1967

John Coltrane quartet records *A Love Supreme* at Van Gelder Studio, December 9, 1964

Cuban singer Celia Cruz ("¡Azúcar!") shapes modern salsa (early 1960s–2003)

"Havana on the Hudson" honors Latin jazz greats

Singer Frank Sinatra (b. 1915) left c. 1939

ng Branch: satirist/poet orothy Parker (b. 1893)

Long Branch: drummer Sonny Greer (b. 1895) raised, works with Duke Ellington, c. 1919–50

Palisades Interstate Pkwy

Englewood

Englewood Cliffs

ackensack

4

80

46

95

I-9

George Washington
Fort Lee Bridge

Edgewater

BRONX

Hudson River

tern Spur

Eastern Spur

Tonnelle Ave

I-9

Union City

MANHATTAN

495

Lincoln Tunnel

Hoboken

Holland Tunnel

East River

QUEENS

Upper Bay

BROOKLYN

Lower Bay

"Hasn't Passaic replaced Rome as the Eternal City?"
—Robert Smithson, 1967

THE SUBURBAN THEORY OF THE AVANT-GARDE
NEW JERSEY'S GREATS

day. My dad was caught on the conundrum of a moral axis. He was driven to succeed by his rage at being classified as second-rate for being a Jew, and his organizing principle was "I will show those cocksuckers. I will fucking show them." He built a life of great baronial elegance. He ran a museum-quality antique store of American and English colonial furniture. Long before Ralph Lauren, he figured out that the style of old money was *the* style. He was a very shrewd imitator and he did very well.

My parents moved out of Manhattan when I was about six months old and settled at 90 Booth Avenue in Englewood, New Jersey. Englewood had been something of a millionaire's playground in the twenties and teens and golden age. The black ghetto was south and west and then, as you moved north up the hill on Woodland Avenue toward the Hudson River, there was a huge panoramic vista of millionaires' homes.

When I was about two and a half, my mother had a shattering nervous breakdown. Life with Dad—what I've pieced together: she probably asked for a divorce. My dad basically told her, "You'll have to leave the kids; I've got judges." He was a powerful, very, very wealthy man until he lost all his money. My mom was sort of a ghost, and my dad was not going to slow down his acquisition of wealth and insulation against being a Jew in America in the 1940s. He was a very competitive guy. He was the sparring partner of Philadelphia Jack O'Brien [the light heavyweight boxing world champion]. He was a black belt in jujitsu. He was Olympic-qualifying level for Greco wrestling. Very brilliant. Went to MIT when he was fifteen.

Susie Howard came from this big clan in Henderson, North Carolina. She came up when she was sixteen and got a job working for the army and sewing coats. In Paterson—on the day she was fired, because they found out her real age—she met my aunt, who hired her. When my mother had the nervous breakdown, my Aunt Ruth said to Sue, "You'll never be able to make enough money on what I can afford to pay you. Why don't you go to my brother's house? He'll pay you $85 a week and he'll give you room and board. He's in a bind and needs someone to look after the children." So that's how Sue Howard came into my life.

She was seventeen or eighteen max. So she came in, and she is as confident as someone who has survived a lightning strike. She just picked up all the suffering in our household and threw it over her shoulder like it was a weightless sack. I transferred my loyalty to her just like a little ol' traitor. So suddenly my house was full of black people. Her friends. John Ellerbee and his wife, Violet. Jules, another half-Cherokee guy, like Sue, from North Carolina. And Chris, my father's chauffeur. They were signifying and laughing and jiving in the kitchen. Jazz was playing. Errol Garner and Teddy Wilson. And the house was full of life. Just full of life. And by being with them I actually got the most singularly valuable lesson of my entire life, which was I got the opportunity to perceive "whiteness." I got to see that there were two different ways that people were treated and different levels of power.

Susie's boyfriend, later husband, Ellsworth "Ozzie" Nelson, was a gospel singer. I would go to the Holy Sanctified Church. We would go to the Battle of the Gospels in Newark. (I still listen to gospel music every Sunday.) Battles of the Gospels were big events where various groups like the Swan Silvertones, or the Dixie Hummingbirds, Clara Ward and the Soul Sisters, Sam Cooke and the Soul Stirrers, would come in and go to these theaters. This is my personal theory, but there's something extremely powerful about gospel that most people don't get. It's call and response. Everybody knows that, but—well, the *response* represents the insistence of law and order in the universe. The chorus that's going, "All night, All day" [*sings*]—they are absolutely on the beat. They are metronomic, together, collective. They never budge. They represent the implacability of what can't be budged in the universe. Within that matrix, and under that pressure, the lead singer is struggling for liberation, seeking a way out. The fact that the music represents both forces simultaneously is what gives it its power.

It was very dangerous to speak in my household. In my first book I described my dad's daily return home as like a hand grenade being rolled into the room. Everybody was galvanized, watching it to discover if the pin was in or out. But music offered a language of expressiveness and feeling. Even today, I would never be an actor or even a writer if I had the musical gifts to express what I can hear. It just short-circuits language. You're not stuck within the prison of syntax, logic, and contradictions. It became a really important life jacket or lifeline.

My father's best friend was a guy named Buddy Jones, who was Charlie Parker's roommate in Kansas City for three years. We met him through a gay dancer in Martha Graham's company named David Campbell, a good friend of Merce Cunningham's. Buddy was a jazz bass player, and I remember coming home one day after school and Al Cohn and Zoot Sims, along with Dave McKenna and Buddy, were playing in my house. The whole house was alive with this musical conversation, and my father was happy and my mother was happy and Susie was happy, and I'd never seen grown-ups have so much fun. I thought that's what I want to do. I want to do that. Well, the creator didn't give me the gift of being that musical. But I did become an artist. I knew that's where I was going. Buddy taught me how life can be improvised.

Prestige and Blue Note records: I started saving my allowance when I was around eleven. Buying records. Buying jazz. Buddy would turn me on to people, and I'd hear people and poke around in record stores, listening to this and that. I knew that Englewood was a center of this, but I didn't have access to it. I didn't know [Blue Note Records engineer] Rudy Van Gelder, and it never would have occurred to me to go up to Englewood Cliffs, but I passed Englewood Cliffs all the time. It gave me some sense that I was in a place where something special was happening. This guy I told you about, David Campbell, who was in Martha Graham's company, a dancer and concert pianist. He was the guy I went to Mexico with when I got arrested and went to jail smuggling back sixteen kilos of weed in 1959. David was really close friends with Sarah Vaughan and Dizzy Gillespie, who lived in Englewood. I went to Dizzy Gillespie's house once with him. We just stopped in for David to give him something or say something. For all I know, he was bringing him dope. I just don't know, but I remember that he had a can of "Nigger Boy Sardines," or something like that, on his mantle with a picture of a black boy eating a watermelon or something, and he pointed out how it was registered at the U.S. Patent Office. That made me think.

So after I was thrown out of the Englewood School for Boys, a tony local prep school, I went to Dwight Morrow, the public high school in Englewood. Nearly 60 percent of the kids were black and from the Fourth Ward, where Susie and Ozzie had moved to. She left our house after she got married, and then she had a son of her own, named Billy. By that time I was over thirteen and a teenager going to Greenwich Village and interested in folk music, old blues, and the life I'd been introduced to by Buddy Jones. I shifted a lot of my attention to Buddy in those years. He introduced me to Miles Davis when I was twelve. He took me to hear Billie Holiday's last concert at Carnegie Hall, took me backstage to meet her. I mean, all my heroes knew these invisible people that were friends of my father. My father couldn't teach me to add two numbers, but he managed to assemble these souls around him that really trained me for life.

When I got old enough, when I got to be about thirteen and collecting Prestige and Blue Note records, I found out about Rudy Van Gelder and about the Englewood Cliffs studios and all that. But the only jazz person in Englewood that I knew was Tyree Glenn Senior. His older son, Tyree Junior, and I were in a group called the Fabulous Imperials.

1950. Skinny black ties. Suits. Playing CYO (Catholic Youth Organization) dances. Friday and Saturday night. Twenty-five dollars a man. I couldn't even drive then. I was the drummer. Tyree [Junior] was the saxophone player. We had a guy named Crazy Louie, who had his two front teeth out, who was a crazy hillbilly electric guitar player in pegged pants. He drove a Cadillac convertible and had a mink-lined beer opener hanging from a key chain on his belt. It was an improbable group of people. My friend Ray Popkin was also a sax player.

I played there until I was about fifteen or sixteen, and then one day I was taking apart my drum kit, and a girl I was interested in left with the guitar player, because all he had to do was slap his guitar in his case and take off, so I shifted my interest to folk music and guitar. Music for me was the path off the sidewalk and out of the suburbs. Rock 'n' roll was just starting. Alan Freed was having wiggy shows at the Brooklyn Paramount—maybe 1953 or 1954, right around then—all sexual energy and ecstasy.

I was old enough to take the subway and bus in and hear the Platters and all these doo-wop groups, and guys like Chuck Berry. Something in the zeitgeist was shifting from the Fabian, Perry Como, and Paul Anka sound to black voices, or guys like Elvis, white guys that sounded black. Jerry Lee Lewis, the Righteous Brothers. Like, real black race music was starting to colonize the hearing nerve circuits of white America. It was sex music. It had everybody like . . . I can remember listening to records with my friends and just being in frenzies and throwing ourselves around the room and smashing into walls. Rock 'n' roll. It was so exciting. You leave the sidewalk, walk out of the suburbs, and go to hootenannies in Greenwich Village and start rubbing shoulders with older bohemians. They start telling you about the Beats and the poets and left-wing literature and the American Transcendentalists and giving you books and education to read, and instead of being this weird, little, goofy Jew with a bell around my neck that felt weird because nobody was into what I was into, I gradually got conscripted into the counterculture. That's where the people were like me. We'd read a book and then talk about it. What could be more fun than that? Girls would take their clothes off with you. It was just thrilling. What could be better? That's where it started for me. That actually got me out of New Jersey. ✺

23 PLANTING LIBERTY

Diversity is the lifeblood of New York City. After all, the metropolis gets its vibrancy, in part, from the mix of people and perspectives that animate it. "Diversity" is also a catchword for those praising New York City; the mere presence of difference is treated as a value that's good in and of itself, as if mixing were without real difficulty. The neighborhood of Flushing, home to some of New York City's most vibrant immigrant communities, and home to some of the city's loveliest horticulture, lies in north central Queens, not far from the former site of the 1964 world's fair, whose theme was "Peace through Understanding." Diversity in the natural world—for example, Flushing's botanical bounty (the neighborhood once had the city's, and some of the nation's, most important nurseries)—is easily celebrated. But people living with different opinions or traditions don't naturally coexist: there is a danger of exclusion and, as a corollary, persecution of minorities whose beliefs are out of step with the status quo. In New York City, many neighbors who get along with each other come from countries where they are trying to kill each other. Thankfully, the rule of law sometimes helps. Otherwise, New York City might explode under old national and ethnic grudges given free rein.

In seventeenth-century New York City, Quakers were persecuted for their religion and (to many) strange behavior, and a few courageous New Yorkers spoke in defense of their rights, making a case for religious liberty. They didn't just argue for toleration—it wasn't enough to stomach those they disagreed with—but they made a case for not excluding anyone based on differences in religious belief. (Though they weren't yet open enough to advocate for Roman Catholics.) In a city with millions of people bumping into each other, where pluralism brings along clashing ideas and innumerable disagreements, this is a lesson and heritage worth holding close: we shouldn't try to bend people's consciences or exclude those who don't share our religious convictions, and ought to stand against tyrants who try to do so.

CARTOGRAPHY: MOLLY ROY; CONCEPT: EMMY CATEDRAL   MAP APPEARS ON PAGES 186–187.

"LAW OF LOVE, PEACE AND LIBERTIE"

BY GARNETTE CADOGAN

Get off at the end of the 7 line—nicknamed "The International Express" because of the many diverse ethnic neighborhoods this train traverses—and marvel at the bouquet that is Flushing, Queens. Step onto Main Street and see the poetry of movement on the sidewalks: the rapid passing of bodies that never bump, mimicking the choreography of industrious ants; person after person who walks from below the knees rather than from under the hips; and the shuffling pedestrian whose to-hell-with-you rhythm cuts through

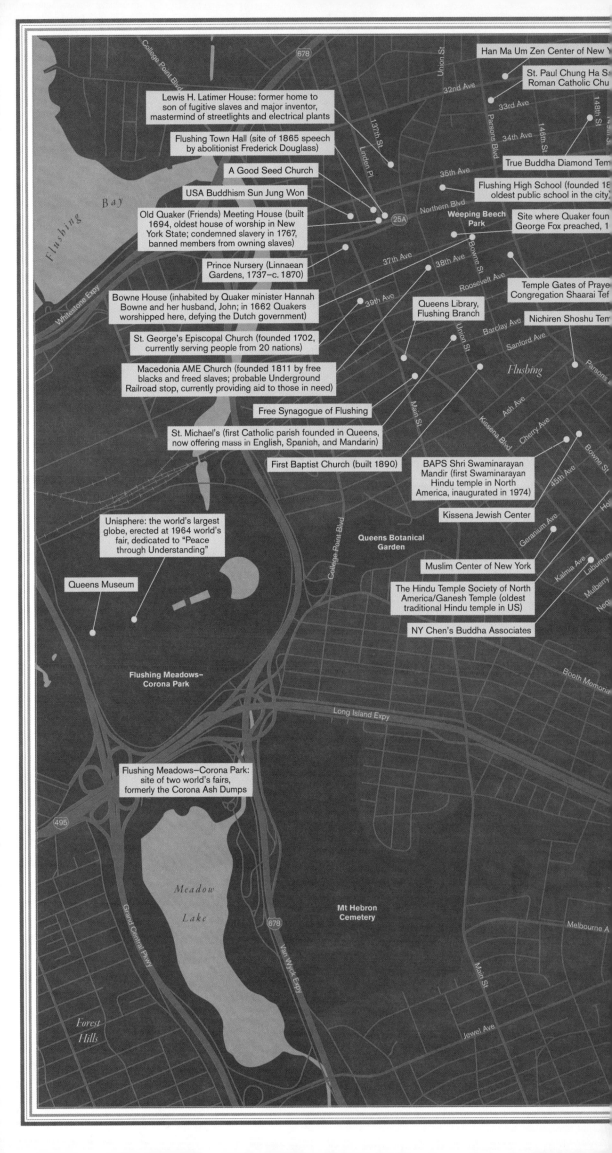

Han Ma Um Zen Center of New Y

St. Paul Chung Ha S
Roman Catholic Chu

True Buddha Diamond Tem

Flushing High School (founded 18
oldest public school in the city)

Site where Quaker foun
George Fox preached, 1

Temple Gates of Praye
Congregation Shaarai Tef

Nichiren Shoshu Tem

Lewis H. Latimer House: former home to
son of fugitive slaves and major inventor,
mastermind of streetlights and electrical plants

Flushing Town Hall (site of 1865 speech
by abolitionist Frederick Douglass)

A Good Seed Church

USA Buddhism Sun Jung Won

Old Quaker (Friends) Meeting House (built
1694, oldest house of worship in New
York State; condemned slavery in 1767,
banned members from owning slaves)

Prince Nursery (Linnaean
Gardens, 1737–c. 1870)

Bowne House (inhabited by Quaker minister Hannah
Bowne and her husband, John; in 1662 Quakers
worshipped here, defying the Dutch government)

St. George's Episcopal Church (founded 1702,
currently serving people from 20 nations)

Macedonia AME Church (founded 1811 by free
blacks and freed slaves; probable Underground
Railroad stop, currently providing aid to those in need)

Free Synagogue of Flushing

St. Michael's (first Catholic parish founded in Queens,
now offering mass in English, Spanish, and Mandarin)

First Baptist Church (built 1890)

BAPS Shri Swaminarayan
Mandir (first Swaminarayan
Hindu temple in North
America, inaugurated in 1974)

Kissena Jewish Center

Unisphere: the world's largest
globe, erected at 1964 world's
fair, dedicated to "Peace
through Understanding"

Queens Museum

Muslim Center of New York

The Hindu Temple Society of North
America/Ganesh Temple (oldest
traditional Hindu temple in US)

NY Chen's Buddha Associates

Flushing Meadows–
Corona Park

Flushing Meadows–Corona Park:
site of two world's fairs,
formerly the Corona Ash Dumps

Queens Library,
Flushing Branch

Queens Botanical
Garden

Weeping Beech
Park

Flushing

Flushing
Bay

Meadow
Lake

Mt Hebron
Cemetery

Forest
Hills

PLANTING LIBERTY
350 YEARS OF FREEDOM IN FLUSHING

35th Ave

Murray Hill

Crocheron Ave

Sanford Ave

Korean American
Church of Love

ch Ave

Northern Blvd

QUEENS

156th St

162nd St

Elm Ave

45th Ave

Temple Beth Sholom

Jesus Tree Presbyterian Church

Hawthorn Ave

46th Ave

Flushing Cemetery

Oak Ave

Poplar Ave

wne St. *Quince Ave*

Parsons Nursery
(1838–1909)

Kissena Park
Historic Grove

Kissena Lake

Rose Ave

Iglesia Evangelica Presbiteriana

Kissena Park

December 27, 1657
31 citizens of Flushing
sign the Flushing Remonstrance,
a manifesto for religious freedom
under Dutch rule,
"The law of love, peace and libertie in the states
extending to Jews, Turks and Egyptians . . . .
for wee are bounde by the law of God
and man to doe good unto
all men and evil to
noe men"

1718
Flushing
Quaker William Burling
publishes a pamphlet
criticizing slavery

1732
Robert William Prince
founds the Linneaean Botanic Gardens,
first commercial nursery in the colonies

1790s
James Bloodgood
founds
Bloodgood Nursery

February 7, 1814
The Flushing Female Association
(disbanded 1989)
starts an unsegregated school
for Flushing's poor children

1906
Samuel Bowne Parsons's
obituary noted,
"It was his boast that he assisted
more slaves to freedom
than any other man
in Queens County"

1838
Founding of Quaker preacher Samuel
Parsons's nursery, which
introduces the Valencia orange,
frost-tolerant honeybee,
weeping beech,
and Japanese
maple

the flow of foot traffic as if protected by an invisible force field. Walk two blocks east past the bustle of Korean and Chinese and Indian and Bangladeshi shoppers, past the gourmands in from Manhattan on their culinary pilgrimages, struggling to orient themselves in the path of swift-moving passersby, past the bottlenecks that develop when customers spill out of restaurants and reflexology shops and reduce sidewalk traffic to little more than a single moving lane, until you reach placid Bowne Street. Here the wide sidewalks are populated with unhurried residents. Walk north on Bowne Street another block and a half until you see a beige wood-framed house, with a sign on its lawn announcing: "Bowne House. Built in 1661. A National Shrine to Religious Freedom." Stand for a while in front of this simple house and observe. You'll notice that hardly anyone cuts pace to look at, much more take in, this building or the historical marker on the sidewalk that spells out its significance: "This house, built by John Bowne in 1661, featured prominently in the early struggle for religious freedom in America."

Shortly after it was built, this house became a place of worship for Quakers, and therefore a place of refuge for them. Yes, spiritual refuge—"God is our refuge and strength, a very present help in trouble," as the Psalmist declared and the Quakers would wholeheartedly affirm—but also a shelter from harassment and persecution in the anti-Quaker climate of Flushing. Peter Stuyvesant, the director-general of what was then New Netherland—of which Flushing was an especially diverse part—was not a fan of religions that weren't his own Dutch Reformed. Observers of other faiths might pray and preach in private homes, but public homage was reserved for the national church of the Netherlands and New Netherland. Such was Stuyvesant's preference, and such was the law: "No other religion shall be publicly admitted in New Netherland except the Reformed." His religious intolerance brought him into conflict with various newcomers to New Netherland who weren't part of his tribe: Lutherans, Jews, Baptists, and others. But he had a special revulsion for Quakers, whose theological populism—their insistence that uneducated men and women could preach, for instance—and egalitarian style—their refusal to be deferential to ecclesiastical and political authority—he detested. Stuyvesant not only forbade Quakers public worship, he also forbade their meeting privately. And in the fall of 1657, the same year the Quakers arrived in New Netherland and made themselves unwelcome by preaching in the streets, Stuyvesant issued a proclamation that ships bringing Quakers to New Netherland would be seized. Anyone attending a Quaker meeting or receiving Quakers would be fined. To help smoke out offenders, he offered snitches a commission.

In response to Stuyvesant's ordinance, a group of thirty-one Flushing residents (only one of whom was a Quaker) got together and drew up a statement of protest. The Flushing Remonstrance called upon Stuyvesant to live up to New Netherland's founding principles. Flushing was supposed to be tolerant of racial, ethnic, and religious differences. Like the colony's namesake, the Netherlands, which recognized that "no one shall be persecuted or investigated because of his religion," Flushing by its very charter was to allow residents "to have and enjoy the liberty of conscience, according to the custom and manner of Holland, without molestation or disturbance from any magistrate." Not only was Stuyvesant intolerant and cruel, therefore—he was a hypocrite. The signers of the Remonstrance not only stood up for other Christians, "whether Presbyterian, Independent, Baptist or Quaker," but they also insisted that "the law of love, peace and libertie" extended to "Jews, Turks and Egyptians." They took their stand at great risk—Stuyvesant had an appetite for torture—and they made their case with respect and eloquence. The document pulsates with a heartbeat of openness and generosity and humility. "If any of these said persons come in love unto us, we cannot in conscience lay violent hands upon them," the signers protested, "but give them free egresse and regresse unto our towne and houses, as God shall persuade our consciences . . . for wee are bounde by the law of God and man to doe good unto all men, and evil to noe men." Thin-skinned and thick-headed, Stuyvesant was unswayed. He called the Remonstrance a "mutinous and detestable letter of defiance" and, true to form, had the town officials who had signed and delivered it arrested.

In 1662, the year after he built his house, John Bowne and his wife, Hannah, began holding Quaker meetings there. Stuyvesant got word of the gatherings and arrested a defiant Bowne and had him deported to Holland. When Bowne arrived in Amsterdam in early 1663, he argued his case before the Amsterdam chamber of the Dutch West India Company, reminding the Dutch of the principle of liberty of conscience that Flushing's charter should have guaranteed. He was later allowed to return to Flushing, mainly out of a fear of "diminishing the population and stopping immigration, which must be favored at so tender a stage of the country's existence." The Dutch West India Company told Stuyvesant to "shut your eyes" to nonconformists and "allow every one to have his own belief." They wanted a "maxim of moderation" in order to create "a considerable influx of people"—they valued free trade much more than freedom of religion—and so they rebuked Stuyvesant and restored Bowne. In spite of the mixed motives that drove it, it was a triumph for liberty of conscience.

. . .

On the street in front of John Bowne's house stands a signboard that lists other significant locations in Flushing. There are directions to Freedom Mile, a pair of self-directed walking tours within a mile's radius. There are places of historical significance (sites that might have been active in the Underground Railroad) and clues to a multicultural present (the word *Welcome* in multiple languages). The sign also notes that in 1664—the year that the British took control of New Netherland, renaming it New York—"Bowne returned to his house, where Quaker meetings were held for another 30 years, until the Friends Meeting House was built." The Friends Meeting House, a modest wooden building around the corner, which Bowne helped build, is the oldest place of worship in continuous use in New York. It's on a street—Northern Boulevard—that's one of the city's "God's Rows" (to borrow the term coined by journalist Tony Carnes, who has spent decades trying to map every religious site in New York City and has counted 372 in Flushing). Places of worship dot the street, as if sprinkled freehandedly from above. Walk on Northern Boulevard past the many spaces where Buddhists, Jews, and Christians of an array of denominations worship, and it's easy to believe that this multifaith world is a creation of the Flushing Remonstrance. You'll feel this even more when you walk a few blocks south of Bowne House past a Church of Christ, a Church of Oversea Chinese Mission, a synagogue, a Sikh Gurdwara, and a Hindu temple.

But the remarkable fact that Flushing is one of the most religiously and ethnically diverse neighborhoods in New York and the United States is not a result of the Remonstrance. (Occasionally there's boosterish talk of that little-known document influencing the drafting of the Bill of Rights more than a century later, but no compelling evidence supports that claim.) The U.S. Immigration and Naturalization Act of 1965, which threw open the gates that immigrants walked through, is more responsible for Flushing's vibrant pluralism. Nonetheless, one Sunday morning, my good friend Joshua, a Jewish American, and I, a Protestant Jamaican, took a walk around Flushing with Emmy Catedral, a Filipino American artist who grew up in Queens and whose work has often focused on Flushing's ethnic and horticultural diversity. We wanted to see how the neighborhood's past influenced its present. We were in search of what people thought of the Flushing Remonstrance and whether it shaped their ideas of pluralism. Was it in their blind spot, the way the Bowne House seemed to be, or had it been dusted off and set before them?

It seemed fitting to plan a route along the locations listed on the Freedom Mile. We met on Main Street in front of St. George's Church, the second-oldest religious organization

Emmy Catedral, garden tags from *Germinalia*, 2008. Weeping beech saplings planted with mulch from religious pamphlets.

in Flushing. Outside was a sign announcing services in English, Chinese, and Spanish. As we hovered in the entrance, shortly after a service began, we were greeted by a charming elderly woman, who invited us to join the congregants. We demurred, explaining we had a lot of ground to cover, and she responded reassuringly, "We welcome everybody."

Onward we went, asking people everywhere we stopped about the Flushing Remonstrance. None of them knew anything about it. We ended up at the Macedonia AME Church, the third-oldest religious organization in Flushing, a block west of Bowne House, on Union Street, another "God's Row." Partway through the service, we were having difficulty wresting ourselves from the centripetal pull of the funky organ, but we managed to break free. On our way out we encountered a deacon who not only knew about the Remonstrance, but regaled us with reminiscences about growing up in Flushing with close friends whose surnames included Lum, Vargas, O'Neal, and DiVecchio. He saw in himself—part African American, part Native American—the story of the place. He told us that John Bowne had been an abolitionist, as were many of his descendants. For the deacon, the significance of the Remonstrance wasn't whether it had bequeathed the diversity he celebrated. It was in providing a model for how that diversity could be preserved: a group of men—many of whom weren't fans of the Quakers—stood up to defend the religious freedom of people with whom they disagreed, refusing to demonize them. They stood up for unity as well as diversity, just like the Chinese and Italian friends who'd come to his defense as a kid, when they traveled together to parts of Brooklyn and Staten Island where his skin color wasn't welcome.

We left the church, more awakened to the diversity around us, seeing it in the faces of many shades that we passed, hearing it in the multiple languages being spoken, observing it in the warm exchanges between Sikhs and Jews who parked beside each other in a synagogue's parking lot. As we walked south, Emmy pointed out emblems of Flushing's horticultural past in the names of the streets. The nation's first commercial nurseries began in Flushing, and some of the streets in the neighborhood celebrate this—Parsons Boulevard, for example, one block east of Bowne Street, was named for the family of Samuel Parsons Jr., a descendant of John Bowne who was head landscape architect for New York City and supplied Frederick Law Olmsted and Calvert Vaux with many plants for Central Park. Parsons learned about horticulture at his family's nursery, which was one of the most important commercial nurseries in the United States in the nineteenth century. The Parsons nursery searched the world for exotic specimens and brought trees and plants from all over to Flushing, which it then supplied to estates and parks in the United States and beyond. A bit north of the Bowne House, Weeping Beech Park honors Samuel Bowne Parsons (father of Samuel Parsons Jr.) and the weeping beech tree that he planted. That tree, which was transported from Belgium, lived there from 1847 until 1998, and is rumored to have produced generations of weeping beeches all over America. As we strolled along, we saw this tree, along with other rare specimens, in yards and on sidewalks. Not much farther south of Bowne House, we crossed Ash, Beech, and Cherry Avenues—and onward they grew alphabetically until Rose Avenue. At Rose Avenue and Parsons Boulevard lies the Kissena Park Historic Grove, a fourteen-acre plot that was part of the original Parsons nursery. It contains over a hundred varieties of trees, including rare ones that originate from Japan, China, and Iran. In that grove a few dozen saplings that Parsons planted have grown to provide a beautiful canopy for walkers sauntering underneath. Looking at Flushing's horticultural heritage in rich display, it was hard for us not to think of nature as corroboration of the diversity the deacon praised. Our walk ended in front of the Queens Public Library, which carries books in dozens of the languages that could be heard outside on Main Street, where we stood in wonderment, fascinated by the mix flooding our senses. Monks, street preachers, and believers on their way from the neighborhood's many places of worship zipped past us, some disappearing into a few of the restaurants that make Flushing smell like the crossroads of many nations, others heading off into the cultural vastness beyond.

. . .

In the face of such resplendent variety, it's impossible not to be enamored of the beauty of difference. Enchantment, however, can slide into naiveté—you gaze at the manifold offerings and ignore the rough textures that chafe. The danger is to forget that diversity often produces conflict. Pluralism, we ought not forget, brings together people with deep convictions and alienating differences. It's not enough that we live alongside each other—we have to learn to live with our differences. The Flushing Remonstrance is not only a moment of historical significance in New York. It is a reminder to New Yorkers today of the intellectual and moral resources we have to combat the challenges brought on by pluralism—particularly the temptation to harass and persecute people who think or look differently than we do. It reminds us that respect ought to be wed to tolerance. Most important, it reminds us of our responsibility to one another. After all, if the authorities come for the Quakers today, they might very well come for their neighbors tomorrow.

Before us in Flushing were hurrying immigrant crowds, some of them from groups that are enemies in their home countries but have learned to coexist without rancor in these packed streets. There was none of the fear-born intemperance one saw, for example, in 2010, when Muslims wanted to build a mosque a few blocks from the World Trade Center site, where terrorists had left a scar in the city's psyche. Some New Yorkers objected, stating that because some of the terrorists who committed that despicable act were Muslim, a mosque so close to Ground Zero was "insensitive." Then-mayor Michael Bloomberg delivered a speech that rejected those claims, saying, "We would betray our values—and play into our enemies' hands—if we were to treat Muslims differently than everyone else." He invoked the Flushing Remonstrance: "Of all our precious freedoms, the most important may be the freedom to worship as we wish." That document's signers still summon us to stand up for others when we disagree with them; to recognize that our city thrives not only despite our differences but because of them; and to affirm with W. H. Auden, "You shall love your crooked neighbour / With your crooked heart." It calls us, above all, to "doe unto all men as we desire all men should doe unto us, which is the true law of both Church and State."

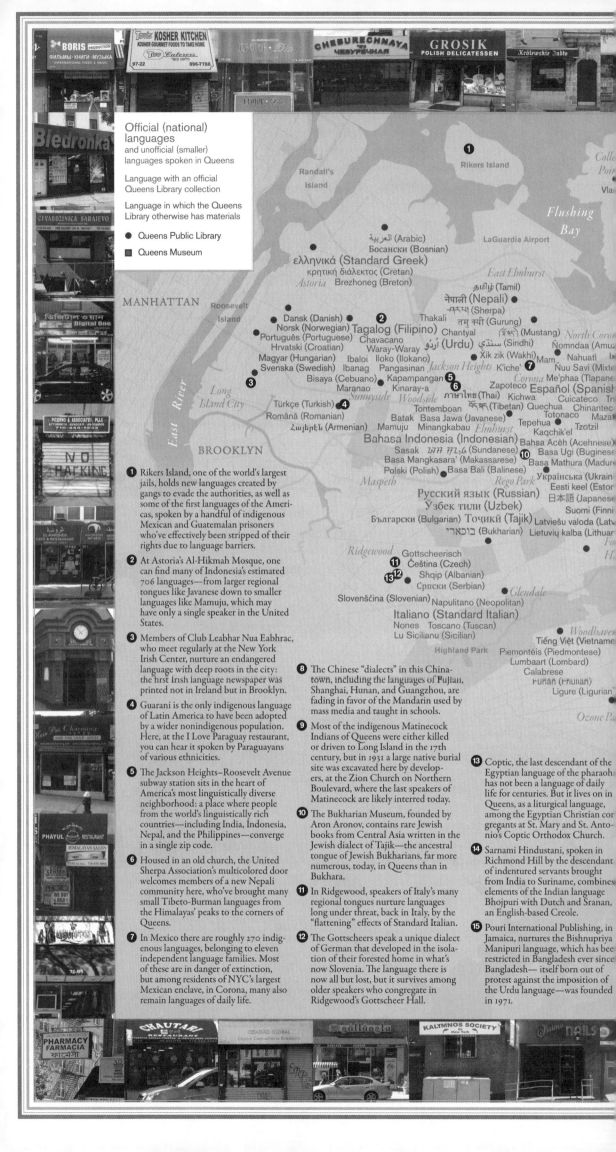

Official (national) languages
and unofficial (smaller) languages spoken in Queens

Language with an official Queens Library collection

Language in which the Queens Library otherwise has materials

● Queens Public Library
■ Queens Museum

MANHATTAN

Rikers Island ❶

Randall's Island

Flushing Bay

LaGuardia Airport

East Elmhurst

Astoria

العربية (Arabic)
Босански (Bosnian)
ελληνικά (Standard Greek)
κρητική διάλεκτος (Cretan)
Brezhoneg (Breton)

Roosevelt Island

தமிழ் (Tamil)
नेपाली (Nepali) ●
নেপালি (Sherpa)
Thakali
தமு क्यी (Gurung)
(मुस्ताङ) (Mustang)

Dansk (Danish)
Norsk (Norwegian)   Tagalog (Filipino) ❷   Chantyal
Português (Portuguese)   Chavacano   (اردو) (Urdu)   سندی (Sindhi)
Hrvatski (Croatian)   Waray-Waray
Magyar (Hungarian)   Ibaloi   Iloko (Ilokano)   *Jackson Heights*   Xik zik (Wakhi)   Mam
Svenska (Swedish)   Ibanag   Pangasinan   Ñomndaa (Amuz
Nahuatl   I
Bisaya (Cebuano)   Kapampangan ❺   Nuu Savi (Mixte
Long Island City   Maranao   Kinaray-a   K'iche' ❼
Zapoteco   Español (Spanish)
ภาษาไทย (Thai)   Kichwa   Cuicateco   Tr
Türkçe (Turkish) ❹   *Sunnyside* *Woodside*   ইউক্কাৰ (Tibetan)   Quechua   Chinantec
Română (Romanian)   Tontemboan   Totonaco   Maza
Հայերեն (Armenian)   Batak   Basa Jawa (Javanese)   Tepehua   Tzotzil
Mamuju   Minangkabau   *Elmhurst*   Kaqchikel
Bahasa Indonesia (Indonesian)   Bahsa Acêh (Acehnese)
Sasak   ᮘᮞ ᮞᮥᮔ᮪ᮓ (Sundanese)   Basa Ugi (Buginese)
Basa Mangkasara' (Makassarese)   Basa Mathura (Madur
Polski (Polish)   Basa Bali (Balinese)   *Rego Park*
Русский язык (Russian)   Українська (Ukrain
Ўзбек тили (Uzbek)   Eesti keel (Eston
日本語 (Japanese)
Български (Bulgarian)   Тоҷикӣ (Tajik)   Latviešu valoda (Latv   Suomi (Finni
בוכארי (Bukharian)   Lietuvių kalba (Lithuar

Maspeth

Ridgewood   Gottscheerisch
Čeština (Czech) ⓫
⓬   Shqip (Albanian)
⓭   Српски (Serbian)
Slovenščina (Slovenian)   Napulitano (Neopolitan)   *Glendale*
Italiano (Standard Italian)
Nones   Toscano (Tuscan)   *Woodhaven*
Lu Sicilianu (Sicilian)   Tiếng Việt (Vietname
Highland Park   Piemontèis (Piedmontese)
Lumbaart (Lombard)
Calabrese
Furlan (Friulian)
Ligure (Ligurian)

Ozone Pa

BROOKLYN

East River

❶ Rikers Island, one of the world's largest jails, holds new languages created by gangs to evade the authorities, as well as some of the first languages of the Americas, spoken by a handful of indigenous Mexican and Guatemalan prisoners who've effectively been stripped of their rights due to language barriers.

❷ At Astoria's Al-Hikmah Mosque, one can find many of Indonesia's estimated 706 languages—from larger regional tongues like Javanese down to smaller languages like Mamuju, which may have only a single speaker in the United States.

❸ Members of Club Leabhar Nua Eabhrac, who meet regularly at the New York Irish Center, nurture an endangered language with deep roots in the city: the first Irish language newspaper was printed not in Ireland but in Brooklyn.

❹ Guarani is the only indigenous language of Latin America to have been adopted by a wider nonindigenous population. Here, at the I Love Paraguay restaurant, you can hear it spoken by Paraguayans of various ethnicities.

❺ The Jackson Heights–Roosevelt Avenue subway station sits in the heart of America's most linguistically diverse neighborhood: a place where people from the world's linguistically rich countries—including India, Indonesia, Nepal, and the Philippines—converge in a single zip code.

❻ Housed in an old church, the United Sherpa Association's multicolored door welcomes members of a new Nepali community here, who've brought many small Tibeto-Burman languages from the Himalayas' peaks to the corners of Queens.

❼ In Mexico there are roughly 270 indigenous languages, belonging to eleven independent language families. Most of these are in danger of extinction, but among residents of NYC's largest Mexican enclave, in Corona, many also remain languages of daily life.

❽ The Chinese "dialects" in this Chinatown, including the languages of Fujian, Shanghai, Hunan, and Guangzhou, are fading in favor of the Mandarin used by mass media and taught in schools.

❾ Most of the indigenous Matinecock Indians of Queens were either killed or driven to Long Island in the 17th century, but in 1931 a large native burial site was excavated here by developers, at the Zion Church on Northern Boulevard, where the last speakers of Matinecock are likely interred today.

❿ The Bukharian Museum, founded by Aron Aronov, contains rare Jewish books from Central Asia written in the Jewish dialect of Tajik—the ancestral tongue of Jewish Bukharians, far more numerous, today, in Queens than in Bukhara.

⓫ In Ridgewood, speakers of Italy's many regional tongues nurture languages long under threat, back in Italy, by the "flattening" effects of Standard Italian.

⓬ The Gottscheers speak a unique dialect of German that developed in the isolation of their forested home in what's now Slovenia. The language there is now all but lost, but it survives among older speakers who congregate in Ridgewood's Gottscheer Hall.

⓭ Coptic, the last descendant of the Egyptian language of the pharaoh has not been a language of daily life for centuries. But it lives on in Queens, as a liturgical language, among the Egyptian Christian cor gregants at St. Mary and St. Antonio's Coptic Orthodox Church.

⓮ Sarnami Hindustani, spoken in Richmond Hill by the descendant of indentured servants brought from India to Suriname, combines elements of the Indian language Bhojpuri with Dutch and Sranan, an English-based Creole.

⓯ Pouri International Publishing, in Jamaica, nurtures the Bishnupriya Manipuri language, which has bee restricted in Bangladesh ever since Bangladesh— itself born out of protest against the imposition of the Urdu language—was founded in 1971.

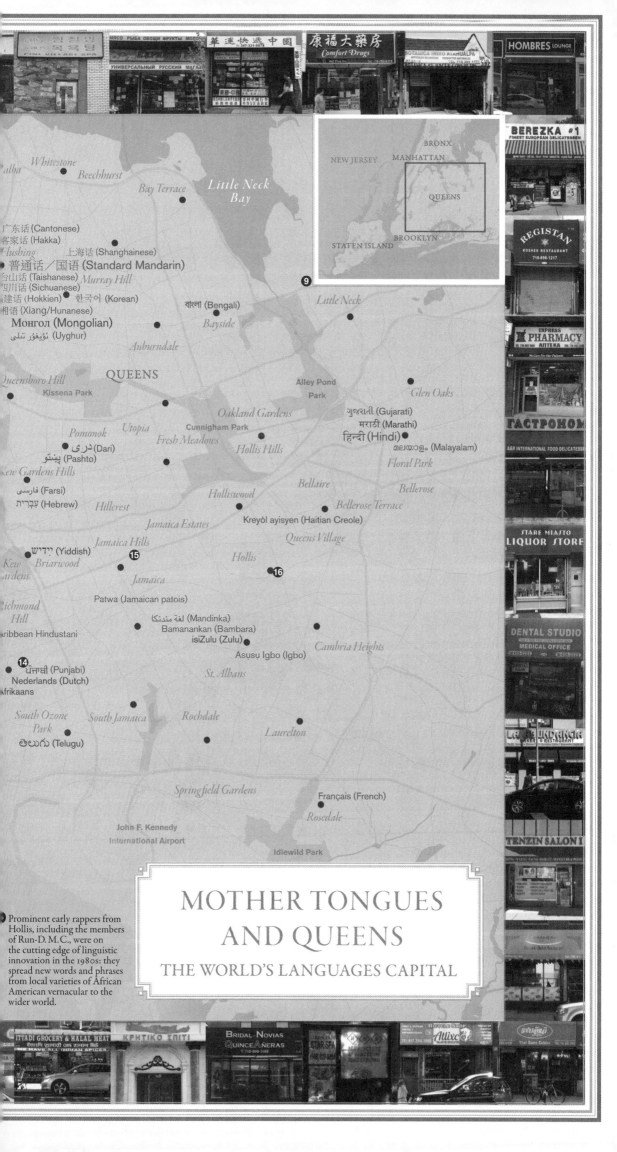

MOTHER TONGUES AND QUEENS
THE WORLD'S LANGUAGES CAPITAL

Prominent early rappers from Hollis, including the members of Run-D.M.C., were on the cutting edge of linguistic innovation in the 1980s: they spread new words and phrases from local varieties of African American vernacular to the wider world.

24 MOTHER TONGUES AND QUEENS

New York is a city that talks. And talks and talks and talks. Not only in different tones—whispers in court, shouts in the subway, grumbles in restaurant queues—but also in many different languages. Language can bridge from the old to the new, but it can also be used as a drawbridge to keep outsiders at bay. In New York, language is an overworked handmaiden preserving immigrants' habits and rituals as they try to create a new home without losing touch with the old. If, as often seems the case, ambition is the one mother tongue shared by every New Yorker, then the various national tongues are the means immigrant New York uses to express its self-worth.

New York City's many languages function like wormholes, taking us to new cultures, but they also close off speakers who are unable to fully participate in New York's economy through its lingua franca, English. This is especially true for people who speak endangered languages and who struggle not to be left behind while safeguarding an important part of themselves and their country. In some cases, a very civilization depends on a few immigrants achieving the balance between survival and preservation.

The Endangered Language Alliance (ELA), our collaborator and great resource in assembling this map of gloriously polyglot Queens, states, "Melting pots like New York are home to hundreds of endangered minority languages, from the Otomanguean languages of Mexico, to the Nilo-Saharan languages of Sudan and everywhere between. Religious liturgies, native-language literatures, ethnic newspapers and radio stations quietly struggle and flourish." The Tower of Babel myth suggests that there's power in homogeneity, but there's another power in heterogeneity, in the variety of languages and the many ways they can describe the world (and time, space, self, others, agency, and similar essentials).

The capital of linguistic diversity, not just for the five boroughs, but for the human species, is Queens. This tower of something better than Babel is a peculiarly blessed and rich place, as well as an unparalleled testament to the possibilities of coexistence among those whose differences are profound. Our map locates many of the borough's languages, as well as the libraries that serve the speakers with collections in those tongues; our photographic map border by Mirissa Neff calls attention to how this linguistic diversity is visible right out on the street; and our essay by Suketu Mehta celebrates the lived experience of polyglot Gotham.

CARTOGRAPHY: MOLLY ROY; PHOTOGRAPHS: MIRISSA NEFF   MAP APPEARS ON PAGES 192–193.

TOWER OF SCRABBLE   BY SUKETU MEHTA

How does a new immigrant learn a new language? As a child does.

It is 1996, and my son Gautama's first day of school, at the Y on 14th Street in Manhattan. The entire class of two-year-olds is speaking English, all except my son, whom we have raised speaking Gujarati. He comes into the class and sees a yellow school bus and runs toward it. But someone else snatches it from him. The teachers lead the kids through a drill, telling them when to raise their hands; they sing songs. My son cannot understand. I sit with him feeling miserable. The kids in my apartment building say about him: "He can't talk." He looks up at them hopefully, but they don't invite him to play with them. When he eats his khichri in the little garden downstairs, the girl across the hall says, "Eeeuww." This is colonialism. This is what it has done to me and to my son: it has rendered our language unspeakable.

I switch him to a new school, the Third Street Music School Settlement (which is actually on 11th Street), where the medium of instruction is music. When I first speak to his teacher, a woman sitting behind a piano in front of a class of little Japanese, little French, little American kids, I caution her that Gautama doesn't speak English; there will have to be a transition. "Don't worry," she says. "When you bring him here, come with a tape of a song he knows in his own language."

So I make a tape, of a lullaby that I have been singing to Gautama almost every night:

Lalla lalla lori
Doodh ki katori
Doodh me batasha
Munna dekho tamasha

Gautama enters the new schoolroom, apprehensive, wondering if all these kids will talk to him, play with him. The teacher listens to the tape. Then she turns to the classroom. "Children, this is Gautama. Let's all sing a song in Gautama's language." She plays it on the piano, leading the chorus. And my son watches in amazement as all the little American and Japanese and French and Indian kids sing this song that he knows so well, this song that soothes him into sleep. My son discovers that his language is no longer unspeakable. If they're willing to learn his language, then . . .

Within a month, Gautama is speaking English.

· · ·

The tallest building of the ancient world was the Tower of Babel. It was so ambitious an undertaking—its monolingual builders wanted its top to reach heaven—that God confounded their tongues, so that they could not understand one another, and they scattered all over the world, abandoning their mighty project. Centuries later, a band of people flew down from the heavens into two equally mighty towers in another splendid city, also invoking God's name. Except this time, the people of the city did not disperse, since they were already speaking in an ungodly babble of tongues. They regrouped, to begin building yet another tower. This is the benefit of diversity: if you have had long experience in working with other cultures, you are less vulnerable to the whims of a jealous god and his cunning machinations to keep you from reaching him.

Not for nothing did the writer O. Henry call New York "Baghdad-on-the-subway." Diversity of language is the clearest indication of diversity of culture, and by this measure New York was from its very beginnings an extraordinarily diverse city. By 1643, only nineteen years after the first Walloon settlers founded New Amsterdam, 18 languages were already being spoken in the city—among a population of a mere 500. Today, over 176 languages are spoken in New York's schools. Nowhere are more of them spoken than in the neighborhood of Jackson Heights, in Queens, where I first came to America with my family, in 1977, and spent eight years of my teenage and early adult years.

.   .   .

On Valentine's Day 2015, I drive out to Jackson Heights for a walkabout with Daniel Kaufman and a friend, Fahima, a visiting Egyptian architect from Cairo.

Daniel is a linguistic raconteur who speaks with a Hebrew accent, because his parents spoke Hebrew at home. It is an example of a language that came back from near-death when the state of Israel came into being. "To revive Hebrew they trampled Yiddish almost to death. In Israel they would beat you up if you spoke Yiddish." Daniel now runs the Endangered Language Alliance, a small but marvelous organization that works with native speakers in New York to save and catalog threatened languages in the city.

Around the corner from where I grew up, on the corner of 82nd Street and 35th Avenue, I point out to Daniel the street sign reading "35TH AVENUE." Each letter has a number below it—the A, a 1; the V, a 4; and so on. "What does that remind you of?"

"Scrabble!" says Daniel.

The sign is in honor of the adjoining Community United Methodist Church, where Alfred Butts invented Scrabble in 1931. The building itself is a polyglot house of worship: a church holding multidenominational services in Indonesian, Spanish, Korean, and Mandarin. God is praised in many tongues in the house where Scrabble was invented.

The number commonly bandied about is that there are 800 languages spoken in New York City—a number that first appeared in an interview with Daniel's partner, who extrapolated it from the linguistic diversity of the countries from which the city's immigrants are now coming. Daniel cautions that the number is a "guesstimate." The official census estimate is that there are some 200 languages spoken in the city, also a wild underestimate.

There are some 7,000 languages spoken on the planet; half of them are in danger of vanishing. In New York between a quarter to a third of the languages are endangered. A language classified as "endangered" could have as many as 40,000 speakers in the city, but it's going to be gone in two generations. There are some that might only be spoken by one or two people in the city, such as the iKota language from Gabon, which Daniel was made aware of by a speaker in Harlem. Another time, Daniel met a man from Eastern Indonesia, which has the highest linguistic diversity of any area on the planet, who spoke a language called Teon Nila Serua. It's very endangered because that part of the country sided with the Dutch during the war of independence, and most people speaking it moved to Holland during the war. The man was now the only speaker of the language in New York.

These are full-fledged languages, not dialects, as many people believe. Daniel explains the difference: any collection of words people use to communicate is a "complete human language"; variants of those languages, intelligible among smaller groups, are dialects. He repeats an old saying I've heard before: "A language is a dialect with an army and a navy." Therefore, as my guru, the Kannada writer U. R. Ananthamurthy, once noted, "An international language is one with an atom bomb."

"New York is the only world city that's ashamed of its own dialect," notes Daniel, because it was associated with lower-class immigrants, mostly Irish and Italian. Only real New Yorkers would say "toity-toid and toid," or "goil" instead of "girl," or "earl" instead of "oil," pronouncing: "I sor a goil at the earl station."

With a Hispanic population of 28 percent, growing at 8 percent a year, the city is increasingly referred to as Nueva York. In some quarters, it's even referred to as "Manhattitlan"— a combination of "Manhattan" and "Tenochtitlan," the Aztec capital. But many Mexicans first learn Spanish only when they move to New York. Mexico has over 200 indigenous languages, placing it among the countries with the highest linguistic diversity in the world. When the indigenous language speakers come to New York, they find that they have to learn Spanish to get a job and an apartment, whether in Corona or Sunset Park or Staten Island.

"What about English?" I ask Daniel.

He laughs. "English is superfluous."

But not knowing even Spanish has real consequences for the children of the indigenous speakers. In school they don't respond to teachers speaking English or Spanish, and so they get left behind, under the assumption that they're not smart, that they can't or won't participate in the classroom. Public school funding for bilingual education has been cut back.

When they do learn English, these children of indigenous Mexican immigrants develop their own variant, which is sometimes hard to decipher by outsiders. The Spanish spoken in New York is its own thing, a blend of different Spanish dialects. The bulk of it is Caribbean Spanish: the tongues spoken in the Dominican Republic and Puerto Rico. It doesn't have much cultural contact with Mexican Spanish.

New York is a sort of language asylum. It allows banned languages to flourish, like Kurdish, the teaching of which is forbidden in Turkey. Daniel has to negotiate these issues carefully, though. He was once invited to make recordings at an event for the Bishnupriya Manipuri speakers, a group of Bangladeshi Hindus. Around forty people showed up. The language is philogenetically related to Bengali but has close social contact with Manipuri, or Meithei, which is a Tibeto-Burman language spoken in the Indian state of Manipur. But the Manipuris scoff at it, and there are political issues around the nomenclature. The Meithei, who want to reserve the term *Manipuri* for themselves, might take umbrage at Daniel's using the term to refer to their neighbors.

Immigrants can be obstinate about holding on to their origin-tongues, because language can also be used for sabotage or as a stratagem. We spoke in Hindi or Gujarati, my best friend Ashish and I, and later my wife and I, when we wanted to talk about or make fun of other people in the subway or on the street, or when we were calling each other from work, foiling eavesdroppers.

The wholesale diamond market on 47th Street, where my parents had an office, was dominated by Gujarati-speaking Indians and Yiddish-speaking Hasidim. The Gujaratis learned Yiddish on the sly, as the Hasidim learned Gujarati, but we did not use it to converse with the people whose native tongue it was. We used our secret knowledge to business advantage, eavesdropping on the others' conversations to find out how much room we had to haggle on a parcel of diamonds.

· · ·

All this tongue-wagging about the tongues of Man has made us hungry. So we repair to a newish restaurant, the Arepa Lady, a small café belonging to a Colombian woman who started with a hugely successful food cart under the 7 train tracks on Roosevelt Avenue, selling the delicious South American pastries. Business flourished to the point where she could afford to expand into this restaurant. There are bottles of sauces on the table, ranging from mildly spicy to not spicy.

As we savor our arepas, we reflect on how most languages spoken in the diaspora die within two generations. An exception is Latvian, which is nourished in upstate summer camps for Latvian children, conducted entirely in Latvian. Amish and Yiddish are other, classic examples, but they're totally socially isolated. Daniel tells us what is lost when a language dies. "Language is a collective instrument, an incredibly unique product of thousands and thousands of years of evolution. It's a very complex piece of technology that can delineate all of the things that need to be delineated in the universe and has many, many centuries of knowledge. The language defines the community and strengthens the community. When people lose that language, they lose a big part of their identity. There are quite real effects for communities that lose their language—you're living with their defeat. Native American groups feel this way—language is the marker of their survival. When you don't have that, you're living with your defeat, your conquest through colonialism."

Most indigenous languages don't have a script, and Daniel and his institute work with the speakers to preserve a written record, usually with Latin characters. He'll also do such things as setting up a radio station for a Guatemalan language—K'iche'—in his office, so that the language is disseminated, has a medium.

Television has had disastrous effects on indigenous languages, but the Internet has been good for them because it's a two-way medium and everyone can create their own Facebook page, writing out the language "however the hell they want."

Daniel "crossed the rubicon" from academia to activism with the first recording in his office at the ELA in 2009. A Peruvian woman had brought in her mother, a Quechua-speaking woman in her sixties, who would go back and forth from her village to New York, selling crafts. Her daughter had grown up in Lima and didn't speak much Quechua. Daniel and two other workers, his colleague Juliette and a young volunteer who had just finished her bachelor's, gathered around the old lady at the mic, waiting for her to speak in her language. "Until that point I was really a grammarian, a specialist in Austronesian languages, interested in nouns, verbs, grammar," recalls Daniel. "I was imagining this as more of an academic enterprise."

Then the Peruvian woman leaned toward the microphone and started speaking in Quechua. Daniel thought they'd get a cute little story about village life. After a few moments the moisture began gathering in her eyes. As the three of them looked on, not understanding a word, the woman, weeping, recited her story. It was, they learned much later through a translator (none of them wanted to press her to translate), a story of the hard childhood she'd had, the abuse and discrimination she'd faced for speaking her language—in Peru, in New York City. For a good half hour the woman spoke and wept, wept and spoke. The act of speaking, the permission to speak in her native tongue, had released something deep inside her, and the tears and the stories flowed. "We got a mountain of stories about sorrow, stories about language endangerment. We were confronted with all of the stories that led to the endangerment—the hatred, the discrimination. Then I realized that grammar is just one small part of the project."

Daniel's Indonesian wife, Amalia, comes into the café with their two small children; she has been teaching an Indonesian dance class nearby.

"Nobody can think of unique words in their own languages," says Daniel. "Can you?" I can't think of one, in Gujarati, on the spur of the moment. "That's because people don't think the words they speak are unique—it's just their language."

But there are certainly languages that might strike most of us as unique, like the click languages of Africa, which are spoken with a series of clicks, delineated in writing as a | or ! or ʘ or || or ǂ. The largest of them is the Khoekhoe, the national language of Namibia. Daniel hasn't found anybody in the city who speaks the language. But the one that really enchants me is the N|uu language of Botswana, where a kissing sound (ʘ) accompanies some of the words. (NYU's Chris Collins is now working with the last couple of speakers of the language.) Daniel demonstrates this sound, and we follow.

Outside the windows, it has begun to snow again. It is falling on every part of the darkening district—on the treeless avenues, on the illegal basement apartments, on the Ecuadorean food carts, on the rusting tracks of the 7 train, on the bailaderos, the Pakistani appliance stores, the Indian sari shops. On Valentine's Day, snow is general all over Jackson Heights. And inside the Colombian Arepa Lady, an Egyptian, an Indian, an Indonesian, and an American who speaks English with a Hebrew accent are making kissing sounds at each other. ✺

25 BLACK STAR LINES

Harlem, like no other neighborhood in the United States, lays claim to being the capital of Black America, the heart of African American culture, and both Mecca and Promised Land for people of African heritage from all over the United States and the world. A short walk through it quickly reveals rituals that all seem arranged to answer Harlem son Countee Cullen's question, "What is Africa to me?" One doesn't pass through Harlem so much as one *arrives* there.

The neighborhood is therefore both place and idea, and to speak of its past—the Harlem Renaissance, for instance—or its future—say, fears over gentrification—is to talk about institutions and people African Americans hold dear: churches, mosques, the Apollo Theater, Marcus Garvey, Malcolm X, Martin Luther King Jr., Adam Clayton Powell Jr., Frederick Douglass. Street names, wall murals, school names, even restaurant menus (where dishes are named after African American religious, political, and cultural leaders) testify to the power of African American heritage in this neighborhood. Arguments about the meaning of Harlem, then, are arguments about what is sacred. And some institutions carry multiple histories and meanings of sacredness—perhaps the most sacred of them all, if judged by the number of murals and expressions of neighborhood sentiment, is the Apollo Theater. In this neighborhood, change is not just about the loss of places and traditions—it is about the loss of memory that is invaluable to African American character. The way one prays or plays or pickets here says multitudes about which institutions and people are considered sacred by Americans of African heritage. This uptown neighborhood, home to many of the most important African American stars, and a place where even a humble resident can often feel like a star, is both destination and constellation—like those depicted in the star chart, behind this map, of the night sky on January 26, 1934, when the hallowed Apollo Theater opened.

CARTOGRAPHY: MOLLY ROY MAP APPEARS ON PAGES 200–201.

HOME TO HARLEM BY CHRISTINA ZANFAGNA

"What is the Black Star?" Mos Def and Talib Kweli ask on their now-classic late-nineties hip-hop record, *Black Star.* "Is it the cat with the black shades, the black car? / Is it shinin' from very far, to where you are?" The New York MCs aren't alone in their wonder. After all, a black star is a kind of impossibility. How can we see a black star against the darkness of the night?

Astronomers and physicists have wondered, too. Some, using the term to explain various galactic phenomena, argue that black stars existed early in the universe, dying off before

SACRED SITES (SECULAR)

1. Cotton Club (1923–35): home to Cab Calloway's *Brown Sugar* revue
2. Savoy Ballroom (1926–58): Langston Hughes's "Heartbeat of Harlem"
3. Renaissance Ballroom and Casino (opened 1924): home to elegant dances, prizefights, and meetings of the NAACP
4. Small's Paradise (1925–86): major jazz place and the first in Harlem to be integrated; Malcolm Little works here as a waiter before becoming Malcolm X
5. Barron's Exclusive Club (opened 1915): Duke Ellington brought to Harlem by Ada "Bricktop" Smith in 1923
6. Schomburg Center for Research in Black Culture (opened 1905): Langston Hughes's ashes now interred beneath the foyer
7. World Headquarters (1919–26) of Marcus Garvey's Universal Negro Improvement Association (UNIA) and his Black Star Line
8. Crescent Theater (Maximilian Zypkes, architect) starts showing films and vaudeville in 1909; original headquarters of UNIA
9. Leroy's jazz club (c. 1920s): Count Basie gets his first steady Harlem gig in 1925
10. Connie's Inn (1923–34): Harlem home of Louis Armstrong, Fats Waller, and Peg Leg Bates
11. Showman's Jazz Club (1942–): Harlem host to jazz legends, including Lionel Hampton and Sarah Vaughan
12. Apollo Theater (1934–): Hurtig and Seaman's New Burlesque Theater changes name and opens to blacks
13. Hotel Theresa (1912–67): Harlem host to Muhammad Ali, Patrice Lumumba, and A. Philip Randolph's March on Washington Movement
14. African-American Wax Museum of Harlem (c. 1990s): black stars immortalized in wax; Raven Chanticleer, proprietor
15. Minton's Playhouse (1938–74): crucial seedbed for bebop cutting sessions of Dizzy Gillespie, Charlie Parker, Thelonious Monk, and others
16. Mount Morris Park renamed Marcus Garvey Park (1973)
17. Harlem World disco (1978–84): home to storied hip–hop battles, including Kool Moe Dee vs Busy Bee Starski in 1981
18. James Reese Europe's Harlem Hellfighters WWI band turns the corner into Harlem and changes its sound from military marches to jazz (1919)
19. Ike Hines's Professional Club (opened 1880): inspiration for James Weldon Johnson's 1912 *Autobiography of an Ex–Coloured Man;* three downtown locations move progressively north toward Harlem

SACRED SITES (RELIGIOUS)

1. The Most Worshipful Prince Hall: Order of the Eastern Star (Freemasons)
2. First Haitian Baptist Church
3. Zion Baptist Church
4. Greater Hood Memorial AME Church (founded 1822): home today to the Hip Hop Church, founded by "rap's first millionaire," Kurtis Blow
5. Timbuktu Islamic Center
6. Mosque of Islamic Brotherhood
7. Victory Tabernacle Seventh Day Christian Church
8. Abyssinian Baptist Church (founded 1808): Calvin Butts III, pastor
9. Mother AME Zion Church (founded 1796): oldest black church in New York City and stop on the Underground Railroad; congregants included Frederick Douglass and Harriet Tubman
10. West Indian Prayer Warriors Deliverance Church
11. Shiloh Baptist Church
12. Pentecostal Faith Church: founded by the great broadcaster and preacher Mother Horn in 1938; James Baldwin attends its opening
13. Muhammad Mosque No. 7: official New York headquarters of Louis Farrakhan's Nation of Islam
14. Presbyterian Church of Ghana
15. Debre Sahel Beaata LeMariam Ethiopian Orthodox Tewahedo Church
16. Commandment Keepers Synagogue (founded 1919): Black Hebrew congregation
17. Mount Olivet Baptist Church (formerly Temple Israel of New York)
18. Masjid Malcolm Shabazz (formerly Mosque No. 7)
19. Bethel Gospel Assembly

SACRED SITES (SECULAR AND RELIGIOUS)

1. Audubon Ballroom (opened 1912, Broadway at 165th St): Malcolm X is assassinated and called home to Allah (1965); now home to the Shabazz Center
2. Liberty Hall of Marcus Garvey's UNIA: formerly Metropolitan Baptist Tabernacle
3. Harlem YMCA: first home of the Nation of Islam's Temple No. 7 (1946)
4. The old Lincoln Theater: now the Metropolitan African Methodist Episcopal Church
5. Lafayette Theater (opened 1912): acquired by Williams Institutional Christian Methodist Episcopal Church in 1951
6. Riverside Church: Martin Luther King Jr speaks against the Vietnam War (1967)
7. Impact Church of Harlem at the Magic Johnson Theater
8. Allah School in Mecca: Five Percenters' Harlem headquarters
9. Greater Refuge Temple: global headquarters of the Church of our Lord Jesus Christ of the Apostolic Faith—previously the Harlem Casino
10. First Corinthian Baptist Church—previously the Regent Theater
11. Church of the Lord Jesus Christ of the Apostolic Faith—previously the Mt. Morris Theater

Riverside Dr
Claremont Ave
Broadway
Riverside Park
Columbus Ave
Manhattan Ave

BLACK STAR LINES
HARLEM SECULAR AND SACRED

conventional stars were able to form. Others contend that quantum effects may prevent true black holes from forming, giving rise instead to dense entities called black stars.

The ancient Hebrews also had a theory. They referred to Saturn as a black star, representing it with six points. It was a precursor to the Star of David, that familiar symbol of modern Jewishness and longing for Zion. It was also a central symbol for Marcus Garvey, the Pan-Africanist pioneer whose Black Star shipping line has coursed through black political thought for almost a century.

In 1917 Garvey planted the headquarters of his Universal Negro Improvement Association in the heart of Black Harlem in the old Crescent Theater on 135th Street. Initiating a global mass movement known as Garveyism, the Jamaican-born visionary launched the literal embodiment of "Back to Africa" ideology—a shipping line intended to transport goods and people back to the motherland. When Joshua Cockburn, the mariner hired to captain the Black Star Line's first boat, visited the Harlem offices two years later, in 1919, he saw a line stretching down the block. Eager job seekers and followers of the Garvey faith waited patiently for a date with their racial and geographic destiny.

Garvey's Afrocentric philosophies were shaped by the "Back-to-Zion" ideology of Jewish Harlemites. His musical director and confidant, Rabbi Arnold Josiah Ford, helped found the Commandment Keepers Ethiopian Hebrew Congregation of the Living God Pillar and Ground of Truth—a sect of predominantly Afro-Caribbean Black Hebrews that worshipped in a synagogue at 123rd Street and Lenox Avenue. The Commandment Keepers' members were guided by the belief that the people of Ethiopia were the descendants of one of the lost tribes of Israel. Black Hebrews, like Garveyites, espoused a brand of black Zionism that would come to shape the feel of Harlem's churches and ballrooms.

Garvey's Black Star Line made only a few voyages. The fleet was undone by continued thievery by employees, acts of infiltration and sabotage by J. Edgar Hoover's Bureau of Investigation, and its founder's five-year prison sentence for mail fraud. The ships ceased sailing altogether in 1922, but they've remained a potent symbol of the black pilgrim's longing for home. "Train to Zion is coming," the reggae musicians Linval Thompson and U Brown sang in the 1970s, when the call for repatriation was widespread across the black diaspora. "Don't want no one to miss it / It's the Black Star Liner / It's going to Zion."

Many seekers from the diasporic cosmos have journeyed to and from Harlem in search of all matters sacred and secular—Jesus and jazz, Allah and hip-hop, freedom and fame. Harriet Tubman tracked the North Star through many dark nights along the Underground Railroad, across the Mason-Dixon line, and eventually to New York's Mother African Methodist Episcopal Zion Church. The oldest black church in New York and now a Harlem holy site, "Mother Zion" has attracted politically influential congregants such as Sojourner Truth, Frederick Douglass, and Paul Robeson.

Black Star Lines continue to crosscut Harlem, the Black Mecca in motion, a place that's at once departure point, rest stop, and final destination. To draw a map of Garvey's Harlem is to conjure multiple territories—Africa, Jamaica, Israel. To draw a map of Harlem is to connect the lines between black stars and Stars of David. For "Planet Harlem," as religious scholar Tony Carnes once told me, "percolates with pilgrims."

· · ·

Before Harlem reigned as the black capital of America, it was a farming village inhabited first by the Lenape, a native community, and then by European settlers of mostly Dutch origin. The first African Americans in Harlem, both freed and enslaved, worked farms in the area known as Nieuw Haarlem, a settlement formally established by Peter Stuyvesant in 1658 and named after the Dutch city of Haarlem. It remained provincial until the development of railroad lines, which drew real estate speculators and builders and linked the northern village to the southern regions of the city. By the advent of a subway line to Harlem in 1904, a slew of other commercial developments and cultural institutions had been erected, especially large-scale theaters and movie palaces.

Harlem's first major theater—the Harlem Opera House—was built in 1889 by inventor and cigar manufacturer Oscar Hammerstein I, just down the block from the vaudeville house, which later became the Apollo Theater. By the early 1900s Harlem was known as an epicenter for entertainment. Crowds flocked to its theaters, clubs, and speakeasies as the Jazz Age reached a peak in the 1920s, with black entertainers the main attraction. But Jim Crow's northern variant, during Harlem's Renaissance heyday, made black stardom a paradox.

African American jazz luminaries such as Fletcher Henderson and Duke Ellington dazzled whites-only crowds at the Cotton Club, but could not walk through the venue's front door. The Cotton Club, like the Savoy Ballroom, showcased black performers while simultaneously propagating racist imagery—presenting African Americans as savage primitives from faraway jungles or good ol' plantation "darkies" from the American South. Black female dancers were forced to take a "brown bag test": only women with skin color lighter than a brown paper bag could score a gig at the Cotton Club or the Savoy. In the white-owned club world, black stars were either too black or not black enough. It wasn't until 1934 that the Apollo, previously known as Hurtig and Seamon's New Burlesque Theater, opened its doors to African Americans. That same year, seventeen-year-old Ella Fitzgerald won its "Amateur Night" to launch her career.

As Fitzgerald took the Apollo stage, she rubbed a bit of varnished wood at stage left, which had just been placed there by Amateur Night's first host, Ralph Cooper Sr., but whose history in Harlem had deep roots. The Apollo's famous stump was once part of the Tree of Hope—a lone elm on Seventh Avenue nestled between the famed Lafayette Theater and Connie's Inn—which beckoned the likes of Ethel Waters and Eubie Blake to the "Boulevard of Dreams," and which aspiring black stars ceremoniously rubbed, as they passed by, for good luck. The tree was chopped down in 1934 and sold off in pieces as souvenirs. One of those pieces, thanks to Ralph Cooper, landed at the Apollo so that performers could touch the sanctified stump before being applauded into stardom onstage or booed back into anonymity's shadows.

A showcase for bona fide black stars from Duke Ellington to Bob Marley, Celia Cruz, George Clinton, and Michael Jackson, the Apollo has also celebrated them after death. This is the stage, across which, in 1959, a youthful James Brown shimmied in his signature one-legged, holy dance frenzy—and where the Godfather of Soul made his final pilgrimage, too. Brown's posthumous homecoming, in 2006, drew thousands of mourners to 125th Street and nearby. They looked on, almost fifty years after Brown's debut, as his motionless body was borne in a white carriage, led by two white Percheron horses with feather-plumed headdresses, in a slow twenty-block procession from the Reverend Al Sharpton's Harlem headquarters, on 145th Street, down to the Apollo. Laid out in a twenty-four-karat gold coffin, Brown was dressed in a glittery blue suit with silver trim and silver shoes to match. The quintessence of black stardom sparkled from his open casket as Reverend Sharpton delivered a rousing eulogy, sending the showman home from Harlem to the Promised Land.

Many other black stars have dressed to impress on 125th Street. In the 1980s Dapper Dan—heralded as the "Hip-Hop Tailor of Harlem"—outfitted a slew of rap artists with custom European-inspired designer apparel from his boutique there. Until, that is, he was forced to close after two heavyweights—Mike Tyson and Mitch Green—got into a brawl at his store and brought undesirable publicity and, with it, lawsuits from Gucci, Fendi, and Louis Vuitton. Dapper Dan's is gone now, but 125th Street still boasts clothing retailers like Jimmy Jazz—a destination for urban streetwear, right next door to the Apollo,

Photographs of Harlem by Mirissa Neff, 2015

where in the same month as James Brown's funeral, I took my friend Alick Macheso, a Zimbabwean music star, to shop. Macheso insisted on going there to get decked out—from cap to kicks—before his flight back to Harare. He sported his new gear along 125th Street, promenading along what is now Harlem's "Walk of Fame"—a stretch of pavement with inlaid plaques featuring the names of black idols. "Now I'm ready to go home, back to Africa," said the visiting musician, "with some of the Black Mecca on my back."

Beyond the hip-hop glamour and bright retail lights of 125th Street, of course, there's also a Harlem fallen from grace. This is a Harlem of collapse and conversion, perhaps epitomized by the slow demise of the Renaissance Ballroom. One of Harlem's only integrated clubs in the 1920s, the "Renny" was home to prizefights, NAACP gatherings, and America's first professional black basketball team. After closing its doors in 1979, the ballroom deteriorated into a wasted ruin and, not surprisingly, was used as the setting of Spike Lee's crack den in his 1991 movie, *Jungle Fever.* Reduced to a pile of rubble in 2015, the lot, presided over by the Neo-Gothic towers of the famed Abyssinian Baptist Church, will soon be home to an eight-story residential tower.

This kind of proximity—between past and present, sacred and secular—is everywhere in Harlem. Often, churches and theaters even occupy the same buildings. The colossal movie palaces and dance halls built in the early 1900s proved unsustainable as houses of entertainment. Declining social conditions in Harlem after World War II likewise precipitated a mass exodus in the 1960s and '70s. Church buildings were destroyed, forcing congregations to take shelter in abandoned theaters. In a way, Harlem churches and theaters have saved each other: old ballrooms and movie houses have allowed religious congregations to be "born again" as churches have simultaneously breathed new life into desecrated theaters. While Harlem has wooed converts to its places-of-prayer, its landscape has also undergone myriad conversions, creating a sort of ever-changing urban palimpsest of both debauchery and devotion.

Of course, many of the superstars who have graced Harlem stages grew up singing and playing in the church. Harlem resident and jazz pianist Mary Lou Williams combined Catholicism and bebop, "praying through her fingers" in a historic jazz mass at St. Patrick's Cathedral in 1975. More recently, the Church of the Intercession in Harlem held jazz concerts in its 2,300-square-foot underground crypt—the first official columbarium built in the United States, in 1915.

When I was a student at New York University in the late 1990s, living downtown in the Village and singing with the All University Gospel Choir, I witnessed this combination of pop and gospel during one of my first ventures into Harlem. In a small, crowded uptown church, I watched Martha Wash—former backup singer for the "Queen of Disco" Sylvester and unrecognized vocal powerhouse on C+C Music Factory's 1990 hit, "Gonna Make You Sweat (Everybody Dance Now)"—belt out gospel classics with earthy efferves-

cence. A black star who did not receive her proper "shine" from the popular music industry, Martha's vocals shimmered, that day, like a disco ball in the sanctuary.

Another time, I watched Kurtis Blow, the Harlem-born MC who became "rap's first millionaire," offer another gloss on the pop-gospel nexus. After founding his Hip Hop Church ministry at Greater Hood Memorial AME Zion Church, Kurtis began leading Thursday night services featuring rap music. An ordained minister clad in baggy jeans, oversized jersey, and silver cross necklace, he warned the congregation: "This is not entertainment; this is not a show. This is ministry." The congregation hollered back—"Word!" Their affirmation, common in hip-hop parlance, was linked to the familiar aphorism "word is bond"—a phrase originating with another group, the Five Percent Nation, whose ideas have been key both to Harlem's spiritual landscape and to recent black culture at large.

An offshoot of Islam, the Five Percent Nation is symbolized by a crescent moon and black star behind the number 7, inside a larger eight-pointed nautical star. The group's headquarters, the Allah School in Mecca, is located just twenty blocks south of Greater Hood Memorial AME Zion Church.

To draw a map of Kurtis's Harlem is to conjure multiple promised lands—Heaven, Mecca, and Zion. A map that connects the lines between black stars, crosses, and crescent moons.

· · ·

Since my student days visiting Harlem churches, I've moved west to California. But whenever I visit New York City, I make a point of returning to Harlem. It's a home of sorts—a place where I feel connected to all the intersecting black star lines that link so many diasporic sites, sounds, and struggles. On one such trip in 2015, I took the 2 train to 116th Street and Malcolm X Boulevard, and emerged onto a corner that used to house the well-known hip-hop disco Harlem World, but is now a branch of the discount chain Conway Stores. Walking along 116th Street, I peeked through the window of Amy Ruth's, a home-style Southern restaurant where Sunday churchgoers enjoy dishes named in honor of African American celebrities: the Rev. Al Sharpton (Chicken and Waffle), the Ruby Dee (Fried or Baked Catfish), the Kid Capri (Salmon Croquettes), the Al Roker (Short Ribs or Beef). On the menu by Amy Ruth's door, black stars of today and yesterday coexist as soul food treats. Even Bronx-born hip-hop guru Afrika Bambaataa has his own special: a dish—fried whiting (a tasty white fish)—that you can also order at the West African–style Accra Restaurant, nearby. At Accra, beneath an awning that reads "Where Food stick to your Soul," Ghanaian immigrants discuss the past and future of their Black Stars, the beloved nickname for Ghana's national soccer team.

I approach Adam Clayton Powell Jr. Boulevard, passing the Senegalese markets that line 116th, and watch the weathered grandeur of the First Corinthian Baptist Church loom into view. Once home to the Regent Theater, one of New York City's first luxurious movie palaces, the church's Venetian palazzo-style shell houses a Spanish-Moorish auditorium, adorned with frescoes, ornate moldings, and elaborate chandeliers. Below the niche on the front façade, where a female muse figure used to perch invitingly, but where Christ has presided since First Corinthian bought this building in 1964, masses of tourists are queuing up for the 9:30 a.m. service. Hundreds of them—Europeans, mostly hailing from Spain, Sweden, Germany, and Russia—form lines wrapping around the block. They're hoping to attend this Harlem church, to witness the Gospel its congregants know each week.

Herded into the "nosebleeds" along with multitudes of foreigners, I make a dash for the front row of the balcony. The choir, donning all-black attire with flourishes of leopard and cheetah prints, high-steps their way onto the stage below. They belt the words "into the darkness we shine!" over a driving backbone of drums, bass, piano, and organ. The sermon today, in honor of the church's eighty-second anniversary, is by a visitor. Pastor Larry E. Covington is from South Carolina. He warms to the pulpit, posing a question to us all: "Why this place?"

The preacher pulls us into a biblical scene: John the Baptist hears a voice calling out in the wilderness—a flash of grace in the darkness. He talks about how *this place,* this Harlem church—First Corinthian—has provided him that same flash of grace in the midst of troubled times. "You can't spell wilderness without wild," he barks, "and there is a residue of wildness in me. That's why I've been called here to this place—because it keeps lifting me higher and higher."

Above his majestic voice, wall hangings bear the phrase "We are the Dark and the Dawn." The choir's soaring harmonies, as he finishes, suggest the same. Sitting in this theater-turned-sanctuary, I begin to feel (again) the coexistence of things—of light and darkness, of this world and the other, of city and wilderness, of churches and mosques, of natives and pilgrims. And when I emerge from the hearth of First Corinthian into the cold, cloudy day, that sense remains.

I walk northeast across 125th and eventually end up, just off Malcolm X by 126th, before what feels like a fitting mural. "Planet Harlem," says the piece's block-lettered title, which is signed by an artist named Paul Deo and which brings together, in colorful collaged form, a pantheon of idols both cosmic and local. In it, the Apollo starship rockets upward above Marcus Garvey wearing a double-breasted jacket. Booker T. Washington sits on his right shoulder. Searchlight beams shoot up into the mural's dark night, ending in the faces of James Brown and Michael Jackson. Jimi Hendrix gallops among stars with a guitar slung over his back while Maya Angelou poses in a white brassiere top and headdress. Langston Hughes types poems on a broken keyboard as Duke tickles the ivories. Adding to this chorus in space-time, Malcolm X deejays for Nina Simone and Muhammad Ali while Arturo Schomburg, the founder of the famed nearby library, strikes golden cymbals that seem to take flight as doves in the sky. Hip-hop constellations link Kurtis Blow and Tupac Shakur, hovering above a friendly jitterbug between Barack Obama and Romare Bearden. Adam Clayton Powell Jr. lunges forward in a blue suit, "climbing towards that higher ground."

One block south, a Whole Foods is being erected on 125th Street. Gentrification continues to creep farther north into the Black Mecca. Against this backdrop, Deo's vision emerges as a mystical and extraterrestrial gathering of black star revelry and fellowship across generations. It feels like the Harlem that perhaps once was, or never was, or could have been. It feels like multiple Harlems remixed—ancient and modern and beautiful, a story still unfolding. ✦

26 OSCILLATING CITY

The famous I ♥ New York logo is based on the old notion of the heart as the seat of sentiment and emotion. But the heart is something else, a tremendous engine of circulation, not hugging or holding on, but keeping things moving, and Manhattan itself pulsates like a gigantic heart, beating once or twice a day to make the human population surge through tunnels, bridges, roads. In the morning it pumps in more people than the population of many states; in the evening these diurnal migrants are pumped out again, but a second shift arrives for nightlife. Manhattan's population is 1.6 million, already one of the densest in North America, but each day, the population more than doubles with commuting workers (1.6 million), day-trip visitors (778,000), and students and patients (88,000). No other U.S. county has such a dramatic daily population flux. The surrounding boroughs lose population during the day; for example, evening rush hour returns 366,000 people to Queens.

Daily the equivalent of the entire population of Seattle—750,000 people—flows through Grand Central Station, while Penn Station is traversed by half a million people every day. The George Washington Bridge—the world's busiest bridge—carries 300,000 cars daily, while the Verrazano-Narrows Bridge is crossed by 200,000, the Queensboro Bridge 180,00, the Brooklyn Bridge 130,000, and the Lincoln Tunnel—the busiest vehicular tunnel in the world—120,000. The Staten Island Ferry carries 19 million people a year back and forth from Manhattan. In 2014 on average 5.6 million people rode the subway each weekday, the highest ridership since 1949; 1.75 billion annually, the equivalent of the entire U.S. population riding the trains more than five times apiece. Nightly Manhattan averages 404,000 overnighting out-of-towners; 32,000 revelers; 17,000 hospital patients; 17,000 night-shift commuters. Citywide, some 57,000 homeless men, women, and children sleep in shelters; 3,200 more on the streets or subways, the majority in Manhattan.

The 8,000 to 10,000 taxis on the streets of Manhattan at 3:00 p.m. have dropped to about 2,000 by 3:00 a.m. There are no statistics on the considerable number of affluent people who leave every weekend and every summer for homes in the country. But there are for midtown's luxury apartments: between East 56th and 63rd, the majority of homes are empty most of the time, night and day. This is a map of Manhattan as a place of coming and going, of restlessness, of micro-migrations on a daily and nightly basis, of the circulation of a bloodstream whose individual cells are janitors and accountants, students and chauffeurs, people in pursuit of a living and a life—of all those individual lives adding up to a city that oscillates like no other.

CARTOGRAPHY: MOLLY ROY   MAP APPEARS ON PAGES 208–209.

OSCILLATING CITY
MANHATTAN, DAY AND NIGHT

Inwood

*Washington
Heights*

Harlem

*Morningside
Heights*

East Harlem

Upper West Side

*Upper
East Side*

MANHATTAN
AT 3 PM

Hell's Kitchen

Midtown

Grand
Central
Station

Penn
Station

Chelsea

Kips Bay

Flatiron

West Village

NoHo

East Village

SoHo

Little Italy

Tribeca

Chinatown

Lower East Side

Wall Street

Hudson River

East River

MANHATTAN
AT 3 AM

Inwood

Washington
Heights

Harlem

Morningside
Heights

East Harlem

Upper West Side

Upper
East Side

Hudson   River

Hell's Kitchen

Midtown

• Penn
Station

• Grand
Central
Station

Chelsea

Flatiron

Kips Bay

West Village

NoHo

East Village

SoHo

Little Italy

Tribeca

Chinatown

Lower East Side

East   River

Wall Street

Population density
(approximate number of people per square mile)

60,000 120,000 180,000 240,000 300,000 360,000 420,000 480,000 540,000 600,000

SCHLEPTROPOLIS BY THOMAS J. CAMPANELLA

Gotham is a centripetal city, with a rhythm as predictable as the tides. Consolidation in 1898 created the modern metropolis with its five boroughs, four of which have ever since orbited Manhattan like supplicants about the polestar. Greater New York City today occupies almost 305 square miles, only 23 of which are Manhattan Island. And though the vast majority of the city's land area—93 percent—is spread across Brooklyn, Queens, the Bronx, and Staten Island, they are the city's supplicant "outer" boroughs. Manhattan— the original New York, it must be admitted—is the sole *inner* borough, though it's never called that. It is simply *The City*. So extreme is Manhattan's gravity that even a subway ride between the other boroughs requires passing through its core. This is because New York is among the few major world cities served only by a "hub and spoke" rapid transit system. Most such systems—the metros of Tokyo, London, Paris, Moscow, Shanghai, Berlin—also have a circular line, making intracity travel easy (Beijing has two). New York's sole subway line that doesn't touch Manhattan is the poor G train—the Gentrificant Local, which slogs between Park Slope and the hipster principalities to the north. Such a geopolitics virtually mandates that Manhattanites be self-absorbed egoists who, like the ancient Chinese, see their demesne as the hub of the heavens, the *axis mundi* around which the rest of us spin. And why not? Manhattan is the island at the center of the city at the center of the world, just as Saul Steinberg drew for a 1976 *New Yorker* cover—"View of the World from Ninth Avenue"—where everything from Hoboken to Hokkaido is compressed into the space of New Jersey.

Brooklyn and Queens both far exceed Manhattan in population—as independent entities, they would be the third and fourth largest cities in the United States, respectively (Manhattan by itself would be sixth). But Manhattan holds the lion's share of regional jobs. So on a typical weekday some 1.6 million commuters pour onto the island to work. Most—about 65 percent—hail from the city's other boroughs; the rest, from the surrounding metropolitan region: Long Island, Westchester, the lower Hudson Valley, New Jersey, Connecticut. A tiny but growing percentage—about 3 percent—come from farther afield, "super-commuters" who travel ninety minutes or more one way on a regular basis (mostly from Philadelphia and Albany). But commuters are only part of Manhattan's daily deluge. There are also those who come to shop. On any given Sunday, stores like Century 21 and B&H Photo, the famed Hasidic-run emporium of discount electronics in Hell's Kitchen, probably see more people than live in all of Central Asia. And then there are all the tourists—not just map-fumblers from afar, prey for Times Square body-painted *desnudas,* but day trippers from Flushing or Forest Hills, in to see a show, walk the High Line, or savor the sea urchin at Cosme. There are also high school and university students, people coming in for medical treatment, those visiting family. Manhattan's average weekday bump is about 2.4 million these days, yielding a total island population of nearly 4 million souls. The influx more than doubles Manhattan's resident population on a daily basis, as if all of Phoenix and San Francisco came to visit at once.

Schlepping about town has been a vital part of Gotham life since even before the days of New Netherland. The Bowery and Broadway were trails used by the Lenni-Lenape Indians before Europeans came to stay; so, too, were Flatbush Avenue and Kings Highway in Brooklyn. But the modern New York commute began, in spirit at least, on August 17, 1807, when an erstwhile painter and mechanical genius named Robert Fulton launched the first commercial steamboat. Fulton later established a regular ferry service across the East River from Lower Manhattan, making Brooklyn suddenly easier to reach than uptown or the Bronx. This encouraged developers to buy up land there and subdivide it for Wall Street's prosperous parvenus. The most ambitious of these entrepreneurs was

Hezekiah Beers Pierrepont, who fortified his investment by helping Fulton monopolize East River ferry operations. Brooklyn Heights, a fifteen-minute ride from Manhattan, thus became New York City's first suburb. A more substantial form of union came in 1883 with completion of the Brooklyn Bridge, a triumph of nineteenth-century engineering, whose gorgeous span Hart Crane hymned as a "harp and altar, of the fury fused," and whose Egypto-Gothic towers and cabled maze have inspired artists—from Marianne Moore to Joseph Stella to Sonny Rollins—ever since. The Great Bridge opened a heroic age of nuptial infrastructure. In the years following consolidation, three major spans—the Williamsburg, Manhattan, and Queensboro Bridges—were erected over the East River to consecrate the municipal union. The 1930s brought another great wave of construction, with six big bridges spanning the city's Depression-troubled waters between 1930 and 1939—the George Washington, Henry Hudson, Bronx-Whitestone, Kosciuszko, Marine Parkway, and Triborough. And Gotham burrowed as busily as it bridged, digging twenty tunnels and transit tubes under the Hudson, Harlem, and East Rivers by 1936—including engineering landmarks like the Holland Tunnel, the first vehicular tunnel in the world to be mechanically ventilated.

To some, bridges and tunnels alone could never make Gotham whole. Far more radical action would be required—filling in the East River, for example. This was first proposed by civil engineer T. Kennard Thomson in a 1916 *Popular Science* article, "A Really Greater New York." Thomson, whose proposals for joining the boroughs also included expanding Lower Manhattan by filling the harbor all the way to Staten Island, recommended "moving" the East River to a new channel across Queens from Long Island Sound to Jamaica Bay. The idea was floated again in 1924 by John A. Harriss, who wanted to build dams at Hell Gate and the Williamsburg Bridge so as to convert the East River into "a five-mile system of automobile and motor-truck highways, subway lines, parking spaces, and city centers." Harriss was no quack. A physician who made a fortune in real estate, he was appointed in 1918 to a post of his own making—Special Deputy Police Commissioner for Traffic. Gushing with ideas both ingenious and absurd, it was Harriss who devised and installed—at his own expense—the city's first traffic lights. He also designed the first pedestrian-crossing signals in America (including the ubiquitous "red hand"), formalized the concept of a no-parking zone, made Central Park West and Fifth Avenue one-way streets, and proposed the "marginal roadway" that later became the West Side Highway— a road overlooking the city's other great river, the Hudson, which had a set of land-filling schemers all its own. One of these schemers was engineer Norman Sper, who urged using WPA funds to drain the great river and turn it into a subterranean transit and street system that could also shelter "practically the entire population of the city" in the event of a poisonous gas attack.

Over the rivers or through the mud, New York's array of water-crossing apparatuses taps Manhattan into a vast regional network of road and rail. Rapid transit was cobbled together at first from a patchwork of rail lines laid into its streets and elevated overhead, but by the 1880s some 2,000 trains a day were speeding around the city. Ridership on the city's "els" jumped from 2 million to 60 million between 1876 and 1880, and tripled again by the end of the nineteenth century. The subway's current system took form in 1940 with consolidation of the city's three subway companies—the IRT, BMT, and IND. The subways helped decant Manhattan's exploding population to the outer boroughs, where tracts of farmland were soon churned into tidy blocks of mock-Tudor homes. The New York City subway system has more miles of track and more stations than any in the world. Along with commuter lines like PATH, Metro-North, and the Long Island Railroad, it carries more than 67 percent of all weekday commuters in and out of Manhattan. And subway use is increasing, with annual ridership in 2014 the highest since the pre-sprawl

1940s. City bus use has fallen slightly in recent years, but still accounts for some 14 percent of the commuter total—slightly less than the 16 percent of Manhattan workers who defy logic and drive their cars to town.

The first threads of Gotham's modern arterial system were sylvan motorways modeled on those—the Bronx River, Hutchinson River, and Saw Mill River Parkways—built in the 1920s by unsung visionaries in Westchester County and later replicated on Long Island by Robert Moses, the mercurial master of Gotham infrastructure. By the 1930s only New York City stood in the way of creating a vast regional system of modern roads. It became Moses's driving ambition to make this happen—to "weave together," as he put it in 1941, "the loose strands and frayed edges of New York's arterial and metropolitan tapestry." In fact, all the key components had been proposed years before. Madison Grant—chair of the Bronx Parkway Commission, whose anti-immigrant screed, *The Passing of the Great Race,* helped bring about the National Origins Act—proposed linking Westchester and Manhattan in 1907 with "a direct, level, and attractive boulevard to the city from the open countryside." A Brooklyn minister named Newell Dwight Hillis—Henry Ward Beecher's successor to the Plymouth Church pulpit—envisioned a shoreline "ocean boulevard" from the Narrows to Coney Island. The great Chicago planner Daniel Burnham recommended that Brooklyn build a "Central Island Boulevard" to extend its reach from the end of Eastern Parkway to the tip of Long Island at Montauk Point, 120 miles distant. Not long after, Thomas Adams and the Russell Sage Foundation launched an exhaustive study of the region that provided a template for metropolitan growth over the next half century. But it took Moses to make such pipe dreams real. ("We have never lacked for plans . . . ," he once wrote. "What we have lacked is unified execution.") He extended the Bronx River Parkway into Manhattan as the Henry Hudson, built Reverend Hillis's shoreline drive as the Belt Parkway, and realized Burnham's Central Boulevard as the Interboro (Jackie Robinson) and Grand Central Parkways. With the Triborough (Robert F. Kennedy) Bridge, he connected Long Island to Manhattan, Westchester, and the Bronx with a great junction box of bridges, roads, and ramps. The Triborough pulled together the metropolitan fabric as radically as the Brooklyn Bridge did fifty years before. However cursed by traffic-bound motorists, the span is not without its devotees—poet Cristin O'Keefe Aptowicz, for example, or composer Mohammed Fairouz, whose 2013 "Mighty Triborough" was commissioned by the New Juilliard Ensemble.

Moses's early parkways did as much for pedestrians and bicyclists as they did for motorists. The vast West Side Improvement transformed the aging Riverside Park into a modern recreation complex whose shoreline motorway was just one of its many "paths and esplanades," judged the urbanist Lewis Mumford, "meant obviously to lure and hold thousands of people at a time." Moses similarly envisioned his Circumferential Parkway (comprising today's Belt and Cross Island Parkways) as not just an automobile road but a "shoestring park" laced with bikeways and amenities for "people in the neighborhoods along the route." But all this changed after World War II, when Moses's ego swelled in step with the surging numbers of cars and trucks demanding access to New York. The lithe prewar parkways, laid gently on the land, yielded to ramrod-straight expressways punched through some of the city's most populous sections, wrecking working-class neighborhoods from Red Hook to the South Bronx. Only in moneyed Brooklyn Heights were residents able to make Moses play nice. He planned to run the Brooklyn-Queens Expressway through the heart of Pierrepont's old subdivision, but instead stacked its lanes below Columbia Heights in a series of cantilevered decks, whose roof is one of the city's finest open spaces—the Brooklyn Heights Promenade.

Commuting in New York is a full-contact sport, and a swift and painless trip to work—no delays on the PATH, no backed-up BQE, nobody off their meds in your subway car on

Richard Renaldi, *05:33*

the Q line—offers the equivalent joy value of a week on the Amalfi coast. More human
emotion is probably spent in a single morning's commute in New York City than in a
decade in a sane, well-adjusted place like Portland or Vancouver. Little of this emotion
could be filed under Altruism, Benevolence, or Charity. But the quotidian slog is not
without its poetry and has yielded more than a few penetrating glimpses into the soul of
the city, if not of humankind. Walt Whitman's "Crossing Brooklyn Ferry" (1856) is a commuter's paean to the universality of life—and to the "simple, compact, well-join'd scheme"
that life, like the city, could still seem on a twilight commute. "I am with you," he versed,
"you men and women of a generation, or ever so many generations hence." A long ride
from Whitman's exuberance is John Cheever, whose rail-bound stories tell of anguished,
gin-addled men carried numbly to leafy hells on the Hudson and Harlem Lines—suburban realms so splendidly removed from the great world that "the only idea of the future
anyone has," laments his antihero Clayton in "The Country Husband" (1954), "is just
more and more commuting trains and more parties." Cheever knew the oscillations of
hope and despair inhering in the daily commute. He shuttled for years between Manhattan and his home in Ossining, struggling in his work to "confront, with forgiveness and
compassion, the terrifying singularity of my own person."

Phyllis McGinley wrote from a sunnier place, publishing mock epics like "Musings
Aboard the Stamford Local" and "A Day in the City" that satirized the suburban commute in both directions. Reviled by feminists, the self-styled "housewife poet" made a

Richard Renaldi, *05:23*

good living with her verse, winning honorary degrees, a Pulitzer Prize, and a place on the cover of *Time*. The countless souls schlepping home each weeknight on the Long Island Expressway found their balladeer in Billy Joel, whose songs tell of mortgaged dreams, suburban lust, and landscapes paved by sprawl: "Give us this day our daily discount outlet merchandise," he sings in "No Man's Land." "Raise up a multiplex and we will make a sacrifice." And then there is Jay-Z, whose name is *not* a reference to the J and Z trains, but might as well be; the rapper grew up in Brooklyn's Marcy Houses, a stone's throw from both. On the final night of his 2012 concert series that opened his home borough's new Barclays Center, he made a celebrated reverse commute—riding to work on the R train from Canal Street, by his luxe downtown Manhattan home, to Atlantic Avenue in downtown Brooklyn. His second song that night was "Empire State of Mind," his hit ode to the city recorded with Alicia Keys in 2009, which crosses boroughs in its very first line ("Yeah I'm out that Brooklyn, now I'm down in Tribeca").

Whitman remains one of the few artists who could see past the infrastructure to the souls it carried. The commuter today, in the world's eyes, remains a haggard soul staring ahead or nodding with exhaustion, as in Reginald Marsh's painting of riders on the Third Avenue el. Without the commuter, New York City would literally cease to work; for the commuter is the caffeinated corpuscle that pumps tumescent Manhattan's drowsy Priapus each morning, rushing across a vast arterial network to engorge the *urbs spongiosum* and ready it to perform. And yet the commuter is as unloved as the tourist or the meter maid. Even kindly old E. B. White, author of *Stuart Little* and *Charlotte's Web,* put down the commuter. In a famous 1948 essay he laid out three constituent Gothams: the city of native-born locals, the city of strivers from elsewhere drawn to New York by their dreams, and the city of commuters—"devoured by locusts each day and spat out each night." If the natives gave New York its constancy and the settlers its "poetical deportment . . . its incomparable achievements," the commuter-locusts were good only for "tidal restlessness." We can perhaps forgive White for this, for he wrote at a time when youthful seekers from afar—not just Russian oligarchs, Chinese billionaires, and people with rent-stabilized apartments—could actually afford a place in Manhattan. Today, as everyone knows, all bright young things from afar live in Brooklyn.

Manhattan is still the glowworm of Gotham, but its monopoly on light is not what it was. And while no one is expecting a flood of commuters heading off the island anytime soon, the relative balance of jobs is beginning to shift—especially in the all-important "creative-class" sector upon which the city's economy is increasingly based. Jay-Z's reverse ride to work on the R train was a symbol of things to come. In 2014 the New York State comptroller's office reported that between 2003 and 2012 the number of private-sector jobs in Brooklyn rose by nearly 20 percent, double the citywide average. And it's not only Brooklyn. The Center for an Urban Future found similar increases in the number of Bronx residents commuting to Queens and Westchester, Staten Islanders working in Brooklyn or New Jersey, Brooklynites commuting to Queens. These trends are changing how Manhattan is seen and how it sees itself. Once upon a time, mocking the "bridge and tunnel crowd" was the way Manhattan trendsetters signaled their insider status. Steve Rubell, the founder of the legendary disco Studio 54, is said to have coined the term. In a 1977 *New York Times* interview he referred dismissively to "people from Queens and Staten Island and those places" who crowded his club on weekends. Rubell himself was from Brooklyn, but "bridge and tunnel" soon became an all-purpose put-down for anyone judged unworthy or ignorant by self-appointed city sophisticates. Today, with once-marginal places like Red Hook, Crown Heights, and Long Island City now trendy and booming, the term has made it full circle, like a virus-laden chicken coming home to roost. For not only is Manhattan schlepping more and more to Brooklyn for food, culture, and even work, but "one can now reside in Manhattan," as Urban Dictionary's Trey Parasuco noted, "and still be considered 'bridge and tunnel.'"

In the end, of course, we all leave town. And even the most committed Manhattanite must leave the mighty isle—unless opting to be scattered there as ashes. Mayor Ed Koch famously refused to spend eternity anywhere outside of the 212 area, but his Trinity Cemetery in Washington Heights—the last on the island still taking reservations—is filling up fast. Lesser souls must settle for a last great schlep, in casket or urn, over the rivers Styx to a resting place upstate, on Long Island, or in Jersey. Since 1838 many of Manhattan's more illustrious souls, from Horace Greeley to Leonard Bernstein, have chosen to cross the East River for Green-Wood Cemetery in Brooklyn, where no less than ten New York City mayors are also buried. Farther east, across Queens and Nassau, the last glacier's terminal moraine is draped with landscapes of terminal repose. At Cypress Hills in far-out Brooklyn, Jackie Robinson, Piet Mondrian, and Mae West all rest. Harry Houdini has yet to free himself from Machpelah Cemetery, just over the border in Queens; Jacob Riis, chronicler of immigrant life, made it a bit farther out to Maple Grove Cemetery. Later

Richard Renaldi, *05:47*

cemeteries farther out on Long Island sprawled over the outwash plain like subdivisions of the departed, replicating in death the geography of suburban life. Just beyond Farmingdale is the Pinelawn complex of burial grounds. In St. Charles Cemetery, tucked beside a commuter airport, and in New Montefiore and Mt. Ararat and Long Island National, are buried tens of thousands of men and women who once called themselves New Yorkers. Among them is Steve Rubell, who joined the bridge-and-tunnel set at last and sleeps beneath the blue jays and squirrels at Beth Moses Cemetery, in West Babylon, just north of Exit 35 on the Southern State Parkway. 🜁

ACKNOWLEDGMENTS

THREE RINGS AND FULL CIRCLE:
A LAST ROUND OF GRATITUDES

REBECCA SOLNIT

This project has come full circle. One day in 2007 Frank Smigiel, a curator at the San Francisco Museum of Modern Art newly arrived from New York, asked me to propose a project for the museum's seventy-fifth anniversary in 2010; I proposed a series of map-broadsides and then scuttled across the bay to convince University of California Press to sign on for a book version of the same; the two institutions co-sponsored what became *Infinite City: A San Francisco Atlas*, and Frank always joked that he had commissioned an atlas to help orient himself. Nine years later, he's a dedicated San Franciscan, and we're finishing up the atlas of his former hometown.

There are so many people to thank for this vast ensemble project. Love of maps and of places brought in a number of people who became part of more than one atlas. No one has been more generous or inspiring in that regard than map scholar, lover, and collector David Rumsey, who during the making of the first atlas let the writers, artists, cartographers, and designer visit his magnificent collection (now mostly housed at Stanford University and online at davidrumsey.com) for inspiration and education more than once, occasions that lit us all up with joy. David provided recommendations, financial support for the second and third atlases, and a generosity of spirit and deep intelligence about what maps do—all forms of encouragement to do our best with our own projects. The Samuel H. Kress Foundation matched David's latest donation. David also introduced us to Matt Knutzen, the map specialist at the New York Public Library, whose enthusiasm and deep knowledge of the cartographic history of New York City were a huge gift.

Serendipity, chance meetings, and luck brought in other characters, like foundation expert Marty Krasney, who sat next to me on a plane to Boston in 2011 or 2012 and turned into a dear friend, a patron who made his own contributions with his wonderful wife, Pamela, and introduced us to other funders, including Manhattanites Jonathan Rose and Josh Mailman, whose generous support early on helped us get going. The J. M. Kaplan Fund's Furthermore grant gave us funding to defray some of the costs of the cartography for the twenty-six maps in this book, all but one done by the steadily excellent Molly Roy, who also did some cartography on the New Orleans atlas (and has done some remarkable atlases of her own).

Making atlases was a—what is the right word? Team effort? Group endeavor? At times I felt like the ringmaster of a very talented circus, as well as a herder of brilliant cats. Each atlas developed its own core group, and some people stayed on through all three. Of course, central to it all was University of California Press's magnificent team: design goddess Lia Tjandra, who determined the look of the atlases the day I met her in 2008 and devoted herself to making every map as beautiful and clear as possible; senior editor and paver-of-the-way Niels Hooper; and angel of accuracy/project manager Dore Brown. Big thanks to them, to Niels's assistant

Bradley Depew, and to Sue Heinemann and the proofreaders who saved us from ourselves and our spelling. Artist Alison Pebworth was one of the very first people I recruited for the first atlas, and it was clear after she did the cover logo and title page for that one that nothing better was possible, so she stayed on to provide the same features for the other two volumes.

Caribbean scholar, geographer, music historian, and man-about-town Joshua Jelly-Schapiro, whom I'd met at UC Berkeley in 2007, researched one map and wrote one stellar essay for the first atlas. He became the editor-at-large for the second, for which he wrote more, researched more, and recruited some superb scholars and writers, notably cultural historian Garnette Cadogan, who in turn became the editor-at-large for this atlas as Josh became its co-director. Dr. J stepped up in September of 2014 to become, in essence, *Nonstop Metropolis's* managing editor—overseeing a lot of the day-to-day production of the atlas—as well as my coequal collaborator in dreaming up and directing the large and small creative decisions every step of the long way toward a finished book. Working with the unflappable and resourceful Dr. J has been a joy from beginning to end, and his depth of knowledge and analytical genius about how cities work as culture, community, racial politics, collective memory, and more shape the book in important ways.

Jonathan Tarleton, then at New York's Architectural League and editor for its *Urban Omnibus,* contacted me out of the blue to see if he could become a researcher for the project. We emailed, and then we Skyped, and by the time we met, I knew I was tremendously lucky to have found an indefatigable, resourceful scholar. His invisible work has been crucial to this book, and it becomes visible in his essay on Olmsted, Moses, and Jacobs, which thoughtfully unsettles our assumptions about the three. Jonathan himself "would like to thank the owners of all the shoulders he stood upon while researching for this book, especially Benjamin Miller, Fred Gitner of the Queens Library, Mariel Villeré of Freshkills Park Alliance, Elizabeth Gaskin of the U.S. Census Bureau, Colleen Alderson of NYC Parks, Emily Colucci, Cara Dellatte of the Staten Island Museum, and Xandra Clark, who provided the crucial leg-up that started it all."

Josh, Garnette, and Jonathan became, with me, the core team that produced this atlas, and the most delightful parts of the project for me were the meetings where the four of us ironed out ideas and the adventures we had together walking the city. Garnette's broad acquaintance with people, places, and books; his own deep relationship with the city, informed by the kind of long-distance walks mapped here; his devotion to precision in language and meaning and to principle and integrity mattered immensely to this project, as does his friendship to this author.

Maybe it's the essence of urban mingling that many of the key players for this atlas were encountered casually, or by coincidence, or through mutual acquaintances. It was a beautiful coincidence that I met up with Laura Raicovich when she was about to announce her appointment as director of the Queens Museum. She immediately recognized that the atlas served the mission of the museum and vice versa, and brought us in as collaborators on a series of projects—installations, events, broadsides—at the museum in 2016. We are grateful to her magnificent staff, including chief curator Hitomi Iwasaki, deputy directors Debra Wimpfheimer and David Strauss, public programs director Prerana Reddy, development director Munira Khapra-Reininger, and communications maven Pema Domingo-Barker. We have been so happy to be associated with that institution, its generous and visionary staff, and a borough whose richness revealed itself to us through research and through many conversations with lovers of the 7 train, Jackson Heights, Flushing, the Unisphere (often said to be the world's largest globe) next to the Queens Museum, and so much more.

Laura reconnected us to the extraordinary and inspired Michelle Coffey of the Lambent Foundation, which became a crucial supporter of the atlas project in our final stretch to go to press. Sociology professor Eric Klinenberg, whose fantastic work on the Chicago heat wave had been essential to an earlier book of mine, met me one summer and invited me to be a scholar in residence at the Institute of Public Knowledge he heads at New York University. He and the staff expanded the invitation to include Joshua Jelly-Schapiro and Garnette Cadogan, so that for several months our three names adorned an office we papered with maps of the city, a beautiful and useful confirmation of our collaboration. The IPK was a superb place for us to work and hold meetings, pile up books on New York, and meet other scholars. It was through Eric and the IPK's auspices that we met, for example, the sociologist Daniel Aldana Cohen, who became an essayist for the atlas and whose immersion in the best research currently being done on climate change and cities led us to, in "Carboniferous," the potent scholarship of Kevin Ummel. IPK's program head Siera Dissmore and associate director Gordon Douglas both became beloved friends of the core group, and before her departure fellow staffer Jessica Coffey was also a warm presence and a big help in our work. We can't thank Eric enough for offering us friendship, space, community, and conversation that made the process and the results immeasurably better.

The vast complication we call New York has inspired many scholars of the place—or, rather, of aspects of the place—whose research was instrumental to this atlas. We were left grateful not only for their knowledge but for the generosity with which they shared it with us and their contagious enthusiasm. Daniel Kaufman, the passionately dedicated executive director of the Endangered Language Alliance, unstintingly shared his own and his organization's knowledge of Queens's linguistic richness for our map "Queens and Mother Tongues" (which also became a broadside circulated by the Queens Museum and inspired a mural inside that institution). Elena Martinez of the Bronx Music Heritage Center and of City Lore provided crucial information, and key guidance, in our efforts to chart the Bronx and its music, as did the Notorious PhD—otherwise known as Professor Mark Naison of Fordham University, who heads up the marvelous Bronx African American Oral History Project there. One benefit of being housed at IPK was that we got to share a floor and water cooler with the New York Institute for the Humanities, to whose fellow, the poet Rowan Ricardo Phillips, we owe deep thanks for a clutch haul of Bronx songs to include on "Singing the City."

Hip-hop scholars Joe Schloss and Jeff Chang shared key information with us, as did Melissa Libran of Windows of Hip Hop, Christie Z-Pabon, and Maxine Gordon, the exemplary scholar of jazz and life whom Garnette and not a few of our era's finest musicians have called "Auntie." Josh's partner, radio producer and New Yorker-of-many-talents Mirissa Neff, conducted interviews with hip-hop's early greats to accompany our map of the Bronx in the 1970s and also took the photographs that frame "Mother Tongues and Queens." Representing Staten Island as the Wu-Tang Clan's Shaolin was a joy, and Josh was helped in the process by RZA assistant Tamika Layton and his editor Sean McDonald—and special thanks to RZA himself for making time to talk with Josh about his formative landscape. The Chinese cultural aspects of the map were researched by Garnette in conversation with Pastor Stephen Ma of the Staten Island Chinese Christian Church. My old friend Thomas Evans introduced us to artist and explorer Emmy Catedral, who in turn introduced us to the mysteries and wonders of Flushing. The great Tony Carnes, who has for decades documented the spiritual and religious life and institutions of the five boroughs, was an important source of information for "Black Star Lines." Big thanks to each and all of them.

Beyond Josh and Garnette, two other holdovers from *Unfathomable City* were a pair of Brooklyn-born New Orleanians—the stalwart Joel Dinerstein and historical geographer extraordinaire Richard Campanella, who, beyond explaining the uncanny similarity between New Orleans and Brooklyn accents, furnished us with brilliant cartography of his home city's growth across time. Richard's brother Thomas, the Cornell urban historian, contributed not one but two essays—including a clutch pinch-hit piece on Brooklyn's physical plant, based in the Campanella boys' home neighborhood of Marine Park.

One of my great influences, Barry Lopez, wrote a Borges-like short fiction some years ago called "The Mappist" about an extraordinary and mysterious cartographer named Corlis Benefideo, which has inspired many of us. There's a beautiful circular logic to the fact that these atlases won the Corlis Benefideo Award for creative cartography from the North American Cartographic Information Society as Barry wrote an exquisite short essay for this atlas about his little-known sojourn as a young New Yorker. His contribution, for me, felt like a special benediction on the project.

We're also grateful to the independent booksellers who have taken such good care of our atlases that are too tall to file on the shelves and often too sui generis to fit in the usual categories.

These books were always made as a celebration of what physical, material books are and can be, of the old miracle of the codex as a way to collect and share information, of the beauties of the form, of the sheer joy of discovery on paper—so love of libraries and bookstores as well as readers and explorers was always a motivating force. I owe a special thanks to Lydia Matthews, Trevor Paglen, Ann Hamilton, Matthew Ernest, and Kat Galasso and Sam Green, whose sofas I surfed at various points in this project.

Finally, for this East Coast project, I owe a mountain of thanks to a consummate westerner back home on the other coast, Charlie McDonald, who listened, encouraged, and inspired me through the years of this project.

Winding down this trilogy that has taken up a good deal of my time over eight years, I'm both relieved to hang up my role as ringmaster of an intricate and sometimes overwhelming operation and sad to say good-bye to working with many of the collaborators named above, who will remain cherished friends. The seventy maps and essays, the three books, the experiments in rethinking cartography live on too; the semi-immortality of books is one of the things we sought to celebrate by returning to making maps on paper. And the cities the three books document continue to change in unforeseen ways, which means that we will never be done exploring.

CONTRIBUTORS

SHEERLY AVNI is a screenwriter and recovering journalist currently living in Mexico City. She gets back home to New York as often as she can, which is never often enough.

GAIUTRA BAHADUR is an award-winning reporter, essayist, and critic. Her book *Coolie Woman: The Odyssey of Indenture* was shortlisted for the Orwell Prize, and her work has appeared in *The Nation, Virginia Quarterly Review, New York Times Book Review, Dissent,* and *Ms.,* among other publications. A MacDowell Colony Fellow, Nieman Fellow, and New Jersey State Council on the Arts Fellow, she was born in Guyana and raised in Jersey City, NJ.

MARSHALL BERMAN was born in the Bronx in 1940 and died in 2013. Educated at New York City public schools, he taught at City College for over forty years and wrote four books: *The Politics of Authenticity, All That Is Solid Melts into Air, Adventures in Marxism,* and *On the Town: One Hundred Years of Spectacle in Times Square.* He also published articles in *The Nation, New York Times Book Review, Village Voice,* and *Dissent,* where he sat on the editorial board.

JOE BOYD is the author of *White Bicycles: Making Music in the 1960s.* He has produced records by Nick Drake, the Incredible String Band, ¡Cubanismo!, Fairport Convention, REM, Pink Floyd, and Ivo Papasov, among many others. He also produced the films *Jimi Hendrix* and *Scandal* and has curated a number of concerts. His work is collected at joeboyd.co.uk.

BETTE BURGOYNE, a visual artist, was born and lives in Seattle. She graduated from Cornish College of the Arts, lived in San Francisco for ten years, and earned an MFA from Mills College. Her drawings of various phenomena are created using black paper and white pencil.

WILL BUTLER is a musician living in Brooklyn. He is a member of the band Arcade Fire, and he released his first solo record, *Policy,* in 2015.

GARNETTE CADOGAN is editor-at-large for *Nonstop Metropolis.* He is a visiting fellow and writer-in-residence at the Institute for Advanced Studies in Culture at the University of Virginia and a visiting scholar at the Institute for Public Knowledge at New York University. He writes about culture and the arts for various publications and is at work on a book on walking.

RICHARD CAMPANELLA, a geographer with the Tulane School of Architecture, is the author of nine award-winning books and scores of articles on geography, mapping, greater New Orleans, and coastal Louisiana. In 2016 the government of France named Campanella a Chevalier dans l'Ordre des Palmes Académiques.

THOMAS J. CAMPANELLA is a professor of city planning at Cornell University and historian-in-residence at the New York City Department of Parks and Recreation. He has received Guggenheim, Fulbright, and Rome Prize fellowships and is the author of the forthcoming book *Brooklyn: A Secret History.* He divides his time between Ithaca and the Marine Park neighborhood of Brooklyn.

HANNAH CHALEW is an artist from New Orleans whose work explores places in the urban environment that exist on the threshold between cultivated and wild. She recently received an MFA in painting from the Cranbrook Academy of Art in Detroit, where she lives.

DANIEL ALDANA COHEN lived for almost a decade in New York City while pursuing a PhD at New York University, where he co-founded the Superstorm Research Lab after Hurricane Sandy. He is now assistant professor of sociology at the University of Pennsylvania and co-hosts the "Hot and Bothered" podcast on climate politics. His writing has appeared in *Public Culture, Jacobin, Dissent, The Walrus, Toronto Star, Public Books,* and elsewhere.

TEJU COLE is a writer and photographer. He is the photography critic of the *New York Times Magazine*, distinguished writer-in-residence at Bard College, and the author of *Open City, Every Day Is for the Thief,* and the forthcoming *Known and Strange Things,* a collection of essays.

PETER COYOTE, an actor in over 145 films, is the author of two books. In 1966 he was a founder of the Diggers, an anarchist family famous for free food, free stores, free medical clinics, and free crash pads. From 1975 to 1983 he served as policy advisor to Governor Edmund Brown Jr. and as a member (and later chair) of the California Arts Council. He lives on a small farm with two dogs and forty fruit trees and is a fully transmitted Zen Buddhist priest.

MOLLY CRABAPPLE is an artist, journalist, and author of the memoir *Drawing Blood.* A contributing editor for *VICE,* she has drawn in and reported from Guantanamo Bay, Abu Dhabi's migrant labor camps, Syria, Lebanon, Gaza, the West Bank, and Iraqi Kurdistan. She has written for such publications as the *New York Times, Paris Review,* and *Vanity Fair,* and her work is in the collection of New York's Museum of Modern Art.

JOEL DINERSTEIN is an associate professor of English at Tulane University and the former James H. Clark Endowed Chair in American Civilization. He is the curator of the exhibition *American Cool* at the Smithsonian Institution's National Portrait Gallery and author of the forthcoming *The Origins of Cool.* He earned the Eugene M. Kayden Book Award for *Swinging the Machine: Modernity, Technology, and African American Culture between the World Wars,* a cultural history of big-band jazz and industrialization.

ALEX FRADKIN, trained as an architect, began his photography career in 1996. His work is frequently published in leading magazines and is held in the collections of the Art Institute of Chicago, Museum of Contemporary Photography, and Portland Art Museum, among others. Fradkin teaches photography at the International Center for Photography in Manhattan and is at work on his third and fourth books.

KELSEY GARRITY-RILEY is an illustrator and artist living in Brooklyn. She grew up in Germany and Belgium and is a graduate of the Savannah College of Art and Design.

FRANCISCO GOLDMAN is the author of *Say Her Name,* winner of the 2011 Prix Femina Étranger; *The Interior Circuit: A Mexico City Chronicle;* and four other books. He has received Cullman Center and Guggenheim fellowships and a Berlin Prize, among other honors. His work has appeared in the *New Yorker, Harper's, The Believer,* and numerous other publications. Every year he teaches one semester at Trinity College in Connecticut and then hightails it back to Mexico City.

CHRIS HENRICK's work encompasses cartography, geospatial information systems, web development, and social justice. Among his projects is a website titled "Am I Rent Stabilized?" which uses open data to help New York City tenants determine if they are being illegally overcharged in rent. He has an MFA from Parsons School of Design and works for Stamen Design.

MARGO JEFFERSON, the winner of a Pulitzer Prize for criticism, was for years a book and arts critic for *Newsweek* and the *New York Times.* Her writing has been widely anthologized and has appeared in, among other publications, *New York, Guernica, The Believer, The Nation,* and *Vogue.* Her memoir, *Negroland,* received the 2015 National Book Critics Circle Award for autobiography. She is also the author of *On Michael Jackson* and a professor of writing at Columbia University School of the Arts.

JOSHUA JELLY-SCHAPIRO, a geographer and writer, is the author of *Island People* and the co-director of *Nonstop Metropolis*. His work has appeared in the *New York Review of Books*, *New York*, *Harper's*, *Artforum*, *The Believer*, and *The Nation*, among many other publications. He was the editor-at-large of *Unfathomable City: A New Orleans Atlas* and is a visiting scholar at New York University's Institute for Public Knowledge. He lives in Queens and the Caribbean.

LADY PINK was born in Ecuador but raised in New York City. In 1979 she started writing graffiti on subway cars and elsewhere, before starring in the classic hip-hop film *Wild Style*. Today she continues to produce paintings on canvas and conducts mural workshops for youth. Her artwork is in the collections of the Whitney Museum of American Art, Metropolitan Museum of Art, the Brooklyn Museum, and the Groninger Museum in the Netherlands.

PAUL LA FARGE is the author of the novels *The Artist of the Missing* and *Haussmann, or the Distinction,* both of which won the California Book Award, as well as *Luminous Airplanes* and *The Facts of Winter,* a book of imaginary dreams. His stories and essays have appeared in the *New Yorker*, *Harper's*, *The Believer*, *McSweeney's*, *Nautilus*, *Conjunctions*, *Fence,* and elsewhere. He has received fellowships from the Cullman Center for Scholars and Writers, the National Endowment for the Arts, and the Guggenheim Foundation.

LUCY R. LIPPARD is a writer/activist and the author of twenty-four books on contemporary art, activism, feminism, place, photography, archaeology, and land use. Born in New York City, she spent several decades in Lower Manhattan but currently lives off the grid in rural Galisteo, New Mexico, where she edits the community newsletter. She is the recipient of nine honorary degrees, a Guggenheim fellowship, and a Lannan Foundation grant, among other awards. Her most recent book is *Undermining: A Wild Ride through Land Use, Politics, and Art in the Changing West.*

BARRY LOPEZ is the author of *Arctic Dreams: Imagination and Desire in a Northern Landscape,* winner of the National Book Award; *Of Wolves and Men,* a National Book Award finalist; several short story collections, including *Resistance* and *Light Action in the Caribbean*; and two essay collections, *Crossing Open Ground* and *About This Life: Journeys on the Threshold of Memory.* The recipient of numerous cultural and literary honors, he regularly visits New York but lives in rural western Oregon with his wife, the writer Debra Gwartney.

VALERIA LUISELLI was born in Mexico City and lives in Harlem. A novelist (*Faces in the Crowd* and *The Story of My Teeth*) and essayist (*Sidewalks*), whose work has been translated into many languages, she is the recipient of the Los Angeles Times Art Seidenbaum Award for First Fiction and the National Book Foundation's 5 Under 35 award.

SUKETU MEHTA is the author of *Maximum City: Bombay Lost and Found* and teaches long-form writing at the Arthur L. Carter Journalism Institute at New York University.

MIRISSA NEFF is a photographer, producer, and journalist for public radio and television. She is at work on her first film, *This Is National Wake.* She was born in New York Hospital and lives in Queens.

ALISON PEBWORTH's work focuses on long-range projects that merge painting, installation, and social interaction. She has made three year-long tours across the United States, exhibiting in numerous nonprofit art spaces and museums, and is the recent recipient of a Louis Comfort Tiffany Foundation Award. Pebworth has drawn the cover logo and title page art for all three atlases in this trilogy.

EMILY RABOTEAU is the author, most recently, of *Searching for Zion: The Quest for Home in the African Diaspora*, winner of the 2014 American Book Award. She lives in Washington Heights and co-directs the MFA program in creative writing at the City College of New York, in Harlem.

SHARIFA RHODES-PITTS is the award-winning author of *Harlem Is Nowhere: A Journey to the Mecca of Black America* and an essayist whose work has appeared in the *New York Times*, *Harper's*, *Vogue*, and *Essence*.

DUKE RILEY received his BFA from Rhode Island School of Design and his MFA from Pratt Institute. Fascinated by maritime history and events around the waterways of New York City, he was commissioned by the Queens Museum, as part of its *Nonstop Metropolis: The Remix,* to create his large work *That's What She Said,* based on this atlas and on Heather Smith's essay accompanying the map "Water and Power."

TINO RODRIGUEZ, who gained his first exposure to the art world in the Catholic churches of Mexico, writes, "I am fascinated by the complexity of human sexuality, transformation, longing, and transgression. I represent our human exuberance and decadence."

MOLLY ROY is a cartographer and artist seeking to create beautiful, communicative graphics that provoke people into thinking more critically about place. She is a founding member of Guerrilla Cartography and a contributor to a wide array of alternative atlases, guides, trail books, and organizational mapping projects. She is based in Sacramento, and her work can be seen at mroycartography.com.

LINNEA RUSSELL is an illustrator and rock climber from Brooklyn who is beginning medical school in the fall of 2016.

LUC SANTE's books include *Low Life: Lures and Snares of Old New York, Evidence, The Factory of Facts, Kill All Your Darlings,* and *The Other Paris.* He teaches at Bard College.

HEATHER SMITH writes about cities, bison, insects, and office parks, among other things. She is a co-founder of the arts collective Shipping + Receiving and a staff writer for grist.org.

REBECCA SOLNIT is the great-granddaughter of four Irish immigrants who settled in New York, where her grandparents remained and her mother was raised. She is a columnist at *Harper's,* a frequent contributor to the *Guardian,* the author of seventeen books, and the instigator of this atlas series.

GENT STURGEON is an artist living and working in San Francisco. A native of Ojai, California, he trained at the Chouinard Art Institute and is currently producing book illustrations and covers, among other projects.

PEACH TAO is a Beijing-born and Brooklyn-based artist specializing in woodblock prints. Inspired by her travels over three continents, her work has been shown in numerous exhibitions in the United States, France, Spain, and United Kingdom and is included in collections around the world.

JONATHAN TARLETON is a writer, oral historian, and urbanist who lives in Brooklyn and maintains roots in the South. He formerly edited *Urban Omnibus,* a magazine covering planning, architecture, art, and policy in New York City.

ASTRA TAYLOR is a documentary filmmaker, writer, and political organizer. She is the director of the films *Zizek!* and *Examined Life* and the author of *The People's Platform: Taking Back Power and Culture in the Digital Age,* winner of a 2015 American Book Award. She co-edited the *Occupy! Gazette* and the book *Occupy! Scenes from Occupied America,* helped launch the Rolling Jubilee debt-abolishing campaign, and is a co-founder of the Debt Collective.

ALEXANDRA T. VAZQUEZ is associate professor in the Department of Performance Studies at New York University. Her book *Listening in Detail: Performances of Cuban Music* won the American Studies Association's Lora Romero Book Prize in 2014. Vazquez's work has been featured in *American Quarterly, Social Text, Women and Performance,* and the *Journal of Popular Music Studies,* and in the edited volumes *Reggaeton* and *Pop When the World Falls Apart.*

CHRISTINA ZANFAGNA is an assistant professor of ethnomusicology at Santa Clara University and author of the forthcoming *Holy Hip Hop in the City of Angels.* She is the co-creator of the San Francisco Bay Area Sound Map and currently resides in Berkeley, where she regularly performs as a flamenco dancer.